Footprintltalia

Sicily

Mary-Ann Gallagher

Introducing
the island

About the island

Palermo &
around

Northern Sicily

Eastern Sicily

Southeastern Sicily

Central & southern Sicily

Western Sicily

Practicalities

Contents

About the author

Mary-Ann Gallagher has written extensively for numerous travel publishers, including five guides for Footprint. She has travelled throughout Italy, but Sicily remains her favourite region. She first visited on an ostensibly short writing assignment and loved it so much that she refused to come home for several months. Although she is currently based in Barcelona, she continues to visit Sicily as often as possible.

Acknowledgements

Mary-Ann would above all like to thank the following people in Sicily for all their help: Giovanna Fichera, Salvatore and Viola; Alessio Creta and Luccio; Alessandro Vito; Patrizia Eggleton and Simi; Karen Abend and Emilio; Marcella Amato at Real Sicily; Rob and Cristina at 5Balconi B&B (Catania); Cindy and Gianni at Casale Lisycon; Josune Garcia Yanguas; Aleix and Max Artigas. Thank you, too, to all the wonderfully generous Sicilian people at tourist offices, bars, cafés, restaurants, boats, and beaches, who generously offered me everything from brilliant tips to free babysitting. *Grazie mille a tutti!*

Huge thanks go to Tim, my outstanding editor, and to endlessly patient and hard-working Alan, Dav and Alice at Footprint.

About the book

The guide is divided into 4 sections: Introducing the island; About the island; Around the island and Practicalities.

Introducing the island comprises: At a glance, which explains how the island fits together by giving the reader a snapshot of what to look out for and what makes this region distinct from other parts of the country; Best of Sicily (top 20 highlights); A year in Sicily, which is a month-by-month guide to pros and cons of visiting at certain times of year; and Sicily on screen & page, which is a list of suggested books and films.

About the island comprises: History; Art & architecture; **Sicily today**, which presents different aspects of life on the island today; **Nature & environment** (an overview of the landscape and wildlife); **Festivals & events**; **Sleeping** (an overview of accommodation options); **Eating & drinking** (an overview of the island's cuisine, as well as advice on eating out); **Entertainment** (an overview of the island's cultural credentials, explaining what entertainment is on offer); **Shopping** (the island's specialities and recommendations for the best buys); and **Activities & tours**.

Around the island is then broken down into six areas, each with its own chapter. Here you'll find all the main sights and at the end of each chapter is a listings section with all the best sleeping, eating & drinking, entertainment, shopping and activities & tours options plus a brief overview of public transport.

Sleeping price codes

€€€€	over €300 per night for a double room in high season
€€€	€200-300
€€	€100-200
€	under €100

Eating & drinking price codes

€€€€	more than €40 per person for a 2-course meal with a drink, including service and cover charge
€€€	€30-40
€€	€20-30
€	under €20

Map symbols

i	Informazioni / Information	🏛	Monumento / Monument
○	Luogo d'interesse / Place of Interest	🚉	Stazione Ferroviaria / Railway Station
🏛	Museo/Galleria / Museum/Gallery	🥾	Escursioni a piedi / Hiking
🎭	Teatro / Theatre	**M**	Metropolitana / Metro Station
○	Negozi / Shopping	🍅	Mercato / Market
✉	Ufficio postale / Post Office	🚡	Funicolare / Funicular Railway
†	Chiesa Storica / Historic Church	✈	Aeroporto / Airport
🌳	Giardini / Gardens	🎓	Universita / University
......	Percorsi raccomandati / Recommended walk		

Picture credits

Assessorato al Turismo Regione Siciliana Pages 17, 101, 157, 166, 198, 239

Alamy Pages 93, 173: Cubolmages srl; page 90: David Lyons; page 44: Gianni Muratore; page 120: Keith Lewis; page 279: Setchfield

fotolia Page 35: apeschi; page 238: Comugnero Silvana; page 60: fibra; page 188: Florian Villesèche; page 45: franger; page 200: Giuseppe Bognanni; page 212: ISABELLE.ESSELIN; page 29: jean claude braun; page 104: Jordan Lewy; page 172: ollirg; page 70: Pierre Juin; page 114: Ralf Gosch; page 249: Yohka91

Hemis.fr Pages 1, 3, 9, 12, 62, 89, 184, 186, 187, 248, 275: Bruno Morandi; page 015: Camille Moirenc; page 068: Emilio Suetone; pages 2, 9, 18, 110, 167: Franci Barbagallo; pages 140, 141: Hervé Hughes; page 197: Imagestate; pages 51, 128, 132: Jean Du Boisberranger; pages 10, 14, 152, 162: Jean Pierre Lescourret; pages 58, 77, 83, 94, 118, 139, 195, 269: John Frumm; pages 47, 52, 66, 115, 137, 190, 255, 284: Patrick Frilet; pages 3, 9, 73, 113, 131, 135, 136, 216, 233: Philippe Renault; pages 76, 84, 88, 97, 192: René Mattes

Shutterstock Pages 220, 244: akva; page 175: Ant Clausen; page 230: Bart Parren; page 267: DUSAN ZIDAR; page 151: Ivan Cholakov; pages 43, 204, 205: Jakub Pavlinec; page 117: Jolanda; page 206: mirabile; page 148: Natalia Macheda; pages 28, 202: ndrpggr; pages 2, 6, 16, 59, 170, 171, 218, 226, 228, 231, 274, 276, 277: ollirg; page 20: René Hartmans; page 281: Sandy Maya Matzen; page 14: slava_vn; page 191: Ventura

SuperStock Pages 3, 9, 11, 13, 17, 30, 40, 42, 63, 109, 182, 191, 211, 214, 227, 242, 250, 253, 257, 271, 272: age fotostock; page 56: Ben Mangor; page 224: De Agostini; page 246: Hemis.Fr; page 143: Mauritius; page 183: Ping Amranand; pages 232, 253: Prisma; page 149: Richard Cummins; page 235: Sergio Pitamitz; pages 169, 251: Silvio Fiore.jpg

TIPS Images pages 219, 234, 241; Adriano Bacchella; page 96: Alberto Rossi; page 144: Andrea Forlani; page 215: Andrea Pistolesi; pages 2, 9, 15, 32, 146, 213: Antonello Lanzellotto; pages 2, 26, 156, 158, 160, 168, 179, 223: Anotonio Zimbone; pages 38, 63, 98, 124, 224: Arco Digital Images; page 19: Charles Mahaux; pages 125, 127, 245, 249: Francesco Tomasinelli; page 34: Gianalberto Cigolini; pages 92, 252: Giancarlo Biscardi; pages 154, 164, 257: Giuliano Colliva; pages 2, 9, 55, 74, 80, 165, 203, 254: Giuseppe Masci; pages 37, 48, 86, 107, 123, 153, 165, 262: Guido Alberto Rossi; pages 116, 261, 263: Imagestate; page 108: Laurence Simon; pages 197, 258: Mark Edward Smith; page 112: Photononstop; pages 72, 100, 109, 260: Roberto Rinaldi; page 142: Sodapix AG RM; page 119: Stefano Lunardi; page 21: Stefano Scata; pages 71, 247: Tommaso Di Girolamo

----

Tetra images front cover

ML Sinibaldi/CORBIS back cover
Philippe Renault/hemis.fr back cover

Contents

Doric column, Agrigento.

Introducing the island

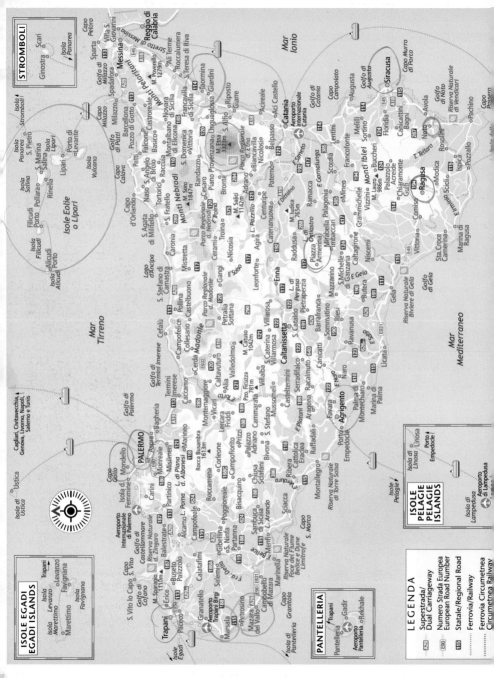

Introduction

Sicily is a sly seductress. You'll fall for her – everyone does – but she won't make it easy. First impressions are intense, but paradoxical: beautiful and brutal, anarchic and serene, exuberant and insular, the island resists all easy definitions. Complex, yes – but also infinitely beguiling.

The Greeks, the first of a long line of foreign rulers, loved Sicily best. They built their cities as though their civilization would last forever – even now, their ancient ruins are breathtaking. The Arabs' subtle legacy is felt in the islanders' generous hospitality and its rich cuisine, and the Normans left golden cathedrals at Monreale and Cefalù.

Tragically for Sicily, everyone else – from the Romans to the Bourbons – was out for what they could get. Grinding poverty, institutionalized corruption and Cosa Nostra have taken a heavy toll. But a renaissance is underway: the historic centres of Palermo and Syracuse are being slowly restored; great swathes of the glorious landscape are now protected in nature reserves; and grassroots organizations have found the collective courage to stand up against the Mafia. There's a heady sense of hope in the air – just one more reason to fall a little more in love.

Palermo.

At a glance
A whistle-stop tour of Sicily

Sicily is an almost perfect triangle, floating just off the toe of Italy. The east has some blockbuster attractions – chic Taormina, Mount Etna, ancient Syracuse (Siracusa), Baroque Noto, and the serene Aeolian Islands. In the northwest, the teeming capital of Palermo is curved around a craggy bay, while ethereal salt pans, fishing villages and ancient ruins are found at the quiet western tip. The south coast boasts long beaches and the magnificent Valley of the Temples in Agrigento.

Palermo
Palermo, Sicily's theatrical, bomb-blasted, anarchic capital, is tightly packed around a wide, curving bay. It was considered one of the loveliest cities of medieval Europe, but centuries of war, neglect and poverty have stripped it of much of its former beauty. Some spellbinding corners survive, particularly the glittering 12th-century Cappella Palatina, in the Palazzo dei Normanni (Norman Palace), one of the great jewels of Arabic-Norman art. There are some interesting museums, but much of the city's allure lies in exploring its crumbling alleys and squares, and visiting the eye-popping markets with their glistening offal and gaping fish. Palermo's seaside suburb, elegant Mondello, is dotted with pretty art nouveau villas submerged in greenery. On a hill overlooking the city, the magnificent cathedral of Monreale is encrusted with dazzling Byzantine mosaics. To the east, the once-chic resort of Bagheria is still scattered with extraordinary follies and whimsical turn-of-the-century villas. Much of Palermo province is former bandit country, and even now towns like Corleone and Prizzi summon up visions of the Mafia (however much they wish they didn't).

The lowdown

Money matters

You could scrape by on €45-60 per person per day if you stay at hostels and cater for yourself. For a modest budget holiday, allow around €90-100 each for food, accommodation and travel. For double this sum, you can live in absolute comfort. Prices are considerably higher on the coast and on the islands, particularly during the intense main season (end-July to end-August) when accommodation prices can double or even triple. The good things in life are still cheap: a scoop of the best ice cream you'll ever taste is as little as €1.20. Stand at the bar for your breakfast *cornetto e cappuccino* and you'll only have to fork out about €1.80-2.00 (double that to sit on a gorgeous, but touristy square).

Opening hours & holidays

Opening hours vary widely across the island, but the following is a very general guide. Shops and businesses are usually open from Monday to Saturday 0900-1300 and then from around 1530-1930. Everywhere is closed on Sunday, apart from bakeries and cake shops. Businesses often close completely for the whole of August. Restaurants usually open at lunchtimes around 1230 and close around 1500, opening again at 1900 until about 2200 or 2300. Pizzerias may not open at lunchtimes, and, if they do, they probably won't serve pizza (this is because it takes such a long time to get the wood-fired ovens going). Museums are usually open during the mornings only (0900-1300) in smaller towns, with afternoon opening just one or two days a week. They are often closed on Sunday afternoons and sometimes on Mondays. The main archaeological sites are usually open from 0900 to one hour before dusk.

Note that opening times in Sicily are, at best, guidelines. Even the biggest and most important sights can close without warning. If there is something you really want to see, ring in advance to ensure it is open – and always, always have a plan B.

Admission fees

There are no useful discount passes in Sicily. Reduced admission fees are usually available to children, students, and seniors. Some museums offer free admission to EU citizens on production of a passport. Museums are, however, generally inexpensive.

Tourist information

Tourist information in Sicily is patchy at best. While a few tourist information offices are well equipped and have multilingual staff on hand to help, most have nothing but the unfailing charm of the attendants. A basic overview of Sicily is provided by the Italian tourist board at italiantourism.com, while the official Sicilian tourism website regione.sicilia.it/turismo is a sometimes outdated but occasionally useful source of information before you travel. There are local tourist information offices in most towns, run by several different bodies, and with a confusing array of acronyms. If you ask simply for the 'ufficio turistico', you will be sent in the right direction. In smaller towns, the municipally run local tourist offices are called Pro Loco. The larger towns may have regional tourist offices – Ente Provinciale per il Turismo (EPT) or Azienda di Promozione Turistica (APT) – which provide information on the province. In big cities, like Catania and Palermo, there are also information offices run by Informazioni e Assistenza ai Turisti (IAT) or Azienda Autonoma de di Soggiorno e Turismo (AAST).

Introducing the island

Northern Sicily

Cefalù, at the very centre of Sicily's northern coast, is one of the prettiest seaside towns on the Mediterranean, with a red-roofed old quarter piled up beneath a cliff. Just inland, the Madonie and Nebrodi mountains, now two adjacent natural reserves, contain some of Sicily's highest peaks, and are scattered with steep, stone villages where old traditions survive intact. The undulating coastline east of Cefalù offers dramatic capes and seductive coves of fine pebbles. Ancient Tyndaris (Tindari), high on a dramatic headland, is one of the most beautifully situated archaeological sites on the island, and the lagoons and beaches below are quiet, empty and utterly magical. From appealing, castle-topped Milazzo, ferries run to the idyllic Aeolian Islands, each of which boasts a different character, from firework-spitting Stromboli to the celebrity haven of Panerea.

Eastern Sicily

At the tip of the island, Messina is a big working port that sits just a few kilometres from mainland Italy. Sicily's eastern coast is spectacularly beautiful, with undulating cliffs overlooking exquisite coves and the startlingly blue Ionian sea. Taormina, Sicily's loveliest and best-preserved hill town, has been the island's biggest tourist magnet since Goethe waxed lyrical about its charms in his 18th-century travelogue *Italian Journey*. One of Taormina's biggest attractions is the superb view of Mount Etna afforded from its elegant squares and terraces. The huge volcano, the largest and most active in Europe, dominates the entire eastern coast – physically, and in other less tangible ways. Even when entirely hidden by cloud, its menacing, unpredictable presence is felt. The trip to the top – whether you choose to hike, take the cable car, or a jeep – is thrilling. The towns and villages that circle Etna's base may be threatened by eruptions, but they are immersed in a sea of orchards, olive groves and vineyards. They are linked by a panoramic railway which culminates in Catania, Sicily's flamboyant second city, where the elegant

Syracuse.

Baroque monuments of the historic centre are now a UNESCO World Heritage Site. Poverty and neglect may have taken their toll, but Catania remains a vibrant and engaging city.

Southeastern Sicily

The southeastern corner of Sicily is packed with enticing sights, including the superb archaeological remains of Syracuse at modern Siracusa and the exquisite little time-capsule island of Ortigia. Then there is the string of superb Baroque cities, awarded UNESCO World Heritage status, built in one glorious surge after a massive earthquake decimated the entire region three hundred years ago. Foremost among them is Noto, a golden city which has recently emerged from extensive restoration, but don't miss nearby Ragusa and Modiza, where gastronomy vies with architecture as the main attraction. These cities are all firmly on most tourist itineraries, but inland, amid the gentle peaks and farmsteads of the Monti Iblei, you can escape the crowds in quiet villages and gorges. Along the coast, you'll find a spectacular nature reserve at the Riserva Naturale Oasi Faunistica di Vendicari, a haven for migratory birds, which boasts some of the wildest and most beautiful beaches on the island.

Villa Romana del Casale.

Central & southern Sicily

There is only one blockbuster attraction in central Sicily, but it is a stunner: the Villa Romana del Casale at Piazza Armerina. Built during the fourth century AD, this magnificent late Imperial villa was probably built for the Emperor Maximianus, and boasts the finest and most extensive Roman mosaic decoration to be found anywhere in the world. Nearby, the ruins of ancient Morgantina are serenely set overlooking the undulating hills of central Sicily, where few visitors penetrate. At the heart of this quiet region is Enna, a citadel city on a lofty crag with a smattering of churches and an enormous medieval castle. To the north, the rugged hills rise up sharply to join the Madonie mountains (see Northern Sicily), and are scattered with quiet, agricultural villages linked by panoramic small roads. The southern coast, an otherwise workaday region with gritty ports and low-key resorts, contains another of Sicily's headlining attractions: the stunning Valle dei Templi in Agrigento. This magnificent and extraordinarily well preserved temple group, dating back to the sixth to fifth centuries BC, is the finest to be found outside mainland Greece. The far-flung Pelagie Islands, closer to Africa than Europe, are barren and windswept, but their glorious beaches draw huge crowds in summer.

Western Sicily

The western coast of Sicily is flat and ethereal, the coastline delicately etched with the pale outline of salt pans. The provincial capital Trapani, with its surprisingly elegant old quarter and an excellent reputation for its cuisine, occupies a slender promontory. Nearby, the magical, medieval hill town of Erice clings to the mountain-top, overlooking the craggy San Vito Lo Capo and the superb Riserva Naturale dello Zingaro. This reserve encompasses a long swathe of deliciously unspoilt, craggy coastline, with hiking trails and tiny coves. Lost in the hills inland, the great Doric temple of Segesta, erected in the fifth century BC, is heart-stoppingly beautiful. The west also boasts two lively and appealing port towns: Marsala, famous for its delicious fortified wine, and Mazara del Vallo, which has an attractive old quarter. There are more spectacular ancient ruins at Selinunte, romantically located on a clifftop amid a profusion of wild flowers. Celebrities in search of peace and seclusion head for the tiny and enchanting island of Pantelleria, closer to Africa than Sicily. The trio of Egadi Islands are more accessible, and the fishing villages, striking coastline and rocky coves draw floods of summer visitors.

Best of Sicily

Top 20 things to see & do

1 Detail from the Palazzo del Normanni.

❶ Palazzo dei Normanni & Cappella Palatina, Palermo

Palermo's 12th-century Norman Palace, built by Roger II, contains one of the most dazzling yet intimate chapels to be found anywhere. Every surface is covered with shimmering mosaics, with bible stories and curious fables exquisitely rendered in miniature, and the ceiling and columns are masterfully worked in gilt and marble. Page 81.

❷ Cattedrale di Monreale

A glorious, golden cathedral crowns the serene hill town of Monreale, high above Palermo. Almost a thousand years ago, the finest Greek mosaicists, aided by their Sicilian pupils, transformed the interior into a breathtaking, gilded masterpiece,

6 A volcano in the Aeolian Islands.

filling it with Byzantine mosaics of such beauty and grandeur that they rank among the finest in Europe. Page 96.

❸ Cefalù

A picture-postcard seaside village curled around the base of a dramatic headland, Cefalù has managed to retain oodles of old-fashioned charm despite the crowds that descend every summer. Chic Italians come for the fabulous beaches, but the ancient town has plenty more to offer – not least a splendid Norman cathedral containing superb Byzantine mosaics. Page 115.

❹ Madonie & Nebrodi mountains

Two magnificent, protected natural parks are found side by side in the northeast corner of the island. Few visitors penetrate the Madonie and Nebrodi mountains, where wild horses and semi-wild pigs roam the forest and eagles wheel over the remote mountain tops, but those who do are rewarded with traditional stone villages and extraordinary views. Page 118 & 126.

❺ Tindari

Of all Sicilian pilgrimage sites, none is as magical as lofty Tindari. The modern church is unappealing, but this dramatic headland is also home to the spellbinding ruins of ancient Tyndaris, where views stretch over olive trees and prickly pears to the endless blue sea. Below, the quietest and best beaches in Sicily await in the lovely Riserva Naturale di Laghetti di Marinello. Page 124.

❻ Aeolian Islands

The mythical home of the wind god and the god of fire, the Aeolian Islands are one of the last unspoilt island havens in the Mediterranean. From steamy Vulcano and remote Alicudi, to verdant Salina and fire-spitting Stromboli, celebrity-favourite Panarea to bubbly Lipari, each island in the archipelago has a very different character. Page 128.

7 **Taormina piazza and cathedral.**

3 **Cefalù.**

❼ Taormina

Writers, aristocrats and celebrities have flocked to fashionable Taormina since Goethe first put the town on the map in the 18th century. The town's palaces, churches and a spectacular Greek theatre have an unforgettable clifftop setting by the sea, with Mount Etna looming in the background. Page 155.

❽ Catania

Catania's gorgeous ensemble of flamboyant Baroque palaces and churches are built of striking black and white lava stone from nearby Etna. Most are in desperate need of restoration, and the poverty is palpable in places, but the city remains one of the most vibrant and forward-looking in southern Italy. Page 161.

9 The Silvestri crater, Mount Etna.

⑨ Mount Etna

Mount Etna is the highest, most active and possibly the most famous volcano in Europe. Reaching the summit is an adventure, whether you take the easy route and go by cable car and jeep, or make the stiff but enjoyable hike yourself. The fertile slopes are covered with orchards and vines, the source of increasingly fashionable Etna wines. Page 166.

⑩ Syracuse (Siracusa)/Ortigia

Ancient Syracuse was one of the mightiest cities of Magna Graecia, and its magnficent ancient ruins attest to its extraordinary wealth and influence. A superb Greek theatre is the finest of its ancient sites, while the tiny island of Ortigia, with its peeling palazzi and narrow streets, is sheer enchantment. Page 188.

⑪ Noto

The finest of a string of Baroque cities erected in the early 18th century after a devastating earthquake rocked eastern Sicily, Noto is a captivating time capsule of honey-coloured stone. The twirling palaces, churches and graceful squares are dominated by an enormous cathedral. Page 200.

⑫ Riserva Naturale Oasi Faunistica di Vendicari

This nature reserve is one of the quietest and most beautiful corners of Sicily, with pristine beaches backed by undulating dunes and barely a soul in sight. The marshy wetlands and lakes attract thousands of migratory birds, including huge clouds of pink flamingoes. Page 203.

⑬ Villa Romana del Casale, Piazza Armerina

This palatial villa contains the finest mosaics in situ anywhere in the Roman world. There are scenes from ancient myths, exquisite designs in glowing colours, and hunting scenes of such extraordinary vivacity that you can almost hear the snap of the hounds' jaws. Page 224.

⓯ Valle dei Templi, Agrigento

The great Greek temples of ancient Akragas, magnificently silhouetted high on a ridge near the modern town of Agrigento, are the finest Doric temples to be found anywhere outside mainland Greece. They date back to the sixth and fifth centuries BC, when Akragas was at the height of its powers. Page 227.

⓯ Riserva Naturale dello Zingaro

Much of the long, craggy finger of the Capo di San Vito is now a stunning nature reserve, offering one of the last unspoilt stretches of Mediterranean coastline. Scramble down to rocky coves of heart-stopping beauty and splash about in the impossibly blue sea. Page 249.

⓰ Mazara del Vallo

The lively, ochre-coloured fishing port of Mazara del Vallo has a distinctly Arabic flavour, thanks in part to its sizable North African population, which occupies the suggestive Casbah in the heart of the old town. The colourful harbour, the elegant *lungomare* (seafront)., and the wealth of inexpensive fish restaurants, make this one of Sicily's most piquant towns. Page 256.

18 Pantelleria.

⓱ Selinunte

Perched magically on a remote, silent headland, Selinunte is among the most poignant ancient sites in Sicily. The soaring columns of its roofless temples and the overgrown tumble of stones are all that survive of what was once one of the most powerful Greek colonies on the island. Page 258.

⓲ Pantelleria

When celebs want to get away from it all in style, they come to the secretive little island of Pantelleria, which is geographically closer to Africa than Italy. The traditional dammusi (domed stone dwellings) that dot the hilly landscape now contain some of the most chic boutique accommodation to be found in the Mediterranean. Page 260.

⓳ Segesta

Travellers have long gasped at their first glimpse of Segesta, emerging like a mirage from a serene and verdant valley. The great temple has stood here for more than two and a half millennia. Above it, on a wind-whipped crag, are the remains of a Greek theatre with views across the hills. Page 250.

⓴ Erice

An ethereal, medieval town of cobbled streets and noble palaces, little Erice is perched so high on its hilltop that it often sits above the clouds. When they part, the views across the coastline far, far below are truly magnificent. Page 252.

20 Erice.

Month by month

A year in Sicily

Etna, winter.

January

The temperature may not fall much below 10°C but Sicily can feel chilly in January, although you can usually rely on bright sunshine. It's a quiet month, when many hotels and restaurants are closed, beach resorts are silent, and some museums are closed for annual repairs. However, you can go skiing on Etna or in the Madonie mountains and enjoy the most celebrated sights without the summer hordes. Some of the best local festivals include the Epiphany celebrations in Piana degli Albanesi (see page 52) and the *Festa di San Sebastiano* in Acireale (see page 53). On the night of 5 January, excited children go to bed and hope that the witch Befana will bring them presents rather than a lump of coal, which is reserved for bad kids.

February

Carnevale, which kicks off Lent, is the biggest event in February, which is otherwise a sleepy month. The two biggest carnival celebrations take place in Sciacca (see page 233) and Acireale (see page 165). Temperatures are still cool, and although sunshine is the norm you may still need your umbrella. The first blossom appears on the almond trees, a particularly beautiful spectacle in Agrigento where a special festival is held in their honour (see page 53). Catania celebrates La Festa di Sant'Agata (see page 163) with a huge procession through the night and special confectionery prepared to century-old recipes available from convents and street stalls.

Easter Holy Week, Enna.

March

By March, clouds of pink and white blossom fill the orchards. The new spring crops – including artichokes, broad beans and asparagus – appear on menus (try the famous *fritella*, a kind of stew made with baby broad beans, peas and artichokes), and are celebrated in local festivals at country towns. This is also the main citrus fruit season, with market stalls piled high with intense Sicilian lemons and succulent blood oranges. The temperature rises a few degrees (averaging around 16°C) and there is less chance of rain.

April

Easter celebrations are taken very seriously in Sicily, with solemn rituals and processions enacted in every town and village. Some of the most unusual or spectacular take place at Trapani, Gangi, Prizzi and Piana degli Albanesi (see page 53). Special Easter foods, including breads and cakes, fill shop windows: look out for the extraordinary Easter lambs made of marzipan or sugar paste (often life-size) and the extravagant bread sculptures (each town has its own variation).

May

By May, the air is warm and balmy and restaurants and hotels in the seasonal resorts have opened for business. Walkers can enjoy mellow temperatures, meadows full of spring flowers and gloriously green hills. Spring is celebrated in Noto, where the streets are carpeted with flower petals (see page 54), and in Caltagirone, which decorates its famous ceramic staircase with more flowers (see page 240). The tuna fishermen are out in force around Trapani between May and June for *La Mattanza*, a brutal but time-honoured ritual in which the tuna are guided through a series of tunnel-like nets before being speared. Tuna features prominently on menus, in recipes like *ragù di tonno*, served with pasta, or *polpette di tonno* (tuna meatballs).

June

June is perhaps the best month to visit Sicily, before the summer heat becomes oppressive and the resorts fill up with tourists. The mountains are still green, the streams have yet to dry up, and the beautiful islands are not yet overrun. The most glittering event on the social calender is the Taormina Film Festival (see page 54) when celebrities and their hangers-on flock to the beautiful little hill town. Summer-long performing arts festivals kick off in Taormina (Taormina Arte, see page 54) and Palermo (Palermo Estate and Verdura Festival, see page 54). Check out the markets for the best summer fruits which are now in season – apricots, cherries, watermelons, and the curious prickly pear (used in a local liqueur and in jams and desserts).

July

Things really start hotting up in July, with average temperatures of 27°C. Cool off with a *granita* (crushed sweetened ice usually flavoured with lemon), strawberries, mint or coffee, or some of Sicily's outstanding, artisanal ice cream. The tourists arrive en masse towards the end of the month, when Italy shuts down until the end of August. Palermo honours its patron saint, Santa Rosalia, with several days of extravagant parades and traditional street fairs (see page 54).

August

In August, you won't find an inch of space on Sicily's popular beaches, particularly on the islands. If you want to party hard, this is the month to come, but expect to pay for the privilege. Many businesses close down completely (except in the tourist resorts) during August. Prices – for everything – are at their highest this month. It's very hot, and the sun is bleaching the hills and fields, but the mountain villages inland can provide cool retreats from the coastal mayhem. Numerous local festivals take place, many in honour of the approaching harvest, with some of the best happening in Erice, Mazara del Vallo, Trapani, Gangi and Petralia Sottano.

September

The harvest is in full swing this month – hazelnuts, almonds, the famous Bronte pistachios, as well as grapes and wheat. On menus, look out for all kinds of delicious treats, including hazelnut tart, or pesto made with vivid green pistachios, or try the classic Sicilian dish, couscous with fish, at San Vito Lo

The Santa Rosalia festival.

Harvesting of grapes, Pantelleria.

Capo's annual festival. It's a beautiful, golden month, when the summer heat begins to relent, and walking in the hills is a delight. Pilgrims flock to Tindari to see the statue of the Black Madonna, and Lampedusa celebrates its patron saint.

October

Temperatures drop as autumn advances, and the weather becomes unpredictable, but it's a good time to visit if you want to enjoy the main tourist attractions in relative peace. The olive harvest begins towards the end of the month, and some of the *agriturismi* invite visitors to join in, or show them how the oil presses work. One of the most charming traditional festivals is the maritime festival at Santa Flavia, in which an image of the Madonna is taken to the water to be blessed.

November

On Tutti Santi (All Saints' Day), families across Sicily visit cemeteries and honour the dead with special pastries and foods. Many villages host parades for small children, and the cake shops are filled with *ossa di mortu* – marzipan treats in the shape of little bones. It's a good time to visit the Riserva Naturale Oasi Faunistica di Vendicari, which attracts thousands of migratory birds on their way to Africa.

December

December can be wet and surprisingly chilly (average temperatures are 16°C), so come prepared. But it's also a magical month, thanks to the Christmas fairs and elaborate decorations that adorn every town and village. The ski resorts open for business, and Syracuse celebrates the festival of its patron saint, Santa Lucia (see page 55).

Screen & page

Sicily in film & literature

Films

La Terra Trema (The Earth Trembles)
Luchino Visconti, 1948

Luchino Visconti's black-and-white Neorealist film is an adaptation of Giovanni Verga's novel *I Malavoglia* (1888), a gritty, unremittingly tragic tale of a poor fishing family in Aci Trezza.

Stromboli
Roberto Rossellini, 1950

Ingrid Bergman plays Karin, who longs to escape the island and its crushing poverty in this dark, Neorealist film. Stromboli obligingly erupted during filming, but it was the fireworks between Bergman and Rossellini which excited the gossip-mongers.

Divorzio All'Italiana (Divorce, Italian Style)
Pietor Germi, 1961

Marcelo Mastroianni is hilarious as a Sicilian aristocrat plotting the death of his wife so that he can marry his nubile cousin. Divorce may not be tolerated, but *delitto passionale* (crime of passion) is always forgiven. He just has to prove his wife is an adulteress.

Il Gattopardo (The Leopard)
Luchino Visconti, 1963

Luchino Visconti's lavish film adaptation of Giuseppe di Lampedusa's magnficent novel *Il Gattopardo* (1958) stars Burt Lancaster, Claudia Cardinale and Alain Delon, and remains a cult classic.

The Godfather I, II, III
Francis Ford Coppola, 1972, 1974, 1990

For Sicilians, impatient with glamorized and romantic images of the Mafia, The *Godfather* cult serves mainly to sell t-shirts and souvenirs. But for non-Italians, the whole island is inextricably linked with Francis Ford Coppola's Oscar-winning film (in three parts) of Mario Puzo's blockbuster novel.

On location

Forza d'Agrò and Sávoca The Sicilian scenes in The Godfather were ostensibly set in Corleone, but the original town was too overdeveloped. Two villages near Taormina were substituted – fans will immediately recognize Sávoca's Bar Vitelli and the church where Michael and Apollonia were married. Mary's murder takes place on the steps of Palermo's splendid Teatro Massimo.

Mount Etna Etna's spectacular eruption in 2002 was filmed by Lucasfilm and used in the 2005 movie *Star Wars Episode III: Revenge of the Sith*.

Palermo Burt Lancaster and Claudia Cardinale waltzed around the lavish ballroom of Palermo's Palazzo Valguarnera-Gangi (on the piazza Croce dei Vespri) in Visconti's superb film adaptation of Lampedusa's *The Leopard*. Wim Wenders' *The Palermo Shooting* (2008) may deserve the critical hammering it received at Cannes, but the camerawork exquisitely evokes Palermo's melancholy beauty.

Pollara The beautiful story of *Il Postino* was filmed at Pollara, on the lush Aeolian island of Salina.

Various locations Michelangelo Antonioni's strange, elusive 1960 film, *L'Avventura*, was badly received when it first appeared but has become a cult classic in recent years. Palermo, Taormina and the Aeolian Islands get starring roles. The modern classic, *Cinema Paradiso*, was filmed at several Sicilian locations, including Palermo, Bagheria, Cefalù, Castelbuono, and Palazzo Adriano (a sleepy country town which is still rather confused by the trickle of film fans who come to admire its main square).

bay that figures in the Oscar-winning movie *Il Postino*. Memorably shot, this nostalgiac evocation of a long-vanished era centres around the unexpected relationship that develops between a reclusive famous poet and his postman.

L'Uomo Delle Stelle (The Star-Maker)
Giuseppe Tornatore, 1995

For more gorgeously shot footage of rural Sicily (mainly Ragusa and around), check out Tornatore's film about a Roman con man offering screen tests to gullible villagers dazzled by the prospect of fame and riches.

Malèna
Giuseppe Tornatore, 2000

Despite mixed reviews from the critics, Tornatore had another international commercial success with this story of a beautiful woman (played by Monica Bellucci) forced into prostitution during the Second World War. It was largely shot in Noto.

Respiro
Emanuele Crialese, 2002

Dusty, remote Lampedusa is the settting for this award-winning film. It's a strange, dreamy and not entirely successful story, centering on an unconventional woman and her young son and ally, but the island is magnificently shot.

Cinema Paradiso
Giuseppe Tornatore, 1988

Giuseppe Tornatore, probably the best known Sicilian film director, made it big with this moving exploration of the relationship between a fatherless young boy and the ageing projectionist (played by Philippe Noiret) in a tiny village cinema in post-war Sicily.

Il Postino
Michael Radford, 1994

Movie buffs flock to Pollara, on the Aeolian island of Salina, to seek out the heart-stoppingly beautiful

`Books`

Fiction

Il Malavoglia (The House by the Medlar Tree)
Giovanni Verga, 1881

An unflinching chronicler of the Sicilian poor, Verga was the founder of the Verismo (realist) school of writing. This bleak novel, describing the trials of the Malavoglia family eking out a living by fishing, is his most famous work, and was filmed as *La Terra Trema* by Visconti (see page 22).

Sei Personaggi in Cerca d'Autore (Six Characters in Search of An Author)
Luigi Pirandello, 1934

This ground-breaking drama won the Nobel Prize for Literature in 1934 and remains Pirandello's most famous work. Six characters invade a rehearsal and start making demands of the 'real' figures, and chaos ensues.

Il Giorno dell civetta (The Day of the Owl)
Leonardo Sciascia, 1961

Writer and politician Leonardo Sciascia was the first to write unflinchingly about the invidious tentacles of the Mafia. In this novel, a murder is investigated by a policeman, who finds links to politicians in Rome before the investigation is quashed.

Volevo i Pantaloni (Good Girls Don't Wear Trousers)
Lara Cardella, 1989

Annetta believes that wearing trousers represents freedom; in her father's eyes they are worn by men and *puttane* (whores) in this frank portrayal of the hypocritical values of a Sicilian town in the 1950s.

La Hunga Vita di Marianna (The Silent Duchess)
Daci Mariani, 1990

Daci Maraini is one of Italy's foremost contemporary writers. This is the story of Marianna Ucria, an 18th-century Sicilian noblewoman, who is both deaf and mute after a childhood trauma, and her stultifying life amid the patriarchal aristocracy.

The Shape of Water (La Forma dell'Acqua)
Andrea Camilleri, 1994

The first in Camilleri's excellent, and beautifully written, series featuring the unconventional detective Inspector Montalbano. It's one of the most enjoyable ways to glimpse the soul of modern Sicily in all its perplexing contradictions.

One Hundred Strokes of the Brush Before Bed (Cento Colpi di Spazzola Prima di Andare a Dormire)
Melissa Panarello, 2003

A superb, brutal, unsettling, and often pornographic account of a girl's sexual awakening.

Non-fiction

Italian Journey (Italienische Reise)
Johann Wolfgang von Goethe, 1817

Goethe described his epic journey through Italy between 1786 and 1788 in journals which were published in two volumes. He travelled extensively in Sicily during 1787 and noted every impression in obsessional, fascinating detail.

The Honoured Society
Norman Lewis, 1964

The great British travel writer Norman Lewis, whose first wife was Sicilian, spent decades exploring the country. This masterful book is a superb, if horrifying, portrayal of the Mafia after the Second World War.

On Persephone's Island
Mary Taylor Simeti, 1995

An evocative, loving but unflinching account of life on Sicily by the American author Mary Taylor Simeti, who came to the island in 1962 to do volunteer work and stayed.

Midnight in Sicily
Peter Robb, 1996

The 'kiss of honour' said to have been exchanged by former Prime Minister Andreotti and Mafia boss Titò Riina in 1987 is the starting point for a brilliant, personal, and insightful portrait of modern Sicily, food and the Costa Nostra.

In Sicily
Norman Lewis, 2000

A thoroughly absorbing introduction to the island by the most insightful of travel writers. Slim enough to keep in a pocket and rewarding enough to re-read many, many times.

Sicily, Through Writers' Eyes
Horatio Clare (ed), 2006

This wonderful book intersperses Clare's own acute, often poetic observations with a selection of writings about the island chosen from a wide range of authors from Homer to Andrea Camilleri.

Sweet Honey, Bitter Lemons
Matthew Fort, 2008

Food writer Matthew Fort travelled around Sicily on Monica, his red Vespa, in an effort to "understand Sicily by eating it". The journey is lustily recorded with humour, perceptiveness and – most of all – greed. The temples of Agrigento don't get a mention: an entire paragraph is dedicated to the antipasti at one of the restaurants he visited. There are recipes too. You'll be booking the plane ticket as soon as you put it down.

Contents

About the island

Etna erupts.

History

Temple of Castor and Pollux.

Early Sicily

The earliest settlements in Sicily date back to around 10,000-8000 BC. The oldest surviving evidence of these early peoples are the delicate cave paintings found at the Grotto dell'Addaura on the outskirts of Palermo (see page 95) and in the Grotta del Genovese (see page 262) on the island of Lévanzo. The paintings depict deer, among other animals, which were the main source of food and skins. By around 6000 BC, settled agriculture was introduced to Sicily, probably by farmers from the eastern Mediterranean, who began to produce wheat and grain, and to raise sheep and goats.

Imported tools and pottery designs indicate that trade with other Mediterranean peoples was becoming increasingly common by 2500 BC. From around 1500 BC, there is evidence of substantial contact with the Minoan culture (modern Crete). The Myceneans, from their home in the Greek Peloponnese, established a flourishing trade in obsidian (a hard, black volcanic glass) with the Aeolian Islands between 1600 and 1150 BC. Ancient artefacts from this period can be found in the excellent Museo Archeologico Regionale Eoliano in Lipari (see page 130). Other settlements, notably Thapsos near modern Siracusa, prospered thanks to trans-Mediterranean trade.

Sicani, Sicels & Elymians

Among the earliest indigenous peoples in Sicily were the Sicani, who originally occupied the northwestern part of the island. They shifted eastwards with the arrival of the Elymians in around 1100 BC, although there is no evidence of conflict between the two tribes. It's uncertain where the Elymians came from, although historians believe that Anatolia in modern Turkey or the Aegean seem most likely. Thucydides, the Greek historian (460-395 BC), would later claim that their ancestors were refugees from Troy. The Elymians established settlements in western Sicily, notably at Erice (see page 252) and Segesta (see page 250) while eastern Sicily was largely occupied by the Sicels. The Sicels arrived around 1200 BC from what is now mainland Italy, and would eventually give their name to the island, *Sicilia*. The Sicels brought iron to Bronze Age Sicily and introduced the domesticated horse. They were also responsible for the vast necropolis at Pantalica, a UNESCO World Heritage Site (see page 198), with more than 5,000 tombs gouged into a cliff face.

Phoenicians

Trading collapsed in the Mediterranean after the demise of the Mycenean civilization some time around 1100 BC and Sicily remained isolated for about three centuries. However, from the 11th century BC the Phoenicians began to explore the western Mediterreanean from their homelands on the Levantine coast (on the land now occupied by parts of modern Lebanon, Syria and Israel). Their first trading partners were the Greeks, to whom they sold a rare purple dye made from crushed shells; it was the Greeks who gave the Levantine traders the name Phoenicians, which means 'purple people'. From the eighth century BC, the Phoenicians began to establish trading posts along the Sicilian coast, most notably at Motya (modern

Trinacria

The symbol of Sicily that appears on the regional flag is a three-legged Medusa called Trinacria by the ancient Greeks. It represents the triangular form of the island, and the Medusa ensures the protection of Athena, patroness of Sicily. As well as referring to the symbol, Trinacria is an alternative name for the island itself.

Mozia see page 251), Solus (modern Solunto, see page 98) and Panormos (modern Palermo, see page 80). They also introduced the Phoenician alphabet, which is considered the basis for Greek and Roman letters. The Phoenicians enjoyed peaceful relations with the Elymians and other local tribes, but trouble was on the horizon. Where the Phoenician traders led, the Greeks would follow, and the first Greek colonizers arrived on eastern Sicily in the eighth century BC.

In the sixth century BC, the Phoenician homeland on the Levantine coast was conquered by the Persians and absorbed into the Persian empire. Many Phoenicians fled across the ocean to Carthage (modern Tunis), which would become the centre of a mighty maritime empire – and a deadly rival to Greece. The Phoenican settlements on western Sicily fell to the Carthaginians, who developed them into walled cities. It was only a matter of time before the Greeks and Carthaginians would clash over territorial and trading rights.

The galleries of Castello Euriàlo.

Greek Sicily

The first permanent Greek colony in Sicily was established in Naxos (see page 158) in 735 BC. During the following century or so, several more would follow: first were those among the eastern coast including Siraco (Syracuse, see page 188) in 734 or 733 BC, Zancle or Messene (Messina, see page 150) in 730 BC, and Katane (Catania, see page 160) in 729 BC. When the best sites on the eastern coast were taken, the settlers moved to the southern coast of the island and established themselves at Selinus (Selinunte, see page 258) in 630 BC, Gela (see page 231) in 688 BC, and Akragas (Agrigento, see page 227) in 580 BC. The Greeks also absorbed several Sicel cities, including Enna, which became identified with the Persephone myth (see page 221).

Akragas rapidly became one of the largest and richest of the new city states, and erected the magnificent temple complex at the Valle dei Templi (see page 227). As the early settlements developed, the Greeks grew bolder, and Dorius of Sparta attempted to establish a colony on Carthaginian territory in western Sicily 514 BC. He was quickly ousted, but the Greeks and Carthaginians began to prepare for combat. The Carthaginians were crushed by Gelon, the powerful tyrant (leader) of Gela and Syracuse, in the battle of Himera in 480 BC, but the Greeks faced new problems with a Sicel uprising led by Ducetius in 452 BC. When the Peloponnesian War (431-404 BC) broke out between Athens and Sparta, Syracuse, allied with Sparta, was on the front line. The Athenians sent a vast fleet, the doomed Sicilian Expedition, to take the island in 415 BC, but were spectacularly defeated. The Carthaginians returned to take their revenge for Himera, which they destroyed in 409 BC, before sacking Akragas (Agrigento) in 406 BC.

Another tyrant emerged in Syracuse: Dionysos I (432-367 BC) took advantage of the confusion to sieze power in 405 BC. He would make Syracuse the greatest city of Magna Graecia, but was known for his cruelty. Tyrant meant simply 'leader' at this time, but Dionysos I was worthy of its modern definitions of despot and oppressor. Dionysos conquered territories across Sicily and southern Italy, and kept the Carthaginians at bay – not least by the erection of mighty walls and the great fortress at the Castello Eurialo – but was eventually poisoned by his own son (according to one account of his death). Dionysos II (c397-343 BC) was a weak ruler and Syracuse collapsed into anarchy. The Corinthians sent Timoleon (c411-337 BC) to impose order, and democratic law was restored in 339 BC.

Meanwhile, the Carthaginians were once again causing trouble. They were defeated in 341 BC, but the death of Timoleon plunged the region back into chaos. A general from Himera, Agothocles, assumed power but achieved little and was assasinated in 289 BC. Several Greek city states including Taormina asked Pyrrhus of Epirus to drive out the Carthaginians in 278 BC. In 277 BC, he captured the Carthaginian stronghold of Eryx (modern Erice, see page 252), but was forced to leave the island after the Carthaginians refused to relinquish their other settlements, and the locals turned against him.

In Messina, an apparently minor crisis would have dramatic repercussions. The Mamertines, former mercenaries who had been granted the city by Agothocles, asked both Carthage and the emerging powers in Rome for support in their struggle with Syracuse. The Carthaginians established a garrison in Messina, but relations between Carthage and Rome, former allies, had deteriorated and the Romans sent an expedition force to Sicily in 264 BC. Thus began the First Punic War (264-241 BC), the first of three major wars fought between Carthage (*Punicus* in Latin, referring to the Phoenician ancestry of the Carthaginians) and the Roman Republic. Hieron II of Syracuse, tyrant from 270-215 BC, negotiated a treaty with the Romans, and, under his rule, Syracuse enjoyed a long period of peace and prosperity. Hieron II was succeeded by Hieronymous, aged just 15, who broke the alliance

with Rome and asked the Carthaginians, who had gained some notable victories in the Second Punic War (218-201 BC), for support. In response, the Romans set siege to Syracuse, which held out for almost three years before finally falling in 212 BC.

Roman & Byzantine Sicily

Sicily became the first Roman overseas province, and was ruled from Syracuse, the capital of the island, by a Roman *praetor* (governor). The city states remained more or less intact, but were required to pay heavy taxes, which took the form of grain, to the empire.

The population of Rome was growing rapidly (even conservative estimates place it at around 1 million), and grain was needed urgently. Sicily would become Rome's 'bread basket'. To this end, the land was expropriated and then parcelled out to new owners favoured by Rome. The Romans became the first of a long line of foreign invaders to ruthlessly exploit Sicily. The local people, who had farmed the land for five centuries, were now dependent on rich, and usually foreign, landowners. The Romans stripped the island of trees, using the timber to build ships, and making more land available for cultivation.

As the number of landholdings increased, more slaves were imported to work in the fields. Thousands of slaves arrived after Carthage (modern Tunis) was razed in 145 BC, at the end of the Third (and final) Punic War (149-146 BC). The wealthy landowners of Sicily were growing richer at the expense of a large and increasingly embittered slave class, who were treated with exceptional brutality. The first Slave Revolt (136-132 BC) was led by Eunus of Enna, whose followers managed to occupy a large swathe of central Sicily before being savagely put down by the Roman army. Another revolt, which took place near Palermo (104-100 BC), was smaller but concluded no less tragically: the slaves were promised mercy if they capitulated, but were sent, instead, to Rome to be torn apart by lions.

Detail from the Sant'Agata carnival, Catania.

Politically, Sicily was a quiet backwater under Roman rule, but it found itself centre stage briefly during the civil wars of the first century BC. Julius Caesar (100-44 BC) had nominated Octavian (63 BC to AD 14) – later known as Augustus – as his successor, but Octavian's claim was challenged by Pompey, who was supported by the Sicilians. After Pompey's defeat, the Sicilians were punished: the entire population of Tauromenium (Taormina) was expelled, numerous other city states lost their privileges, and large swathes of land were expropriated as imperial estates.

From the first century AD, much larger landholdings developed, called *latifundia*, which relied heavily on vast amounts of slave labour. Local smallholders were forced to find other occupations, as their land was swallowed up by the great estates, and the inland towns declined notably as the rural population migrated to the coastal cities. However, the wealthy landowners lived in considerable splendour, as evidenced by the dazzling mosaic decoration of the Villa Romana del Casale in Piazza Armerina (see page 224).

Rise of Christianity

Sicily was one of the first Roman regions to become Christianized. St Paul preached in Syracuse in around AD 52, and two of the earliest Christian martyrs were Sant'Agata of Catania (AD 230-251) and Santa Lucia of Syracuse (AD 283-304). Although Christians were persecuted for many years, by AD 380 the official religion of the Roman Empire was Christianity.

By the late third century AD, Diocletian had divided the vast and unwieldy Roman Empire into east and west, each administered by an emperor. The practice continued erratically for a century, but Theodosius (AD 347-395) was the last emperor to rule both eastern and western portions. After his death, the Empire would split decisively, with the Eastern Roman Empire ruling independently from its capital at Constantinople (modern Istanbul), which had been founded in AD 324.

Several Germanic tribes flooded into the declining Western Empire's territories on the Italian peninsula. In AD 440, the Vandals landed on Sicily, only to be ousted in AD 476 by the Ostrogoths. The Goths remained until AD 535, when the island was recovered by the Byzantines (by which name the former Eastern Roman Empire would become known) in AD 535. From AD 663 to AD 668, Syracuse had another moment of glory, when it briefly became the capital of the Empire under Constans II. It was also appointed metropolis of the whole Sicilian Church. In AD 652, an Arab force landed briefly, but soon left. They would return again to conquer the island in the ninth century.

Medieval Sicily: from Arab to Spanish rule

Arab invasion

A Byzantine governor, Euphemius, proclaimed himself emperor in Syracuse in around AD 826. He was rapidly ousted, and fled to north Africa, where he asked the Arabs for support. In AD 827, Euphemius returned to Sicily with a vast fleet and more than 10,000 men under the command of Asad ibn al-Furat, but his own ambitions ended when he was killed later that year. The Arabs, who had conquered huge Mediterranean territories including most of the Iberian peninsula in the preceding century, had long dreamed of ruling Sicily. Palermo (called Bal'harm under the Arabs) fell in AD 831; Messina in AD 842; Enna in AD 859; Syracuse in AD 878; Catania in AD 900; and the last Byzantine stronghold at Taormina, in AD 902.

Sicily had suffered famine and depopulation before the arrival of the Arabs, who revitalized the island's economy by introducing mulberries for silk-making, as well as oranges, pistachios and sugar cane. The Sicilian Emirate allowed freedom of worship to the native Christians, but levied a special tax for the privilege. By AD 902, Palermo had replaced Syracuse as Sicily's capital, and was considered one of the most beautiful and cultured cities of the Mediterranean. But only a century later, the Emirate was destabilized by dynastic disputes, and the Arab leaders of Catania and Agrigento hired Norman mercenaries to support them in battle. The battle was won, but the Normans, who had already conquered much of southern Italy, didn't leave.

Norman Sicily (1091-1194)

Led by the brothers Robert Guiscard and Roger Hauteville, later Roger I of Sicily, the Normans took Messina in 1061, Syracuse in 1086, and Palermo in 1072. Roger was invested as Count of Sicily, and the entire island was under Norman control by 1091. Roger's son, Roger II of Sicily (1095-1154), would unite all the Norman conquests in Italy into one kingdom with a strong, centralized government. Under his enlightened rule, the Kingdom of Sicily enjoyed a golden age, particularly in the arts, and its extraordinary mix of peoples – Byzantine Greeks, Muslim Arabs, Jews, Normans, Lombards and Sicilians – coexisted peacefully. However, under Norman rule, Roman Catholicism would become the predominant religion, partly owing to considerable Lombard immigration from northern Italy. When Roger II's grandson, William II

The trial of Verres

Although most Roman officials saw Sicily as ripe for plunder, none was more grasping than Gaius Verres (120-43 BC). As governor of Sicily, he stripped the temples of their finest treasures, executed enemies on trumped-up charges, and embezzled and extorted vast sums. He was prosecuted for corruption in 70 BC by the Roman lawyer and orator Cicero (106-43 BC), but fled to Marseilles before the trial's conclusion. He was merely one in a long line of corrupt officials who have blighted Sicily right up to the present.

(Guglielmo II, 1155-1189), known as 'The Good', died without issue, the throne of Sicily was claimed by Henry VI (1165-1197), of the German Hohenstaufen dynasty, rulers of the Holy Roman Empire. He was succeeded by his son Frederick II (1194-1250), who became King of Sicily at the age of four.

Hohenstaufen & Angevin rule (1194-1282)

Frederick II (Federico II) was known as 'Stupor mundi' ('Wonder of the world'), and his court at Palermo was famous for its magnificence and academia. He was locked in continuous battles with the papacy throughout much of his reign (paid for partly by heavy taxation on the Sicilians), and constructed a chain of mighty fortresses across the island. The premature death of Frederick's son precipitated another succession crisis, which ended when Sicily came briefly under Angevin rule (1266-1282). Charles of Anjou was deeply unpopular with Sicilians, and the crushing taxation imposed by his French officials further alienated locals. They revolted in 1282, in the uprising known as the Sicilian Vespers (triggered outside a church in Palermo, when a French soldier dared to address a Sicilian woman), during which thousands of French inhabitants were massacred. The Sicilians begged Peter III of Aragon (1239-1285) – Peter the Great – for help. After ousting the Angevins, he was crowned King of Sicily, initiating over 400 years of Spanish rule.

About the island

Catania.

including Sicily. Another outbreak of plague in 1656 decimated the island's population (Trapani was completely abandoned), and a terrible earthquake shattered the eastern portion of the island in 1693, killing more than 60,000 people. Several cities, notably Catania and Noto, were handsomely rebuilt in the Sicilian Baroque style (see page 41). In 1713, the Spanish lost Sicily at the conclusion of the War of the Spanish Succession (1701-1714), and the island passed briefly to Savoy (1713-1720), then to the Austrian Habsburgs (1720-1735), and finally to the Bourbons of Naples in 1735.

Bourbon Sicily & Italian Unification

Bourbon rule (1735-1860)
The Bourbon King Charles V (who would become Carlos III of Spain in 1759) made some efforts at dismantling Sicily's anachronistic feudalism and modernizing its agriculture, but had little success. The status quo remained unchanged: the barons owned the land, which was farmed by the poor, who were entirely dependent on their overlords. The old-fashioned farming methods resulted in poor yields, and most Sicilians lived at subsistence level. When the harvest failed, famine ensued: 30,000 people died in 1763 alone. Charles V and his son Ferdinand (who would become known as Ferdinand I of the Two Sicilies) attempted to alleviate the problem by banishing the Jesuits in 1759, and offering their land for sale in smaller parcels. Unfortunately, the poor still couldn't afford it, so the land was snapped up by the barons. Several reforms were enacted under Viceroy Caracciolo, who crushed the Inquisition (which had become yet another weapon in the armoury of the manipulative barons), but he was forced to resign after the Palermitani revolted when he tried to shorten the religious festival in honour of Santa Rosalia, their patron saint.

The court remained at Naples, capital of the Kingdom of the Two Sicilies (comprising the island and southern Italy). Although largely indifferent to the fate of the island, the royal family were forced to move briefly to Palermo in 1799, and again

Spanish rule (1282-1713)
For much of the 14th century, Sicily was ruled as an independent kingdom, and a sense of a Sicilian nationhood began to emerge. Catalan (spoken by the Aragonese) was the language of the court, but Sicilian was spoken in parliament and by the people. When Aragon became part of Spain (through marriage) in 1409, the Sicilian crown passed with it. Once again, Sicily was reduced to an unimportant backwater, governed by a viceroy and a handful of feudal barons. The Black Death reached Europe through Messina in 1347, and famine, revolt and epidemics continued throughout the 15th century. In 1492, Muslims and Jews were expelled from all Spanish dominions,

between 1806 and 1815, when their capital was threatened during the Napoleonic Wars. As Ferdinand II was unable to raise an army in Sicily, they were protected by the British military, notably Lord Nelson, who was handsomely rewarded with a large estate in Bronte, near Mount Etna (see page 170). The Sicilians were impressed by the British (not least for the cash they brought to the island), and some nobles even raised the possibility of annexing the island to Britain. They also asked for British help drafting the new Constitution in 1812; Ferdinand, threatened with a French invasion and pressured by the irksome presence of the British protectors, was forced to accept it. Under the Constitution, Sicily was granted independence, and the parliament was allowed to make laws and raise taxes. Most importantly, the feudal system was abolished, and landowners were finally required to pay taxes.

Once the Napoleonic threat diminished and Ferdinand was back in Naples, the Constitution was quickly repealed, but the issue of Sicilian independence gained increasing acceptance. Angered by Bourbon neglect, the Sicilians revolted several times, most significantly in 1820 and in 1848, Europe's 'year of revolutions'. Ferdinand was once again forced to accept the 1812 Constitution but, after just 16 months of heady independence, he sent in the army. Messina and Palermo were subjected to such heavy bombardment that Ferdinand was nicknamed 'King Bomba', but he had control of the island once again.

Union with Italy

Dissatisfaction with Bourbon rule was increasingly underpinned by a growing nationalism, and the Italian peninsula was caught up in the wars and struggles of the Risorgimento ('the revival'), a radical movement dedicated to the reunification of Italy. In 1860, Giuseppe Garibaldi (1807-1882), who had enjoyed considerable success against the Austrians and the French in the north of Italy, led his troops against the Bourbons. He took Palermo and Messina, gaining the support of the Sicilian peasants by promising land reform. But land

Giuseppe Garibaldi.

reform had to wait, while Garibaldi crossed to the mainland to take Naples and defeat the Bourbons, and the peasants grew impatient. Rebellion broke out as the peasants attempted to take land by force, particularly at Bronte, but were rapidly put down. In 1861 Italian Unification was officially complete, and the Piedmontese Victor Emmanuel II was proclaimed King of all Italy.

Garibaldi believed Sicily deserved regional autonomy within the new Italian nation, but it quickly became apparent that the politicians in Turin thought differently. Sicily, like the rest of Italy, was taxed heavily and conscription was imposed. Garibaldi confiscated church land in order to give it to the poor, but Turin was desperate for money and sold it to the highest bidder. The Sicilians found themselves poorer than ever, and also, for the first time, forced to leave their homes and their land to fight on the peninsula. In 1866, they revolted and marched on Palermo, but the insurgency was rapidly crushed by the royal navy.

Dissatisfaction continued to simmer, often boiling over into small rebellions, and the northern rulers, who viewed the wretched peasants as bandits, imposed martial law.

The economic gap between the industrial north and the poverty-stricken south grew ever wider. Although Sicily was still overwhelmingly agricultural, sulphur had become the island's biggest export. The profits, of course, lined the pockets of the landowners, while the poor, including children as young as six, worked in nightmarish conditions in the mines. By the 1890s, an economic recession crippled Europe, and Sicily's sulphur industry collapsed (although a few mines would limp on until the 1960s). This coincided with a phylloxera blight that decimated the vineyards, and conditions in Sicily became desperate. Sicilians developed their own version of the socialist workers' organizations called *fasci dei lavoratori* that had sprung up on the mainland. The *Fasci Siciliani* demanded land reform and fairer working practices, but, when a peaceful demonstration degenerated into a riot, it was viciously put down and the movement's leaders imprisoned. Emigration began in earnest, as despairing miners and farm labourers left for America and the promise of work: 14,626, around 6% of the island's population, left in 1893 alone. By 1910, more than a million and a half Sicilians (roughly a third of the total population) had emigrated.

Modern Sicily

During the First World War (1914-1918), Sicily was industrialized to some extent in order to provide munitions for the war effort. The organized crime clans known as the Mafia had become increasingly powerful during the last decades of the 19th century and, as well as engaging in extortion, robbery, and murder, they also controlled elections. They were tolerated by the Fascist leader Benito Mussolini until he declared himself dictator in 1925 and no longer required their support: then,

he sent in the army to throw anyone suspected of Mafia ties in prison.

Italy allied with Germany during the Second World War (1939-1945) and Sicily was bombed heavily by the Allied powers in preparation for an invasion. The cities, particularly Palermo and Messina, were devastated and thousands of civilians died. Operation Husky, the Allied invasion of Sicily by British, Canadian and American forces, took place in 1943, and the island was quickly subdued. Mussolini was toppled soon after, and Italy's new regime capitulated. The Americans took the western side of the island with little bloodshed, thanks, it is widely believed (although never conclusively proved), to Mafia protection arranged by the American-Sicilian gangster Lucky Luciano. The Mafia also made recommendations for the post-war administrative appointments across the island, instituting a political entrenchment which was cemented when they ensured the victory of the Christian Democrats in the 1948 elections. (The Christian Democrat party was eventually dissolved in 1993, after the government was toppled in a huge corruption scandal and many of its leading politicians were accused of Mafia connections.)

Sicily was granted some autonomy within the Italian republic in 1948, and there was some attempt at land reform. But the promised redistribution of land was a long time coming, and more than 400,000 Sicilians (10% of the population) emigrated between 1951 and 1953. There was a brief boom in the 1950s, when the American Marshall Plan provided funds for reconstruction. Under the massive government programme *Cassa di Mezzogiorno* (Fund for the South), hotels, schools, roads and hospitals were built, and homes provided with electricity. Unfortunately, political corruption and the influence of the Mafia in the construction industry led to shocking abuses, including the (continuing) illegal developments in the supposedly protected Valle dei Templi in Agrigento. Corruption and Mafia-style nepotism remain endemic in almost every area of public life. The Sicilian governor, Salvatore Cuffaro, was found

The destroyed buildings of Calza, Palermo.

guilty of Mafia collusion in 2008 and forced to resign. Vote-buying remains common practice, and was widely blamed for Cuffaro's victory over the anti-Mafia candidate for governor, Rita Borsellino, in 2006.

Although the crushing poverty of 50 years ago is a thing of the past, Sicily remains one of the 10 poorest regions in the EU, with an unemployment rate of 26% (some observers believe it to be considerably higher). There has been very little investment in agriculture, the fishing industry is declining, and the discovery of oil did not lead to the much-hoped-for boom. Despite this, there is room for cautious optimism. There is slow improvement in the island's infrastructure (the main motorway between Palermo and Messina was finally completed in 2005 after 35 years), gradual renovation of the historical centres of Palermo and Siracusa, and implementation of protected reserves to preserve the island's extraordinary natural heritage.

But perhaps most important is the sea change in public opinion towards the Mafia and systemic corruption. The Sicilians, particularly young Sicilians, are refusing to accept the status quo, and are speaking out – unthinkable only a generation ago. The murders of the anti-Mafia magistrates Giovanni Falcone and Paolo Borsellino (brother of Rita) in 1992 shocked the islanders profoundly, and triggered a widespread backlash against the Mafia, with several businesses refusing to pay the *pizzo* (protection money), and popular demonstrations in the streets. Estates confiscated from Mafia members are now being converted into agricultural cooperatives and even *agriturismi*. Tourism is on the increase, and, although emigration is the only option for many Sicilians, several return, often to open the stylish guesthouses and country estates that have become increasingly popular.

Tip...

For an overview of Sicilian history in just 100 seconds, check out Salvatore Scandurra's film at salvatorescandurra.com/video/movie.php?v=10 . Turi is a mult-media artist and film-maker whose home town is Giardino-Naxos.

Art & architecture

The Greek theatre at Taormina.

The Greeks left an extraordinary architectural legacy on Sicily, including some of the best preserved Doric temples to be found outside mainland Greece. The island also preserves magnificent mosaics at Villa Romana del Casale and gleaming Byzantine decoration at the Norman cathedrals of Monreale and Cefalù, and in the exquisite Capella Palatina in Palermo. And the cities of the Val di Noto, built in the wake of the terrible earthquake of 1693, are perfect showcases for lavish Sicilian Baroque architecture.

Graeco-Roman

Most of the architectural marvels that continue to dazzle visitors were built by the Greeks over 2,000 years ago. Sicily was home to some of the biggest temples in the ancient world, notably the great shrine to Demeter in Enna, once celebrated throughout Magna Graecia but long destroyed, and the Temple of Jupiter (Zeus) in Akragas (Agrigento). This was the largest Doric temple of the ancient world, and the few surviving columns, which measure a massive 4 m in diameter at the base, are testament to its scale. It is now part of the superb Valle dei Templi (Valley of the Temples) (see page 227) at Agrigento, a magnificent complex built between the sixth and fifth centuries BC and still astonishingly intact. The Tempio della Concordia (built around 450 BC) is one of the best preserved Greek temples anywhere in the world, a perfect example of the Doric style, characterized by tapering fluted columns with plain capitals; almost all of Sicily's temples were built in this style. Once, the temples would have been elaborately painted (apart from the columns), and contained statues of the deities. It's thought that early temples were often decorated with an image of Medusa, and whose face would later be incorporated into the Triancria symbol (see page 29).

Like the temples of Agrigento, those of Selinunte (see page 258), magically poised on a wild and unspoiled headland, were built between the sixth and fifth centuries BC. Segesta (see page 250), in the northwest of Sicily, occupies a quiet valley, and was undoubtedly the work of master craftsmen. Although never roofed, it is also substantially intact. Above the temple, crowning the hill, is an elegant theatre, gouged out of the rock. It is one of several panoramic Greek theatres to survive in Sicily, of which the most beautiful is perhaps that of Taormina (see page 154).

The Teatro Greco (see page 155) at Syracuse was one of the biggest theatres in the ancient world, and the complex also includes a (if rather worn) Roman amphitheatre, built between the third and fourth centuries AD. This was also the period in which the landowners were constructing luxurious country mansions and decorating them lavishly. The grandest of these was the Villa Romana del Casale (see page 224), a late-Imperial villa with the finest mosaic decoration to survive in situ anywhere in the world. Two other villas have been discovered at Patti (see page 125) and Tellaro. There are some Roman remains incorporated into the historic heart of Taormina, including the ruins of the Odeon (21 BC) on the piazza Vittorio Emanuele, and the Naumachia ('sea battle'), a brick wall with niches, which, despite its rousing name, was simply a boundary wall, perhaps of a well or a spring dedicated to the nymphs.

Five of the best

Graeco-Roman treasures

Sicily boasts five excellent archaeological museums: those at Palermo, Siracusa, Lipari, Agrigento and Gela. They contain some extraordinary ancient treasures, including ceramics, statuary, stone carvings from the ancient temples, and mosaics. The best pieces are:

❶ Bronze ram from Syracuse, third century BC, in Palermo museum (see page 84).

❷ Metopes of Selinunte, a series of sculpted panels that once adorned the temples of Selinunte's friezes, sixth to fifth centuries BC, in Palermo museum.

❸ *Venus Anadyomene*, a sensuous headless statue of Venus from the Temple of Athena at Sircusa, Roman copy of a Greek original, in Siracusa museum (see page 196).

❹ *Ephebus of Agrigento*, the marble statue of an athlete from the fifth century BC, in Agrigento museum (see page 229).

❺ *Il Giovane di Motia*, an outstanding Greek sculpture of a young man with delicately rendered garments, in the Museo Whitaker (see page 251).

Norman, Gothic & Renaissance

After the Romans, Sicily was invaded by Germanic tribes, then by the Byzantines and finally by the Arabs. But none of these cultures would leave their mark on Sicilian art and architecture until the arrival of the Normans, who built splendid churches and invited the Byzantines and Arabs to decorate them. The first Norman churches in Palermo were small and rounded in the Arabic style and topped with pierced cupolas – as in La Martorana (see page 84) and San Catalado (see page 84) – but later churches displayed Romanesque influences from northern Italy. The Byzantines added the sublime mosaics, which still decorate some of Sicily's most beautiful monuments.

Foremost among these is the Cappella Palatina in Palermo's Palazzo dei Normanni (see page 81), built for Roger II, which achieved a perfect synthesis of Norman, Arabic and Byzantine styles.

About the island

The walls glitter with intricate mosaic work, while a graceful cupola soars overhead. This tiny chapel is a miniature jewel of what was known as Sicilian Romanesque, a style that would become refined in the construction of the great cathedral at Cefalù (see page 115). The finest craftsmen from Greece and Constantinople were commissioned to work on the vast mosaic filling the apse, which features a huge and unusually gentle image of the Christ Pantocrator. In the lovely cloister, slender columns are adorned with exquisitely carved capitals, which illustrate a distinct Arabic influence in the intricately wrought flowers and garlands. The great apotheosis of the Sicilian Romanesque is undoubtedly the Duomo of Monreale (see page 96). Every surface of the vast interior gleams with gold, and the enormous cloister is fringed with superbly carved columns, each delicate capital depicting a fabulous creature, or a riot of flowers and palm fronds.

The arrival of the Hohenstaufen rulers in the 13th century marked the end of Sicily's artistic golden age. Art and architecture were no longer prized, and the biggest architectural contributions of Emperor Frederick II were the hulking castles that he erected across the island: Castello Maniace in Siracusa (see page 171), Castello Ursino in Catania (see page 164) and Castello di Lombardia at Enna (see page 221) still survive.

Sicily passed to the Spanish crown in the early 15th century, just as the Renaissance was reaching its apex on the Italian mainland. But the Renaissance would pass Sicily by, with the exception of one outstanding painter: Antonello da Messina (1430-1479). The Messina-born artist travelled through northern Europe, and, on his return, introduced oil painting and Flemish realism to Sicilian art. One of his finest paintings, *Portrait of an Unknown Man* (1470), can be seen at the Museo Mandralisca (see page 116) in Cefalù. Other works

Detail from the Palatine chapel, Palermo.

Where to see Norman, Gothic and Renaissance art

Capella Palatina in Palazzo dei Normanni, Palermo A jewel of the Norman-Arab-Byzantine decorative style (see page 81).

Cathedral, Palermo Catalan-Gothic portal, statues by Gagini family (see page 82).

La Martorana and San Cataldo, Palermo Exquisite, Arabic-style early Norman churches (see page 84).

Cathedral and cloister, Cefalù Among the earliest and best preserved Byzantine mosaics in Sicily (see page 115).

Cathedral and cloister, Monreale The greatest example of Byzantine art (see page 115).

Museo Mandralisca, Cefalù Antonello da Messina's *Portrait of an Unknown Man* (see page 116).

Museo Regionale, Messina Renaissance paintings (see page 152).

are found in the Museo Regionale in Messina (see page 152), which contains the best collection of Renaissance art on the island, and in the Palazzo Bellomo in Siracusa (see page 194). The great artistic achievements of 16th- and 17th-century Spain, where Velázaquez was painting at the Habsburg court, would have no impact on Sicilian art. Some elements of Spanish architecture, in particularly the Catalan Gothic style imported by the Aragonese in the early years of their rule, still survive, particularly in the sculpted porch of Palermo's Duomo (see page 82) and in a string of handsome palazzi – Palazzo Ajutamicristo, Palazzo Chiaramonte, and Palazzo Abatellis (see page 92).

Domenico Gagini (1420-1492), a sculptor from northern Italy, moved to Sicily and became the founding father of a dynasty of artists which would have considerable influence on the island. Their work still adorns Palermo's Duomo and the church of San Domenico (see page 87).

Sicilian Baroque

In 1693, a devastating earthquake rocked eastern Sicily, killing thousands and destroying more than 45 towns and cities. The new Baroque style, which had recently come into vogue, swept the island as cities like Catania were raised from the rubble. The Sicilians refined Spanish and Italian Baroque, creating a distinctive style characterized by lavish ornamentation. Volcanic lava was used in much of the new construction, and architects played with its myriad shades of grey and black in the decoration of the new buildings.

This is particularly evident in the historic heart of Catania (see page 161), which was largely the work of the Sicilian architect Giovanni Battista Vaccarini (1702-1768). Vaccarini, who studied in Rome before returning to Sicily, designed Catania's beautiful Duomo (see page 163) and the nearby church of Badia di Sant'Agata, as well as the pediment topped by the city's symbol, the lava-stone elephant, which still sits in the centre of the piazza del Duomo.

Generally regarded as the greatest jewel of Baroque architecture in Sicily, the city of Noto (see page 200) was rebuilt in a different location after the earthquake. Several remarkable architects worked on the new city, but the acknowledged master was Rosario Gagliardi (1698-1762), who oversaw the plans for reconstruction. Although his best churches are in other towns, Gagliardi's vision is reponsible for the architectural harmony that characterizes Noto's beauty. Gagliardi's greatest works were the churches of San Giorgio and San Giuseppe in nearby Ragusa (see page 205) and the spectacular Duomo di San Giorgio atop a sweeping flight of stairs in Módica (see page 206). Another of the great architects of Noto was Vincenzo Sinatra (1720-1765) who was responsible for Noto's Palazzo Ducezio.

Noto, Catania, Ragusa and Módica are the best known of the great Baroque cities of the Val di Noto (see page 200) which are now protected as a UNESCO World Heritage Site: the other four cities singled out are Caltagirone, Militello in Val di

Five of the best

Baroque balconies

❶ University of Catania, Catania Pouting *putti* support the balcony, decorated with lava-stone in shades of grey, in this building designed by Vaccarini (see page 160).

❷ Palazzo Zacco, Ragusa This very decorative balcony is supported by an extraordinary cast of musicians, cherubs and grotesques pulling faces (see page 205).

❸ Palazzo Beneventano del Bosco, Siracusa A late Baroque building, with restrained decoration, this features elegant wrought-iron balconies.

❹ Palazzo Iudica, Palazzolo Acreide This enormous palace features one of the longest balconies in Sicily, thickly covered with an array of *putti*, masks and grotesques sticking their tongues out (see page 198).

❺ Palazzo Nicolaci Villadorata, Noto More gamboling *putti* and leering grotesques support the wrought-iron balconies of this once lavish Baroque palace (see page 202).

Palazzo Nicolaci Villadorata, Noto.

Catania, Palazzolo Acreide and Scicli. The lavish adornment intrinsic to the Sicilian Baroque style was not restricted to sacred buildings: secular architecture was equally lavish, and exterior decoration included elaborate balconies, notably in Noto's Palazzo Villadorata, or those lining the via Garibaldi in Palazzolo Acreide.

The Baroque style developed differently in Palermo, where the influence of the Spanish dons was strongest. The lavish Quattro Canti crossroads (see page 83) remains the best example of *Spagnolismo* (a very ornamental style beloved by the Spanish) in all its splendid, overblown glory. Churches and palaces were decorated profusely, every surface thickly covered with elaborate decoration. The great artist Giacomo Serpotta (1656-1732) transformed many of Palermo's oratories, notably the magnificent Oratory of the Rosary in the church of San Zita, with its swarms of stucco cherubs.

Stile Liberty

Sicily sunk into decline at the end of the 18th century and there was no great art or architecture for another hundred years. The island witnessed a brief renaissance at the turn of the 20th century, with the Liberty style. This movement swept through Italy and became popular in Palermo. So many Liberty-style villas were built on one street that it was named after the movement, via Libertà. Although most of the villas were razed during the 'Sack of Palermo' in the 1960s (see page 46), the city still boasts a large Liberty heritage. Giovanni Battista Basile, who designed the Teatro Massimo, was an early exponent of the style, and his home Villa Favoloro (in piazza Virgilio off via Dante) was built to his designs in 1889. Ernesto Basile created some of the best surviving Liberty villas, including the Villa Igiea, now a hotel (see page 102), and the Villino Florio (see box page 91).

Architectural glossary

Aedicule A frame around a doorway or window made up of columns or pilasters and an entablature on top. It can also be a mini decorative structure housing a statue. It is used in both Classical and Gothic architecture.

Arcade A row of columns that support arches.

Architrave The lower part of an entablature, which meets the capitals of the columns.

Baglio A large, sometimes fortified, building set around a courtyard. It also came to mean a warehouse.

Baldachin A canopy over a tomb, supported by columns.

Campanile Bell tower.

Capital The crown of a column.

Cloister Usually part of a church, this is a covered passage around a courtyard, lined with columns or arches.

Chiesa Madre Parish church.

Choir The chancel of a church, which is used by the clergy and the choir; it is occasionally separated from the nave by a screen.

Colonnade A series of columns.

Columns The Greeks had three orders of columns: the **Doric** order, characterized by straight up-and-down plainness is meant to symbolize man (the grooves are called fluting); **Ionic**, characterized by scrolls, symbolizes women, and **Corinthian**, which has a bell-shaped top (or capital) and is adorned with acanthus leaves and volutes, symbolizes virgins. The Romans added the **Tuscan** order, which is without decoration, while the **Composite** order is a mish-mash of the three Grecian orders. In Sicily, the predominant order is Doric.

Cornice A horizontal ledge or moulding. Practically, it's a gutter, draining water away from the building; aesthetically, it's a decorative feature.

Cupola A dome on a roof.

Duomo A cathedral.

Krater An ancient Greek vase, used to mix water and wine.

Nave The central body of the church, between the aisles.

Pediment The gable end or front of a Grecian-style structure, above the frieze and cornice, that supports the columns.

Pilaster A rectangular column that only slightly protrudes from a wall.

Pinnacle A small often ornate turret, popular in Gothic architecture.

Plinth The lower part or base of a column.

Portico A roofed space that serves as an entrance to a building.

Putti Figures of plump babies, usually naked, sometimes with wings.

Sacristy A room off the main or side altars in a church or, occasionally, a separate building that houses the sacred vessels, vestments and records.

Temple These are named according to the numbers of columns: a **distyle** temple has two columns, a **tetrastyle** temple has four, an **octastyle** temple has eight, etc.

Tessera An individual tile used in a mosaic, usually cube-shaped.

Tracery Ornamental stonework that supports the glass in Gothic windows.

Tympanum The decorated area above a door, usually semicircular or triangular in shape.

Sicily today

Passport control, Palermo airport.

Immigration crisis – on the front line

Concern over illegal immigration has become a political hot potato throughout Europe in recent years, but nowhere more so than in Italy. Silvio Berlusconi was returned to power in 2008 as part of a coalition which includes the fiercely anti-immigrant Lega Nord, and an 'immigration emergency' was promptly declared. In response to this state of emergency, 3,000 troops were deployed on the streets of major cities (including Palermo) as part of a nationwide crackdown on illegal immigration, which the government has linked to rising crime figures. International opinion has widely condemned these draconian tactics, but they have the support of a surprisingly large percentage of Italians, particularly in the context of the global economic recession. Italy counts 3.7 million foreign residents among its population, of whom 650,000 are said to be *clandestini* (immigrants without papers). Numbers rose dramatically in 2008, partly as a consequence of

Addio Pizzo

Spain tightening its border outposts in North Africa. Of those processed through the detention centres, about half are economic migrants, mainly from Tunisia, who are usually deported, while the rest are political refugees fleeing war or persecution.

Sicily is on the front line of the immigration crisis – literally. The tiny island of Lampedusa is 250 km from mainland Sicily, but just 113 km from the Tunisian coast, and thousands of people, crammed into unseaworthy craft, attempt the desperate journey annually. Many don't make it: the UNHCR (the UN refugee agency) believes at least 2,000 die at sea every year. Lampedusa has a reception centre for the boat people, which was built to accommodate 850 detainees, but has frequently sheltered up to twice that number. The island is home to around 5,000 people, but an average of 15,000 migrants pass through the detention centre annually. Locals have long complained about the pressure on the island's limited resources (particularly the lack of fresh water and the insufficient sewage facilities) and, especially, the impact on tourism, which is Lampedusa's major industry. Things reached fever pitch in late 2008, when the immigration system was changed as part of Berlusconi's crackdown: new arrivals were no longer sent to the mainland for dispersal but forced to stay in the centre until their asylum applications were processed. This led to terrible overcrowding, and the inmates broke out of the centre in early 2009 to protest against the appalling conditions. They were joined in the protest by locals, who have found themselves in an unexpected alliance with the migrants against government plans to expand detention facilities in the island.

Plans to build a second detention centre, and expand the one currently in use, have caused uproar on the little island. The government's response to the immigration crisis is to seal Italy's porous borders, and turn migrants away at the door – and Lampedusa has become the country's front door. But locals, led by mayor Dino de Rubeis, are determined that Lampedusa won't become a "prison island". The islanders have organized

Lampedusa.

themselves into a pressure group, SOS Pelagie (sospelagie.it), and the mayor has visited Brussels and appealed to the European Union for help. "After all," he says, "this is a European problem."

Europeans, however, are no closer to finding a solution to the prickly issue of immigration. Just as Berlusconi was sending the army onto the streets in the summer of 2008, Europe's interior ministers reached agreement on a *Pact on Immigration and Asylum* which sets out guidelines for a common immigration policy. It was endorsed in October, with several amendments, but has been heavily criticized by human rights NGOs, particularly with regard to the controversial 'Return Directive', which would crack down on illegal immigrants and increase forced deportation.

Meanwhile, back on Lampedusa, the people anxiously await bookings for the summer after months in the glare of the media.

The Mafia & Mafiosità

Opinions may be divided on the origins of the Mafia, but most agree that it had taken on the form recognizable today by the end of the 19th century. The Mafia developed from the *gabellotti*, agents engaged by the barons to administer their lands and collect taxes. As well as the infinite possibilities for skimming, they were perfectly placed for a little extortion: both from the peasants whose livelihoods they controlled, and from the landowners who required protection from a potentially restive populace. Mussolini almost wiped out the Mafia in the 1920s, but it returned with a vengeance after the Second World War, when Mafia leaders could prove their impeccable anti-Fascist credentials and were accordingly placed in important administrative positions by the Allied powers. In 1948, the Mafia (who had long been proficient at 'persuading' voters) ensured the victory of the Christian Democrat Party, thus cementing the influence of Cosa Nostra in the corridors of power.

The relationship between the Christian Democrats and the Mafia was extremely profitable for many years. This reached its peak during the 1960s, when Salvo Lima was mayor (first in 1958-1963 and then again 1965-1968), and Vito Ciancimino was the deputy in charge of public works. Between them Lima and Ciancimino oversaw the wholesale destruction of the city in the so-called 'Sack of Palermo', in which the historic centre was left to rot while Mafia-run construction firms were given contracts to erect the shoddy, soulless cement apartment blocks that still blight the city's suburbs. Lima, who was widely regarded as seven-times Prime Minister Giulio Andreotti's main contact with Sicily's Costa Nostra, was gunned down by his former 'friends' in 1992. Andreotti himself was not only accused of Mafia connections but also put on trial three times for the murder of a journalist (the case was originally dismissed for lack of evidence, but he was found guilty the second time, only for the judgement to be overruled by a higher judge. He remains a member of the Italian senate). The Christian Democrat Party was dissolved in 1994 amid a massive corruption scandal uncovered by the *Mani Polite* (Clean Hands) investigations of the early 1990s.

Astonishingly, the very existence of the Mafia was in doubt until the 1980s, when Tommaso Buscetta, originally of the Porta Nuova crime family, became the first *pentito* (Mafia turncoat) to break the code of *omertà*. Finally, the extent of Cosa Nostra organization was revealed in all its tentacular duplicity, and hundreds of public figures implicated in its criminal activities. As a result of evidence given by the *pentiti*, hundreds of Mafiosi were tried in a special bunker courthouse built inside Palermo's Ucciardone prison during the 1990s. At the forefront of the investigations were the magistrates Giovanni Falcone and Paolo Borsellino, brutally murdered in 1992 by order of Totò Riina, the notoriously violent Mafia boss nicknamed 'The Beast'. Riina was captured after 20 years on the run in 1993, and his successor as *capo di tutti capi* (boss of all bosses) Bernard Provenzano

was finally caught in 2007 after evading police for 43 years. (The fact that Riina was arrested at home, and Provenzano was widely known to be living in a villa in Bagheria, have led most observers to speculate on the extent to which they were protected by high-ranking public officials.) A wave of Mafia arrests followed in 2008 and 2009, and officials are proclaiming the demise of the Mafia. But the battle has only just begun. More than 80% of Palermo's businesses still pay the *pizzo* (protection money), although several brave individuals have stood up against the practice – and, in the case of Libero Grassi, a shopkeeper from Palermo, paid for their courage with their lives.

But the tragedy of modern Sicily is not just the continued existence of the Mafia, but the prevalence of the so-called *Mafiosità* (mafia mentality). Corruption and nepotism remain endemic in every area of public life. Bribery and *bustarellas* (kickbacks) are normal. Who you know is indubitably more important than what you know. Double the number of posts advertised at

academic institutions have been filled, and, until recently, some jobs at the Banco di Sicilia were hereditary. The patient lists at Sicilian hospitals and medical centres are padded with the names of more than 50,000 dead citizens (some of whom passed away more than 35 years ago) at an estimated cost to the state of €14 million. And yet, in 2008 all the street lights went out in Catania because the city hall couldn't afford to pay the electricity bill.

However, there is some cause for cautious optimism: several anti-Mafia groups, including Libera Terra and Pio La Torre, which develop confiscated Mafia lands into farms and *agriturismi*, and Addio Pizzo, which supports businesses that choose not to pay protection money, have enjoyed considerable success in recent years, indicating a profound shift in public opinion. The backlash is not just directed at organized crime, but at the institutionalized culture of corruption and patronage. Whether real, lasting reform will follow, remains to be seen.

Nature & environment

Etna.

At nearly 26,000 sq km, Sicily is the largest island of the Mediterranean, and has been coveted for its beauty and fertility for more than 2,000 years. Mountainous in the north and east, the island's topography undulates gently south and west, where it becomes flatter and emptier. After years of neglect, the Sicilian regional government has finally begun to protect the island's natural heritage by implementing natural parks and marine reserves, but there is still a way to go. Illegal building remains a problem, and fly-tipping is endemic (visitors will be shocked by the site of dumped fridges in beauty spots).

Volcanoes

Eastern Sicily is dominated by the commanding, usually snow-capped bulk of Mount Etna (3329 m), one of the most active volcanoes in the world. It is part of a fiery volcanic chain that begins at Vesuvius (near Naples) in the north, continues southwards through the volcanic archipelago of the Aeolian Islands, and culminates in the tiny volcanic islet of Linosa in the south.

Mount Etna is Europe's highest volcano, and is at the centre of Sicily's only national park, Parco dell'Etna (see page 166) – there are other natural parks, but they are protected at the regional rather than the national level. This measure was introduced to curb the illegal building that was proliferating Etna's flanks in the 1980s, and has been largely successful in preserving the region from unregulated development. The eerie volcanic landscape makes for some superb walking, and even skiing in winter, when the lava glows red-hot beneath the ice. The volcano is in an almost constant state of eruption, and sinuous streams of molten lava are clearly visible at night (they provide entertainment for the crowds at Taormina's elegant terrace cafés and bars). Massive eruptions in 1992 and 2002 badly damaged the two main tourist centres of Rifugio Sapienza and Piano Provenzano, but they have been largely rebuilt.

The second-most famous volcano in Sicily is Stromboli (see page 132), part of the Aeolian archipelago in the northeast. The volcanic island has been rumbling for two millennia and its spectacular fireworks draw huge crowds. Most arrive on one of the regular tour boats that cruise the islands, while a hardy few make the climb up to the main crater for an unforgettable glimpse into the heaving belly of the volcano. On Vulcano (see page 131), the volcanic black-sand beaches are famous for their sulphur mud baths, where the pungent (and mildly radioactive!) clay is said to be good for the health.

The tiny island of Linosa (see page 235) is part of the Pelagian archipelago – formed by Lampedusa, Linosa and Lampione – between Sicily and Tunisia. It's the only volcanic island of the trio, and is remarkable for its beaches of black sand and incredibly clear waters.

Mountain ranges

Sicily's highest mountain peaks dominate the northeast of the island, stretching from Etna to the Tyrrhenian coast. The Madonie, Nebrodi and Peloritani ranges are the last gasp of the great Apennine range that forms the backbone of the Italian peninsula.

Cefalù (see page 115) is the main access town for the Madonie mountain range, which includes two of Sicily's highest peaks (after Etna), and is dotted with beautiful mountain towns. The area is a vast protected natural park, the Parco delle Madonie (see page 118), which stretches for 400 sq km and is home to the indigenous Sicilian fir (*Abies nebrodensis*), plus an extraordinary array of butterflies and wild orchids. It offers fabulous opportunities for hiking (the park information offices have leaflets describing walks), and even skiing in winter.

Adjoining the Madonie is the Nebrodi range, less dramatic but equally beautiful, and protected as the Parco dei Nebrodi (see page 126). The Nebrodi wolf has long been hunted to extinction, but the griffon vulture (see box, page 127), wiped out here in the 1960s, has been successfully reintroduced. San Fratello horses live semi-wild in the northern reaches of the park, and the black-footed pigs that root around the woods are used for excellent local charcuterie. To the east, the Nebrodi range merges with the Peloritan mountains, which stretch towards Messina.

There are two much gentler mountain ranges in Sicily: the Monti Iblei (see page 198) in the southeast and the Monti Erei in the centre of the island (see page 222). These regions are quiet and

Natural parks

Information in Italian and English at parcs.it.

❶ Parco delle Madonie Sicily's highest mountain range, sprinkled with historic towns and villages, is one of the best places to spot Sicilian wildlfe (see page 118).

❷ Parco dei Nebrodi The Nebrodi mountains are not as high as the neighbouring Madonie, but they are covered in beautiful forest and traditional villages (see page 126).

❸ Parco Fluviale dell'Alcantara The Alcantara river valley is lush and green, perfect for hiking, or swimming in the dramatic gorge (see page 159).

❹ Riserva Naturale Oasi Faunistica di Vendicari This coastal wetland is a paradise for birdwatchers, and also boasts glorious, wild, sandy beaches (see page 203).

❺ Riserva Naturale dello Zingaro This occupies a craggy headland, with walking trails linking lovely coves with crystal-clear waters overlooking turquoise waters and perfect coves (see page 249).

rural: the Monti Iblei are greener, dotted with olive groves enclosed by snaking walls, while the more exposed peaks of the Monti Erei are scrubbier and sun-bleached.

Caves & gorges

Eastern Sicily is well endowed with dramatic gorges, which offer some excellent opportunities for walking and swimming. North of Taormina, the Gola dell'Alcantara – part of the Parco Fluviale dell'Alcantara (see page 159) – is a deep gorge of basalt sides, formed when the Alcantara river forced its way through a stream of solidified lava. The banks are green and leafy, and, despite the constant traffic of visitors, popular with myriad birds (including the elusive kingfisher) and animals such as pine martens and porcupines.

Southeast of Siracusa, the Vall dell'Anapo is a verdant river valley with a steep gorge honeycombed with thousands of ancient tombs, the Necropoli di Pantalica (see page 198). Quiet and suprisingly little visited, it's a wonderful place to hike. The island's largest limestone gorge cuts a dramatic, pale swathe just south of Siracusa in the Riserva Naturale Cavagranda del Cassíbile (see page 202).

Another gorge stretches between Ispica and Mòdica, the Cave d'Ispica (see page 207), which is pocked with cave dwellings and rock tombs.

Islands, wetlands & marine reserves

Off the coast of Sicily are several islands and islets. There are three main archipelagos: the Aeolian Islands to the northeast, the Pelagie Islands to the south, and the Egadi Islands to the west. Off Palermo is the large island of Ustica, and west of the Egadis, closer to Africa, is Pantelleria, a favourite hideaway for international celebrities.

The Aeolian Islands (see page 128) – comprising Lipari, Vulcano, Salina, Panarea, Stromboli, Filicudi and Alicudi – is a volcanic chain located north of Milazzo; only Stromboli (see above) is permanently active. The waters are protected as a marine reserve, the presence of minerals making them very clear.

The Pelagian Islands (see page 234) – Lampedusa, Linosa and Lampione – are also protected. More by luck than good management, the waters here are among the cleanest in the entire Mediterranean. Lampedusa and Lampione are calcerous, with white cliffs and beaches, while Linosa is volcanic. Lampedusa and to a lesser extent Linsosa are among the few remaining places where the loggerhead turtle (*Caretta caretta*), which is endangered in the Mediterranean, still lays its eggs.

The Egadi Islands (see page 260) – Favignana, Levanzo and Marettimo – are quieter than their flashier counterparts, but are just as protected in an attempt to preserve them from overdevelopment.

Pantelleria (see page 263), located closer to Africa than to Sicily, is the largest of Sicily's offshore islands. Hot springs bubble up to the surface on this volcanic island (last erruption 1891), which is excellent for birdwatching as it is perfectly located on the migration paths between Africa and mainland Europe.

Innumerable tiny islands and rocky outcrops dot the Sicilian coastline, including the Faraglioni del Ciclope on the Ionian coast north of Catania.

Two of Sicily's most spectacular natural parks are coastal: the Riserva Naturale dello Zingaro (see page 249) in the northwest, and the Riserva Naturale Orientata Oasi Faunistica di Vendicari (see page 203) in the southeast. The latter is another major destination for birdwatchers, with thousands of migratory and resident birds, including flamingos, spoonbills and herons.

Sicilian wildlife

Centuries of intensive farming, deforestation and hunting have taken their toll. Many species, such as the Nebrodi wolf, have disappeared, although an attempt is being made to reintroduce the roe deer (there's a centre near the Nebrodi village of Galati Mamertino). Smaller animals can be spotted in the mountains and forests of the adjoining Madonie and Nebrodi natural parks: look out for porcupines, pine martens, and, after heavy rainfall, the huge Sicilian toad. These forests are also home to an extraordinary variety of butterflies and numerous birds of prey including golden eagles and griffon vultures. For waterbirds, the Vendicari nature reserve is best, particularly during the migration seasons of spring and autumn. Loggerhead turtles are endangered throughout the Mediterranean, but protected on the Egadi island of Lampedusa. In spring, whales come to mate off the Egadis, and dolphins can be spotted year-round. The waters of the Egadi Islands teem with marine life, as do the maritime reserves of the island of Ustica near Palermo, and the Aeolian Islands.

Festivals & events

At the Bachelors' festival, Terrasini.

January

Festa Nazionale della Befana (6th)

Epiphany, which marks the end of the Christmas celebrations, is traditionally the day on which Italian children are given presents. An old witch, Befana, who refused to accompany the Magi to find Jesus in the stable, rewards good children with sweets, and bad children with a lump of coal. There are special masses and celebrations throughout the island, and each town prepares its own bread and cakes. The most famous are those in Bordonaro (just outside Messina), where locals erect the *Pagghiaru*, a tree topped with a huge cross, which is thickly hung with cakes and fruit. After Mass, the kids scramble up the tree and grab the treats.

Arbëresh (6th)

The feast of the Epiphany (12 days after Christmas) is celebrated in Piana degli Albanesi according to ancient rites and traditions passed down from the first Albanian immigrants who arrived here in the

15th century. Exquisite embroidered Balkan costumes, made by hand, are worn in elaborate processions and religious rites. The highlight is a solemn re-enactment of the Baptism of Christ.

Festa di San Sebastiano (20th)
The feast of the martyr San Sebastiano, patron saint of Acireale, is celebrated with fireworks and a lively street party.

February

Festa del Mandorlo (first week)
This festival celebrating the almond blossom in Agrigento, where thousands of almond trees fill the Valle dei Templi with their pale pink blooms. There are puppet shows, music, parades and street parties, and bakeries and street stalls sell all kinds of delicious almond treats.

Carnevale (10 days before Ash Wednesday)
carnevaledisciacca.it
Carnival is celebrated across the island, but the best events are famously held in Acireale and in Sciacca. In Acireale, a magnificent procession of elaborate floats brings huge crowds from across the island. Townspeople spend the entire year decorating the floats with vast historical, mythical or allegorical scenes made of papier-mâché, many of which feature popular TV personalities, celebrities or politicians. Each neighbourhood vies to produce the winning float. In Sciacca, the anarchic figure of Peppe 'Nnappa begins the carnival celebrations by dancing through the streets and inviting the crowds to join in. He leads another fabulous procession of elaborate floats, often hilarious spoofs of contemporary scandals. As in Acireale, the floats are created by neighbourhood collectives, who vie with each other to build the best float.

Festa di San Corrado (19th)
The patron saint of Noto, St Corrado, is celebrated with a procession through the streets of the beautiful Baroque city. An effigy of the saint, accompanied by a silver urn containing his ashes, is carried through Noto, stopping at each of the city's finest churches.

La Festa di Sant'Agata (3rd-5th)
Catania celebrates its patron saint, St Agatha, on the anniversary of her martyrdom, with a huge and very moving procession of her effigy through the city. It is one of the biggest and most lavish festivals on the island, attended by vast crowds. The statue is accompanied by *candelore*, huge elaborate Baroque candle-holders, each of which requires at least two bearers. As dusk falls, hundreds of thousands of candles are lit. It's not all solemn: there is also plenty of street theatre, as well as fireworks, and a carnival atmosphere at the food stalls, where delicious pastries and snacks are sold through the night.

March/April

Pasqua (Easter)
La Settima Santa (Easter week) is celebrated with solemn processions throughout the island, with each town or village preparing special cakes and breads according to time-honoured recipes. The most famous Easter celebrations take place in Trapani, where the *Processione dei Misteri* – the procession of enormous floats bearing sculptural depictions of the Passion of Christ by members of different trade guilds – lasts from 1400 on Good Friday to 1200 on Saturday.

In the mountain town of Gangi, there is an unusual competition between supporters of the Madonna and supporters of Jesus, who vie to produce the most beautiful decorations on the cathedral square on Easter Sunday.

In Piano degli Albanesi, Easter celebrations follow Greek Orthodox traditions and begin with the arrival of the archbishop on horseback on Palm Sunday. There are processions, choirs sing sacred songs, and full-immersion baptisms are performed by white-robed priests. On Easter Sunday, the

About the island

What the locals say

One of my favourite memories of the Taormina film festival is being in the Teatro Greco one July night, with Tom Cruise on stage and the beautiful panorama of Mount Etna behind him. It was his birthday, and the entire cavea was filled with candles as everyone sang 'Happy Birthday'. It was so beautiful and he was very moved.

Giovanna Fichera, Taormina resident.

festival culminates with Mass in the cathedral of San Demetrio followed by a huge feast.

In Terrasini, near Palermo, the Festa degli Schietti (Batchelors' Festival) is celebrated on Easter Sunday. Batchelors lift a beautifully decorated orange tree with just one hand to show their strength to their fiancées.

Prizzi also has its own unusual tradition, the *Aballu de li Diavoli* (Dance of the Devils) which dates back to medieval times and culminates in a horde of 'devils' in masks rampaging through the town.

May

Infiorata (third Sunday)
Noto's via Corrado Nicolaci is carpeted with elaborate 'paintings' made entirely of flower petals, the start of a week-long festival including art exhibits, classical music concerts, and a parade of antique carriages decorated with flowers.

June

Taormina Film Festival (mid-June)
taorminafilmfest.it
The week-long Taormina film festival is the island's glitziest event, with premieres taking place nightly in Taormina's Teatro Greco. From 2009, events are also held on other parts of the island, including Palermo, Siracusa and Agrigento.

Taormina Arte (June to August)
taormina-arte.com
A summer arts festival takes place in Taormina's Teatro Greco, with opera, ballet and theatre performances by internationally renowned names.

Palermo Estate & Verdura Festival (June to September)
The Palermo Summer Festival takes place from June to September, with a varied programme of events including street theatre, concerts and puppet shows. The Teatro Massimo runs a varied programme of opera, pop, flamenco, jazz and theatre during the summer months. Ask the tourist office for information.

July

Festino di Santa Rosalia (9-15th)
The festival in honour of Palermo's patron saint, Santa Rosalia, is one of the biggest and most popular traditional events in Sicily. The saint is believed to have saved the city from plague in 1624, and her feast is celebrated with processions, concerts, street theatre and fireworks.

August

Palio dei Normanni (13-14th)
Piazza Armerina re-enacts the arrival of Count Roger I in a two-day festival featuring pageants, jousting and medieval-style street fairs.

September

Madonna di Lampedusa (first Sunday of month to 22nd)
On the first Sunday of September, the fishermen of Lampedusa carry the statue of their patron saint, the Madonna of Lampedusa, through the streets to the town church where it is hidden. On the 22nd

it is processed back to the sanctuary, and the town erupts with fireworks and street concerts.

Il Pellegrinaggio alla Madonna del Tindari (8th)

The Black Madonna of Tindari is one of the most venerated statues in Sicily, and thousands join the annual pilgrimage to the sanctuary, which begins on the night of the 7th. On the 8th, there is a Mass with choirs from across the island, a lively street fair and a huge fireworks show.

Couscous Fest (22nd-27th)

sanviticouscous.com
The famous Sicilian dish of couscous with fish, a fusion of North African and Mediterranean influences, is the focus of a huge, popular festival in San Vito Lo Capo, where there are tastings, concerts and street parties.

October

Festa di Maria SS del Lume (14th)

Santa Flavia
One of the most picturesque local festivals takes place in Santa Flavia, in honour of the Madonna of the Holiest of Light. A procession of fishing boats, lit with torches, is followed by the blessing of the statue, which is submerged in the port.

November

Tutti i Santi (All Saints' Day; 1st)

All Saints' Day is a national holiday celebrated across Sicily. This is the Italian version of Halloween (which is increasingly celebrated), when children often dress up in frightening costumes, and *pasticceries* are full of traditional confectionery. The following day, the Day of the Dead, children traditionally hunt for sweets and toys left overnight by the 'souls of the dead', and families take picnics and visit their relatives' graves, decorating them with candles and flowers.

December

Festa di Santa Lucia (13th)

Siracusa
The patron saint of Siracusa, Santa Lucia, is celebrated during a week-long festival beginning with a solemn procession of the much-venerated silver statue of the saint through the city streets. Hundreds of white doves are freed on the piazza del Duomo and there are also puppet shows, fireworks and concerts.

Presepi di Natale

One of the most unusual features of the Christmas period in Italy, including Sicily, are the 'living' nativity scenes, or *presepi viventi*, which take place in several towns including Caltagirone, Noto, Palazzolo Acreide and Montalbano Elcano. Costumed townspeople re-enact the arrival of the Magi. Manger scenes can be found in most towns.

The Infiorata Festival, Noto.

Sleeping

A room with a view.

Whether you want to hobnob with the stars in a palazzo in Taormina, or help out with the olive harvest on a country estate, you'll be spoilt for choice in Sicily, which offers a wide range of accommodation for all tastes and pockets. Not so long ago, the pickings weren't so rich, but recent years have seen the rise of the boutique hotel, the quirky B&B, and the stylish *agriturismo*. Unfortunately, these options are largely confined to the cities, coastal resorts and major tourist attractions: as soon as you head off the beaten track, the options become more limited. Many towns and villages of the interior have no accommodation at all, although, if they like the look of you, staff in the tourist offices may be able to put you in touch with someone offering *camere* (rooms). If you are travelling with your own transport, *agriturismi* are often the best rural options, but anyone travelling by public transport should plan acccommodation carefully in advance.

Villas & apartments

Self-catering is often a good idea if you are travelling with the family or in a large group. Sicily offers a range of splendid seaside villas (one tour company offers a particularly luxurious option which is voted 'best villa in the Mediterranean' year after year), with most concentrated around the tourist meccas of Cefalù and Taormina. Self-catering apartments by the sea are very popular with the Italians, particularly on the islands, and you'll be hard pressed to find any available in August unless you book well in advance. These are usually much cheaper than hotels, although they are often basic and located in the standard concrete holiday blocks that are a feature of every Italian seaside resort. Increasingly, *agriturismi* are offering self-catering accommodation, often in attractively converted stables or outhouses. See also Useful websites, page 59 – thinksicily.com and opensicily.com are both highly recommended.

Tip...

Prices soar in the high season, particularly on the islands and along the coast. For four weeks in late July and August, expect everything to cost three or four times what it would a month later, and plan accordingly. Affordable accommodation is often booked solid for this period, so reserve quickly. Many hotels require full or half board during the peak season, and it's wise to check before you book. Note that many of the island hotels close in winter.

Five of the best

Agriturismi

❶ **Masseria Maggiore, Pettineo** A 19th-century family farm has been beautifully converted into a luxurious retreat with superb home cooking (see page 136).

❷ **Monaco di Mezzo, Petralia Sottana** A gem in the Madonie mountains, with horse riding (see page 136).

❸ **Tenuta San Michele, Santa Venerina** Gaze out across the snaking vines to the enormous silhouette of Mount Etna from this comfortable farm (see page 176).

❹ **Agriturismo La Frescura, Siracusa** A friendly, family-run farm on the edge of historic Siracusa, with delicious meals prepared with their own organic produce (see page 208).

❺ **Masseria Mandrascate, Valguarnera** Stylish, welcoming, with a heavenly setting in green hills near piazza Armerina and the Villa Romana del Casale (see page 236).

Agriturismi

Perhaps the best way to visit Sicily is to stay on one of the island's superb *agriturismi* (farm accommodation). There is a huge range available, from palatial accommodation with pool and restaurant (to rival any luxury hotel) to simple farms with rustic rooms. Farm holidays have become increasingly popular throughout Italy over the last few years, particularly with families, and some offer plenty of child-friendly extras such as play areas and children's pools. Most are on working farms, and some allow guests to take part in the harvest, or prepare meals with produce grown on the estate. Others include specific activities, such as horse riding, or tours of Mount Etna. A new initiative has seen the lands confiscated from Mafia leaders being transformed into working farms with accommodation: the idea behind the scheme is to provide much-needed work for locals so that they can resist joining the Mafia through poverty. See also Useful websites, page 59.

About the island

Hotels

The swankiest hotels are clustered in Taormina, followed by the main cities and resorts. Four- or five-star accommodation is virtually unheard of in Sicily's interior, although some *agriturismi* offer luxurious hotel-style services. The craze for boutique hotels that has swept the rest of the world in the last decade has been slow to reach Sicily but, finally, the word is out and the island can now offer some sumptuous designer accommodation. There is still plenty of dreary, chain-hotel-style accommodation, so popular in the 1970s and 1980s, but the classic peeling palazzo with creaking furniture and a rosary on the wall has almost had its day.

There are scores of hotel-booking websites (see Useful webites, page opposite, for a small selection). These tend to concentrate on mainstream hotels and the more expensive ones.

Note that the star rating refers to services rather than difficult-to-rate features such as charm or service. This can lead to anomalies such as a stunning little hotel with rooms filled with antiques but no lift earning a lower rating than a concrete monstrosity with a cafeteria and as much soul as an airport waiting lounge. Star ratings are also rarely an indication of price, particularly on the islands, where some of the most expensive hotels on Sicily have only a two- or three-star rating.

B&Bs

The biggest recent change in the Sicilian accommodation scene has been the proliferation of B&Bs. These vary wildly, from a simple room in a converted palazzo to private homes full of chintzy flounces. Many of the smaller towns without hotel accommodation will have a few B&Bs. Tourist

The Sul Mare hotel, Castel di Tusa, has 15 rooms decorated by renowned artists.

information offices can usually provide details. Like hotels, there has been a definite swing towards the cool and stylish in recent years. Prices are usually very reasonable, and B&Bs will usually offer better accommodation than hotels for the same price. See also Useful websites, right.

Hostels & *rifugi*

There are only five official youth hostels on Sicily. These can be found in the major tourist centres Palermo, Catania, Piazza Armerina and Noto, and in the rural town of Castroreale. Siracusa, Taormina and the Aeolian Islands offer independently run backpacker accommodation. Prices start at around €16 for a dorm bed. Only official youth hostels (ostellionline.org, including online reservations) require membership of a hostelling organization. For suggestions on independent backpacker hostels, check out Useful websites, right.

For walkers and climbers, Italy's system of *rifugi* (mountain huts) offer basic (usually extremely basic) accommodation in rural mountainous areas: in Sicily they can be found in the Madonie and Nebrodi ranges, and also on Mount Etna. The *rifugi* are run by the Club Alpino Italiano (cai.it, some sections of the website are exclusively in Italian) and are open to non-members. Advance booking is essential.

Convents & monasteries

Several convents and monasteries offer simple accommodation to visitors. These are rarely advertised and it can be hard to find information, but the Italian tourist office can provide lists in advance of your trip. An easier way of arranging a monastery stay may be to contact a specialist tour operator, such as Monastery Stays (monasterystays.com), which can arrange rooms at seven properties throughout the island (prices range from €82 to €200 for a double room, which includes the booking fee).

Useful websites

Villas & apartments
discoversicily.com.
opensicily.com
ownersdirect.co.uk
perfectplaces.com
solosicily.com
thinksicily.com

Agriturismi
agriturismo.com.
agriturismosicilia.it
agriturist.it
siciliariturismo.com (Italian only)
toprural.com

Hotels
destinia.com
hotels.com
travelnow.com.
venere.com

B&Bs
bbplanet.it
bedandbreakfast.com
bed-and-breakfast-sicilia.it

Hostels & *rifugi*
ostellionline.org
bug.co.uk
hostelbookers.com
realadventures.com

Tip…

The website tripadvisor.com is an excellent resource, thanks to its numerous warts-and-all consumer reviews.

Eating & drinking

Even in a country famed for its passion for food, the Sicilians stand out. Andrea Camilleri's hugely popular fictional detective and gourmand, Inspector Montalbano, can be silenced by a perfectly prepared dish of *caponata*, and spends at least as much time pondering what to eat and where to eat it as he does capturing criminals.

Sicilian cuisine

The island's cuisine is wonderfully rich, combining the wide range of local ingredients with an infusion of flavours bequeathed by Greeks, Normans, Spanish and, perhaps most pervasively, Arabs and, later, North Africans. It's not surprising that the Slow Food Movement (founded in Italy in the 1980s as a protest against 'fast food') flourishes in Sicily; few cuisines place such emphasis on the importance of fresh, seasonal produce, or so carefully cherish their traditional foods.

Every town and village has its street market, with stalls piled high with seasonal produce: zingy blood oranges and citrus fruit in winter, mounds of artichokes and broad beans in spring, then melons and peaches, and the bursting figs and *fichi d'india* (prickly pear) of late summer, and then the pungent mushrooms of autumn. By the side of every road is a little three-wheeled truck (known as *ape*, meaning bee) overflowing with whatever is in season. And even if you don't speak a word of Italian, you can bet your last euro that the impassioned exchange between the stallholder and the client has something to do with food.

The cuisine follows the landscape, as well as the seasons. On the coast, fish predominates, particularly swordfish and tuna, although octupus, squid and a dazzling range of shellfish is also available. In some of the smaller coastal towns, you can head to the quay to buy the catch of the day directly from the fishermen. A visit to Catania's celebrated fish market is one of the best experiences to be had on the island. Inland, meat features more prominently on the menu, particularly pork and lamb, which is often served simply grilled, barbecue-style over hot coals. The inland regions, particularly the Madonie and Nebrodi mountains, also enjoy a superb reputation for artisanal cheeses, including *provola*, *ragusano* and *caciocavallo*, and all kinds of hams and cured sausages. Black Nebrodi pigs, which live semi-wild in the forest, are the source of highly regarded *prosciutto* and other pork products.

Great, universally known Sicilian dishes include: *pasta alla Norma*, named apparently after Bellini's opera, and prepared with aubergine, tomatoes and a pungent, cured ricotta cheese; *caponata*, a sort of ratatouille made with aubergine, peppers and tomatoes; *cuscus al pesce*, North African-style couscous served with fish rather than meat; and *pasta con le sarde*, which is made with sardines, anchovies and fennel.

Sicily is also famous for its snack foods, including *arancine*, stuffed, fried rice balls which usually contain a filling made with minced meat, peas, tomato sauce, and mozzarella, although there are many variations. Palermitan specialities include *sfincione*, a kind of pizza made with tomatoes, onions and anchovies, and *panella*, slivers of fried chickpea dough (the best are served at the little stalls in the the city's markets).

So the history of Sicily is written on the plate, in the granitas, cannoli, bread, pasta; in the vegetables and fruits; in the crespelle, pannelle, fave, lenticchie, sesame seeds and framento duro; in the methods of preservation – salted, sun-dried, sott'olio, sott'aceto; in the chocolate, rice, tomatoes, melanzane and peppers; in the spices, cloves, cinnamon, nutmeg; in the stuffed vegetables, fried fish, grilled meats and the fancy French-inspired styles of the aristocracy…

Matthew Fort, *Sweet Honey, Bitter Lemons*.

Desserts & pastries

Sicilians are famous the world over for their outstanding sweet pastries. Top desserts include *cannoli*, pastry tubes filled with a creamy, sweet ricotta filling, and *cassata*, a rich cake stuffed with more creamy ricotta, but every town and village has its own particular speciality and a visit to the *pasticceria* is always a treat. The ice cream (*gelati*) is outstanding, and often freshly prepared with whichever fruit is in season; try it local style, served inside a soft brioche roll.

When & where to eat

Colazione (breakfast) in Sicily usually consists of a *caffè latte* or an *espresso* accompanied by a pastry, usually a croissant-shaped cornetto with fillings – *alla crema* (pastry cream), *al cioccolato* (chocolate) or *alla marmellata* (marmalade). At weekends, particularly on Sundays, Sicilians will enjoy a long *pranzo* (lunch), which will inevitably be followed by a siesta in the deadening heat of summer. In the evenings, after the *passeggiata*, locals might head to a café terrace for an *aperitivo*.

Although traditionally *ristoranti* were a cut above less formal *trattorie*, this distinction has now been blurred to the point at which it is no longer any indication of the quality of an establishment.

About the island

Ristorante-pizzerie serve pizzas (which are almost as good as those in Naples), but will often also offer a wide range of local meat, fish and pasta dishes. A full lunch or dinner Italian-style usually begins with antipasti, often a selection of cold dishes at a self-service buffet. For the first course, *il primo*, it's usual to have a pasta dish or perhaps some soup. *Il secondo* is the meat or fish dish, which will probably be served unaccompanied, so you will probably have to order vegetable *contorni* (side dishes). Curiously, in a region famed for its sweet delicacies, restaurant *dolci* (desserts) are rarely good, and it's best to stick to fresh fruit (and head to the nearest *pasticceria* after the meal) unless you know the desserts are home-made.

Restaurants usually serve lunch from 1200 to 1530 and dinner from 1900 to 2300. If you get the munchies between meals, look for a *távola calda* ('hot table'). These simple snack bars sell all the delicious Sicilian fast foods, from *arancine* to mini-pizzas.

Wines of Sicily

Sicily is one of Italy's largest wine-producing areas, and local wine, once a byword for cheap plonk, has become increasingly sophisticated in recent years, with a full spectrum of wines being made from both indigenous (such as Nero d'Avola and Grillo) and international grape varieties. There are several regional liqueurs, made from almonds, or prickly pear, and Sicilian *limoncello* is deliciously zesty. Few of the DOC (*Denominazione di Origine Controllata*) areas are well known outside the island – the most prominent wine regions are Etna in the east, Alcamo in the northwest in Trapani province, and Marsala in the west.

Alcamo Perhaps best known for its dry yet fruity Bianco di Alcamo, the perfect accompaniment to seafood.

Cerasuolo di Vittoria A pale-coloured yet full-bodied, dry red with aromas of cherries from the Ragusa region.

Etna Currently the hottest wine-producing area with a range of reds, rosés and whites from fashionable new wineries, including one belonging to Mick Hucknall of Simply Red.

Faro A popular, medium-bodied red grown in the Messina region.

A wine cellar in Marsala.

Malvasia delle Lipari This is a stunning sweet wine produced in the Aeolian Islands, particularly on Lipari.

Marsala Sicily's most famous tipple, the key ingredient in that most popular of Italian desserts, *zabaglione*. An Italian equivalent to sherry and port, this fortified wine was popularized by the British in the early 19th century. It comes in a variety of forms including dry, medium or sweet, and is available as *oro* (golden), *ambra* (amber) and *rubino* (ruby). It is most commonly drunk as an aperitif, or to accompany dessert.

Moscato Sweet dessert wines are made in Siracusa and Noto, but the most celebrated wines come from Pantelleria, where sweet wines of varying styles – *passito* (from dried grapes) and *non-passito*, some fortified, some sparkling – are made from the Zibibbo (Muscat of Alexandria) grape, much as they were five hundred years ago.

Some of the most famous wine producers include Regaleali, which spearheaded the revival of Sicilian wines and is still probably the most popular producer on the island, as well as Rallo (Donnafugata), Planeta (Noto), Pellegrino (Marsala), Moncada Rudini (Pachino) and Murgo (Etna).

The €10 picnic

Go to any *alimentari* (and every town will have several) and pick up a loaf of the typical Sicilian sourdough bread, available everywhere and utterly delicious. Ask for a couple of slices of *prosciutto dei Monti Nebrodi*, a few slivers of the *Provola* cheese (the creamy variety is a perfect counterpoint to the ham), a handful of olives (you can usually try a few varieties before deciding on the ones you like best), and a plump tomato. Rub the tomato on the bread, add a drizzle of olive oil, pile on the ham and cheese, and wash down with some local wine. Finish up with a ripe peach or a handful of purple figs.

Palermo market.

The famous local honey of Etna.

Menu reader

General

affumicato smoked
al sangue rare
alla griglia grilled
antipasto starter/appetizer
arrosto roasted
ben cotto well done
bollito boiled
caldo hot
contorni side dishes
coppa/cono cup/cone
cotto cooked
cottura media medium
crudo raw
degustazione tasting menu of several dishes
dolce dessert
fatto in casa homemade
forno a legna wood-fired oven
freddo cold
fresco fresh
fritto fried
piccante spicy
primo first course
ripieno stuffed
secondo second course

Drinks (bevande)

acqua naturale/gassata/frizzante still/sparkling water
birra beer
birra (alla spina) beer (draught)
bottiglia bottle
caffè coffee (ie espresso)
caffè macchiato/ristretto espresso with a dash
  of foamed milk/strong
spremuta freshly squeezed fruit juice
succo juice
vino bianco/rosato/rosso white/rosé/red wine
vin santo a dark, sweet, fortified wine

Fruit (frutta) & vegetables (verdure)

agrumi citrus fruits
anguria watermelon
arance oranges
carciofio globe artichoke
castagne chestnuts
ciliegie cherries
cipolle onions
fagioli white beans
fichi figs

finocchio fennel
fragole strawberries
funghi mushrooms
lamponi raspberries
legumi pulses
lenticchie lentils
mandorla almond
melagrana pomegranate
melanzana eggplant/aubergine
melone melon
mele apples
noci walnuts
nocciole hazelnuts
patate potatoes, which can be *arroste* (roast),
  fritte (fried), *novelle* (new), *pure' di* (mashed)
peperoncino chilli pepper
peperone peppers
pesche peaches
pinoli pine nuts
piselli peas
pomodori tomato
rucola rocket
spinaci spinach
tartufi truffles
zucca pumpkin

Meat (carne)

affettati misti mixed cured meat
agnello lamb
bistecca beef steak
carpaccio finely sliced raw meat (usually beef)
cinghiale wild boar
coda alla vaccinara oxtail
coniglio rabbit
involtini thinly sliced meat, rolled and stuffed
lepre hare
manzo beef
pollo chicken
polpette meatballs
polpettone meat loaf
porchetta roasted, stuffed suckling pig
prosciutto ham – *cotto* cooked, *crudo* cured
salsicce pork sausage
salumi misti cured meats
speck a type of cured, smoked ham
spiedini meat pieces grilled on a skewer
stufato meat stew
trippa tripe
vitello veal

Fish (*pesce*) & seafood (*frutti di mare*)

acciughe anchovies
anguilla eel
aragosta lobster
baccalà salt cod
bottarga mullet-roe
branzino sea bass
calamari squid
cozze mussels
frittura di mare/frittura di paranza small fish, squid and shellfish lightly covered with flour and fried
frutti di mare seafood
gamberi shrimps/prawns
grigliata mista di pesce mixed grilled fish
orata gilt-head/sea bream
ostriche oysters
pesce spada swordfish
polpo octopus
sarde, sardine sardines
seppia cuttlefish
sogliola sole
spigola bass
stoccafisso stockfish
tonno tuna
triglia red mullet
trota trout
vongole clams

Dessert (*dolce*)

cornetto sweet croissant
crema custard
dolce dessert
gelato ice cream
granita flavoured crushed ice
macedonia (di frutta) fruit salad
panettone type of fruit bread eaten at Christmas
semifreddo a partially frozen dessert
sorbetto sorbet
tiramisù rich dessert with cake, cream, coffee and chocolate
torta cake
tozzetti sweet, crunchy almond biscuits
zabaglione whipped egg yolks flavoured with Marsala wine
zuppa inglese trifle

Useful words & phrases

aperitivo a pre-dinner drink, often served with free snacks
posso avere il conto? can I have the bill please?
coperto cover charge
bicchiere glass
c'è un menù? is there a menu?
aperto/chiuso open/closed
prenotazione reservation
conto the bill
cameriere/cameriera waiter/waitress
che cosa mi consegna? what do you recommend?
cos'è questo? what's this?
dov'è il bagno? where's the toilet?

Other

aceto balsamico balsamic vinegar, always from Modena
arborio type of rice used to make risotto
burro butter
calzone folded pizza
formaggi misti mixed cheese plate
formaggio cheese
frittata omelette
insalata salad
insalata Caprese tomatoes, mozzarella and basil
latte milk
miele honey
olio oil
polenta cornmeal
pane bread
pane-integrale brown bread
panzanella bread and tomato salad
provola smoked cheese
ragù a meaty sauce or ragout
riso rice
salsa sauce
sugo sauce or gravy
umbricelli thick spaghetti
zuppa soup

Entertainment

San Pietro by evening.

Nightlife is generally confined to the bigger towns and cities, but comes into its own on the coast in summer. The main theatres of Palermo and Catania have a varied year-round programme, and classical drama festivals are held at the ancient sites of Syracuse (Siracusa), Tyndaris (Tindari) and Segesta.

Bars & clubs

The bar and club scene in Sicily is not as hip or design-conscious as in other parts of Europe, although there are some great summer clubs in the islands. Most of the action in mainland Sicily is concentrated in the big cities, but heads to the beach in summer. For the rest of the island, the local bar is still the heart of the village and its role has hardly changed in decades.

Children

Children are adored throughout Sicily. Menus rarely feature children's dishes, but few kids turn their noses up at pizza or pasta, and you can usually ask for half portions (*mezzo piatto*). High chairs, however, are extremely rare. Kids will love the enormous range of outdoor activities on offer, particularly anything to do with volcanoes. The museums are rarely child-friendly, but the classical sites can capture a child's imagination. The Sicilian tradition of puppetry (see page 85) will also enchant children. There are few kid-specific attractions, but your children might enjoy the **Aqua Splash** water park at Campobello di Mazara (acquasplash.net) or the **Etnaland** combined adventure and water park near Mount Etna (etnaland.info).

Cinema

Films are almost always dubbed into Italian in Sicily, which makes going to the cinema a frustrating experience. At Taormina's annual film festival (see page 54), the lucky few can enjoy film premieres in the company of international stars.

Gay & lesbian

Attitudes towards homosexuality are still generally repressive in Sicily, although the prevalent attitude is 'out of sight, out of mind' rather than active disapproval – at least when it comes to tourists (the locals have a harder time). Taormina remains the most popular gay destination, although it has no exclusively gay establishments (apart from one gay-friendly guest house, Isoco, T0942-23679, isoco. it), while Catania and Palermo also have small gay scenes. A few websites have local information, including the Italian gay and lesbian association, **arcigay** (arcigay.it, Italian only).

Tip…

It's difficult to find out what's on in Sicily. The tourist office or your hotel may be able to help. There are no good listings guides, although you can pick up freebie leaflets (in Italian) in the bigger cities.

Music

Sicily produced the great composer Vincenzo Bellini (1801-1835), and opera and classical music remain close to Sicilian hearts. The island's monasteries and churches, particularly Monreale (famous for its magnificent organ), host concerts of classical and chamber music.

The island enjoys a strong folk-music tradition, and almost every festival will feature local folk bands and brass bands. The most famous Sicilian folk group is Taberna Mylaensis (tabernamylaensis. com), whose repertoire includes everything from medieval laments to 20th-century protest songs, as well as their own compositions. Although there are few big-name Sicilian pop bands, the singer and violinist Mara Eli straddles the pop and jazz worlds and is popular throughout Italy. Carmen Consoli, a singer-songwriter from Catania, fuses folk, rock and pop in her unconventional, beautiful songs. Jazz is popular, and Catania hosts a popular winter jazz season (cataniajazz.it).

Festival & events

The main cultural festivals in Sicily take place in summer. These include festivals of performing arts in Taormina (see Taormina Arte, page 54), Palermo's Verdura Festival at the Teatro Massimo (see page 54), and the festival of Classical Theatre in Siracusa (see page 195). Other festivals include the Classica e Dintorni festival in Catania which features weekly chamber music concerts in the Castello Ursino (mid-March to mid-May, classicaedintorni.com), and the WOMAD festival of World Music held in Taormina in December.

Shopping

Vucciria Market, Palermo.

Local foods make the best souvenirs: dip a hunk of bread in Sicilian olive oil, or pair a slice of pungent cheese with a good red from Etna, and the island is immediately evoked. A small jar of Salina capers, or some pesto made with Bronte pistachios are memory-triggers to pull out on a dull, rainy day. If you prefer something more permanent, pick up some colourful ceramics in Caltagirone, or some hand-painted greeting cards made from papyrus grown in Siracusa.

Food

Sicilian food is intrinsic to the island's appeal, and one of the best ways to take a little bit of Sicily home with you is to purchase some local delicacies. Sicilian olive oil is excellent, and, if you are in Sicily in early December, you might be lucky and find the vivid green oil – fragrant and intensely flavoursome – from the first pressing. Olives prepared in many different ways can be vacuum-packed by delicatessens for easy transport, or you could buy jars of olive pates, sauces and tapenades.

Tip...

Delis will usually vacuum-pack hams and cured sausages as well as some of the harder cheeses Sweeter treats include the divine, granular chocolate from Módica, or the incredibly realistic marzipan fruits that adorn most *pasticceria* windows. Every town and village has its own sweets or biscuits, which can be bagged up for the plane home – try the nutty biscuits prepared with the Bronte pistachios. The green pistachio kernels can be purchased on their own in bags, or you could pick up a jar or two of the pistachio pesto to take home; look too for *pesto alla Trapanese* from the other side of the island. The salty capers from Salina are also available in jars, and their zesty flavour will enliven all kinds of dishes.

Wine

Sicily produces a fabulous range of wines, and wineries are increasingly opening their doors to tourists. If you are given the opportunity to pick up some house wine, don't miss it: these wines are often the best, and are simply not marketed because they are produced in insufficient quantities. A glass or two of a sweet dessert wine such as Malvasia is a wonderful way to evoke Sicily once you're back home. If you want to take large quantities of wine home, consider having it shipped. The main wineries and enotecas can arrange this, but remember that the shipping price may be more than the value of the wine itself. You could shop for Sicilian wines via the internet in your home country, which, though short on charm, may cut down costs considerably.

Five of the best
Markets

❶ Pescheria, Catania The island's most vibrant, raucous, colourful, eye-popping market, with all manner of creatures from the briny depths taking centre stage (see page 163).

❷ Piazza Carlo Albert, Catania Whatever you want, this market will have it, although it might not be immediately clear where it is in the jumble of stalls and swirling crowds.

❸ Vucciria, Palermo The mother of all street markets, the Vucciria has been going for more than 700 years and is still the place for a tripe sandwich (see page 87).

❹ Ballarò, Palermo A souk-like street market in the run-down, atmospheric warren of the Albergheria, in Palermo's piquant centro storico (see page 82).

❺ Capo, Palermo A gloriously gritty and authentic street market, selling everything from fresh cheese to dried fruit to neon-coloured undies (see page 89).

Other gifts & souvenirs

Painted ceramics are produced in Santo Stefano di Camastra (see page 125) and Caltagirone (see page 225). On the Aeolian Islands, and around Etna, you won't be able to miss the kitsch knick-knacks made of lava. Siracusa has tasteful objets d'art crafted from papyrus, including handmade notebooks and lampshades. The Sicilian art of fine embroidery is dying out but you'll still find evidence of it in the east of the island. You could also pick up a *coppola*, the flat cap associated with Sicily, which has made an ethical comeback in recent years after its reputation was besmirched by its association with the Mafia (see lacoppolastorta.com).

In Baghdad, Valencia or Palermo, a market is more than a market...it's a vision, a dream, a mirage.

Leonardo Sciascia (1921-89)

Activities & tours

Sicily provides plenty of trekking opportunites.

icily's wealth of superb ancient monuments, many of which enjoy glorious and largely untouched natural settings, entice thousands of culture-seekers every year. The island's increasingly fashionable cuisine brings foodies from around the globe to sample what Sicilians have always known to be one of the richest cuisines in the Mediterranean. As for outdoor activities, Sicily's spectacular volcanic landscapes make for unforgettable walks and climbs, and the protected waters of the offshore islands offer extraordinary opportunities for diving and snorkelling. Sicily truly has an embarassment of riches when it comes to activities, but facilities and infrastructure are erratic – sometimes excellent, often downright poor – and almost anything requires a generous measure of fatalistic acceptance and a Sicilian shrug of the shoulders. If you haven't got much time, or just want to smooth your path, it might be worth booking a holiday with a specialist tour operator.

Cultural

Guided tours are available for the biggest cultural sights, including Agrigento's Valle dei Templi. Guides are available for half-day tours (from €90) at the ticket and information office on the via Panoramica dei Templi. **Michele Gallo** (T360-397930, sicilytravel.net) is a reputable, English-speaking tour guide who offers private tours of the Valley of the Temples, the archaeological museum and can arrange tailor-made excursions to the surrounding area. Half-day tours start at around €90. In Palermo, the **Associazione Guide Turistiche di Palermo e Provincia** (palermoguide. eu) offers a range of tours, but they are geared towards larger groups and cost from €200 for a two-hour tour. Much cheaper is the hop-on hop-off bus service run by **City Sightseeing Palermo** (palermo.city-sightseeing.it, T091-589429, €20). In Siracusa, the official city tourist guides (information at the park ticket office) are, like Palermo, geared to larger groups and are prohibitively expensive for individual travellers. However, there is such a high volume of tourist traffic here, including bus load after bus load of organized groups, that it's easy to tag along with a guided tour in your language of preference. **Hermes** (hermes-sicily.com, T329-373260) offer tours within Siracusa as well as day trips to some of the major sights in southeast Sicily (including Noto, the Vendicari Reserve and the Pantalica necropolis). In Piazza Armerina, contact **La Casa Sulla Collino d'Oro** (lacasasullacollinadoro.it, see page 236), a B&B which can also organize visits to the Villa Roman del Casale with an accredited guide.

Cycling

There is some excellent cycling to be had on Sicily, although it's not to be recommended in the crazy city streets. The best areas for cycling (particularly mountain biking) are around Etna, in the Madonie and Nebrodi mountains (for strong cyclists), and on the islands, particularly Pantelleria. Very few places hire out bikes, although there are a handful of rental agencies on the islands and a handful of mainland *agriturismi* offer bikes to guests (see relevant chapters). Sicilians rarely cycle for pleasure, but organized biking holidays on the island have become increasingly popular in recent years and are offered by several specialist tour operators including **Hooked On Cycling** (hookedoncycling. co.uk), **Iron Donkey** (irondonkey.co.uk), **Inn Travel** (inntravel.co.uk), **Cycling Safaris** (cyclingsararis. com), **Headwater** (headwater.co.uk), and **Exodus** (exodus.co.uk). Self-guided biking tours around Etna are offered by **Blue Stone** (via Felice Paradiso 62, Acireale, T095-765 8945, bluestonesicily.com), who also rent bikes. The best online resource is sicilybiking.com.

Cycling around the Egadi Islands.

About the island

Diving

Sicily offers some spectacular diving and many of its offshore islands are protected marine reserves. The main diving centres are at Ustica, the Aeolian Islands, Lampedusa (in the Pelagian Islands), Pantelleria, and around Giardino Naxos and Taormina on the east coast. There are countless PADI diving centres, offering a range of options suitable for beginners through to experienced divers, and **Diving Cala Levante** (calalevante.it) on Pantelleria even run an underwater archaeology course. Good online resources include **Sicilia Diver** (siciliadiver.com), with information on diving on the Aeolians and Sicily's eastern coast.

Food & wine

Exploring Sicily's multicultural cuisine, with its regional specialities, and sampling the local wines is a richly rewarding aspect of holidaying in Sicily. For those keen to make it the focus of their time in Sicily, there are numerous gourmet-themed holidays available, while many of the *agriturismi* listed in the regional chapters offer guests the chance to join in with the harvest, or watch the pressing of the olive oil. There are also many establishments offering cookery lessons or residential courses, the most prestigious of which is the cookery school run by celebrated cook and author **Anna Tasca Lanza** (T0934-814654, annatascalanza.com, see also page 108). The school is based in an old farmhouse on the Tasca d'Almerita family's estate, Regaleali, one of Sicily's top vineyards. **WineCook Italy** (T349-007 8298, cookitaly.com), based in Siracusa, offers cooking holidays (€1250 for six days) and can arrange private cookery lessons. **Love Sicily** (lovesicily.com), based in Módica, offers cooking holidays, but can also arrange tailor-made tours from a day to a week. **Blue Stone** (T095-765 8945, bluestonesicily.com), in Acireale, can arrange winery tours and cookery classes. **Allakatalla** (allakatalla.it), based in Noto, offer a range of tours, including wine tours of Etna, plus cooking lessons. **Egata** (T0923-194 1523, egata. it) offer a range of courses, including half-day classes (two-day to one-week courses are also available) at two centres, one near Trapani and the other near Siracusa.

Diving in Lipari.

Walking

Sicily offers unforgettable opportunities for walking and hiking – from the volcanic drama of Etna and Stromboli to the silent gorge of the Vall dell'Anapo, from the forested peaks of the Madonie to the stunning cliffs of the Zingaro Reserve. If you are walking in the natural parks, visit the park information offices for leaflets. Some areas are considerably better signposted than others for hiking (the Nebrodi, for example, is poor, while the trails on Mount Etna are generally well signposted). If you intend to climb Stromboli or around the summit of Mount Etna, note that you must be accompanied by a qualified guide (see pages 167 and 183 for details of guides). Other beautiful walks include the ascent to the twin peaks of Salina (see page 134), or around the wetlands of the Vendicari Reserve (see page 203).

Mondello.

Watersports

The main resorts, particularly Mondello, Giardino Naxos and Cefalù, are the only places where you will find activities such as jet-skiing or waterskiing. These resorts also have pedaloes and banana boats for kids. Surfing, kitesurfing and windsurfing are most popular at Cape Possaro, the southeastern top of the island, but possibilites for renting kit are limited, apart from a few shops in Pozzallo. Sailing is popular, particularly after the success of the trials for the America's Cup were held in Trapani in 2005. Sicily's islands are a paradise for sailors, and sailing lessons, yacht charter (skippered and unskippered) are available at all the larger marinas, particularly on the smaller islands.

Wellbeing

Sicily boasts a couple of swanky resort hotels with plush spas for some serious relaxation, including the **Kempinksi Giardino de Costanza**, near Mazara del Vallo (see page 256) and the newly opened

Verdura Golf & Spa Resort (verduraresort.com), which boasts one of the biggest spas in Europe. On Vulcano, some hotels offer special beauty treatments that use the black, local clay (see page 131). Several smaller boutique hotels can arrange massages and beauty treatments.

Sicily has been famous for its thermal waters since Roman times, and still boasts a number of spas. These tend to be clinical, even institutional, and feel quite unlike the scented, candlelit oases in, say, the UK or USA.

The island is a popular destination for yoga retreats, with several tour operators offering courses every year. The **Farm Ospitalà de Campagna** (Contrada Strada, Butera, T0934-346600, farm-ospitalitadicampagna.it) in southern Sicily offers massages, yoga and plenty of wonderful pampering.

The **Arya Retreat** (T338-397 4827, aryaretreat.com) offers yoga, organic food and a beautiful location between Noto and the sea.

Contents

Palermo cathedral.

Palermo & around

Introduction

Take a deep breath before plunging into Palermo: this beautiful but ravaged city doesn't surrender its charms easily. Give it a chance, and you'll be rewarded by one of the most unique and thrilling cities in the Mediterranean.

Palermo is sprawled around a magnificent bay, backed by the great rock of Monte Pellegrino. It has been capital of the island since the end of the ninth century, when the Arabs made Bal'harm a gilded metropolis famed for its beauty and culture. Very little survives of its Arabic heritage, but later rulers bequeathed glittering cathedrals, Gothic palazzi and Baroque churches. The historic centre, already poor and neglected, was bombed during the Second World War. Greedy politicians, hand in glove with the Mafia, spent post-war reconstruction funds on concrete suburbs and left Palermo's ancient centre to rot.

But Palermo's renaissance has begun: the historic heart is slowly being returned to its original splendour. And this city, where the anti-Mafia magistrates Falcone and Borsellino were murdered in 1992, is at the forefront of a grassroots campaign to throw off the yoke of Cosa Nostra. Around Palermo lie a string of delights, from the relaxed little island and diving Mecca of Ustica to the golden mosaics that encrust the great cathedral at Monreale.

Piazza Pretoria, Palermo.

What to see in...

...one day
Begin with the **Palazzo dei Normanni** and its exquisite Palatine chapel, then visit the Royal tombs in the cathedral. Dive into the **Albergheria** to soak up the colourful **Il Ballarò market**, and have lunch. Refreshed, head for the archaeological museum, followed by a spot of shopping around **via Libertà**. Dine in the rapidly gentrifying **Kalsa** district.

...a weekend or more
In a weekend, you could add a morning exploring the **Kalsa**, with its bombed-out churches and Gothic palazzi, plus a jaunt to the seaside suburb of **Mondello**. Don't miss the extraordinary cathedral at **Monreale**, one of the finest Norman churches anywhere.

Palermo listings

● Sleeping

1 **28 Butera** *via Butera 28*, H3
2 **Al Borgo Fiorito** *via Benedetto Gravina 59*, D1
3 **Ambasciatori Hotel** *via Roma 111*, E5
4 **BB22** *Palazzo Pantelleria, Largo Cavalieri de Malta 22*, E3
5 **Centrale Palace** *corso Vittorio Emanuele 32*, D5
6 **Chez Jasmine** *vicolo dei Nassaiuoli 15*, H4
7 **Giorgio's House** *via A Mongitore*, C7
8 **Grand Hotel et des Palmes** *via Roma 398*, C1
9 **Grand Hotel Villa Igiea** *salita Belmonte 43*, D1
10 **Palazzo Ajutamicristo** *via Garibaldi 23*, F6
11 **Palazzo Conte Federico** *via dei Biscottari 4*, C6
12 **Sole Luna Della Solidarietà B&B** *via Vincenzo Riolo 7*, E1

● Eating & drinking

1 **Aboriginal Internet Café** *via Spinuzza 51*, C2
2 **Antica Focacceria San Francesco** *via Paternostro 58*, F4
3 **Bar Alba** *piazza Don Bosco 7c*, D1
4 **Caffè Letterario** *vicolo della Neve all'Alloro 2/5*, G4
5 **Caffè Spinnato** *via Principe del Belmonte 107-115*, B1
6 **Cin Cin** *via Manin 22*, D1
7 **Golosandia** *via Vittorio Emanuele 101*, F3
8 **Ilardo** *Foro Italico 11-12*, H3
9 **Il Maestro del Brodo** *via Pannieri*, E4
10 **Il Mirto e la Rosa** *via Principe de Granatelli 30*, D1
11 **Kursaal Kalhesa** *via Foro Umberto Primo 121*, D1
12 **La Cambusa** *piazza Marina 16*, F4
13 **Osteria dei Vespri** *piazza Croce dei Vespri 6*, F5
14 **Piccolo Napoli** *piazzetta Mulino a Vento 4*, D1
15 **Pizzeria Italia** *via Orologio 54*, C2
16 **Ristorante Risi e Bisi**
   vicolo Gesù e Maria a Palazzo Reale 15, B6
17 **Sant'Andrea** *piazza Sant'Andrea 4*, E3
18 **Taverna Azzurra** *via Scina Domenico*, D1
19 **Trattoria ai Cascinari** *via d'Ossuna 43-45*, A5
20 **Trattoria Bellin** *piazza Bellini 6*, E5

Palermo

When the 12th-century traveller Ibn Jubayr first saw Palermo, sprawled around a vast bay, he exclaimed "it dazzles the eyes with its perfection". A thousand years have taken their toll, but the 20th century came close to sounding the city's death knell: wartime destruction was followed by postwar desecration, as corrupt officials tried to rip out its ancient heart. Crushing poverty and the stranglehold of the Mafia almost wiped out what was left. But modern Palermo is experiencing an extraordinary revival. Bomb-blasted ruins are now exciting cultural centres and galleries. Parts of the historic centre are being transformed from no-go areas to places to see and be seen, and the famous markets assault every sense with their noise and colour. Palermo may still be poor and chaotic, but it's also utterly intoxicating – and, for the first time in decades, optimistic.

Cappella Palatina.

The Palazzo dei Normanni (Norman Palace), now seat of the Sicilian parliament, contains the ravishing Cappella Palatina, a jewel of Romanesque art. The palace is flanked on one side by the cathedral and a line of splendid palazzi along corso Vittorio Emanuele. On the other is the Albergheria, one of Palermo's poorest yet most historic districts, with a colourful market.

Palazzo dei Normanni & Cappella Palatina

Piazza Indipendenza, T091-705 6001, ars.sicilia.it. Mon-Fri 0900-1200, 1400-1700 (last entry 1630), Sun and holidays 0830-1400, Cappella €4, plus Royal Apartments €6, €2.50/4 18-25, free under 18 and over 65. May close without warning for official functions.
Map: Palermo, A7, p78.

Phoenicians and Romans built a fortress on this gentle incline, but the Arabs were the first to build a palace, after they moved the Sicilian capital to Palermo from Syracuse in the ninth century. The Normans remodelled and enlarged it considerably in the 12th and 13th centuries, and the Spanish added the grand façade in the 1600s. The main reason to visit is the stunning Cappella Palatina, with its wealth of Byzantine mosaics. In order to see the exquisite little Sala di Re Ruggero upstairs, you will have to submit to the otherwise dull tour of the palace's 19th-century Royal Apartments.

The **Cappella Palatina** is a royal chapel, built for Roger II in the mid-12th century by the finest mosaic artists, sculptors and wood-carvers of the age. The differing styles and techniques – Greek, Byzantine, Arabic and Norman – are perfectly synthesized in this chapel, considered the apogee of the Sicilian Romanesque style. The chapel may be tiny, but it is so thoroughly enthralling that you could easily spend a couple of hours here (even though some sections are under scaffolding as part of an ongoing restoration project). Look up to see the superb ceiling, intricately carved, and down

Essentials

❶ Getting around AMAT (T848-800817, amat.pa.it) run a comprehensive network of local buses. Buy tickets from bars and shops with the AMAT ticket before boarding for €1.20, or onboard at €1.60. Tickets cover 90 mins of journey time, including transfers. Most buses start from the train station, or the piazza Indipendenza behind the Royal Palace.
❷ Bus station There is no central bus station, but the main regional and inter-urban services stop near the train station, mostly along via Balsamo and via Gregorio.
❸ Train station Stazione Centrale, piazza Stazione, T091-617 5451, to the south of the Kalsa district.
❹ ATM ATMs are everywhere, including along via Roma and via Libertà. **Banco di Sicilia**, via Roma 185, T091-331249, and via Libertà 46, T091-626 7511.
❺ Hospital Ospedale Generale, via Messina Marine 197, T091-479111, ospedalebuccherilaferla.it.
❻ Pharmacy Several around via Roma, including **Farmacia Simonetti**, via Roma 323, T091-584067, Mon-Fri 0900-1230, 1630-2000, Sat 0900-1230.
❼ Post office Palermo's massive Fascist-era post office is at via Roma 320, T091-753 5183, poste.it, Tue-Sat 0800-1830.
❽ Tourist information Information booths can be found at piazza Politeama, piazza Marina and the train station, Mon-Thu 0900-1400, 1500-1900, Fri-Sat 0830-2030, Sun 0900-1300, 1500-1900. The freephone city tourist information line is T800-234169. The main provincial tourist office is at piazza Castelnuovo 34, T091-583847.

Tip...

Palermo's two circular minibus services make a cheap, do-it-yourself bus tour. Both start at the train station. The yellow line (Linea Gialla) circles the Kalsa and the red line (Linea Rossa) heads down the via Libertà.

to see the inlaid marble floor. The walls, columns and domes are entirely filled with mosaic decoration, with stories from the Bible unfolding magically across the breadth of the chapel. Upstairs, a guided tour of the **Royal Apartments** takes you through a series of dull 19th-century salons awhirl with velvet and gilt before arriving at the other great jewel of the palace: the **Sala di Re Ruggero** (Salon of King Roger), filled with exotic mosaics depicting peacocks and palm trees, all delicately picked out in glowing colours.

Albergheria

Map: Palermo, C6, p78.

The Albergheria – defined roughly by via Maqueda, corso Tukory and corso Vittorio Emanuele – is one of the city's oldest and poorest districts, still badly scarred by bomb damage from the Second World War. Many of the surviving tenements are tenuously propped up with rusty supports, and the poverty is tangible. However, it's deeply atmospheric, not least thanks to the presence of the 1000-year-old street market, the **Mercato di Ballarò**, located on and around piazza Ballarò. There are a couple of handsome churches, including **Chiesa del Gesù** (Mon-Sat 0800-1130, 1700-1830, Sun and holidays 0800-1230), the first Jesuit church in Sicily. The multi-coloured, tiled dome of the **Chiesa di Santa Maria del Carmine** (daily 0830-1230) rises above the rooftops on the piazza del Carmine and contains more splendid Baroque decoration, including stucco work by Giacomo Serpotta (see page 86).

Tip...

For superb views over the rooftops of the Albergheria, climb the 13th-century Torre di San Nicolò attached to the church of the same name at via Nunzio Nasi 18.

Cattedrale

Corso Vittorio Emanuele, T091-334373, cattedrale.palermo.it.
Cathedral for worship Mon-Sat 0700-1900, Sun and holidays 0800-1300, 1600-1900. Tourist visits, treasury and crypt 0930-1730. Cathedral free, treasury and crypt €2.50/2 concession, €0.50 2 to 10, free under 2; €5 combined ticket with Museo Diocesano
Map: Palermo, B5, p78.

On the other side of the royal palace, a short stroll down corso Vittorio Emanuele, looms Palermo's enormous cathedral. It was begun in the 12th century, when the ambitious Archbishop of Palermo, Gualtiero Offamiglio (an Englishman, whose name translates as Walter of the Mill), decided that a lavish cathedral to rival Monreale was the most effective way to trumpet the extent of his own power. Since then, the cathedral has acquired a hotch-potch of architectural styles, with a predominantly Catalan-Gothic exterior topped by an overblown 18th-century dome. The main entrance is a very beautiful early Gothic work, with three delicately sculpted arches, and superb 15th-century wooden doors.

The cavernous interior is a disappointment. A team of 18th-century meddlers stripped out what was left of its original decoration (the Norman mosaics had gone in the 1600s) and imposed their own bleak, Neoclassical vision. The only interesting side-chapel contains the reliquaries of Palermo's beloved Santa Rosalia, patroness of the city.

Medieval royal tombs are gathered at the back of the church. Roger II (1095-1154) is here, along with Frederick II (1194-1250) (see History, page 33) and his first wife Constance of Aragon (1179-1222). The pair were an odd couple: Constance was a 30-year-old widow when she married the 15-year-old king, but they were happy. Constance of Aragon's jewel-encrusted 13th-century crown takes pride of place in the Treasury, and there are more fine tombs in the crypt, including the mosaic-encrusted tomb of Walter of the Mill.

Cattedrale, Palermo.

Museo Diocesano

Via Matteo Bonello 2, T091-607 7111,
museodiocesanopa.it.
Tue-Fri 0930-1330, Sat 1000-1800, Sun 0930-1330, €4.50/3 concession, €2 children under 6, €5 combined ticket with Cathedral, no concessions.
Map: Palermo, B5, p78.

The imposing Palazzo Arcivescovile (Archbishop's Palace), opposite the cathedral, houses a collection of religious art and sculpture, much of which was salvaged from ruins after the Second World War.

Palazzo Asmundo

Via Pietro Novelli 3, T091-651 9022,
palazzoasmundo.it.
Mon-Sat 0930-1300, hours may be extended for special exhibitions.

Opposite the cathedral, this Baroque palace was begun in 1615 and enlarged by Giuseppe Asmundo Paternò, Marquis of Sessa, in the late 18th century. The opulent salons contains a superb collection of porcelain and *objets d'art*.

Linking the old port La Cala to the Palazzo dei Normanni, corso Vittorio Emanuele has been the city's main artery since Arabic times. No longer quite the grand address it once was, the corso is now blackened by traffic fumes, and amiable stray dogs sleep in the doorways of once-lavish palazzi.

Museo d'Arte Contemporanea della Sicilia

Palazzo Belmonte-Riso, corso Vittorio Emanuele 365, T091-320532, palazzoriso.it.
Tue-Sun 1000-2000, Thu-Fri until 2200, €5, €3 students, free under 25 and over 60 with EU passports.
Map: Palermo, D5, p78.

A beautifully restored 18th-century palazzo makes a fabulous setting for Palermo's newest museum (opened in 2009), dedicated to contemporary art, including paintings, photography and sculpture.

Quattro Canti

Map: Palermo, D5, p78.

Halfway down corso Vittorio Emanuele, at the intersection with via Maqueda, Quattro Canti (Four Corners) marks the centre of the old city, the meeting point of its four historic districts. The grand Baroque palazzi at each corner of the junction are decorated with extravagant sculptures, each depicting one of the four seasons, a local saint, and various kings. Unfortunately, there's nowhere to get an overview, as the intersection is always choked with traffic.

Nearby, the impressive **piazza Pretoria** is named after the much-remodelled 15th-century Palazzo Pretorio (city hall), which overlooks a 16th-century Florentine fountain whose frolicking nymphs and satyrs so scandalized Palermitan society that they called it the **Fontana della Vergogna** (Fountain of Shame).

Detail from Chiesa di Santa Caterina.

Tip...

Come in the morning to see La Martorana, when the light is at its best to admire the delicate mosaics in the central cupola.

Piazza Bellini

Via Maqueda.
Map: Palermo, E5, p78.

Close to piazza Pretoria, piazza Bellini could be one of the very prettiest squares in Palermo if some enlightened city official would ban the traffic. The late 16th-century **Chiesa di Santa Caterina** belies its restrained exterior with a fabulously ornate Baroque interior, but is closed to visitors. Opposite, half-hidden by palm trees, sit two of Palermo's oldest and most beautiful churches: La Martorana and San Cataldo (see below). At the far end is the winsome **Teatro Bellini**, inaugurated in 1742, which still offers light opera.

Chiesa della Martorana

Piazza Bellini, T091-616 1692.
Mon-Sat 0800-1300, 1530-1730, Sun 0830-1300, free.
Map: Palermo, E5, p78.

Palermo's most celebrated medieval church, La Martorana, was founded in 1143 by George of Antioch, admiral to Roger II, and later given to a nearby convent endowed by Eloisa de Martorana. The nuns were responsible for the heavy-handed Baroque remodelling that took place in the 17th century, destroying the Norman apse and its irreplaceable mosaics, but fortunately they didn't demolish the delicate bell tower or strip the central cupola of its beautiful gilded depiction of Christ enthroned. These mosaics date back to the early 12th century and were probably carried out by artists from Constantinople. Other fragments of the original mosaics have been preserved near the entrance, including the only known portrait of Roger II in Sicily, which depicts him receiving his crown from Christ. The church is still used for Greek Orthodox services (held on Sunday mornings).

Chiesa di San Cataldo

Piazza Bellini, T091-616 1692.
Apr-Oct Mon-Sat 0930-1300, 1530-1830, Nov-Mar daily 0930-1300, €1.
Map: Palermo, D5, p78.

Next to La Martorana, with its trio of small red domes peeping above the palm trees, San Cataldo was founded in the mid-12th century by Maio da Bari, hated advisor to William I. He died before its completion and so the interior was never finished; it remains almost completely bare, with just the mosaic floor to hint at its potential.

La Kalsa

Beyond piazza Bellini spreads the Kalsa district, one of the oldest neighbourhoods in Palermo. A thousand years ago, under the Arabs, it was a walled, exclusive district of palaces and gardens. Now it is poor and decrepit: ancient palazzi sag alarmingly, only the bombed-out shells of others survive. But the Kalsa is on the up, with new bars, clubs and galleries opening all the time.

Tip...

Peer through the gates of Palazzo Bonagia (via Alloro 54), where only the Baroque staircase survives.

Galleria di Arte Moderna e Restivo

*Via Sant'Anna 21, T091-843 1605,
galleriadartemodernapalermo.it.*
Tue-Sun 0930-1830, last entry 1730.
Map: Palermo, E5, p78.

Just off piazza Santa Anna, at the western end of
via Alloro, the gallery of modern art contains
paintings and sculpture from the 19th to the early
20th centuries, all beautifully laid out in light-filled
galleries. It's a fashionable hang-out for arty young
Sicilians, with a great café.

Galleria Regionale della Sicilia

*Via Alloro 4, Palermo, T091-623 0011,
regione.sicilia.it/beniculturali.*
Closed at time of writing: due to re-open end 2010.
Map: Palermo, H4, p79.

The 15th-century Palazzo Abatellis contains the
Galleria Regionale Siciliana, with the best collection
of Sicilian painting and sculpture on the island.
Among the highlights of the collection is the huge
and terrifying fresco *The Triumph of Death*, by an
unknown artist, in which Death careers wildly
through a crowd on his skeletal steed. The finest
work in the museum is Antonello da Messina's
outstanding *Annunciation* (c1474), in which the
Virgin is beautifully depicted trying to absorb the
news which the angel has just imparted.

Piazza Marina & La Cala

Map: Palermo, G4, p79.

The piazza Marina is a symbol of the Kalsa's
regeneration: a decade or so ago, this square was
squalid, dangerous and piled high with rubbish.
Now it boasts good restaurants and a lovely public

Tip...

Just off the piazza Marina, you can sip coffee and
ponder on Giuseppe di Lampedusa's classic *The
Leopard* in Caffè Letterario (see page 106).

Opera dei pupi

The roots of Sicilian puppet theatre date back to the
15th century, but it only took on its current form in
the early 1800s. The stories are rousing, epic tales,
drawn from *La Chanson de Roland* (which describes
the exploits of the knights of Charlemagne) or Sicilian
folklore. The *pupi* (marionettes) are huge, each one
carved and painted by hand, and exquisitely dressed
in medieval costumes. There are marked differences
between the Catanian and Palermitan styles: the
marionettes used in Palermo's theatre, for example, are
smaller and more mobile than those of Catania, which
are 120-140 cm tall. Although the stories are ostensibly
geared towards children, the vigorous fighting scenes
might be a bit much for more sensitive kids. Good
places to see puppet shows or find out more about
the art include Palermo's *Museo Internazionale della
Marionetta Antonio Pasqualino* (see below) and *Teatro di
Mimmo Cuticchio* (see page 107) and the *Piccolo Teatro
dei Pupi* in Syracuse (see page 212).

garden, the **Giardino di Garibaldi** (always open),
where old-timers play dominoes under the banyan
trees. One end of the square is dominated by the
Palazzo Chiaramonte (occasionally open for
exhibitions), once the seat of the Inquisition. At the
opposite end, near via Merlo, is the 16th-century
Chiesa di Santa Maria dei Miracoli. Behind the
square is La Cala, the former port, now home to
glossy yachts but still overlooked by the 15th-
century Catalan-Gothic **Chiesa di Santa Maria
della Catena** (open for mass).

Museo Internazionale delle Marionette Antonio Pasqualino

*Piazzetta Niscemi 5 (just off piazza Marina),
T091-328060, museomarionettepalermo.it.*
Mon-Fri 0900-1300, 1600-1830, Sat 0900-1300,
€5/3 concession.
Map: Palermo, G3, p79.

There are more than 3000 puppets from around
the world in this thoroughly enjoyable museum,
which is run by a venerable family of puppeteers.
Regular performances are held in summer.

Walking through the heart of Palermo

This walk takes you through one of Palermo's oldest and most interesting neighbourhoods, La Kalsa, where the ravages of time and neglect are slowly being reversed. The bomb damage of the Second World War is still evident, but now the blasted churches are used for concerts and festivals, and some Gothic palazzi accommodate boho-chic cafés and stylish restaurants. The walk culminates in beautiful public gardens.

Start at the **Quattro Canti** (see page 83) – where corso Vittorio Emanuele joins via Maqueda – which marks the intersection of Palermo's four historic quarters (*canti*). Of these, only the Albergheria (to the southwest) and the Kalsa (to the southeast) have survived. Walk down the via Maqueda, keeping the piazza Pretorio with its

fountain on your left – aristocrats heading for the high-society church of San Giuseppe dei Teatini (on the right, opposite the square) were deeply offended by the fountain's ecstatic nymphs, and nuns from a nearby convent attacked it with sticks.

Turn left into the **piazza Bellini** (see page 84), where a pair of superb Norman churches, **La Martorana** (see page 84) and **San Cataldo** (see page 84), are framed by palm trees. Head towards the charming 18th-century **Teatro Bellini** and take the small street that skirts its left flank, the via Discesa di Guideca, which crosses via Roma and becomes **via Sant'Anna** by the Baroque church of the same name. You are now entering the Kalsa. Palermo's modern art gallery **Galleria di Arte Moderna e Restivo** (see page 85) is set in a restored former convent at via Sant'Anna 21, and

contains a great café for a break. From the gallery, continue down via Sant'Anna, which soon becomes **via Alloro**, which is the Kalsa's main artery. Turn immediately right down **via Aragona,** which passes through the **piazza Rivoluzione** (so named because it was here that the first uprising against the Bourbons broke out in 1848), where a fountain is topped with the *Genio di Palermo*, a bearded figure which has become one of the city's symbols. Just off the square, on via Garibaldi, is the vast bulk of the **Palazzo di Ajutamicristo**, one of Palermo's best surviving Catalan-Gothic mansions (to stay there, see page 102).

Turn left after the palace to reach the **piazza Magione**, controversially grassed over and turned into a park in the 1990s. It's still etched with the ruins of streets flattened during the wartime raids.

Overlooking the square, set in a palm-shaded garden, is the 12th-century Norman church of **La Magione** (Mon-Sat 0930-1900, Sun 0900-1330, donation requested). At the furthest end of the square, walk down **via dello Spasimo** to reach the poignant ruins of the **Chiesa di Santa Maria dello Spasimo** which are now a sublime open-air cultural centre and concert hall. Beyond it is the palm-shaded **piazza Kalsa**, a little green oasis.

For more extensive gardens, turn right down via Nicolò Cervello (the continuation of via Torremuzza) and cross the Via Lincoln to reach the gardens of the **Villa Giulia** (also known as La Flora), first laid out in the 18th century. The adjoining **Botanical Gardens** (daily 0900-1330, 1430-1900, €4, ortobotanico.palermo.it), which opened in 1795 have more than 30 acres filled with tropical plants.

Chiesa di San Francesco d'Assisi.

The mystery of Caravaggio's lost Nativity

On the night of 17 October 1969, someone stole into the Oratory of San Lorenzo and crudely cut Caravaggio's painting of the Nativity from its frame. The painting was never seen again. Francesco Marino Mannoia, one of the most high-profile *pentiti* (Mafia turncoats) to emerge during the 1980s, admitted to the theft of the masterpiece. He claimed it was damaged beyond repair and that the person who had commissioned the theft burst into tears when he saw it. But according to the *carabiniere*, Mannoia 'mis-remembered'. They believe, along with many art critics, that the Caravaggio is still out there, waiting to be returned to its rightful place.

Palazzo Mirto

Via Merlo 2, T091-616 0571.
Daily 0900-1900, €3.
Map: Palermo, G4, p79.

Duck down the via Merlo, off piazza Marina, to find one of the few Palermitan palazzi open to visitors. The palace was built for the Lanza-Filangeri family in the 16th century, although most of the furnishings date from the late 18th and early 19th centuries. The visit includes sumptuous public salons, the bijou Chinese room, and a collection of historic carriages in the stables.

Chiesa di San Francesco d'Assisi

Piazza San Francesco d'Assisi, T091-616 2819.
Daily 0800-1200, 1600-1830, free.
Map: Palermo, F4, p78.

Around the corner from the Palazzo Mirto, the 13th-century Chiesa di San Francesco d'Assisi boasts a fine portal and a huge rose window. The graceful interior contains the delicately sculpted *Cappella Mastrantonio* (1468), a Renaissance masterpiece by Francesco Laurana and Pietro da Bonitate. There are some sculptures by Serpotta in the nave; to see more, head to the oratory next door.

Oratorio di San Lorenzo

Via dell'Immacolatella (corner with piazza San Francesco d'Assisi).
Daily 1000-1800, €2.
Map: Palermo, F4, p78.

The Oratory of San Lorenzo was built in the mid-16th century and splendidly remodelled a century or so later, when Giacomo Serpotta (1652-1732), the outstanding Rococo stucco artist, filled it with vivid depictions of events from the lives of St Lawrence and St Francis. An altarpiece depicting the Nativity, painted in 1609 by Caravaggio (1571-1610), was stolen in 1969 and has never been traced: a copy now hangs in its place.

Porta Felice & Foro Italico

Map: Palermo, H3, p78.

Corso Vittorio Emanuele culminates by the seafront at the Baroque Porta Felice. From here, a modern seafront promenade, the Foro Italico, stretches along the coast.

The eye-popping spoils of the famous Vucciria market are displayed in all their fleshy splendour along a mesh of narrow streets and squares enclosed by the via Roma and the corso Vittorio Emanuele. There are other unmissable sights here too, from sumptuous Baroque oratories to the superb archaeological museum.

Mercato della Vucciria

Via Roma, la Cala, piazza del Garraffello, via Argenteria nuova, piazza Caracciolo, via Maccheronai.
Mon-Sat 0700-1400.
Map: Palermo, E4, p78.

Rumours of the demise of Palermo's oldest and most celebrated market have been rife for many years, but, even as the stall-holders lament the 'old days', it remains an exuberant, pungent, noisy spectacle. Come to see stalls of offal, the skinned heads of unidentifiable animals, enormous swordfish, and fruit and vegetables of every variety.

Chiesa di San Domenico

Piazza S Domenico (just off via Roma), T091-329588.
Tue-Fri 0900-1130, Sat-Sun 1700-1900.
Map: Palermo, E3, p78.

This enormous Baroque church was completed in 1640, although the lavish façade was tacked on in 1726 when the square in front was widened to offer a better view. It's often called Sicily's Pantheon, although few visitors will have heard of most of the worthies buried here. They include former Italian prime minister Francesco Crispi and the painter Pietro Novelli.

Five of the best

Palermitan street foods

❶ *Frittula* Fried meat scraps, usually dished up on a scrap of waxed paper.

❷ *Pane con la milza* Veal spleen sandwiches. In Palermitan dialect, they're called *pani cà meusa.*

❸ *Panelle* Chick-pea fritters: delicious stuffed in a soft roll.

❹ *Sfincione* Pizza-like snacks.

❺ *Stigghiola* Roasted intestines of sheep or goat, cooked on a skewer. Much better than it sounds!

Mercato della Vucciria.

Tip...

For a quick lunch Palermo-style, head for one of the *friggitorie* (fried-food stands) at the markets, and order a few hot *panelle* (chick-pea fritters) stuffed into a hot roll (*mafaldina*).

Detail from Oratorio di Santa Zita.

Oratorio di San Domenico & Oratorio di Santa Zita (Cita)

Via del Bambinai/via Valverde 3, T091-332779.
Mon-Sat 0900-1300, €3/1.50 concession, free under 11, includes admission to both oratories.
Map: Palermo, E3, p78.

Directly behind the Chiesa di San Domenico, the 16th-century Oratory of San Domenico is endowed with a superb altarpiece by Anton van Dyck, the *Madonna del Rosario* (1648). Giacomo Serpotta created the stucco decoration in this chapel, and the entrance ticket includes admission to his great masterpiece, the breathtaking Oratorio di Santa Zita (also known as Cita) inside the nearby church of the same name. It's impossible to hold back a gasp as you enter: the walls seem to pulse with life. The battle of Lepanto (1571) is played out vigorously on one wall, while swarms of *putti* cavort playfully around the doors. It's said that Serpotta used street urchins for his models, and his nonchalant little angels, swinging their legs in their patched boots, seem only a moment away from jumping down and skedaddling.

Museo Archeologico Regionale Salinas

Piazza Olivella 24, T091-611 6805.
Tue-Fri 0830-1345, 1500-1845, Sat-Mon 0830-1345, €6/3 concession, free under 18 and over 60.
Map: Palermo, D2, p78.

Palermo's excellent archaeological museum, located at the corner of via Cavour and via Roma, contains some extraordinary ancient treasures, most gathered from the great sites of western Sicily, including Segesta, Himera and Selinunte (see pages 250, 99 and 258). The best works are on the ground floor. These contain a slab of inscribed stone, part of the *Pietra di Palermo*, a 5000-year-old delivery note confirming the safe arrival of some cedar wood for the Pharaoh, which has proved invaluable for determining ancient Egyptian chronology. Other highlights include fifth-century BC water spouts in the form of lions' heads, which once adorned the Temple of Victory at Himera. Best of all are the magnificent *metopes* (stone carvings) brought from the temples of Selinunte. These carved panels were part of a long, decorative frieze and are beautifully displayed to illustrate how they might have looked 2500 years ago. The most famous carving depicts Perseus slaying the Gorgon as Athena looks on.

Upstairs, the collections continue with finds from the main archaelogical sites of western Sicily, including Selinunte and Lilybaeum (modern Marsala). There are countless terracotta figures, from various sites across the island, but one room contains an eye-popping selection of votive offerings brought from the sanctuary of Demeter Malophorus at Selinunte. The top floor (not always open) contains some superb Roman mosaics.

Il Capo

The Capo district is run-down, but remains one of central Palermo's liveliest and most authentic neighbourhoods. Its life blood is the Mercato del Capo, a noisy, exuberant street market that has existed here since Palermo was Bal'harm.

Mercato del Capo

Porta Carini, via Sant'Agostino, via Cappuccinell.
Map: Palermo, A4, p78.

The market begins at the porta Carini (the oldest of the three surviving medieval gateways into the city) and fans out into surrounding side streets. As well as fresh produce, it also sells clothes, saucepans, candles, car batteries and almost anything else you can imagine.

Teatro Massimo

Piazza Verdi, T800-655858/T091-605 3555, teatromassimo.it.
Guided tours (25 mins) Tue-Sun 1000-1530, €5/3 concession, held in several languages.
Map: Palermo, B2, p78.

Palermo's opera house sits at the junction of via Maqueda and via Volturno. It was begun by Giovanni Battista Basile in 1875 and completed by his son Ernesto in 1897. Ernesto Basile, who would become the city's greatest exponent of Italian art nouveau, known as *stile Liberty*, endowed his father's splendid Neoclassical edifice with some beautiful *stile-Liberty* details. You might recognize the theatre from the *The Godfather (Part III)*.

Around via Libertà

The smartest neighbourhoods of modern Palermo unfold north of the Teatro Massimo. Another lavish 19th-century theatre overlooks the main square at piazza Ruggero Settimo, and beyond it stretches the viale della Libertà (usually known as via Libertà), now lined with chic shops. The street culminates in the refreshing gardens of the Giardino Inglese.

Piazza Ruggero Settimo

Dominated by the extravagant Teatro Politeama Garibaldi (1891), piazza Ruggero Settimo is the main hub of modern Palermo. It merges with the adjoining piazza Castelnuovo, and is commonly known as the Piazza Politeama. This is the heart of the city's smartest shopping district.

Via Libertà & the Giardino Inglese

This street, which stretches for 2½ km between Politeama and the Giardino Inglese, gets its name from the lavish *stile-Liberty* villas which bloomed in this vicinity at the turn of the 20th century. Many were destroyed by bombs during the Second World War, and many more were demolished, shamefully, during the 'Sack of Palermo' in the 1950s and 1960s. It's now the fanciest shopping street in town. The street culminates in the **Giardino Inglese** (0900-1700, until 1800 in summer), Palermo's loveliest public gardens, which were laid out in the 19th century. There are more charming gardens at the **Villa Trabia** (enter from the via Salinas).

It's a fact...

There are lots of cafés on the via Principe di Belmonte, which links via Ruggero and via Roma.

Around the island

Palermo fringes

On the fringes of Palermo are a string of fascinating sights, all accessible on Palermo's comprehensive public bus system, or by taxi. These range from an Arabic-style medieval palace, to a shiver-inducing crypt full of desiccated bodies.

Castello della Zisa

Piazza Guglielmo il Buono, T091-696144.
Mon-Fri 0900-1830, Sat-Sun 0900-1300, €3/1.50 concession, free under 18.
Bus 124 from piazza Ruggero Settimo.
Map: Palermo, A2, p78.

The name of this exquisite palace comes from the Arabic word *al-Aziz*, meaning 'splendid', and it is the best example of Arabic-Sicilian secular architecture on the island. The Norman king William I of Sicily (1131-1166) commissioned the finest Arabic craftsmen to build the palace, which was begun around 1164 and completed for his son William II. The Ziza features richly textured vaulted

Castello della Zisa.

Five of the best

Stile-Liberty villas

❶ **Villino Florio, via Regina Margherita 38** A pretty pavilion designed by Ernesto Basile between 1899 and 1902, see page 91.

❷ **Villa Malfitano, via Dante 167** A sumptuous home built for Joseph 'Pip' Whitaker between 1885 and 1889, see below.

❸ **Villino Ida, via Siracusa 15** This was built by Ernesto Basile, the leading exponent of *stile-Liberty* in Palermo, as a family home.

❹ **Palazzo Dato, via XX Settembre 36** Fans of art nouveau should visit this red and yellow mansion.

❺ **Villa Igiea, salita Belmonte 43** Now one of Palermo's most luxurious hotels, see page 102.

arches known as *muquarnas*, as well as gilded mosaics and intricately carved capitals. The cool salons, shaded with carved wooden screens, provide an exquisite backdrop for the small collection of Islamic art – mainly ceramics and metalwork. The most extravagant room is the Sala della Fontana, which once boasted an internal fountain, while outside the modern fountains and gardens provide a refreshing retreat from the heat.

Villa Malfitano

Via Dante 167, T091-681 6133.
Mon-Sat 0900-1300, €6 house (guided visits only) and gardens.
Buses 106, 108 (from piazza Politeama), 122 (from Stazione Centrale).

This luscious, *stile-Liberty* villa set in extravagant gardens was built in 1887 by Ignazio Greco for Joseph 'Pip' Whitaker, whose family made a fortune in Marsala wine (see box page 257). Its gilded salons were at the centre of the social whirl at the turn of the 20th century, and visitors included several British royals. The exquisite interior can be admired on guided tours, but the blissful gardens are the real draw.

Villa Malfitano.

Convento dei Cappuccini

Via Cipressi 1, T091-212633.
Daily 0900-1200, 1500-1700, €2.
Bus 327.
Map: Palermo, A6, p78.

Beneath this nondescript church on Palermo's western outskirts is one of the creepiest and most surreal sights on the island: thousands of skeletons, all dressed up in their finery. Quite why Sicilians chose to preserve and display their dead remains a mystery. The practice was finally abandoned in 1881, but the most famous occupant arrived (illegally) in 1920: two-year-old Rosalia Lombardo lies in her glass coffin like a pretty doll, her blonde curls topped with a yellow bow.

It's a fact...

The enchanting Villa Florio, a short walk from the Villa Malfitano on viale Regina Margherita, was designed by Ernesto Basile in 1899. The seat of the Sicilian government, it's closed to visitors, but the gardens are open to the public.

Parco della Favorita

Main entrance on piazza Miscemi.

This former 18th-century royal pleasure garden is now an extensive public park in the northern reaches of Palermo. It sits at the foot of Monte Pellegrino and contains the city's hippodrome and football stadium as well as some charming follies. Among them is the recently restored **Casina Cinese** (T091-707 1248, casinacinesepalermo.it), occupied in the early years of the 19th century by King Ferdinand of Naples during his enforced exile. At the **Museo Etnografico Pitrè** (via Duca degli Abruzzi 1, T091-740 4879, Sat-Thu 0830-2000, €5), a folklore museum named after the great Sicilian ethnologist Giuseppe Pitrè, there's a wonderful collection of Sicilian puppets, *caretti* (colourfully painted carts), costumes and musical instruments.

Around Palermo

A string of very different sights surrounds Palermo, from the seaside delights of Mondello to the magnificent Norman cathedral at Monreale. Inland is Piana degli Albanesi, which retains the unique customs of its Albanian forebears, and the hill town of Corleone, forever linked in the popular imagination with *The Godfather* films. To the east, Bagheria is still dotted with elegant Baroque mansions, and beyond it, on a headland overlooking the sea, are the serene ruins of ancient Solunto.

Mondello.

Mondello

12 km north of Palermo.

Seaside Mondello, linked by regular local buses, is curved around a perfect bay with a sandy beach. It's been a popular resort since the late 19th century, when it was transformed from a fishing village into a chic summer retreat for wealthy Palermitani. It is still strewn with lavish villas.

Monte Pellegrino & Grotto dell'Addaura

14 km north of Palermo.

The great mountain that dominates Palermo's wide bay is topped by a sanctuary dedicated to the city's beloved patron saint, Santa Rosalia. On Sundays, families drive up to picnic near the sanctuary and enjoy views. On the northern side of the mountain is the **Grotta dell'Addaura** (T091-671 6066, closed indefinitely), famous for its prehistoric cave paintings, which provide the earliest evidence of human settlement in the Palermo area.

Piana degli Albanesi

24 km south of Palermo.

This tranquil town was founded in 1488 by Albanian immigrants, and the inhabitants have preserved their dialect, customs, and Orthodox religious rites. Signposts are in Albanian and Italian, and the cake shops are full of unusual Albanian goodies. The town is famous for its Easter celebrations, featuring embroidered costumes, examples of which can be seen in the **Museo Civico** (via Guzzetta, Tue-Sat 0900-1300, 1500-1900, free). Peek in to the 15th-century Chiesa di San Giorgio, the town's oldest church, to see the iconostasis with its gilded icons. About 4 km southwest of Piana degli Albanesi is the mountain pass where the **Portella della Ginestra** massacre took place.

The Beast

The most notorious *capo di tutti capi* to emerge from Corleone is Salvatore 'Totò' Riina (born 1930), nicknamed La Belva (The Beast), who is currently serving life in Milan. It's believed that he killed 40 people, and ordered the deaths of hundreds more. During the 1980s, he also presided over a power struggle known as 'the Riina terror': at its height, between 1981 and 1982, there were more than 200 murders on the streets of Palermo and more than 300 disappearances.

Corleone

60 km south of Palermo.

Nowhere in Sicily is more associated with the Mafia than Corleone, about 60 km from Palermo, reached by a potholed country road. Millions know Corleone's name thanks to Mario Puzo's novel *The Godfather*, on which Coppola based his celebrated film trilogy, but the town has long been home to one of Sicily's most important Mafia families and once had the highest murder rate in the world. Modern Corleone is home to an anti-Mafia museum and documentation centre, currently under threat owing to insufficient funds. If you find it open (ask at the tourist office on the main square, piazza Falcone Giovanni e Borsellino Paolo, T091-846-3655), the photographs showing Mafia victims are a grim reminder that the realities of Cosa Nostra are a world apart from the glamorous rogues portrayed by Hollywood. There's little else to do, apart from perhaps a quick look at the **Museo Civico** (Palazzo Provenzano, via Orfanotrofio, T091-846 4907, Mon-Sat 0930-1300, 1530-1930, Sun 0930-1300, free).

If you're driving from Palermo (there's no public transport), you could drop in to the **Palazzo Reale di Ficuzza** (signposted off the SS118, 8 km north of Corleone). This late-18th-century royal hunting lodge is closed indefinitely for restoration, but it's the starting point for several easy walking trails through the **Bosco di Ficuzza** (parks.it/riserva. bosco.ficuzza), Sicily's most extensive forest, and a nature reserve.

The cloister at Cattedrale di Monreale.

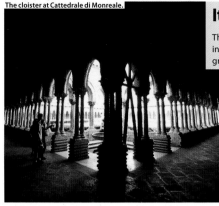

Cattedrale di Monreale

Piazza Duomo, Monreale, T091-640 4413.
Cathedral 0800-1800, free; Treasury 0930-1200, 1530-1730, €2; Cloister Mon-Sat 0930-1900, Sun 0900-1230, €6.
Bus 389 from Piazza Indipendenza, behind Palazzo dei Normanni.

Hilltop Monreale is just a 20-minute bus ride from the centre of Palermo, and provides a peaceful retreat from the city chaos below. The meandering lanes and alleys are a delight to explore but all roads lead back to the celebrated cathedral, one of the finest Norman churches anywhere, which is still the heart of the town.

The cathedral was begun in 1174 by William II of Sicily who proclaimed that the Virgin Mary had come to him in a vision and asked that a church be built in her honour. (In reality, William II sought to curb the power of his former tutor, Gualtiero Offamiglio, the Archbishop of Palermo, by building a cathedral to outshine anything the capital could offer.) It was almost complete by 1182, an incredible feat for the age. The finest artists and craftsmen from around the Mediterranean were gathered to create this masterpiece of Sicilian Romanesque, which is an exquisite fusion of Arabic, Byzantine and Norman decorative techniques. The exterior

barely hints at the magnificence within: step inside, and the impact is quite literally dazzling. The lofty nave and its supporting columns are completely encrusted with gleaming mosaics, which culminate in the huge Christ Pantocrater (Christ in Majesty) which entirely fills the apse. Among the saints and apostles ranked beneath Christ is the first image of an English saint, Thomas à Becket, who was canonized in 1174, only four years after his murder was instigated by William II's own father-in-law, Henry II. William II can be seen, on the curved wall on the left transept, being crowned by Christ, in a deliberate echo of the mosaic depiction of his father Roger II's coronation in La Martorana (see page 84). On the right transept, he is seen handing the cathedral to Mary.

Several royal tombs, including those belonging to William II, his mother Margaret of Navarre, and his father William I ('the bad') of Sicily, are found within the cathedral. A chapel contains an urn said to hold the entrails of King Louis IX, the only canonized king of France, who died in Tunis in 1270. The most lavish of the cathedral's reliquaries can be seen in the Treasury, which also displays some richly embroidered vestments. For giddy but far-reaching views (not for the faint-hearted), you can climb the steps to the cathedral roof.

Along with the cathedral, the astonishingly beautiful cloister is all that is left of the 12th-century Benedictine monastery. There are 228 paired columns (with four columns at each of the corners), all with exquisitely sculpted capitals and reliefs, or richly gilded mosaic inserts. They are utterly enchanting, each miniature scene breathing life and vitality. In one corner, there is a fountain, which looks like a palm tree stripped of its fronds, where the monks would wash their hands.

Tip...

An excellent map locating the principal mosaics of the cathedral, and another with the finest carvings in the adjoining cloister, can be downloaded from the informative website bestofsicily.com.

Detail from inside the cathedral.

Solunto.

Coast towards Cefalù

Bagheria

18 km east of Palermo.

Designed as a model Baroque town in the 18th century, Bagheria was once an elegant enclave of aristocratic palazzi and graceful villas. Now, however, concrete development threatens to choke its elegant core, and many of the villas are sadly neglected. Some, however, have been preserved, including most famously the **Villa Palagonia** (T091-932 088, villapalagonia.it, daily Nov-Mar 0900-1300, 1530-1730, Apr-Oct 0900-1300, 1600-1900, free), the only place in Sicily that Goethe really hated. Begun in 1715, the palace is a classic example of the Sicilian Baroque style – but for one major difference: the exterior walls and parapets are covered with an eye-popping array of stone monsters, which cavort eerily across the garden walls. Part of the interior can also be visited.

Shake off the memory of the grotesques at Bagheria's light-hearted toy museum, the **Museo del Giocattolo** (via Consolare 105, T091-943801, Tue-Fri 0900-1300, 1600-1830, Sat-Sun 0900-1300, museodelgiocattolo.org, €4, €2 children aged 4-6, free under 4), where over 700 toys spanning four centuries are housed in the 18th-century Villa Aragona Cutò. The **Museo Guttuso** (via Rammacca 9, T091-943902, winter Tue-Sun 0900-1300, 1430-1900, summer Tue-Sun 0930-1400, 1500-1900, museoguttuso.com, €5/4 concession, free under 6), in the Villa Cattolica, is dedicated to the works of the most celebrated 20th-century Sicilian painter, Renato Guttuso (1911-1987), and other contemporary Sicilian artists.

Solunto

Via Collegio Romano, Località Solunto, Santa Flavia, T091-904557.
Mon-Sat 0900-1730, Sun 0900-1400, €2/1 concession. Train from Palermo to Santa Flavia (€2, 17 mins), then walk 2 km uphill.

On the slopes of a gentle hill, about 20 km east of Palermo, ancient Solus overlooks the sea near the fishing village of **Porticello** (which has a fantastic daily fish market). It was one of the three main Phoenician settlements on the island, but fell to the Greeks at the end of the fourth century BC, when it became a satellite of Himera (see below). Most of what survives dates from the Roman colony of Soluntum which developed here from the third century BC. There isn't much to see, but it's a peaceful and atmospheric spot, and the views across the undulating coastline are wonderful. Some of the finds are displayed in a small museum at the entrance.

Termini Imerese

39 km east of Palermo.

Termini Imerese is an ancient spa town with a delightful old centre, where you can still take the waters at the 19th-century Grand Hotel delle Terme (see Wellbeing, page 109). The town is split in two, with the old village (Termini Alta) arranged in terraces on a rocky promontory and a modern resort (Termini Bassa) splayed along the beach below. The focus of the old town is the 15th-century Duomo, which overlooks the main square. Nearby the **Museo Civico** (via del Museo, Tue-Sun 0900-1300, free) contains finds from the ancient Greek city of Himera (see below). Don't miss the wonderful coastal views from the Principe di Piemonte Belvedere, near the cathedral.

Himera

Località Buonfornello, T091-814 0128.

Mon-Sat 0900 till 1 hr before sunset, Sun 0900-1300, €3/1.50 concession.
Just off the SS113 (or take the Buonfornello exit on the A19 motorway), 12 km east of Termini Imerese. Randazzo buses (T091-814 8235), run a twice-daily bus service to Himera; check times with tourist offices in advance.

Confronted by a straggle of stones lost in sun-bleached grass, it requires some imaginative effort to recreate the once powerful Greek colony that occupied this site. Himera was founded in 648 BC by Greek colonists from Zankle (modern Messina), but was dangerously close to the Carthaginian settlement at Solunto, just 30 km away. In 480 BC, the Carthaginians attacked Himera but the invaders were repelled by an enormous Greek army that included troops from Agrigento and Syracuse. The Carthaginian army was led by the famous general Hamilcar, whose grandson Hannibal led a second attack on Himera in 409 BC. This time, the Carthaginians were victorious: Himera was utterly destroyed, and its inhabitants slaughtered or deported. The only substantial ruins to survive are those of the **Tempio della Vittoria** (Temple of Victory), which celebrated the Greek victory of 480 BC. Himera hit the news in 2008, when a vast necropolis was discovered containing more than 10,000 skeletons, including adults, children and babies (the babies, touchingly, were buried with their 'bottles').

Caccamo

14 km south of Termini Imerese.

The little town of Caccamo is set on the northeastern slopes of Monte San Calogero (1326 m), which rises dramatically from the coastal plain, making it appear considerably higher than it is in reality. Dominating the town is its fabulous medieval castle, the **Castello di Caccamo** (via Termitana, daily 0900-1230, 1500-1830/1600-2000 in summer, €2), with its fairy tale crenellations and ramparts. The interior has been substantially remodelled and only a small section is open to the public, but the views from the ramparts are particularly outstanding.

Ustica

The tiny volcanic island of Ustica, floating 60 km north of Palermo, provides an ideal contrast to the mayhem of the Sicilian capital. Once a pirate lair and then a prison (right up until the 1950s), the island is now a popular, but deliciously slow-paced, tourist destination. A mecca for divers, Ustica is protected as a marine reserve, and the turquoise coves are also perfect for snorkelling and swimming.

Punta Gavazzi.

Ustica town

Most of the 1300 inhabitants of Ustica live in this small town, its multi-hued houses arranged in neat rows around the port. There's only one main street, which winds up from the port to the Chiesa Madre, passing colourful murals painted by artists in the 1970s. Most of the cafés, shops, bars and restaurants are concentrated around piazza Umberto I, focus of the evening *passeggiata*. On a cliff overlooking the port, the Torre Santa Maria, formerly a watchtower and prison, is now a small archaeology museum, with underwater finds. An easy path leads up to the ruined Castello Saraceno, for stunning views.

Around the island

Ustica is greener than might be expected of a volcanic island, and much of it is tamed by cultivated fields. A single road makes the 9-km journey around the island, but the interior is criss-crossed with mule tracks, which are perfect for gentle walks. A coastal path winds from Ustica town along the northern half of the island for about 4 km to reach the Punta di Megna. The whole island is a marine reserve, but it is divided into three zones with varying degrees of protection: the Punta di Megna is the northern boundary of Zone A, the most highly protected section of the reserve. Boats are prohibited, and swimming is only allowed in two small areas. The best way to see Ustica is by boat: fisherman at the harbour offer daily boat tours to coves, with black lava rocks reflected in translucent waters.

It's a fact...

The last prisoner on Ustica was convicted Mafioso Giovanni Amato, who sipped an espresso as he told *Time* reporters in 1961, "My family and I have enjoyed it here. I'll surely come back to Ustica for vacations."

Essentials

◑ **Getting there** Siremar (T091-582403, siremar. it) operates a ferry and hydrofoil service to Ustica from Palermo's **Stazione Marittima**. The ferries are slower but cheaper (2 hrs 40 mins, €15 one way) than hydrofoils (1 hr 15 mins, €20). Siremar also operates a summer-only ferry service between Ustica and Naples.

❶ **Getting around** There is a limited local minibus service on the island (routes run clockwise and anti-clockwise). Buy tickets on board (€1).

⑤ **ATM** On the main square, including the **Banco di Sicilia**, piazza Capitano Vito Longo 5, T091-844 9010.

⊕ **Hospital** First-aid surgery at Largo Gran Guardia 1, T091-844 9248.

✛ **Pharmacy** Farmacia Zattoni, piazza Umberto I 30, T091-844 9382, Mon-Fri 0800-1230, 1700-1900, Sat 0800-1230.

⤵ **Post office** Piazza Armeria 9, T091-844 9394, poste. it, Mon-Fri 0800-1330, Sat 0800-1230.

❶ **Tourist information** No tourist office on the island.

Diving on Ustica

There are several diving companies operating on Ustica, most open from May to October. The island is a protected nature reserve, and numerous species including barracuda, amberjack and grouper are commonly seen. Prices are fairly standard: around €40 for a single dive; €330 for a 10-dive package; or €360 for a six-day open water course. All dive companies rent out equipment. Recommended establishments include the following:

Profondo Blu Ustica, via Cristoforo Colombo, T091-844 9609, ustica-diving.it.

Orca, T338-888 2236, orcasub.it.

Mare Nostrum Diving, via Cristoforo Colombo, T330-792589, marenostrumdiving.it.

Sleeping

Palermo

Grand Hotel Villa Igiea €€€€
Salita Belmonte 43, T091-631 2111, hilton.com/Italy.
Map: Palermo, D1, p78.
A lavish art nouveau villa, designed by Ernesto Basile, this hotel sits in gardens on the edge of Palermo bay. The public salons are gorgeous, but bedrooms need updating.

Centrale Palace €€€
Corso Vittorio Emanuele 327, T091-336666, centralepalacehotel.it.
Map: Palermo, D5, p78.
A plush hotel in an 18th-century palazzo by the Quattro Canti, this boasts marble floors and glittering chandeliers. The bedrooms are elegantly furnished and spacious, but some can be noisy. Amenities include a gym, fabulous sun terrace, and a smart restaurant.

Grand Hotel et des Palmes €€€
Via Roma 398, T091-602 8111, hotel-despalmes.it.
Map: Palermo, C1, p78.
This villa belonging to the Ingham-Whitaker family, was converted into a hotel in the late 19th century and then lavishly remodelled in *stile Liberty* by Ernesto Basile. Much-needed renovation (ongoing at the time of writing) will hopefully return it to its former glory.

Palazzo Ajutamicristo €€€
Via Garibaldi 23, T091-616 1894, palazzo-ajutamicristo.com.
Map: Palermo, F6, p78.
The owners offer guided tours of their 15th-century palazzo as well as B&B accommodation in the former servants' quarters. The rooms are comfortable, and guests can breakfast on the splendid terrace.

Palazzo Conte Federico €€€
Via dei Biscottari 4, T091-651 1881, contefederico.com.
Map: Palermo, C6, p78.
Another sumptuous palace tucked away in Palermo's old quarter, this dates back to the 12th century although most of what exists today is from the 17th and 18th centuries. The count and countess offer B&B accommodation in rooms that retain their original beams but are otherwise simply furnished.

BB22 €€
Palazzo Pantelleria, Largo Cavalieri de Malta 22, T091-611 1610, bb22.it.
Map: Palermo, E3, p78.
Perhaps the most stylish B&B in the city, with a handful of beautifully designed bedrooms which mix neo-Baroque chandeliers with chrome. It's next to the church of San Domenico, but ongoing neighbourhood restoration may mean unwanted noise. No lift.

Ambasciatori Hotel €€-€
Via Roma 111, T091-616 6881, ambasciatorihotelpalermo.net.
Map: Palermo, E5, p78.
This modest, three-star hotel is family-run and perfectly located in the heart of the city. While it may not have oodles of character, it does offer immaculate rooms, charming service, and a roof terrace (where breakfast is served) for splendid rooftop views.

Al Borgo Fiorito €
Via Benedetto Gravina 59, T091-612 4625, alborgofiorito.com.
Map: Palermo, D1, p78.
About a five-minute walk to the central via Roma, this is a pretty B&B painted in bright tones. It's on the third floor with no lift, but rooms are sunnily furnished, with balconies and bright prints.

Sole Luna della Solidarietà B&B €
Via Vincenzo Riolo 7, T091-581671, solelunabedandbreakfast.org.
Map: Palermo, E1, p78.
This friendly little B&B can be found near the Teatro Politeama, about a five-minute walk from the central via Roma. It's run by delightful Patrizia, who spent years working with deprived children in Palermo (5% of the profits from the B&B goes to the children's charity Arciragazzi). No credit cards.

Giorgio's House €
Via A Mongitore, T091-525057,
giorgioshouse.com.
Map: Palermo, C7, p78.
Effervescent and irrepressible,
Giorgio is a Palermitan fixture. His
budget B&B is colourful and
pristine, and he can't do enough
for his guests, providing a free
pick-up service at the train
station, and happily dispensing
insider tips on where to eat and
what to do.

Self-catering
28 Butera
28 via Butera, T333-316 5432,
butera28.it.
Map: Palermo, H3, p78.
Avid fans of *The Leopard* can stay
in Giuseppe di Lampedusa's
former home, which has been
lovingly restored by his nephew.
The upper levels of the house
have been divided into
comfortable self-catering
apartments. Prices start at €50
per day/€300 per week for a
studio apartment, rising to €120
per day/€770 per week for the
largest apartment with terrace.

Chez Jasmine €€
Vicolo dei Nassaiuoli 15, T091-616
4268, chezjasmine.biz.
Map: Palermo, H4, p78.
This little hideaway is at the top
of a palazzo in the Kalsa district.
The apartment is split over two
levels, linked by a spiral staircase,
and there's also a pretty little roof
terrace (€110-130 per night for
two people).

Around Palermo

Casale del Principe €€
Contrada Dammusi, Monreale,
T091-857 9910,
casaledelprincipe.it.
This working farm on the edge of
Monreale offers elegant rooms
(three of which have stunning
private terraces) with views over
vines and orchards. Their own
produce is served in the
restaurant, and activities include
hiking, horse riding and archery.

Villa Cefalà €€
SS113 No 48, T091-931545, Santa
Flavia, T091-931545,
tenutacefala.it.
This *agriturismo* sits in hills near
the village of Santa Flavia, a
30-minute drive east of Palermo.
It offers a selection of beautifully
decorated rooms, suites, or
self-catering apartments. There's
a pool, and restaurant serving
the estate's own produce.

Domus Notari €
Via Duca degli Abruzzi 3,
Monreale, T091-640 2550,
domusnotari.it.
Tucked away in the old centre of
Monreale, this little B&B has just a
couple of elegant rooms,
decorated with wooden
furniture and paintings, and it's
handy for the cathedral.

Home from Home €
Contrada Scozzari, Bolognetta,
T091-872 4848,
homefromhome-sicily.com.

Owners Kathy and Toto will
ensure that their guests are
comfortable. Although
Bolognetta is off the tourist trail,
it's only 23 km from Palermo and
32 km from Corleone.

Portella della Ginestra €
San Giuseppe Jato, T091-857
4810, liberaterra.it.
Located near Piana degli
Albanesi, 22 km south of
Monreale, this estate formerly
belonged to Mafia boss Giovanni
Brusca; it is now run by the *Libera*
Terra (Free Earth) cooperative.
The B&B is set in the renovated
farmhouse, and activities include
horse riding and hiking.

Self-catering
Masseria Pernice
Contrada Pernice, Camporeale,
T092-436797, sallierdelatour.it.
A vineyard in hills south of Piana
degli Albanesi, this is both a
winery and an *agriturismo*. There
are four apartments set around a
courtyard. Prices start at €190 per
night for an apartment for two,
rising to €250 in the high season.
Minimum stay of three nights,
although this is negotiable in the
low season.

Sant'Agata Agriturismo,
Località Sant'Agata, SP5 Km
17.800, Piana degli Albanesi,
agriturismosantagata.pa.it.
Overlooking sun-baked fields of
wheat 28 km south of Palermo
and 9 km south of Piana degli
Albanesi on the SP5 this

Eating & drinking

19th-century *masseria* has been restored. There's a pool in the gardens, and a restaurant serving the estate's own produce.

Ustica

Hotel Clelia €€
Via Sindaco I 29, T091-844 9039, hotelclelia.it.
A modern establishment with well-equipped bedrooms. The top-floor restaurant is one of the best on the island, and offers views to go with the seafood.

Albergo Ariston €
Via della Vittoria 5, T091-844 9335, usticahotels.it.
A small inn with functional rooms offered at modest prices, particularly in the low season.

Self-catering
Agriturismo Hibiscus
Contrada Tramontana, T091-844 9543, agriturismohibiscus.com.
This working farm on Ustica's northern coast offers four delightful apartments, all simply but stylishly furnished. The apartments sleep two (€350-840 per week) or four (€350-1300).

Palermo

Cin Cin €€€€
Via Manin 22, T091-612 4095, ristorantecincin.com.
Mon-Sat 1230-1500, 2000-2300, lunch only Jul-Aug.
Map: Palermo, D1, p78.
'Sicilian Baroque' cuisine is the speciality at this restaurant. This translates into traditional recipes such as *spaccatelle* with pesto Ericino, or fresh fish of the day served with mussels and clams.

Osteria dei Vespri €€€€
Piazza Croce dei Vespri 6, T091-617 1631, osteriadeivespri.it.
Mon-Sat 1230-1500, 1930-2300. Closed Aug.
Map: Palermo, F5, p78.
One of the city's smartest choices, with a vaulted dining room in the Palazzo Gangi and a summer terrace on one of the old city's loveliest squares. Try dishes such as black ravioli stuffed with mussels, or Nebrodi pork with wild fennel. The desserts are fabulous, as is the wine list, but service is erratic.

Kursaal Kalhesa €€€
Via Foro Umberto Primo 121, T091-616 2111.
Mon-Sat 1300-1530, 2000-2330. Café open from 1130.
Map: Palermo, D1, p78.
In a stunning medieval palazzo in the Kalsa district, this restaurant boasts a beautiful summer terrace, set in a 'secret' courtyard. Dine on market-fresh, seasonal cuisine, which might include grilled vegetables topped with smoked cheese or tenderloin in Sicilian wine.

La Cambusa €€€
Piazza Marina 16, T091-584574, lacambusa.it.
Mon 1930-2300, Tue-Sun 1230-1500, 1930-2300.
Map: Palermo, F4, p78.
Looks deceive at this apparently simple little restaurant, which is renowned for its fresh fish. Book early to get a seat on the plant-fringed terrace. Start with the seafood salad and follow up with simply grilled sea bass – or whatever is fresh that day.

Piccolo Napoli €€€
Piazzetta Mulino a Vento 4, T091-320431.
Mon-Thu 1230-1530, Fri-Sat 1230-1530, 2000-2230.
Map: Palermo, D1, p78.
A superb, traditional restaurant about a five-minute walk from

the Teatro Politeama, with a spectacular seafood display at the entrance. Everything here is seasonal and fresh, from the antipasti to the fish and shellfish.

Sant'Andrea €€€
Piazza Sant'Andrea 4, T091-334999.
Mon-Sat 2000-2330.
Map: Palermo, E3, p78.
Book in advance for this rustically furnished trattoria in the Vucciria neighbourhood which prepares excellent Sicilian cuisine. Try the outstanding *pasta con le sarde*, a Sicilian classic made with fresh sardines, wild fennel, pine nuts and raisins, and finish up with home-made desserts.

Il Maestro del Brodo €€
Via Pannieri, T091-329523.
Tue-Sun 1300-1500, 1930-2230.
Map: Palermo, E4, p78.
On the fringes of Vucciria, this traditional tavern draws locals and tourists alike with its good value menu of Palermitani favourites. Try the spaghetti with sea urchins and *neonata* (tiny baby fish) and the seafood mixed grill (*grigliata mista*).

Il Mirto e la Rosa €€
Via Principe de Granatelli 30, T091-324353, ilmirtoelarosa.com.
Mon-Sat 1230-1500, 1930-2300.
Map: Palermo, D1, p78.
This vaulted restaurant also serves as an art gallery. The menu changes according to what's freshest in the market.

Ristorante Risi e Bisi €€
Vicolo Gesù e Maria a Palazzo Reale 15, T091-652 1037.
Tue-Sun 1200-1500, 1900-2300.
Map: Palermo, B6, p78.
Just a stone's throw from the Palazzo dei Normanni, this restaurant specializes in fish and seafood. The menu changes, but, if available, you should try the risotto with prawns and champagne.

Trattoria ai Cascinari €€
Via d'Ossuna 43-45, T091-651 9804.
Tue, Wed, Sun 1300-1500, 1930-2300, Thu-Sat 1930-2300.
Map: Palermo, A5, p78.
A great place for lunch after a stroll through the Capo market, this buzzy trattoria celebrates Palermo's delicious specialities. Try *sarde a beccafico* (sardines stuffed with breadcrumbs, pine nuts, and lemon) and follow up with a plate of home-made pasta or some fresh fish.

Trattoria Bellini €€-€
Piazza Bellini 6, T091-616 5691.
Tue-Sun 1230-1500, 1930-2300.
Map: Palermo, E5, p78.
There are always queues at this relaxed, family-run trattoria, with a terrace overlooking the cupolas of La Martorana and San Cataldo. In the evenings, outstanding pizzas are also on the menu, but there's also a good range of pasta, fish and meat dishes.

Antica Focacceria San Francesco €
Via Paternostro 58, T091-320264, afsf.it.
Map: Palermo, F4, p78.
This is *the* place to get your *pane con la milza* (veal spleen sandwiches), with focaccia offered for less adventurous palates. It's been going since 1834, and the family owners are currently in the news after refusing to pay the Mafia *pizzo* (the police car at the door is for their protection).

Pizzeria Italia €
Via Orologio 54, T091-598885.
Tue-Sun 2000-2300.
Map: Palermo, C2, p78.
You'll have to get here early to beat the queues and grab a prime people-watching spot on the terrace. The fabulous pizzas are perhaps the best on the island, and are accompanied by a very affordable wine selection. A great option for families.

Cafés & bars
Aboriginal Internet Café
Via Spinuzza 51, T091-662 2229, aboriginalcafe.com.
Daily 1000-0300.
Map: Palermo, C2, p78.
A friendly, colourful café. Internet access costs a very reasonable €3.50 per hour, and includes free coffee.

Bar Alba
Piazza Don Bosco 7c, T091-309016, baralba.it.
Tue-Sun 0700-2200, Sat 0700-2400, daily in summer.
Map: Palermo, D1, p78.
The coffee served at this unassuming modern café is regularly voted the best in Italy. Try it for yourself with a pastry.

Caffè Letterario
Vicolo della Neve all'Alloro 2/5, T091-616 0796.
Mon, Wed-Fri 1630-2400, Sat-Sun 1030-0200.
Map: Palermo, G4, p79.
Just off the piazza Marina, you can sip coffee and ponder on Giuseppe di Lampedusa's *The Leopard* in this café, which is the headquarters of the Parco Culturale del Gattopardo, parcotomasi.it.

Caffè Spinnato
Via Principe del Belmonte 107-115, T091-583231.
Daily 0700-2100.
Map: Palermo, B1, p78.
Sit out at an umbrella-shaded table on the summer terrace at this legendary café, and order from the extensive menu.

Golosandia
Corso Vittorio Emanuele 101, T091-611 5082.
Summer daily 1000-2200, reduced hours in winter.
Map: Palermo, F3, p78.
This artisanal gelateria, just off piazza Marina, is a member of

Addio Pizzo, so treat yourself with an extra large helping of the heavenly *nocciola* (hazelnut).

Ilardo
Foro Italico 11-12, T091-616 4413.
Summer daily 1100-2200, weekends only in winter.
Map: Palermo, H3, p78.
The city's oldest gelateria, Ilardo was founded in 1860 and still enjoys a seafront location.

Taverna Azzurra
Via Scina Domenico, T091-583541.
Mon-Sat 0900-2200.
Map: Palermo, D1, p78.
It's always a squeeze at this traditional tavern in the Vucciria market, but well worth the effort for a draught of beer to wash down the street-food snacks.

Around Palermo

Da Calogero €€€-€€
Via Torre 22, Mondello, T091-684 1333.
Daily 1230-1500, 1930-2230.
This restaurant has been offering seafood specialties such as *spaghetti con ricci* (sea urchin) and *insalata di polpo* (octopus salad) for almost 80 years. Pizzas served in the evenings.

Antica Stazione Ferroviaria Ficuzza €€
Via Vecchia Stazione, Ficuzza, T091-846 0000, anticastazione.it.
Daily 1300-1500, 1930-2300.

Traditional cuisine prepared with local ingredients is the hallmark of this excellent restaurant set in an old railway station. Try pasta in a rich tomato and aubergine sauce, followed by an organic pork chop, and then finish with a delicious dessert.

Don Ciccio €
Via del Cavaliere 87, Bagheria, T091-932442.
Mon, Tue, Thu-Sat 1300-1500 and 1900-2200
Map: Palermo, D1, p78.
This trattoria serves Sicilian classics like *sarde a beccafico* (sardines stuffed breadcrumbs and pine nuts), pasta with tuna sauce (in early summer), and cannoli and cassata. It's near the villa Palagonia.

Cafés & bars
Il Baretto
Viale Regina Elena, Mondello.
Usually daily in summer, weekends in winter, subject to weather.
This little beachfront kiosk sells fantastic artisanal ice cream.

Sweet Temptation
Piazza Falcone Giovanni e Borsellino Paolo 1, Corleone, T091-846 1570.
Daily 0900-2100.
This place plays up Corleone's *Godfather* connection: you'll see a few bottles of *The Godfather* liqueur. Otherwise, it's a friendly spot for coffee, gelati and snacks.

Entertainment

Children

Most children will enjoy Sicilian puppet theatres (see box, page 85). Recommended theatres include the following:

Teatro di Mimmo Cuticchio
Via Bara all'Olivello 95, Palermo, T091-323400, figlidartecuticchio.com.
This puppet theatre and workshop is run by one of Palermo's most celebrated and accomplished theatrical families.

Teatro di Ippogrifo
Vicolo Ragusi 6, Palermo, T091-329194.

Teatroarte-Cuticchio
Via del Benedettini 9, Palermo, T091-323400, teatroarte-cuticchio.com.

Clubs

I Candelai
Via Candelai 65, Palermo, T091-327151.
Daily 2100-0300, usually free.
One of the city's first clubs, on a street now filled with bars and pubs, this still offers nightly entertainment in the form of live gigs or massive DJ sessions.

Kursaal Kalhesa
Via Foro Umberto Primo 121, Palermo, T091-616 2111.
Daily 1900-0300.
This boho-chic haunt is a great place to start the night. Sit beneath the vaults of this medieval palazzo and enjoy a drink. Upstairs is a restaurant.

La Cuba
Viale Francesco Scaduto 12, Palermo, T091-309201.
Lounge bar open daily 1900 till late.
This lounge bar and club is found in the Villa Sperlinga halfway between the Giardino Inglese and the Parco della Favorita. This is where the beautiful people come, so dress up.

MiKalsa Bar
Via Torremuzza 27, Palermo, T348-973 2254.
Tue-Thu 2030-0100, Fri-Sat 2030-0200.
A stylish option in the Kalsa neighbourhood, with live gigs, and an enormous selection of international beers. Programme at myspace.com/mikalsa.

Festivals & events

Kals'Art festival
Palermo.
Jul-Aug.
This summer cultural festival takes place in the Kalsa district, with theatre, dance, concerts, film screenings and more.

Festino di Santa Rosalia
Palermo.
10-15 Jul.
A five-day celebration dedicated to Palermo's patron saint.

Settimana di Musica Sacra
Monreale.
Late Nov or early Dec.
A week-long programme of classical music concerts in the sublime surroundings of Monreale's cathedral (settimanamusicasacra.info).

Music

Teatro Massimo
Piazza G Verdi, Palermo, T091-605 3111, teatromassimo.it.
Palermo's opera house (see page 89) offers a superb programme of ballet and opera.

Teatro Politeama
Piazza Ruggero Settimo, Palermo, T091-605 3421.
This grand 19th-century theatre (see page 89) is a major venue for classical music.

Shopping

Activities & tours

Beachwear & clothing

Giglio Donna
Piazza Francesco Crispi 3,
T091-611 4102, giglio.com.
Mon-Sat 1000-1300, 1630-2000.
Giglio have hip boutiques
around the city. This is the cool,
pale, designer establishment for
women – just the place to pick
out that little black dress you'll
need to party with the
well-dressed Sicilians.

Food & drink

For picnic supplies, you'll be
spoilt for choice at Palermo's
three street markets – Vucciria,
Capo and Ballarò, see pages 87,
89 and 92 respectively.

Enogastronomia
Badalamenti

Viale Galatea 55, Mondello,
T091-982 0380.
A huge selection of cheeses,
hams, cured meats and other
gourmet delights, along with
more than 1000 wines. It's near
the beach, and perfect for
picking up picnic supplies.

Enoteca Picone di Palermo

Via Marconi 36, Palermo,
T091-331300, enotecapicone.it.
Mon-Sat 0730-1400, 1600-2100.
Closed Aug.
Perhaps the finest and most
extensive wine selection in the
city, which also doubles as a
superb gourmet wine bar
(there's another at viale
Strasburgo 235).

I Sapori e i Saperi della
Legalità

Piazza Castelnuovo 1, Palermo,
T091-888 8859, liberaterra.it.
Mon-Sat 1000-1400, 1700-2000.
Palermo's first *alimentari* (food
shop) dedicated to the organic
products grown on estates
confiscated from the Mafia,
opened in Palermo in early 2009.

L'Emporio

Corso Vittorio Emanuele 172,
Palermo, T329-091 7791.
Mon-Sat 1000-1230, 1700-2000.
This unique gift shop cum
grocery store is stocked with
pizzo-free products: blood
orange honey, organic olive oil as
well as anti-Mafia slogan T-shirts.

Outdoor equipment

Adventure Time
Via Volturno 27, Palermo,
T091-611 8857, adventuretime.it.
Mon-Sat 1000-1230, 1700-1930.
Everything you need to enjoy
the great outdoors at this
centrally located shop.

Cultural

City Sightseeing
T091-589429,
palermo.city.sightseeing.it.
A hop on, hop off open-topped
sightseeing bus makes the circuit
of central Palermo with a
multilingual audio commentary.
Tours depart roughly every 20
minutes/1 hour (depending on
the season) from near the Teatro
Politeama.

Real Sicily

T347-480 9632, realsicily.com.
Marcella Amato is an
experienced and multilingual
guide who offers individual and
small group tours in Palermo and
the surrounding area. Cookery
classes and visits to wineries can
also be arranged.

Diving

See Ustica, page 101.

Food & wine

Anna Tasca Lanza/Regaleali
Contrada Regaleali, Sclafani
Bagni, T0934-814654,
annatascalanza.com,
tascadalmerita.it.
Anna Tasca Lanza was born in
the Villa Tasca and grew up on
the vast family estate, Regaleali.
Her father began the celebrated
Tasca d'Almerita winery, and her
cooking school is now world
famous. Prices start at €150 for a
cooking lesson (a full-course
meal), plus lunch with Anna's
family, and a wine tasting.

Transport

Ristorante Cin Cin
*Via Manin 22, Palermo, T091-612
4095, ristorantecincin.com.*
This prestigious restaurant (see
Eating & drinking, page 104)
offers one-day cooking classes,
which include a visit to the
market to choose ingredients,
then the preparation of the feast.
€150 per person in small groups
of two to eight people.

Eating & drinking, page 104

Wellbeing
Grand Hotel delle Terme
*Piazza delle Terme 2, Termini
Imerese, T091-8113557,
grandhoteldelleterme.it.*
Treat yourself at this luxurious
19th-century hotel, which draws
on hot springs that have been
famous since Roman times for
their curative properties. A
weekend spa package, including
thermal baths and a massage,
costs from €65. Bed and
breakfast in a double room costs
€160-200 for two.

Palermo

The two main hubs for local bus
services (run by **AMAT**,
T848-800817, amat.pa.it) are the
train station and piazza
Indipendenza (behind the
Palazzo dei Normanni), see
Getting around, page 81. The
airport bus leaves from piazza
Giulio Cesare (by the train
station) and piazza Ruggero
Settimo (by the Teatro
Politeama). Palermo's so-called
'Metro' is actually an above-
ground railway line: Metro Line
A, also called the Trinacria
Express, links the city centre with
the airport, while the very short
Metro Line B (Stazione
Notarbartolo to piazza Giachery)
is not useful for tourists.

Getting around, page 81

Around Palermo

Regular AMAT buses link central
Palermo with **Mondello** (buses
806 and 833 from piazza
Politeama, or several services
from the piazzale de Gasperi by
the Parco della Favorita) and
Monreale (bus 389 from piazza
Indipendenza). Tickets €1.20 if
pre-purchased from bars or
ticket kiosks, or onboard €1.60.
   Bagheria (11 mins) and
Termini Imerese (35 mins) are
most conveniently reached by
regular train services from
Stazione Centrale. Both are also
linked by bus with **AST**
(T840-000323,
aziendasicilianatrasporti.it).
   The hills behind Palermo are
most easily explored by your
own transport, but there are bus
services to **Corleone** (3-5
services Mon-Sat, 1 hr 30 mins),
via Ficuzza (1 hr 15 mins), with
AST and **Gallo** (T091-617 1141).
Presti (T091-586351,
prestiaecomande.it) operate bus
services to **Piana degli Albanesi**
(6 a day Mon-Sat, 45 mins) from
via Balsamo.

Ustica

See Essentials, page 101.

See Essentials, page 101.

Contents

Lipari island.

Northern Sicily

Introduction

What to see in…

…one day
If you've just got a day, explore elegant **Cefalù** in the morning, and spend the afternoon in **Castelbuono** in the Madonie mountains. If you are based in northeast Sicily, you could also consider a day trip to **Lipari** on the Aeolian islands.

Sicily's rugged northern coastline once lured pirates, but now its stunning capes and secret coves are a magnet for holidaymakers. A string of resorts dot the bays between Cefalù and Milazzo – most are smallish, family-orientated and delightful (at least if you avoid August).

Cefalù, with its immaculate old centre and magnificent Norman cathedral, has the most to offer if sun, sea and sand begin to pall, or you could while away an afternoon amid the beautiful ruins of ancient Tindaris, high on a craggy headland. Alternatively, head inland to explore the glorious adjoining nature reserves of the Madonie and the Nebrodi mountains. These forested peaks comprise Sicily's most unspoilt region, the slopes carpeted with wild flowers in spring and dusted with snow in winter. It's a blissfully tranquil landscape, scattered with stone villages which have barely changed in centuries.

If you prefer your peace and quiet with a few fireworks and perhaps even a frisson of danger, head for the Aeolian Islands. The islands are utterly idyllic, their transluscent waters a protected marine reserve, but the most famous of the group, the storybook volcano of Stromboli, continues to rumble and spew a nightly shower of red-hot lava.

…a weekend or more
In a weekend, you could explore Cefalù, spend a little time on the beach, and then plunge into the remote **Madonie mountains** to experience traditional Sicilian country cooking, historic hill towns, and some fine hiking. Alternatively, spend the whole weekend island-hopping in the Aeolians, taking a mud bath on **Vulcano**, watching **Stromboli** spit fire, or simply snorkelling around the coves.

Left: Cefalù

Cefalù & the Madonie

If you had to invent the perfect Sicilican seaside town, chances are it would look just like Cefalù. The red roofs of the old town are huddled around a golden cathedral, painted wooden boats are drawn up on the sands, a glorious beach stretches seemingly forever; and an enormous castle-topped rock provides a dramatic backdrop. In August, this stretch of coast is busy, but, fortunately, escape is on hand in the form of the verdant peaks of Madonie mountains. Sicily's highest mountain range, now an extensive natural park, stretches inland south of Cefalù. Scattered across the hills are old-fashioned towns and villages, mostly dedicated to the traditions of rearing livestock and cultivating olives and other crops. It's the perfect location if you're looking for a walking, riding or mountain-biking holiday, with some wonderful *agriturismi* offering a range of activities.

The waterfront at Cefalù.

The popular summer resort of Cefalù has a charming, perfectly preserved historic centre, presided over by a beautiful cathedral containing some of the finest Byzantine mosaics in Europe. Lively beaches extend along the coast, with a host of blaring discos and restaurants in summer, but you can escape the crowds by making the stiff climb up La Rocca. This massive headland boasts stunning views in all directions.

Duomo

Piazza del Duomo, T0921-922021.
Summer 0800-1200, 1530-1900, winter 0800-1200, 1530-1700, free.

Cefalù's golden cathedral rises serenely above the red-tiled roofs of the old town. It was built, according to local legend, to honour a promise made by the Norman count and future king of Sicily, Roger II (1130-1154), whose ship survived a terrible storm to land virtually unscathed on Cefalù's beach. Constructed between 1131 and 1267, the original, grandiose plans were substantially scaled down after Roger's death in 1154. Nonetheless, the cathedral remains one of the finest in Sicily.

Its restrained beauty is infused with just a hint of menace: the cathedral was begun, after all, just a year after Roger II was crowned King of Sicily, when he was still unsure where the loyalties of his new subjects lay. The fortress-like exterior stands testament to the might of the king. The façade is flanked with a pair of sturdy Norman towers, each topped with a pointed steeple added in the 15th century. Behind it rises the sheer face of La Rocca. It's a stunning picture, which you can drink up over a coffee or a glass of wine at one of the numerous terrace cafés on the piazza del Duomo.

Through the heavy doors, the vaulted interior is dimly lit, but the impact of the glittering Byzantine mosaics above the main altar is undiminished by the gloom. Dominating the entire apse is the huge,

Essentials

❶ Getting around The old centre of Cefalù is very small, and easy to get around on foot. It's largely pedestrianized, so you will have to leave your car in the modern part of town (it's usually fairly easy to find roadside parking along the seafront via lungomare G Giardino) and make the short walk into the centre.

❷ Bus station Local and regional bus services arrive outside the train station at the piazza Stazione, T0921-421169. The main bus companies in this region are SAIS (T800-211020, saisautolinee.it) and AST (T800-000323, aziendasicilianatrasporti.it) which have services to Palermo and many of the inland towns of the Madonie (including Castelbuono, Gangi, and Polizzi Generosa).

❸ Train station Stazione FS, piazza Stazione, T0921-421169, trenitalia.it.

❹ ATM There are several ATMs along corso Ruggero, in the old town, and several more along via Roma, including Banco di Sicilia, via Roma 139, T0921-931410.

❺ Hospital Fondazione Istituto San Rafaele Ospedate G Giglio, Contrada Pietrapollastra, Pisciotto, T0921-920111, hsrgiglio.it.

❻ Pharmacy There are several pharmacies, including Farmacia Battaglia, via Roma 13, T0921-421789, Mon 1600-1900, Tue-Sat 0900-1300, 1600-1900.

❼ Post office Via Vazzana 2, T0921-925511, poste.it, Mon-Fri 0800-1830, Sat 0800-1230.

❽ Tourist information AST, corso Ruggero 77, T0921-421050, comune.cefalu.pa.it. There's also an information office for the Parco delle Madonie in Cefalù: corso Ruggero 116, T0921-923327, parcodellemadonie.it.

Tip...

Buses serve some of the Madonie's towns and villages but there are very few services, particularly on Sundays. It's definitely worth renting a car, even for a couple of days, in order to explore this region properly, not just to find the smaller villages but also to reach the hiking trails. It is just possible to see the main towns of the Madonie by public transport if you plan well in advance: you'll need to be very organized, and juggle bus times with accommodation options (which are limited, if you don't have your own transport to get to the *agriturismi*. It's worth contacting the *agriturismi* to see if a lift can be arranged).

unusually benign, image of Christ Pantocrator (Christ the All-Powerful) his right hand raised in blessing. Christ's gaze – steady and deeply compassionate – is incredibly humane and lifelike. Beneath the Christ figure is a sensitively rendered Virgin Mary, in robes of dazzling blue, flanked on either side by archangels. Beneath her are the Twelve Apostles, each minutely rendered in shimmering tiles. These sublime mosaics were created between 1148 and 1170 by master craftsmen specially summoned from Greece and Constantinople, and are among the earliest and best preserved on the island. Near the belfry, a door leads to the graceful 12th-century cloister, with its pairs of slender columns carved with fabulous beasts.

Museo Mandralisca

Via Mandralisca 12, T0921-421547, museomandralisca.it.
Daily 0900-1300, 1500-1900, €5/3 concession, children under 6 free, €1 children 6-10, €3 children 11-15.

The Baron of Mandralisca (1809-1864) was a politician, philanthropist, amateur archaeologist, and passionate mollusc fan. While his extensive collection of shells (more than 20,000 at the last count) and cabinets full of stuffed animals will leave most visitors cold, the Baron's magpie instincts did lead him to acquire two outstanding masterpieces. The first is a Greek vase from the fourth century BC, painted with a comical scene of a fishmonger hacking away at a large fish as his customer quakes before him. The second is a masterly portrait by Sicilian Antonello da Messina (1430-1479), *Portrait of an Unknown Man* (1470), which depicts its sitter slyly gazing out at the viewer with an enigmatic smile. Only a few dozen examples of this accomplished painter's work survive, most of them found in the world's great museums, making it all the more extraordinary that such a splendid painting is on display in the provincial Museo Mandralisca.

Cefalù beaches

❶ **Lungomare** Cefalù's *lungomare* stretches from the old town all the way along Cefalù's modern extension. The beach is crammed in summer, and access is almost entirely limited to expensive lidos: the further you walk from town, the cheaper they get. It's a good family beach, with shallow waters.

❷ **Caldura** The locals prefer the pebbly Caldura beach (on the eastern side of town, beyond the harbour), which is prettier and less crowded but has considerably fewer facilities.

❸ **Mazzaforno** If you're driving, consider the lovely little beaches around Mazzaforno, 5 km from Cefalù.

❹ **Salinelle** This popular beach is 7 km west of Cefalù. There are several lidos (admission), bars and restaurants, but it's not suitable for families with small children as the beach shelves abruptly.

❺ **Capo Playa** The 15-km-long Capo Playa, a popular surfing beach, stretches west from Cefalù all the way to the little town of Campofelice di Roccella, where the ruins of an ancient castle dot the shoreline.

Cefalù's *lungomare*.

Città vecchia

Shop-lined corso Ruggero is the main street of the worn yet charming *città vecchia* (old town), which is laid out in a simple grid pattern and scattered with handsome old buildings. The finest of these is the 13th-century **Osteria Magno** (corner of corso Ruggero and via Amendola), traditionally (if erroneously) believed to have housed Roger II, and

The magician and Cefalù

Of all the colourful characters to have passed through Cefalù, Aleister Crowley (1875-1947) was perhaps the strangest. This dabbler in the black arts, writer, yogi and hedonist came to the town in 1920 to set up a commune, the Abbey of Thelema. It was dedicated to Thelema (a religion he had founded in 1904), whose central tenet was "Do What Thou Wilt". Locals, who were terrified of Crowley, discovered his followers left naked on the beach or bound to the great rock behind the town. Crowley was finally expelled in 1923, reputedly after a young member of the commune died as a consequence of drinking cat's blood.

now restored and used for occasional exhibitions. Perhaps the most atmospheric corner of the old town is the little beach, where fishing boats are perfectly framed by the ancient **porta Marina**, the only surviving gateway in the medieval walls. Colourfully painted boats are pulled up onto the strand, from where you'll enjoy enchanting views of the town in the shadow of the great rock.

La Rocca

The vast rock that dominates the town can be reached via a steep flight of steps from buzzing piazza Garibaldi. Huff and puff your way to the top (it takes roughly an hour, bring plenty of water) for stunning views. There are few vestiges of the settlements that crowned this rock before the Normans built their town at the base of the headland. The best preserved is the **Tempio di Diana** (Temple of Diana), a megalithic construction of pale cubes dating back to the ninth century BC, adapted four centuries later and dedicated to the goddess of the hunt and the moon. Little survives of the recently restored, once-mighty Arab fortress that so impressed early travellers, but the views over the red-tiled rooftops and the cathedral far below are unforgettable.

Central square in Cefalù.

Castel di Tusa.

Around Cefalù

Castel di Tusa

27 km east of Cefalù.

Stacked up around a harbour, this coastal resort is locally famous for its collection of enormous contemporary sculptures, the *Fiumara d'Arte* (Rivers of Art), which are scattered around the town (you'll need a car to visit them all). The artists behind the sculptures have designed some of the rooms in the ART Hotel Atelier sul Mare (see page 136), which has become a minor tourist attraction. On the way to the pretty hill town of **Tusa**, 10 km inland from Castel di Tusa, are the remnants of **Halaesa**, a Greek settlement from the fifth century BC now reduced to a scattering of stones beneath gnarled olive trees, with lovely views over the valley.

Santuario di Gibilmanna

Daily 0730-1300, 1515-1930, free. Three buses daily Mon-Sat (with Sommatinese, T0921-42430, sommatinese.it), journey takes 20 mins.

The 18th-century sanctuary at Gibilmanna, 13 km south of Cefalù, enjoys views over the Madonie mountains and out to sea. It contains one of Sicily's most venerated statues, an image of the Madonna credited with numerous miracles, and is the focus of an pilgrimage on 8 September. There are lots of picnic spots under the surrounding trees.

Parco delle Madonie

Information: Parco delle Madonie, corso Paolo Agliata 16, Petralia Sottana, T0921-684011, parcodelleMadonie.it; also corso Ruggero 116, Cefalù, T0921-923327, parcodellemadonie.it.

Named after the Madonie mountain range, this beautiful 40,000-ha natural park encompasses forest-covered mountains dotted with medieval villages and traditional farmsteads. Some of the highest peaks in Sicily are found within the borders of the park, including the Pizzo Carbonara (1979 m), Pizzo Antenna (1977 m), Monte San Salvatore (1912 m) and Monte Ferro (1906 m). In summer, the park's meadows are carpeted with wild orchids, and an extraordinary variety of butterflies dance in the sunlight. Skiing can be enjoyed for a few weeks in January and February.

Castelbuono, the principal town in the Madonie and one of its most beautiful, tumbles magically down a hillside, its steep streets of rosy stone crowned by a medieval castle. The castle was built by the powerful Ventimiglia family, who ruled this region for two centuries, and has been converted into a rambling, but appealing, museum (May-Sep Tue-Sun 0830-1400, 1600-1900, Oct-Apr Tue-Sun 0900-1300, 1500-2000, €2). Little **Collesano** has a splendid Gothic Duomo, and a smattering of medieval churches.

A ski resort is the last thing you might expect to find in Sicily, but **Piano Battaglia**, complete with Alpine-style chalets, is just that. Perched at around 1,600 m, it's surprisingly popular, and also attracts plenty of walkers during the summer months.

Tucked away in the south of the park, lofty **Petralia Soprana** and its neighbour **Petralia**

It's a fact...

A relatively new tradition, the Madonie mountains hosts an annual 'Ecomarathon', a 42-km run through magnificent countryside which departs from Polizzi Generosa. More information at ecomaratonadellemadonie.it.

Walking in the Madonie

The park information offices can provide leaflets and general maps describing walks in the Madonie region. But the hiking trails are still in their infancy, and signposting is still relatively rare and often poor. If you are unfamiliar with the region, it's best to follow the most popular trails, which include the hike up to the Santuario della Madonna dell'Alto (reached from Petralia Sottana); Piano Pomo, famous for its gigantic and ancient holly trees (the hike starts at the Rifugi Crispi, 11 km from Castelbuono); and the walk through the Vallone Madonna degli Angeli, with its beautiful and endangered fir trees (access 8 km from Polizzi Generosa towards Piano Battaglia on the SP119). Piano Battaglia, a ski station in winter, is also a great place to hike, with several popular trails.

Sottana are two of the loveliest and best-preserved medieval towns in the Madonie, with wonderful views stretching all the way to Etna on clear days. The Parco delle Madonie information centre can be found in Petralia Sottana, while there is a small museum on the Madonie (usually open mornings only, mam.pa.it) in **Polizzi Generosa**, a hilltop town of creamy stone.

Petralia Soprana.

A circular drive in the Madonie

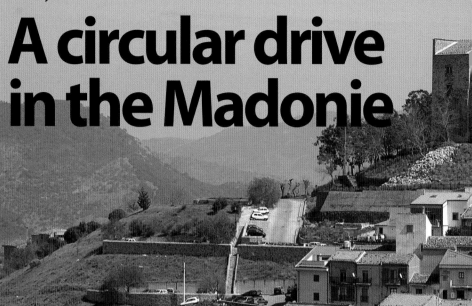

From Cefalù, take the SP15 which wriggles up towards the Sanctuary of Gibilmanna (the sanctuary is signposted up a narrow road on the left). Soak up the views, and then continue on towards Castelbuono (see page 118), turning left onto the SP9 at the junction. As you amble through Castelbuono's lovely cobbled streets and squares, you might come across the curious but very charming sight of Valentina the donkey and her pals, who took over the town's rubbish-collection service at the end of 2007. The museum in the vast Ventimiglia castle is worth a visit, and the town boasts several excellent shops selling delectable local treats, including hams and cheeses.

From Castelbuono, the SS286 continues southwards to **Geraci Sículo**, perched at 1,077 m with a breathtaking mountain backdrop. Wander around its old centre and admire the worn but handsome Chiesa Madre. The ruins of another castle built by the Ventimiglia family dominate a massive basalt rock, and include the remnants of a14th-century chapel with a Byzantine fresco.

Follow the SS286 south to the junction with the SS120 and turn right to reach Petralia Soprana and Petralia Sottana. **Petralia Soprana**, one of the highest villages in the Madonie park, is a beautiful tumble of pale stone, brightened by the scarlet blooms of geraniums. The main park information office is here (see page 118) and it's a good base if you want to stop a while and enjoy some hiking. Below it, reached either by the tiny, crooked local road, or by circling around on the SS120, is **Petralia Sottana**, not quite as striking as its big sister but still a charmer, piled on a gentle, green hill and fringed with pine forest. It is dotted with handsome churches, including the 17th-century Chiesa Madre. Nearby is a belvedere, offering wonderful views over the valley

Continue west along the SS120 and then right onto the SS643 to reach **Polizzi Generosa**, a

Five of the best

Views in the Madonie

❶ Santuario di Gibilmanna
On the fringes of the Madonie park, this sanctuary gazes out over hills covered in forest, see page 118.

❷ Madonna dell'Alto, Petralia Sottana.
Climb up behind Petralia Sottana to reach a sanctuary on one of Madonie's highest peaks, see page 119.

❸ Belvedere, Petralia Sottana.
Visit the superb *belvedere* (viewing area) near the Chiesa della Madonna di Loreto, see page 119.

❹ Vallone Madonna degli Angeli, between Polizzi Generosa and Petralia Sottana.
This lofty valley (1550 m) is famous for its endangered fir trees and jaw-dropping views, see page 119.

❺ Rocche del Crasto, between Longi and Alcara li Fusi.
A jagged crag offering an incomparable panorama of the surrounding hills, see page 127.

dreamy town built on the edge of a spur overlooking the Imera valley. Often, the *maretta* (low cloud) fills the entire valley and the little town seems to float above a sea of white. The 16th-century **Palazzo Notarbartolo** (Tue-Fri 1000-1300, Sat-Sun 1000-1300, 1600-1900, free) houses a museum dedicated to the animal and plant life of the Madonie mountains.

Follow the SS643 north to **Collesano**, another delightful country town piled on a hilltop. Its narrow streets and alleys are coiled around a central square, piazza Garibaldi, and it boasts several fine churches. There's also a small **museum** (summer daily 0930-1230, 1600-1930, winter Mon 0930-1230, Tue-Sun 0930-1230, 1300-1830, €2/1 concession, museotargaflorio.it) dedicated to the famous Targa Florio, a death-defying motor race whose circuit through the Madonie mountains featured over a thousand bends and some awesome drops. It ran from 1906 until, prompted by several deaths, it was abandoned in the 1970s.

Each May, participants in the Rally Targa Florio take to the mountains in their classic and vintage cars in honour of the original race. Locals are almost as passionate about the *palio del Pipiu*, a bizarre turkey race that takes place on 14 September and is the occasion of some very heated betting.

Head north, towards the coast, to **Láscari**, topped by the ruins of a medieval castle and surrounded by olive groves and citrus fruit orchards. The town is famous for its lemons, which are celebrated annually in August in a big local festival. From Láscari, head to the coast and return to Cefalú along the coastal SS116.

Tip...

This circular drive of about 130 km could be done in one hectic day but is best done in two, three or even four days: it's slow-going along the narrow mountain roads and you'll want time to explore the villages, and perhaps take in a hike or two.

Milazzo & the Tyrrhenian Coast

Milazzo, a piquant port city spread along a narrow isthmus, is the main departure point for ferries to the Aeolian Islands. Most visitors simply pass through, which is a shame, because Milazzo has more to offer than its grim industrial outskirts might suggest. The shabby but appealing old centre is piled up above the port, and crowned with the remnants of a massive castle offering superb views. Even better are the views from the tip of the headland, at Capo di Milazzo, still relatively undeveloped. The coastline west of Milazzo is punctuated with plunging cliffs and idyllic bays, and still dotted with the remnants of important ancient settlements such as Tyndaris. Most of the resorts have managed to hang on to some old-fashioned charm, and, when the seaside bedlam gets too much, you can head inland to the Nebrodi mountains, to explore sleepy towns and breathtaking countryside.

The heart of the old town is the castle, in a panoramic position at the top of the hill. The Borgo, the 16th-century Spanish town that grew up around the castle, is now rather dilapidated but still exudes a ramshackle charm. Work is underway on transforming the scruffy, so-called 'Riviera de Poniente' (the beaches on the western side of the isthmus) into something vaguely worthy of the name. There are lots of little coves by the Capo di Milazzo.

Castello di Milazzo & Borgo Antico

T090-922 1291, ilcastellodimilazzo.it.
The castle is a 20-min walk from the port, entrance off via Duomo Antico. Guided tours hourly Mar-May Tue-Sun 0930-1700; Jun-Aug Tue-Sun 1000-1900; Sep Tue-Sun 1000-1700; Oct-Feb Tue-Sun 0930-1530. Visits restricted to Duomo Antico 1630-1800.

The enormous castle that dominates the Milazzo peninsula was built by the Normans over the vestiges of the Greek acropolis and an Arabic fortress and later expanded by the Spanish. In the

Essentials

❶ Getting around The centre of Milazzo is small and easy to get around, but you'll need to catch an AST bus for the Capo di Milazzo (No 6, every 30-60 mins) or the train station (see below). For ferries to the islands, see page 145.

❷ Bus station The main bus service provider in Messina (both regional and local) is **AST** (T090-662244/ T840-000-323, aziendasicilianatrasporti.it). All AST services culminate in the piazza della Repubblica by the port.

❸ Train station Stazione Ferroviaria Milazzo, piazza Stazione, T89-2021, located 3 km from the city centre and port; take local bus No 5 (roughly every 30 mins) or a taxi to the centre.

❹ ATM There are several ATMs clustered near the tourist office, on piazza Caio Diulio 10, one block back from the port.

❺ Hospital Ospedale Civile di Messina, Contrada Grazia, Milazzo, T090-929 0111.

❻ Pharmacy Farmacia Vece, piazza Caio Diulio 10, T090-928 1181, Mon 1600-1900, Tue-Fri 0900-1300 1600-1900, Sat 0900-1300.

❼ Post office Main post office is at via Medici 2, T090-923 0901, poste.it, Mon-Fri 0800-1830, Sat 0800-1330.

❽ Tourist information AAST, piazza Caio Duilio 20, T090-922 2865, aastmilazzo.it, Mon 0830-1330, 1530-1830, Tue-Sat 0830-1330.

Castello di Milazzo.

Around the island

16th century it was the heart of the city, packed tightly within the massive walls. The **Duomo Antico** was built in the 17th century and was abandoned in the 1950s when the Duomo Nuevo in the modern town was constructed. Now wild flowers run riot over the romantic ruins, and the beautiful views extend as far as the Aeolian Islands. Huddled against the castle walls are crumbling houses, part of the Borgo Antico that grew up around the citadel in the 16th century. Now they are dotted with outdoor cafés and, on the first Sunday of the month, a colourful flea market.

Capo di Milazzo

The aptly named Strada Panoramica leads through olive groves and prickly pear to the tip of the cape, a spectacular headland with stunning views. Near the lighthouse, steps lead to the little **Santuario di Sant'Antonio da Padova**, a 16th-century chapel built into a cave. Beyond it is one of the prettiest beaches on this stretch of coast.

Tyrrhenian Coast

A series of rugged capes undulate along the Tyrrhenian coastline east of Cefalù. The modest resorts, popular with Italian families, are gathered around pebbly beaches, some still overlooked by watchtowers which once guarded against Saracen pirates. The sanctuary at Tindari shares a headland with the ruins of ancient Tindaris. Inland stretch the forests and peaks of the Nebrodi mountains, a gentle landscape where life has changed little in generations.

Tindari & around

Crowning the beautiful Capo Tindari, 35 km west of Milazzo, the huge **Santuario della Madonna Nera** (Sanctuary of the Black Madonna) (Mon-Sat 0730-1230, 1430-1900, Sun 1230-2000) is one of the most important pilgrimage sites in Sicily. Close up, the church is garish, a mid-20th-century construction built with more enthusiasm than taste, but it does contain the exquisite statue of a dark-skinned Madonna. On the Madonna's feast day (8 September), there are processions and singing, and a wonderful carnival atmosphere. The most committed pilgrims come barefoot, many travelling across the mountains through the night, hoping that the Madonna will perform a miracle.

Essentials: the Nebrodi

❶ Getting around Public transport is even more limited in the Nebrodi than it is in the neighbouring Madonie. A car is essential to explore the region properly. There are four panoramic main roads though the Nebrodi, connecting the Tyhrrenian coast with the Catania plain near Etna. These roads (going west to east) are: the SS117, which links Santo Stefano di Camastra with Nicosia (see Central and Southern Sicily, page 222); the SS289, from Santa Agata di Militello to Cesarò and Bronte (see Eastern Sicily, page 170); the SS113 (which becomes the SS116), from Capo d'Orlando to Randazzo (where there's another park information office, see Eastern Sicily, page 171); and the SS185, from Terme Vigliatore to Francavilla di Sicilia.

Just beyond the sanctuary lie the enchanting ruins of **Tyndaris** (daily 0900 till 1 hr before sunset, €2), a Greek settlement founded by Dionysos the Elder in 396 BC to house refugees from the Peloponnesian War. The ancient stones, shaded by cypress and olive trees, occupy an unforgettable clifftop setting. The Greek-Roman theatre is the focus of a festival of classical drama held in June (see page 195). There is a small museum on site, with finds from the excavations. The ruins provide a magnificent vantage point from which to gaze down on the shifting sea lagoons at the base of the cliff. Enclosed by banks of pinkish sand, the lagoons are protected as a natural park, the **Riserva Naturale di Laghetti di Marinello** – some of the quietest and most beautiful beaches in the Mediterranean can be found here.

Coastal resorts: Tindari to Santo Stefano di Camastra

The undulating coastline that stretches west from Tindari to Capo d'Orlando is pocked with the remnants of medieval fortresses, built as defence against the Saracen pirates. **Patti** was badly shaken by an earthquake in 1978, but preserves a fine old centre and the remnants of a once-lavish Roman villa in Patti Marina. The little towns of **Goiosa Marea**, **Piráino** and **Brolo** are some of the nicest, low-key resorts in Sicily. **Capo d'Orlando** is a well-kept modern resort with fabulous beaches which stretch around the headland (particularly the little bay of San Gregorio to the east). **Sant'Agata di Militello** has a little more charm than the cement jungles that have sprouted elsewhere on Sicily's coast, and is one of the main

The Greek theatre at Tindari.

entry points to the Parco dei Nebrodi, with park information offices in the main town as well as inland, in pretty **Militello Rosmarino**. The seaside town of **Santo Stefano di Camastra** is famous throughout the island for its ceramics, and the shops are full of colourful pottery.

Parco dei Nebrodi

Information offices: via Ruggero Orlando 126, Caronia, T0921-333211; via Ugo Foscolo 1, Alcara Li Fusi, T0941-793904; Strada Nazionale, Cesarò, T095-696008.
The Cesarò information office organizes free guided walks during the summer, parcodeinebrodi.it.

The Nebrodi mountains may not be the highest in Sicily but they encompass some of the most unspoilt scenery on the island. Since 1993, this 85,000-ha natural wonderland has been protected as the Parco Regionale del Monti di Nebrodi. The mountains are carpeted with extensive forest and traced with rivers and waterfalls. Golden eagles and griffon vultures soar over the highest peaks, and the villages are small, old-fashioned and proudly traditional.

On the western edge of the park, **Mistretta** (16 km inland from Santo Stefano di Camastra on the SS117) is a sea of red-tiled rooftops punctuated by the florid spires of its Baroque churches. The nearby lake **Urio Quattrocchi**, which overlooks beech woods, is a perfect picnic spot and the starting point for some great walks. Further east along the coast and just inland is **Caronia**, prettily coiled around a conical hilltop and overlooked by a battered Norman castle, privately owned and still inhabited. The narrow SP168 from here wriggles steeply for about 35 km through wooded hills to reach one of the highest villages in Sicily, **Capizzi** (1138 m), where there is a fountain whose waters are credited with miraculous powers.

One of the main routes into the mountains is the SS289, a stunning climb through forest and undulating pastureland, which links Sant'Agata di Militello on the coast with Cesarò (where the park's

Burning issue

Nothing much happens in the seaside town of Canneto di Caronia, just below Caronia village. At least not until 2004, when the townspeople experienced a perplexing series of apparently spontaneous fires and explosions. Washing machines, radiators, and fridges simply erupted in flames, even when disconnected from the mains. The electricity supply was cut off, the townspeople evacuated, but the fires continued. The Vatican sent an exorcist – to no avail. The Italian government sent an investigative team, but, after three years of study, they were no closer to an explanation. Its final report suggested that aliens were responsible!

central office is located). Heading inland for about 17 km, you will reach **San Fratello**, a winsome town of dark stone which grew up around a sanctuary dedicated to three martyred brothers (saints Alfio, Filadelfio and Cirino). The sanctuary was founded by Queen Adelaide, wife of Roger I, and the town was settled by her Lombardi compatriots – the locals still speak an unusual Gallic dialect. If you are here on 10 May or the first Sunday in September you'll see the Sanfratellano horses, the oldest breed in Sicily, parade as part of the town's festivals. From San Fratello, the SS289 eventually brings you to **Cesarò**, a fine Nebrodi town spread around a jutting crag with staggering views of Mount Etna. It's a good base for excursions, and the park information office organizes free guided walks during the summer. The town also enjoys a big reputation for its cured hams, made with the free-range black-footed pigs that roam through the forest.

The village of **Longi**, up a twisting mountain road (the SP157 from Castell'Umberto) may be small, but it is a good base for excursions in the Nebrodi, with several simple *agriturismi* in the area, which can organize special-interest tours such as horse riding and birdwatching. There's also a helpful information centre (Centro Naturalistico, T0941-485631).

Time has stood still in peaceful **Floresta** (38 km inland from Capo d'Orlando on the SS116) a huddle

Trekking in Nebrodi park.

of grey stone, where old men gather at cafés on the main street, and ladies sit in doorways with their embroidery. It's a very peaceful town, and its tiny streets are perfect for a gentle amble. Heading out of town on the SS116 towards Randazzo (see Eastern Sicily, page 171), Mount Etna appears like a vision, beautifully framed by wooded hills.

A beautiful country road, the SP10, leads from grim, unlovely Fúrnari near the coast, past delightful **Bàsico,** to exquisite **Montalbano,** dominated by a magnificent castle. This was built by the Normans and expanded in the 14th century under the Spanish, when it served as the Imperial residence. A restoration project, which has already transformed the castle, will hopefully return the haunting old town to its former glory. **Novara di Sicilia**, along the SS185 to the east, hugs a pine-fringed outcrop, the tiled roofs spiked with church spires. Scramble up to the remnants of a Saracen castle to enjoy a picnic and stunning views all the way to the coast and beyond.

Griffon vultures of Rocche del Crasto

Nine kilometres from the village of Longi is the **Rocche del Crasto**, a wild, craggy outcrop which, at 1315 m, is one of the highest peaks in the Nebrodi. It is home to numerous birds of prey, including griffon vultures, reintroduced here after they were accidentally wiped out in the 1960s, and offers heart-stopping views. To get there from Longi, take the signposted trail (7 km, a walk of some 2½ hours) from Portella Gazzana, on the little PR157 road that links Longi and Roca di Caprileone. To reach the Voliere dei Grifoni (the griffon-rearing site), it's easiest to approach from Alcara Li Fusi (ask for directions at the park information office).

The Aeolian Islands

The stunning Aeolian Islands (Isole Eolie), an archipelago formed by violent volcanic eruptions thousands of years ago, were named by the ancient Greeks after Aeolus, keeper of the winds. Although the islands lie only a few kilometres off the coast of mainland Sicily, they feel like a different world. Each of the seven inhabited islands – Lipari, Vulcano, Salina, Panarea, Stromboli, Filicudi and Alicudi – has a distinct personality, from the chichi little celeb-haunt of Panarea to verdant Salina, and from remote Alicudi to fire-spitting Stromboli. If you want to be a beach bum, there's nowhere better than this idyllic island chain, but more active souls will also enjoy some excellent hiking, and superb diving and snorkelling.

Lipari Island.

Lipari is the largest (about 10 km long by 5 km wide) and busiest of the Aeolians, with a lively capital topped by a superb castle, as well as sparkling obsidian beaches and white cliffs of pumice stone. Lipari's main town (also called Lipari) is home to about half the island's population (11,000), but that number doubles during July and August, when it's wise to book accommodation and excursions well in advance.

Lipari town

The town of Lipari, with its cobbled streets and ice-cream coloured villas, is curled around a huge rock surmounted by the remnants of the original fortified town, or citadel. Local people refer to its simply as 'the castle'. The ferry port (Marina Lunga) sits to the north of the rock, while the smaller and prettier fishing port (Marina Corta), where the excursion boats dock, is found to the south. Marina Corta is overlooked by piazza Mazzini, an expansive square packed with terrace cafés, and the place to find out about the boat excursions available. From here, shop-lined via Garibaldi winds up to the citadel, the ancient heart of the town, which is still encircled by thick walls and is where you'll find most of Lipari's historic sights.

The citadel can be reached either from piazza Mazzini at the end of via Garibaldi, or from the impressive flight of steps which lead off the same street and frame the graceful Baroque façade of the **Duomo** (Cathedrale di San Bartolomeo, via del Concordato, daily 0900-1300, free). The original cathedral, built in the 11th century under Count Roger, was destroyed by the pirate Barbarossa, and most of the current edifice dates back to the 18th

Tip...

In August, the islands are overwhelmed with people and prices triple or even quadruple, so come, if you can, during the shoulder seasons (June and September) to enjoy them at their peaceful best.

Essentials

❶ Getting around

Ferries Lipari is the main transport hub of the islands. Ferries (navi, which can transport vehicles) and faster hydrofoils (aliscafi, passengers only) link the Aeolians with Milazzo (the main access point on mainland Sicily), and with the other islands in the archipelago. From Milazzo, there are at least 10 hydrofoils a day in summer, and 2 or 3 ferry services. In winter, there are considerably fewer services (about 5 hydrofoils and 1 ferry service daily to Lipari). Check timetables (which change regularly) carefully in advance. Most hydrofoils from Milazzo stop at Vulcano (40 mins) and Lipari (1 hr from Milazzo, 10 mins from Vulcano); from Lipari, some services continue to Salina (20 mins from Lipari), and others to Alicudi (1 hr 40 mins from Lipari) and Filicudi (2 hrs from Lipari). At least one service daily goes directly from Milazzo to Stromboli (1 hr 5 mins). There are several hydrofoil services between the islands, with Lipari as the main hub. Fares between Milazzo and Lipari cost €16 one-way per passenger on a hydrofoil, or €13 on a ferry; to transport an average car is €28.50 one-way between Milazzo and Lipari. For ferry connections to Naples, Milazzo and Palermo, see Transport page 145.

Buses services on Lipari are run by Urso, T090-981102, ursobus.com. They run the daily summer sightseeeing bus (daily in summer at 0930, 1130, 1700, prior reservation required), as well as local services to the main villages of Canneto, Acquacalda, San Calagero and Quattropani. Timetables are available from the tourist office or online (Italian only).

Scooter one of the best ways to explore the island is by scooter, available to rent from **Maurizio Mondello**, via PE Carnevale 23, Lipari, T090-981 4248, noleggioeolie.it, or from the numerous outlets overlooking the Marina Corta. Scooter rental costs €15-30 per day, depending on the season.

❺ ATM There are several ATMs clustered along Lipari's main street, via Vittorio Emanuele.

⊕ Hospital Ospedale Civile, via Santa Anna, Lipari, T090-988 5111.

✛ Pharmacy Farmacia di Sparacino Mariano, via Vittorio Emanuele 174, Lipari, T090-981 1392, Mon-Fri 0900-1300, 1700-1900, Sat 0900-1300.

❷ Post office Via Vittorio Emanuele s/n, Lipari, T090-981 0051, poste.it, Mon-Fri 0800-1830, Sat 0800-1230.

❶ Tourist information Pro-Loco, via Vittorio Emanuele 55, Lipari, T090-988 0306, eolieproloco.it, May-Oct Mon-Sat 0900-1330.

century. It is dedicated to the patron saint of the islands, and contains a silver statue of San Bartolomeo. Flanking the cathedral are the buildings of the archaeological museum (see below). Beyond them to the south, the **Parco Archeologico** (daily 0900 till 1 hr before sunset, free) is a grassy vantage spot, scattered with Greek and Roman sarcophagi, which overlooks the fishing port below.

Back down in the lower town, the pedestrianized **corso Vittorio Emanuele** is packed with shops and bars, and stays busy long into the night during the high season. Duck down one of the side streets, trimmed with flower-filled balconies, to escape the hubbub.

Museo Archeologico Regionale Eoliano

Via Castello, T090-988 0174.
Daily 0900-1330, 1500-1900, €6, check in advance whether all sections are open.

Lipari's superb archaeological museum occupies a handful of buildings around the cathedral and is the major sight on the island. The Sezione Archeologica in the 18th-century bishop's palace contains the earliest finds, from tools and weaponry made of obsidian (a black volcanic stone prized for its strength and sharpness) to ceramics discovered in ancient burial sites. In the building opposite, the museum continues with prehistoric finds from the smaller islands, and an explanation of their explosive formation through volcanic activity. The most exciting and accessible displays are found in the Sezione Classica (on the other side of the Duomo, often closed in the afternoons), which covers the period from the Bronze Age to the third century BC. There are fascinating recreations of burial grounds from the 14th and 11th centuries BC, a mountain of barnacle-encrusted amphorae, and scores of elaborately painted vases, theatrical masks and statuettes. The galleries culminate with a selection of artefacts, mainly ceramics, that date back to the Norman and Spanish rule.

Getting around Lipari

The best way to tour Lipari is by boat. Numerous companies offer excursions, which depart from the Marina Corta; they allow stops for swimming and snorkelling in some gorgeous coves. Prices vary very little between companies. The second-best option is probably a scooter, although be aware that islanders drive fast and carelessly. There are several scooter rental outlets by the Marina Corta. Tourist buses leave three times a day in summer from the ferry port making an anticlockwise circular tour of the island during the high season, but local buses terminate in Acquacalda and Quattropani during the rest of the year.

Around the island

Three kilometres north of Lipari, **Canneto** is a quiet little resort, virtually deserted outside high season. It has a couple of good beaches, including the main beach of fine pebbles along the seafront, or another slightly quieter and less accessible beach just beyond the town. Beyond Canneto, the pumice quarries of **Campo Bianco** have left white scars and a flurry of white dust across the landscape. The beaches below at **Porticello** are scattered with the remnants of long-defunct quarries and spindly jetties, once used to load the pumice onto boats. Local kids whizz down makeshift pumice 'slides' into the sparkling waters. Down-at-heel **Acquacalda** was also dedicated to the pumice trade, and is strung out untidily along the northern bay. There's a viewpoint at **Puntazze**, with a sweeping panorama of five islands – Alicudi, Filicudi, Salina, Panarea and Stromboli. Just before the scattered little village of **Pianoconte**, a small road splinters off to the **Terme di San Calogero**, old Roman baths, where intrepid locals still splash themselves with the hot, mineral-rich water that bubbles from the ground. The best views of the island are to be had from **Quattrocchi** ('Four Eyes'), a fabulous look-out point which gazes down towards Lipari town and out to sea.

Vulcano

1 km south of Lipari, about 20 mins by hydrofoil.

The Greeks believed that Hephaestus, the god of fire, tended his forges beneath this smouldering island, but it was the god's Roman name – Vulcan – that stuck. With its puffs of dark smoke, the eerie rocks of yellow, green, red and black, and the pungent odour of sulphur that wafts across the mud pools, it is an incredibly alien landscape. Although the island's last major eruption occurred in 1890, the volcano continues to smoulder theatrically. The main reason to visit these days is to soak up the sun on the black beaches, or slather yourself with stinky mud in the Fanghi.

The ferries dock at **Porto di Levante**, which is flanked on either side by surreal rock formations (there's a seasonal tourist information office on via Porto di Levante, Jun-Sep 0800-1400, 1630-2230). From here it's a short walk to the **Fanghi** (daily 0700-2300, €2), the celebrated mud pool where crowds wallow, slapping on the thick clay, and

Five of the best

Activities on the Aeolians

❶ **Climbing** Stromboli at sunset, to see the furious spurts of lava against the night sky.

❷ **Bathing** In volcanic mud on the black beaches of Vulcano.

❸ **Diving** To Filicudi's Museo sottomarino (underwater museum) – Greek and Roman ships found 75 m down off the Cape of Graziano.

❹ **Scrambling** Over Basiluzzo, a tiny islet off Panarea, with the remnants of a Roman port visible beneath the transparent waters.

❺ **Boating** Around Alicudi and Filicudi, stopping for a dip in a turquoise cove.

rinsing it off in a bubbling natural spa nearby. The sulphurous smell – think rotten eggs – is overwhelming, and you might reconsider its apparently health-giving properties when you spot signs warning that the level of radioactivity present makes bathing inadvisable for pregnant women and young children.

Vulcano.

Around the island

Four legs good, four wheels bad on Stromboli.

A clutch of shops, cafés and hotels occupy the narrow isthmus that divides the Porto di Levante from the **Porto de Poniente** on the western side, which overlooks **Spiaggia Sabbie Nere**, a stunning beach of black sand, perfectly curved between two jagged headlands – you won't find an inch of space in summer. Beyond is the little islet of **Vulcanello**, which was created by a mighty volcanic eruption in the second century BC. The eastern flank is scattered with strange, sculptural lava formations that resemble grotesque beasts, and is called the **Valle dei Mostri** (Valley of the Monsters). There's an easy and enjoyable walk up to the **Fossa Grande**, the island's main crater, which still hisses and belches sulphuric fumes. The views from up here stretch across the whole Aeolian chain.

The best beaches are at **Gelso** on the south coast, which is difficult to reach by public transport (although there is a limited local bus service), but several tour operators, including those based on other islands, run day excursions by boat to the bay. It's an enchanting little place, particularly out of season, with a smattering of whitewashed villas and a couple of *trattorie* overlooking the crystal-clear waters. You'll find a pair of even more secluded beaches on either side if you're prepared for a scramble.

Stromboli

45 km northeast of Lipari, about 65 mins by hydrofoil.

Stromboli is a storybook volcano that emerges from the sparkling sea in a perfect truncated cone. At dusk, a wisp of smoke dances around the crater, looking for all the world as though it had been added by a child with a fat grey crayon. Stromboli has been continuously active for the past two thousand years, and puts on an impressive nightly display of stunning, natural fireworks. In 2002 the island was evacuated after a huge eruption created two new craters and resulted in a 10-m-high tsunami that wiped out much of the main village. In early 2007, a state of emergency was declared once again when another massive eruption spewed a sheet of lava into the sea.

Stromboli offers little in the way of cultural sights; visitors are drawn by its harsh natural beauty, the excellent opportunities for hiking, snorkelling and diving, and the stunning beaches of fine black sand. At the end of August, the island plays host to the fortnight-long **Teatro Del Fuoco** (International Firedancing Festival, argomentisas.it). Most of all, people come to witness the unforgettable spectacle of the leaping fires erupting from the belly of the great volcano. During the day the volcanic activity is barely visible but, come nightfall, the sky erupts with shooting jets of red-hot magma every few minutes. You'll get a dramatic view of the crater eruptions from an excursion boat (numerous tours are available, departing from all the islands, see page 144) which moor off the **Sciara del Fuoco** (Slope of Fire) – a sheer, black cliff scoured over time by a sea of lava. But to really feel the power of this spectacular natural phenomenon, make the climb to the mouth of the crater.

Visits to the **Gran Cratere** must be accompanied by an officially approved guide, and tour numbers are strictly limited, so try to book at least a couple of days in advance (see page 144). The climb takes around five hours (a couple of hours each way for the ascent and descent, with about an hour to admire the volcanic activity). The climb culminates at the summit (916 m), where a natural balcony provides mesmerizing views of the bubbling crater 200 m below. The smell of sulphur hangs in the air, and every few seconds a thunderous rumble is followed by a jet of molten lava that shoots up into the sky. It's a truly unforgettable experience.

Across the island from Stromboli town, the little village of **Ginostra** (population 30) is accessible only by sea. The string of whitewashed houses are clamped like barnacles to the cliffs, and donkey taxis take the place of cars and scooters – to really get away from it all, few places compare. With the expansion of the small port, it is now able to accommodate ferries and hydrofoils, but the pace remains decidedly relaxed and laid-back.

Panarea

22 km northeast of Lipari, about 70 mins by hydrofoil.

Little Panarea, with its pretty tumble of low, whitewashed villas, is the chicest of the Aeolians. This is where the jet set come to kick back, mostly at the exclusive Hotel Raya, although some prefer to stay on their luxury yachts. Cars are not allowed on the island, but little electric golf-carts do service as taxis and even police vehicles.

When the earth moved…

Stromboli is famous in movie-making lore for being the location where Ingrid Bergman and Roberto Rossellini began their stormy love affair in 1949. Rossellini was directing Bergman in *Stromboli – Terra di Dio* (1950), a Neorealist epic in which the volcano played a starring role and obligingly erupted for real during filming. The affair (Rossellini was married), and particularly the fact that Bergman fell pregnant and bore them a son, so scandalized the American critics that Bergman didn't get another acting job for seven years.

Boats arrive at the main village of **San Pietro**, with its stepped rows of whitewashed houses swathed in bright bougainvillea. From here, a lovely coastal path wends south past **Drauto** to reach the remnants of a Bronze Age village, spectacularly set on the Capo Milazzese promontory. Excavations have revealed the remnants of 23 huts (the finds are displayed in Lipari's excellent archaeological museum, see page 130). Steps lead down the cliff to reach the **Cala Junco**, an idyllic bay almost completely enclosed by volcanic rock formations, where the pristine waters are perfect for snorkelling and swimming. (This cape was bought by a wealthy businessman in the 1970s, and was the first donation to Italy's Fondo Ambiente, which preserves sites of historic, artistic and ecological value from thoughtless development.) Another enjoyable stroll will bring you to the highest point on the island, the **Punta del Corvo** (421 m), which offers stunning views, including an unforgettable vision of smoking Stromboli if you come at dusk.

North of San Pietro, a path from Ditella leads to the **Calcara beach** where *fumaroles* still bubble. There are also some natural thermal springs near the village of **Punta di Peppe e Maria**. Panarea's offshore islets provide superb scuba diving opportunities, particularly around **Lisca Bianca** and **Bottaro.**

Around the island

Salina

22 km northeast of Lipari, about 40 mins by hydrofoil.

Serene and lovely Salina is the only island with its own source of fresh water and is consequently the lushest of the Aeolians. Two perfectly conical, extinct volcanoes sit at either end, connected by a green saddle where the famous *capperi* (capers), intrinsic to island cuisine, are cultivated. The hills are terraced with vines for making the delicious, sweet Malvasia wine. Salina may be the second largest island of the archipelago, but life here is still enjoyably slow-paced and tranquil. You might recognize some of the scenes from the Oscar-winning film *Il Postino*, shot here in the early 1990s. Salina sits at the centre of the archipelago, making it a convenient base for exploring all the islands, and its two lofty peaks (the highest in the Aeolians) offer some fine walking.

Most ferries arrive in the main port, **Santa Marina**, a pretty little town of low, Aeolian-style villas in pastel shades at the foot of a verdant hill. The elegant main street, via Risorgimento, is lined with fancy boutiques and souvenir shops. About 3 km to the south, the romantic seaside hamlet of **Lingua** is a whitewashed jumble of cube-shaped houses overlooking a popular beach. The **Museo Civico**, in a typical Aeolian home, describes traditional life on the island. The nearby salt lake gave the island its modern name: in Greek times, it was known as Dydime, meaning 'twin', which referred to the two volcanic peaks that still give the island its distinctive silhouette. The **Monte dei Fossa delle Felci** is the highest of the pair, covered with a lacy fir forest which is now a natural reserve. A fantastic two-hour walk from the Santuario della Madonna del Terzito on the centre of the island (accessible by bus from Santa Marina) leads to the top, where you'll be rewarded with unforgettable views across to the Monte dei Porri.

Malfa, on the northern coast, is a chic, tranquil resort with some of the island's fanciest accommodation and a functioning fishing port

(early risers can even take their pick of the day's catch from fishermen at the harbour). It sits high on a wave-whipped cliff overlooking a small beach of fine pebbles. The whitewashed streets are now home to upmarket boutiques and smart restaurants, but a glimpse of just how hard life was for the islanders a century or so ago is revealed in the **Museo dell'Emigrazione Eoliana (Museum of Emigration)**, currently located in the town library.

Continuing west, the road culminates in **Pollara**, a picturesque scattering of traditional Aeolian homes overlooking a curving bay formed by a volcanic crater. *Il Postino* has made the village famous, but at a price: the celebrated little beach has suffered erosion from boats churning up the stones and enthusiastic fans regularly making off with bags of pebbles as souvenirs. The 10-m-wide strand visible in the film is now reduced to just 4 m and, as a result, public access – already forbidden to the destructive boats – has been officially withdrawn, even though everyone ignores the signs anyway.

On the south of the island, **Rinella** – the smaller of the island's two ports – is a scruffy but endearing jumble of pink, blue and white houses set against a scrubby hillside overlooking the bay. The sandy beach and campsite make it popular in the high season (particularly August), but it's virtually deserted during the rest of the year.

Filicudi

23 km west of Salina. Hydrofoils from Lipari via Salina about 1 hr.

Filicudi is the larger and greener of the two islands to the west of Salina, with a resident population of just 300, most of whom are concentrated in **Filicudi Porto**. The harbour is overlooked by **Capo Graziano**, where the vestiges of a pair of prehistoric settlements are scattered across the headland. The only other village of any size is romantic **Pecorini Mare**, a miniature harbour town of whitewashed fishermen's houses overlooking a long pebbly beach. Much of the island is a designated natural reserve, and it boasts some great walking trails, including hikes up to the highest peak, the Fossa del Felci (774 m). An amazing coastal path leads to **Zucco Grande**, a haunting old village abandoned during the mass emigrations of the early 20th century, which clings vertiginously to the hillside. Circular boat trips around the island are very popular, and most offer wonderful swimming opportunities as well as the chance to admire the extraordinary coastal scenery – particularly the enormous stack of **La Canna** and the natural arch at the **Punta Perciata**. There is some spectacular diving in these waters, including special dives to the **Museo Sottomarino**, a collection of Greek and Roman shipwrecks lying at the foot of a headland. This underwater museum opened in 2008 and divers must be accompanied (contact I Delfini diving school, see page 144).

Alicudi

20 km west of Filicudi. Hydrofoils from Lipari via Salina about 1 hr 35 mins.

To really get away from it all, head to beautiful Alicudi, which, like Stromboli, is another perfectly conical volcanic island. The tiny harbour town, **Alicudi Porto**, clings to the steep slopes, which still bear the vestiges of terraces laid out in centuries past. There are no other villages and no roads, just a smattering of mule tracks criss-crossing the hills. Electricity only arrived in 1990 and donkeys are still the main form of transport and haulage. Facilities are minimal: a single hotel with restaurant (see page 139), a couple of stores for basics, and a pebbly beach. There is little to do besides making the scramble to the **Filo dell'Arpa**, the island's highest point, and gazing out to the rest of the archipelago.

Tip...

The smallest, wildest and least visited islands in the Aeolian archipelago are Filicudi and Alicudi. Visitors swarm to these islands in the high season, particularly in the middle of August, but they are usually blissfully quiet at other times of the year.

Alicudi.

Sleeping

Relais Santa Anastasia €€€

Contrada Santa Anastasia,
Castelbuono, T0921-672233,
santa-anastasia-relais.it.
A luxurious rural retreat in a
handsomely restored 12th-
century stone abbey, whose
amenities include a pool with
views of surrounding Madonie,
gardens and a decent restaurant.
The hotel is about 15 minutes'
drive out of Castelbuono, and 30
minutes from Cefalù.

ART Hotel Atelier sul Mare €€

Via Cesare Battisti 4, Castel di
Tusa, T0921-334295,
ateliersulmare.it.
Antonio Presti, who organized
the outdoor sculpture park, the
Fiumara d'Arte (see page 118), is
also the man behind the ART
hotel. Choose between the
striking artist-designed rooms, or
standard rooms at a lower price.
The best offer sea views, but be
prepared for the sound of trains.

Masseria Maggiore €€

Contrada Stranghi, Pettineo,
T380-5451891 (mobile),
masseriamaggiore.it.
This *agriturismo*, 20 minutes'
drive from Cefalù, has a pool,
gardens and restaurant. Take to
the hills and explore the natural
parks on foot, mountain bike or
horseback. Choose from suites or
a small self-catering cottage
(€60-115 per person per night).

Villa Gaia €€-€

Via V Pintorno, T0921-420992,
villagaiahotel.it.
Book early for a room at this
modern hotel in Cefalù, which
fills up quickly thanks to its
central location across the road
from the beach, friendly staff and
smart rooms and suites.

Dolce Vita B&B €

Via CO Bordonaro 8, T0921-
923151, dolcevitabb.it.
This B&B is located up a flight of
stairs in the heart of Cefalù's old
quarter, with lovely sea views
from the shared terrace and from
some of the rooms.

Giardino Donna Lavia €

SS643, Polizzi Generosa,
T0921-551104,
giardinodonnalavia.com.
A friendly *agriturismo*, this is set
in a beautifully restored stone
farmhouse in the Madonie with a
stunning mountain backdrop.
Family-run, it offers four simple
rooms, plus a larger suite in a
13th-century watchtower.
Activities can be arranged,
including horse riding, hiking

and even skiing in nearby Piano
Battaglia. The restaurant serves
traditional cuisine every evening,
and is open to non-guests.

Villa Rainò €

Contrada da Rainò, Gangi,
T0921-644680, villaraino.it.
This old manor house 4 km
outside Gangi boasts simple
rooms and a superb restaurant.
There's a pool, with great views,
and some fine walking in the
Madonie mountains.

Self-catering

Monaco di Mezzo

Resuttano, 32 km south of
Petralia Sottana, T0934-673949,
monacodimezzo.com.
At this 18th-century farmhouse
you can choose between nine
bedrooms (€€) and six self-
catering apartments of various
sizes (€990-1200 per week for a
two-bedroom apartment
sleeping four). The farm
produces its own olive oil, hams
and cheeses. The *agriturismo*
offers riding excursions into the
Madonie natural park, or you
could just laze by the pool.

Antico Feudo San Giorgio

Contrada San Giorgio, SS120 Km 45.990, Polizzi Generosa, T0921-600690, feudosangiorgio.it.

This hilltop farm gazes out across the Madonie mountains, and is paradise for hikers and mountain bikers. Kids will love the animals, the pool and playground, and the chance to join in with the harvest. The *agriturismo* can accommodate up to 50 guests – from B&B (€) to self-catering (€145-170 per day for an apartment sleeping four to six) – and there's a restaurant, with the opportunity for cookery lessons.

Milazzo & the Tyrrhenian coast

Cassisi Hotel €€€-€€

Via Cassisi 5, T090-922 9099, cassisihotel.com.

Located right next to Milazzo port, the Cassisi is a boutique hotel which is much more stylish inside than you might guess from the plain exterior. Breakfast is served in the small bar area, but there's no restaurant. However, you'll find plenty of dining options on the doorstep.

Green Manors Country Hotel €€

Via Porticato, Castroreale, T090-974 6515, greenmanors.it.

A manor house surrounded by extensive gardens, this family-run hotel is set in rolling, green hills 9 km from the medieval town of Castroreale. There are nine guest rooms and a restaurant serving classic, local specialities. Ideal for a luxury break (minimum of two nights).

Petit Hotel €€

Via dei Mille 37, T090-928 6784, petithotel.it.

A few steps from Milazzo's port, the Petit occupies an elegant 18th-century building that has been completely overhauled using 21st-century technology. The hotel is proud of its excellent eco-credentials, which include the use of renewable energy, natural fabrics and materials. There's a restaurant and bar, with a terrace overlooking the port.

Il Vicolo B&B €

Via Salemi 14, T349-504 6851, ilvicolobeb.it.

A great budget option, this is a very welcoming, family-run B&B, with impeccably clean rooms (all with en suite bathrooms and satellite TV). It's in a modern suburb, near the beaches on the west of the peninsula, about a 15-minute walk from Milazzo's port and the old town.

Volver B&B €

Via Maria Provvidenza 34, Montalbano Elicona, T348-800 2303, volverdaniela.it.

Tucked away down one of the narrow medieval alleys that make up Montalbano, this sweet little B&B has three light and airy rooms. Painting and cookery

classes can be arranged. The hauntingly beautiful mountain town is the perfect base for exploring the Nebrodi (guided tours are available), while the coast is only 20 km away.

Self-catering

Antico Casale di Lisycon €€-€

Contrada Nunziata, Sant'Angelo di Brolo, T0941-533288, lisycon.com.

Cindy and Gianni have transformed their lovely stone farmhouse in the Nebrodi hills into a relaxed, simple B&B with three double bedrooms. Full board is also available, while several old buildings scattered around the same valley have been converted into rustic self-catering properties (considerably more basic than they appear on the website, from €80 per night). The agriturismo is surrounded by forest, and is only 12 km from the coast.

See also the Hotel Ericusa and Pensione La Sirene, page 141.

Therasia Resort €€€€
Loc. Vulcanello, Vulcano, T090-985 2555, therasiaresort.it.
If you can cope with the whiff of sulphur that hangs over Vulcano, there's nowhere nicer to stay than this five-star spa hotel. It has been built in the traditional style, using volcanic rock and terracotta, but the decor is 21st century and palely minimalist.

Hotel Raya €€€€
Via san Pietro, Panarea, T090-983013, hotelraya.it.
A chic, surprisingly simple, celebrity hang-out, the Raya is a typical Aeolian-style villa, with a light-filled interior with gleaming white and cobalt-blue decor. If you want to arrive in style, there is a helicopter landing pad, and the open-air Raya nightclub is legendary on the islands.

Capofaro Malvasia & Resort €€€€-€€
Via Faro 3, Salina, T090-984 4330, capofaro.it.
This retreat occupies a remote headland between the villages of Malfa and Santa Marina. Owned by the Tasca d'Almerita family, who have been at the forefront of fine Sicilian wines for over 100 years, the airy rooms and suites (€170-450) are set in whitewashed Aeolian-style cottages amid a sea of Malvasia vines. The facilities include a beautiful pool and tennis court, and the restaurant is one of the best in the islands.

Mamma Santina €€€-€€
Via Sanità 40, Santa Marina, Salina, T090-984 3054, mammasantina.it.
This hotel is set on a hillside overlooking Salina's main port. Hammocks are slung beneath the bougainvillea and some offer gorgeous views out to Stromboli. There's a pool and a moderately priced restaurant which is among the best on the islands.

Hotel La Canna €
Via Rosa 43, Filicudi, T090-988 9956, lacannahotel.it.
One of the quietest hotels on the Aeolian islands, this has just 10 rooms with sun terraces. Book in advance for a room in July and August (when half-board is obligatory). Closed from mid-November to early January.

Pensione La Nassa €
Via Marina, Fico Grande, Stromboli, T090-986033, lanassastromboli.it.
A great budget option on Stromboli, this offers plain rooms (all with shower and private terraces) in a series of Aeolian-style cottages just a stone's throw from the beach.

Self-catering

I Faraglioni
Lipari, T339-444 7646, ifaraglioni.it.
This local firm rents out simple apartments and villas on Lipari and Vulcano. Prices are sky-high in August (€650 per week for a one-bedroom apartment in Lipari between 1-22 Aug, €350 per week the rest of Aug), but very good value (€150-250 per week) for the rest of the year.

Appartamenti Russo Gaetano
Via Giuseppe Cincotta, Stromboli, T090-986017.
A typical, whitewashed Aeolian villa, set in gardens shaded by palm trees, this is divided into apartments sleeping between four and six (€300-800 per week). Simply furnished, they are located between the centre of the old town and the beach.

Casa Mulino
Via Regina Elena, Alicudi, T090-988 9681, alicudicasamulino.it.
Closed Nov-Mar.
The 19th-century Casa Mulino sits close to the water's edge on the tiny island of Alicudi. It contains four immaculate apartments which sleep between two and six (prices in August range from €100 for two people to €250 for an apartment for six; low season prices are €70-140 per apartment per day).

Eating & drinking

Cefalù & the Madonie

Nangalarruni €€€
Via dell Confraternite 5, Castelbuono, T0921-671428.
Thu-Tue 1230-1500, 1930-2200.
This traditional restaurant is a classic, tucked away in one of the narrow streets that make up Castelbuono's medieval core. Superb dishes from the Madonie feature meat (including wild boar), wild mushrooms, cheeses and charcuterie from the mountains. Finish with *testa di turco*, cream-filled pastries.

Ristorante Trappitu €€€
Via Ortolani di Bordonaro 56, T0921-921972, lutrappitu.it.
Wed-Mon 2030-2230.
Set in a stylishly converted olive oil mill in Cefalù, this has a stunning terrace overlooking the sea. Fresh seafood is the main draw, innovatively prepared – try

the shellfish salad, or the sea bass in a courgette crust. Pizzas also available. Book early to get a table on the terrace.

La Brace €€
Via XXV Novembre 10, T0921-423570, ristorantelabrace.com.
Tue 2000-2230, Wed-Sun 1300-1500, 2000-2230, closed 15 Dec to 15 Jan.

Just off Cefalù's piazza Duomo, La Brace serves refined Sicilian cuisine in a rustic, cosy dining room. House specialities include chicken and Madeira paté, roast rabbit with chestnuts, and marinated swordfish.

Osteria del Duomo €€
Via Seminario 5, T0921-421838, ostariadelduomo.it.
Tue-Sun 1230-1500, 2000-2300.
With a grandstand view of Cefalù's main square and the handsome cathedral, this is a popular choice with visitors. There's a well-priced tourist menu, and the food is reliably good, classic Sicilian fare.

Da Salvatore €
Piazza San Michele 3, Petralia Soprana, T0921-680169.
Wed-Mon 1230-1500, 1930-2200.
At this friendly trattoria and pizzeria, a big favourite with locals, you'll find delicious local products from the Madonie mountains, including superb cheeses (rich, milky *provola* and a

creamy ricotta among them), plus a wide range of pasta dishes flavoured with wild mushrooms and local vegetables. Pizzas served evenings only.

Trattoria Itria €
Via Beato Gnoffi 8, Polizzi Generosa, T0921-688790.
Thu-Tue 1230-1500, 2000-2300.
This friendly, family-run trattoria serves up delicious pizzas baked in a wood-fired oven, along with wonderful local dishes such as tagliatelle with wild mushrooms, or roast lamb. Desserts are delicious, particularly the rich *torta al formaggio* (cheesecake).

Cafés & bars

Fiasconaro
Piazza Margherita 10, Castelbuono, T0921-67713, fiasconaro.com.
Try the local speciality, *testa di turco* ('Turk's head', a cake which dates back to the Turkish pirate attacks in the 16th century) or pick up *mannetto*, a cake made with manna, a natural sweetener derived from ash trees.

Pietro Serio
Via G Giglio 29, T0921-422293, pietroserio.it.
Cefalù's best pasticceria, with mouthwatering cakes and pastries, including scrumptious *cannoli*, plus hand-made ice cream in a range of flavours. Stand at one of the counter tables to sample them, or take away for a picnic.

Antica Filanda €€€€
*Contrada Raviola, Capri Leone,
T0941-919704, anticafilanda.net.*
Tue-Sun 1300-1500, 2000-2230,
closed mid-Jan to end Feb.
This award-winning restaurant
has moved to a modern building
and has added a hotel, but the
food is still the highlight. The key
is their reliance on the freshest
local produce – from artichoke
ravioli with lamb ragout to
cutlets from the black-footed
pigs that roam the forests of the
Nebrodi hills.

Doppio Gusto €€€
*Via Luigi Rizzo 44-45,
T090-924 0045.*
Wed-Mon 1300-1500,
2000-2300.
Located overlooking the port in
Milazzo, this is the city's best
seafood restaurant. It's famous
for its *carpaccios* – raw slivers of
ultra-fresh fish and shellfish. It's
relaxed and family-friendly.

Al Bagatto €
*Via Massilmiano Regis 11,
T090-922 4212.*
Daily 1900-2300.
If you've got an hour or two to fill
in Milazzo, this *enoteca* handily
located for the port is a great
place to spend it. There is a range
of Sicilian wines on offer,
accompanied by the island's
cheeses and cured meats.

Il Fienile €
*Via Vittorio Emanuele 70,
Floresta, T0941-662313.*
Tue-Sun 1230-1500, 1930-2200.
Enjoy produce from the Nebrodi
mountains at this old-fashioned
trattoria, with its wooden-
beamed ceiling and
whitewashed walls. Tasty dishes
include succulent *tagliatelle al
Fienile*, with wild mushrooms,
pancetta and courgette,
followed by oven-roasted lamb
or kid.

Trattoria La Rocca €
*Contrada da Rocca di San Marco,
Ucria, near Floresta, T0941-
662228.*
Daily 1230-1500, 1930-2200.
Just off the roadside, with long
wooden benches shaded by tall
pines, this serves huge portions
of superb home cooking,
including home-made spaghetti
with wild mushroom sauce, and
platters of lamb chops grilled
over hot coals. It's a great spot for
families, with plenty of room for
kids to run around. Advance
booking recommended.

Cafés & bars
Bar Albatros
Via dei Mille 38, T090-928 3666.
Right next to Milazzo port, this
bar serves ice cream (try the
hazelnut), and has a good *tavolá
calda* (hot table) with pizza,
sandwiches, *arancine* and more.

Da Pina €€€€
Via san Pietro 3, Panarea,
T090-983032, dapina.com.
Open year round, Tue-Sat
1230-1500, 2000-2300.
One of the most famous places
to dine in the Aeolians. Try the
linguine al pesto eoliano, made
with wild greens, or *vitidduzzu chi
chiappiri* (veal with local capers).

E'Pulera €€€
Via Diana, Lipari, T090-981 1158,
pulera.it.
Daily Jun-Sep 1900-2300.
Seafood features prominently
here, with langoustines with
lemon sauce, fettucini with
prawns and wild fennel, or local
fish tossed in batter.

Ericusa €€
Via R Elena, Alicudi, T090-988
9902, alicudihotel.it.
Closed Oct-May.
One of the most reliable
restaurants on the islands. The
menu features traditional
Aeolian cuisine, and leans heavily
towards fresh seafood.

La Sirena €€
Localita Pecorini Mare, Filicudi,
T090-988 9997,
pensionelasirena.it.
Open Mar-Oct.
Book early for a table on terrace
at this rustic, island restaurant.
Tuck into inventive cuisine, such
as home-made gnocchi with
pistachio pesto, or swordfish

rissoles suffused with a hint of
orange. There are rooms
available (€€-€), and they also
rent out villas around the village.

Cafés & bars

Pasticceria Subba
Corso Vittorio Emanuele 92,
Lipari.
For some of the best pastries and
ice cream on the islands, don't
miss Subba.

Ingrid Bar
Stromboli, T090-986385.
This bar is the centre of village
life, and sits opposite the church
on the main square. The views
from the terrace are reason
enough to come, but a superb
mojito makes it even better.

Da Alfredo
Piazza Marina Garibaldi, Lingua,
Salina, T090-984 3075.
Closed Nov-Mar.
Giorgio Armani and Sean
Connery send staff out from their
yachts to bring back *granite*
(crushed ice with fresh fruit or
nuts) from Da Alfredo. The café's
terrace is the heart and soul of
the village: people hang out here
between swimming and
sunbathing in the afternoons, or
pop in later for aperitivi or
after-dinner *granite*. It's also
famous for its gargantuan *pane
cunzato*, bread piled high with all
kinds of toppings.

Entertainment

Shopping

Clubs

Le Calette
*Porto Presidiana, Cefalù,
lecalettediscoclub.it.*
Jun-Sep 2200-0300, €10 entry
includes a drink.

An upmarket club and bar
beautifully set right on the rocks,
this is one of the most
sophisticated nightlife options in
Cefalù. It's part of the hotel of the
same name. In summer, there are
bars along the whole length of
Cefalù's *lungomare* (seafront).

Festivals & events

Sherbeth Festival
Cefalù.
Early Sep.

Ice cream lovers shouldn't miss
the annual Sherbeth Festival
(sherbethfestival.it), which
celebrates ice cream in every
imaginable flavour. Tastings,
competitions and concerts.

Sagra del Cappero
Salina.
First Sun in Jun.

A festival held in honour of
Salina's famous capers, which are
beloved by gourmets
throughout Italy.

**Festa de la Madonna de la
Provvidenza**
Montalbano.
24 Aug.

This traditional festival, one of
the oldest in the Nebrodi,
honours the town's patron saint.
The wooden statue is covered
with jewels and paraded through
the streets.

Festa di San Bartolomeo
Lipari.
24 Aug.

Lipari celebrates the feast day of
its patron saint with a procession
of the statue of the saint through
the streets, and a fabulous
fireworks show over the sea.

Books

*La Galleria, Via XXV Novembre
22-24, Cefalù, T0921-420211,
lagalleriacefalu.it.*
Daily 1100-2400.

This light, bright stylish café
combines bookshop, gallery,
restaurant and internet café in
one. There is a small selection of
books in foreign languages,
including a decent choice of
English books. The food is fresh,
tasty and modern, although
rather expensive. Best of all is the
lovely courtyard, which is an
enchanting dining venue in
summer.

Ceramics

Ceramiche d'Angelo
*Contrada Soprane, Polizzi
Generosa, T0921-649173.*
Mon-Fri 1000-1300, 1700-1900,
Sat 1000-1300.

The ceramics of the Madonie are
famous. In this workshop on the
edge of the old town, you'll find
hand-painted ceramics in a
range of styles, from traditional
tableware to contemporary
decorative objects.

Food & drink

Fattoria Villa Briadi
*Via Piave 59, Capo d'Orlando,
T0941-676000.*
Mon-Sat 0900-1300, 1630-1900

Mountain cheeses, hams, cured
meats, as well as olives,
preserves, fresh bread and more,
are on offer in this deli in Capo
d'Orlando. Perfect for picnics.

Pick of the picnic spots

Bastione Capo Marchiafava, Cefalù Get some picnic supplies from Sapori di Sicilia and perch on this lovely stone bastion, with a medieval fountain, overlooking the sea.

La Rocca, Cefalù Climb to the top of La Rocca (bringing food and water supplies with you) and find a spot in the grass to enjoy lunch with tremendous views of the sea and back to the Madonie mountains, see page 117.

Tyndaris The beautiful ancient site of Tyndaris is magnificently set on a cliff edge, making it a panoramic picnic spot, see page 125.

Madonna dell'Alto, Petralia Sottana There is plenty of room to picnic near this lofty shrine, which enjoys stunning mountain views, see page 119.

Stromboli You'll deserve your picnic after making the stiff three-hour climb to Stromboli's seething crater – few picnic areas can compare for sheer drama, see page 132.

Gelso, Vulcano This lovely little beach of black sand is a perfect spot for a lazy lunch, especially out of season, see page 132.

Monte dei Fossa delle Felci, Salina Pick up supplies and hike up through forests of fir trees to reach Salina's highest peak, see page 134.

Tyndaris ruins.

Salumificio Sapori di Sant'Angelo
Via Sant'Elia 17, Sant'Angelo di Brolo, T0941-533016.
Mon-Fri 1000-1300, 1700-1900, Sat 1000-1300.
This modern building on the outskirts of Sant'Angelo di Brolo may not look much but it belongs to one of the last old-fashioned salami-makers, who still make the traditional local sausage in the time-honoured way.

Sapori di Sicilia
Via Vittorio Emanuele 93, Cefalù, T0921-422871.
Mon-Sat 0900-1300, 1630-1900.
All the Sicilian treats you could want to make a truly gourmet picnic, from fine olive oil and wine, to a great selection of cheeses, hams and paté. The selection of jams, pesto (including pistachio pesto) and other goodies make great presents.

Outdoor equipment
Decathlon
Via Firenze, Presso Parco C le Corolla, Milazzo, T090-939 2063, decathlon.it.
Daily 0900-2100.
This outpost of the huge French sports goods chain is handy for well-priced outdoor clothing and beachwear, as well as snorkelling equipment to take to the Aeolians. It's on the edge of town, just off the main approach road from the motorway.

Totem Trekking
Piazza San Vincenzo 4, Stromboli, T090-986 5752.
Daily 1100-1300, 1600-2000.
If you are making the trek up Stromboli, this is the place to hire equipment. It also sells a range of outdoor gear (boots, jackets, backpacks and more) if you prefer to purchase.

Activities & tours

Boat trips
There are scores of boat trip operators on all the Aeolian islands, all of whom offer much the same excursions at much the same price. They are all, unsurprisingly, gathered around the ports.

Amici del Mare Eoliano
Marina Corta, Lipari, T339-4738808 (mobile), isoleolie.eu/amicidelmareeoliano/index.htm.
This co-operative offers a range of half- and one-day boat excursions, including a one-day excursion to Panarea and Stromboli, with stops for diving and snorkelling, plus the chance to watch the volcano in action from the water. Prices for this excursion are €25 per person.

Nautic Center
Via M Garibaldi 125, Canneto, Lipari, T090-9811656, nauticcenter.it.

For boat (and scooter) rental. A small motor-boat for up to four people costs €50 for a half day in the low season, or €100 in the high season (petrol costs extra).

Onda Eoliana
Malfa, Salina, T090-984 4222, ondaeoliana.com.
Small motor boats for rent on Salina. Prices depend on the size of the boat, starting at €80-140 per half day.

Diving
Scores of diving companies operate in the Aeolian Islands, which together form a protected marine reserve and diving and snorkelling opportunities in the Mediterranean.

Dive Sirenetta
Hotel Sirenetta, via Marina 33, Stromboli, T090-986025, lasirenettadiving.it.
Open end May mid-Sep.
Attached to a good hotel of the same name, this is a reliable dive centre. It offers PADI courses in English, plus some excellent dives in small groups (four people maximum). Prices for accompanied dives cost from €35, excluding equipment hire.

I Delfini
Pecorini a Mare, Filicudi, T090-988 9077, idelfinifilicudi.it.
This is the only company allowed to offer trips to Filicudi's *museo sottomarino* (underwater

museum) – a collection of ancient ships off the Capo Graziano. They also rent out boats, canoes, and scooters.

La Gorgonia
Salita San Giuseppe, Lipari, T090-981 2616, lagorgoniadiving.it.
Guided dives around the island from €32 for a single dive to €280 for 10, excluding equipment hire; PADI courses also available.

Horse riding
Vallegrande Ranch
Contrada Vallegrande, Cefalù, T0921-420286, vallegrande.it.
This ranch is set in rolling hills 7 km outside Cefalù and can arrange excursions for riders of all levels (in English, French and Italian). Prices start at €15 per person for a one-hour excursion. They also offer accommodation – either B&B or self-catering.

Walking
Sicilian Experience
Discesa Decano Martino 10, Sant'Ambrogio, T0921-999011, sicilianexperienc.com.
This company offers information on walks in the Madonie mountains, or can arrange guided hikes in the Madonie, Mount Etna and the Vall dell'Anapo (Pantalica necropolis) with English-speaking guides. Mountain hikes often include the chance to meet locals engaged in traditional tasks.

Transport

A.G.A.I.
Piazza San Vincenzo, Stromboli, T090-986211.
One of the three official guide companies authorized to take hikers to the top of Stromboli. Contact well in advance at the height of summer as places fill up quickly. Participants are required to bring suitable footwear, a jumper and waterproof jacket, a torch with spare batteries, a spare T-shirt, long trousers, a handkerchief (for the dust and fumes), a picnic and plenty of water. If you don't have these, they can be hired from Totem Trekking (see above). Helmets are compulsory but are provided free by the guides.

Magmatrek
Via Vittorio Emanuele, Stromboli, T090-986 5768, magmatrek.it.
Another of the official guide companies leading treks up Stromboli. See A.G.A.I. above for equipment requirements.

Wellbeing
Hotel Fonte di Venere
Viale delle Terme 85, Vulcano, T090-978 1078.
The volcanic waters on Vulcano are reputed to have curative properties (see page 131). The Romans had a spa at Terme Vigliatore, and you can still take the waters at the Hotel Fonte di Venere, which is institutional and bracing.

Cefalù

Cefalù lies on the main Palermo–Messina train line. There are several daily departures from Palermo (1 hr) and Messina (2 hrs). There are only two direct buses a day (with SAIS, 1 hr) from Palermo. **Ustica** (T091-333333, usticalines.it) runs a daily hydrofoil service linking Palermo to Cefalù (1 hr 10 mins), and a summer service from Cefalù to Lipari on the Aeolian Islands (3 hrs 15 mins).

Monti di Madonie

Buses depart from Gibilmanna (3 daily, 20 mins), for Castelbuono (6 daily, 45 mins), and Geraci Siculo and Gangi (1 daily, 1 hr 30 mins).

Along the Coast: Cefalù to Milazzo

The train is the most convenient way to reach most towns along Sicily's northern coast, with hourly trains from Palermo to Capo d'Orlando (2 hrs) and other resorts. Regular trains (at least hourly) stop at Milazzo (2½ hrs from Palermo, 45 mins from Messina), although it's a bus (AST buses leave every 30 mins) or taxi ride to the city centre and the port. Inter-city buses (including the **Giuntabus**, T090-673782, giuntabus.com, from Messina, 45 mins) are more direct and arrive at the piazza della Repubblica next to the port.

The Aeolian Islands

Milazzo is the main port for the Aeolians, but there are also direct services from Naples and Reggio Calabria on the mainland, and from Cefalù and Palermo on Sicily. The main operators from Milazzo are **SNAV** (T091-6014211, snav.it), **Ustica** (T090-928 7821, usticalines.it) and **Siremar** (T090-928 3242, siremar.it), who all have offices overlooking the ferry dock in the harbour. Between July and September, you can't bring cars to the islands unless you have booked a hotel for at least seven days. No cars are allowed on tiny Panarea. You may find it easiest and cheapest to leave the car in Milazzo (the **Garage delle Isole** is reliable, costs around €14 per day, and will shuttle you to and from the port, garagedelleisole.it, T090-928 8585) and rent a scooter on the islands. **Air Panarea** (T090-983 4428, airpanarea.com) run a helicopter taxi service between the main airports and Panarea, as well as offering panoramic flights over the islands.

Contents

Eastern Sicily

Catania cathedral.

Introduction

Mount Etna, Europe's largest and most active volcano, dominates the entire eastern swathe of Sicily – both physically and in the local psyche. Even when its famous silhouette is shrouded in cloud, menacing Etna is ever present.

Despite the constant danger of eruption and earthquakes, this coast has long attracted settlers: it was the first to be colonized by the Greeks almost 3000 years ago, and its rugged beauty was eulogized in the *Odyssey*. Some extraordinary ancient sites have survived, including the Greek theatre in clifftop Taormina (Sicily's chicest resort since Goethe became the first in a long line of celebrity visitors). You can watch the glowing lava curl languidly across Etna's peak from Taormina's belvederes, or tramp to the summit itself for a close-up look at the other-worldly landscape. It's an entirely different story lower down: the verdant slopes are carpeted with orchards and vines, and dotted with peaceful country towns.

Catania, Sicily's most effervescent city, sits right in the shadow of Etna. Its beautiful, if battered, Baroque centre owes its unique black-and-white decoration to the lavish use of lava. Perhaps because of the constant threat of eruption, Catania, in the spirit of carpe diem, is the best place to party on the island.

Left: Messina.

What to see in...

...one day
With just a day, you'll have to choose between ascending Europe's biggest volcano **Mount Etna**, or the romantic clifftop delights of Sicily's most glamorous destination, **Taormina**. (If it's raining or cloudy, leave Etna for another time.)

...a weekend or more
Take the cable car up Etna and tramp around the surreal lava fields and then spend another day taking in the sophisticated delights of elegant Taormina. Spend at least an afternoon in the Baroque city of **Catania**, and catch some of the city's famous nightlife in the evenings, either by treating yourself to a **night** at the opera, or joining the beautiful people at Catania's nightclubs.

Messina & around

Nestled between green hills on the island's northeastern tip, Messina curves around a fine natural harbour and gazes out across the Strait of Messina to the big toe of mainland Italy, just 5 km away. It has been an important port for millennia, doggedly rebuilding itself time and again after the destruction wrought by earthquakes, pirate attacks, plagues and countless other disasters. The 20th century was particularly brutal. More than 80,000 people were lost in a powerful earthquake that razed the entire city in 1908; it had barely been rebuilt when the Second World War began, and Messina was obliterated by heavy bombing. Modern Messina is decidedly workaday, with low buildings laid out in a grid pattern to guard against earthquake damage, and very few embellishments in the name of historical nostalgia. The seafront, which in any other city might have been prettified for the tourists, is largely industrial (apart from one comparatively small pocket north of the city hall) and geared towards the busy harbour traffic: Messina knows which side its bread is buttered. Nonetheless there are some sights to savour if you have some time to kill before your ferry, including the reconstructed Norman Duomo and an interesting art collection in the regional museum.

Duomo

Piazza del Duomo, T090-668 4111, diocesimessina. net/duomo.
Duomo, Mon-Sat 0700-1900, Sun 0730-1300, 1600-1930; Treasury, daily 0930-1300; Campanile, Mon-Sat 0900-1300, 1500-1830, Sun 1600-1830. Duomo free, Treasury €3, Campanile €3 (€5 combined ticket).

Messina's handsome cathedral, in the heart of the city and just a five-minute walk from the port, was first erected in the 12th century under Norman king Roger II. It was once one of the finest on the island, but fire, earthquakes and war have taken their toll, and this 20th-century copy is only the latest of many reconstructions that have been necessary over the last nine centuries. The elegant façade faithfully replicates the striped marble effect of the Romanesque original, and is inset with a fine 16th-century Catalan-Gothic doorway. The impressive, if rather dim, interior has been handsomely restored but almost everything you see is a copy of the Norman original. Of the gilded mosaics, only those in the apse are original. The **Treasury** contains a collection of vestments and liturgical plate, plus the 17th-century Golden Mantle designed to cloak the painting of the Madonna della Lettera, the city's patron saint, which sits above the main altar. Next to the church, the free-standing **Campanile** was first erected in the 16th century, and replaced after the catastrophic earthquakes of 1783 and 1908. The huge astrological clock, reputedly the largest in the world, roars (literally!) daily at noon, and was built in 1933. Climb to the top for superb views. The expansive square in front of the Duomo is Messina's finest, embellished with the splendid marble **Fontana di Orione** (1551) by Montorsoli (1507-1563), which depicts the city's mythical founder, Orion, cavorting with cherubs and nymphs.

Essentials

❶ **Getting around** Messina's main sights are concentrated in the centre, near the train station and the port, all easily reached on foot except for the regional art museum, which is best reached by tram (No 28, for timetables see atmmessina.it) which can be picked up at piazza Cairoli or at the train station.
❷ **Bus station** The main hub for local ATM buses is the piazza Repubblica, outside the train station.
❸ **Train station** Stazione Ferroviaria Messina Centrale, piazza Repubblica, T892021.
❹ **ATM** Numerous along via Garibaldi, with more concentrated around plaza Cairoli.
⊕ **Hospital** Azienda Ospedale Piemonte, via Gazzi, T090-222 4393.
✚ **Pharmacy** Farmacia Centrale di Calcaterra Giovanni, via Garibaldi Giuseppe 135, T090-679911, Mon-Sat 0830-1300, 1600-1930.
➋ **Post office** Main post office at corso Cavour 138, T090-601581, Mon-Fri 0830-1830, Sat 0830-1230.
❶ **Tourist information** AAPT, via Calabria 301, T090-640221, provincia.messina.it, comune.messina.it (both Italian only).

Messina.

Tip...

If you're here in August, the whole region erupts for the Ferragosto, particularly in Messina itself, where a pair of 'giants' (the legendary founders of the city) are paraded around the city, and there's a huge fireworks show over the sea.

Around the island

Messina Duomo.

Via Garibaldi

North of the Duomo, Messina's main thoroughfare, via Garibaldi, runs parallel to the seafront, and is home to a smattering of buildings that survived the terrible earthquake of 1908. The city's opera house, the **Teatro Vittorio Emanuele** (via Pozzoleone 5, T090-45935, teatrodimessina.it), built in 1842, is once again the centre of Messina's cultural life after major refurbishment. Continuing north along via Garibaldi, the **Villa Mazzini** public gardens on the left host free concerts, film screenings and festivals in summer. The stodgy Prefettura building dominates the piazza Unita d'Italia, whose centrepiece is the the lavishly decorated **Fontana di Nettuno** (1557, by Montorsoli). Neptune, holding his trident in a classical pose, calms the writhing sea monsters Scylla and Charybdis (who guard the Strait of Messina) with an authoritive hand.

Chiesa Annunziata dei Catalani

Piazza Catalani, T090-668 4111.
Mon-Sat 0930-1130, Sun 0900-1130.

Not far from the Duomo a small, pedestrianized street off the via Garibaldi leads to the exquisite late-Norman Chiesa Annunziata dei Catalani. It now sits below pavement level, a consequence of centuries of earthquake damage, but otherwise the beautiful exterior, with its delicate stone decoration, remains enduringly lovely. Although the church was built under the Normans, the ornamentation is clearly Arabic in inspiration, with intricate star-shaped designs and lacy detailing.

Museo di Messina

Viale della Libertà 465, T090-361292.
Mon and Fri 0900-1330, Tue, Thu and Sat 0900-1330, 1600-1830, Sun 0900-1230. €5/3 concession (€2.50/1.50 during remodelling). Tram: Museo.

Messina's regional museum contains a precious hoard of treasures saved from earthquakes, one of the finest collections of Renaissance paintings in Sicily, and an array of poignant fragments of long-destroyed historic buildings, including the cathedral. Highlights from the earliest artworks include a small but evocative section of a 13th-century painted ceiling and Goro de Gregorio's strange sculpture of the *Madonna of the Crippled* (1333), both rescued from the cathedral. Look for the outstanding *St Gregory Polyptych* (1473) by Antonello da Messina (1430-1479), whose works were clearly influenced by van Eyck and Flemish realism – the brocade robes are so exquisitely rendered that you almost expect to hear the rustle of fabric. The museum also boasts a pair of paintings by Caravaggio, including a murky *Raising of Lazarus*. The museum is currently being enlarged, but public access is still possible; some galleries may be closed unexpectedly.

Bridging loans

According to legend, the Strait of Messina is guarded by the six-headed monster Scylla and the terrifying whirlpool of Charybdis. Now these treacherous waters are to be spanned by the world's largest suspension bridge, which will finally link Sicily with mainland Italy. Construction of the 3-km-long bridge should be completed in 2016, and will cost an estimated €6.1 billion. The project has already drawn considerable controversy: detractors say that the money would be better spent improving Sicily's woeful infrastructure, but the bridge's supporters believe it will bring a much-needed economic boost to the region. Commentators on either side of the political divide believe that much of this supposed cash will be lining the pockets of the Mafia on both sides of the Straits.

Around Messina

A wonderful coastal road (which runs parallel to the SS113) heads north of Messina, passing fishing villages-cum-resorts with poetic names like Paradiso, Pace and Contemplazione, before reaching the popular lakeside resort of **Ganzirri**. In summer, the bars and restaurants hum night and day, but out of season it's tranquil and low-key. The two lakes on this headland, which form the **Riserva Natural Laguna di Capo Peloro**, are linked to the sea by short canals, and are a refuge for all kinds of birds, including herons and egrets. The lighthouse blinks at the tip of Capo Faro (also known as Capo Peloro), but it is dwarfed by the gigantic pylon that supports the great cables that sway across the Straits to the mainland. The supporting tower for the new Messina Strait bridge is slated for construction here, despite concern for the currently protected landscape: at an estimated 382.6 m, the tower (and its twin across the Straits) will be taller than the Eiffel Tower (324 m).

Ganzirri.

It's a myth...

The expression 'between a rock and a hard place' echoes the much older phrase 'between Scylla and Charybdis', which derives from the *Odyssey*, in which Homer describes a narrow sea passage guarded by the six-headed monster Scylla on one side and the whirlpool of Charybdis on the other. Sailors negotiating the passage could avoid one fearsome terror only by sailing close to the other.

Taormina & around

In the shadow of Mount Etna, Sicily's most captivating town curls along a ridge overlooking the Ionian Sea. The cobbled streets are lined with elegant palazzi and churches, and a magnificent Greek theatre, breathtakingly set on the cliff edge, stands testament to its importance in antiquity. Goethe eulogized Taormina so passionately that it became an essential stop on the Grand Tour, and soon attracted painters, artists and intellectuals from across Europe. It has shaken off its rakish reputation to become Sicily's swankiest destination, home to luxurious hotels, chic boutiques and upmarket restaurants, and a star-studded film festival every summer. A host of great day trips beckon, from the pools and waterfalls of the Alcantara gorges to time-capsule villages in the Peloritani mountains, and, of course, Etna herself.

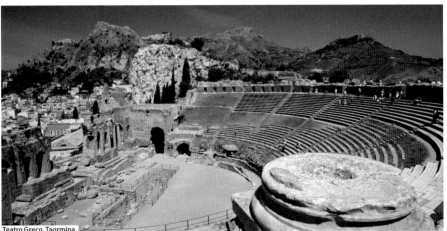

Teatro Greco, Taormina.

Taormina's churches and palazzi of weathered stone are strung out on a high ridge with astonishing views of Mount Etna. The firework show, performed nightly by the vast volcano, can be enjoyed from the town's glamorous café terraces. Such riches attract huge crowds, which throng the main street, corso Umberto I; as soon as you step off it, silence falls, and tiny squares and narrow passages reveal their ancient secrets.

Teatro Greco

Via Teatro Greco, T0942-232220.
0900 till 1 hr before sunset, €6/3. Teatro Greco leads off piazza Vittorio Emanuele.

A perfect arc of golden stone suspended between sea and sky, this ancient amphitheatre was built in the third century BC by the Greeks, when Taormina was one of the most powerful cities on the island. The theatre was thoroughly remodelled by the Romans a century or so later, who erected the elaborate stage and double-columned portico behind it. From the top of the auditorium, the view on clear days perfectly frames the majestic outline of Etna in one direction and stretches out endlessly to the Calabrian mountains in the other. Goethe, who saw this view in 1797, gasped "Never did any audience, in any theatre, have before it such a spectacle," and few modern visitors will disagree. The theatre is the main venue for Taormina's prestigious performing arts festival, Taormina Arte (taormina-arte.com), which takes place annually between June and August (when the stage and scaffolding can obscure the amazing views).

Tip...

Taormina exerts its magic best after dusk, when the hordes of day trippers have gone, so stay the night if you can.

Essentials

❶ **Getting around** The centre of Taormina has been pedestrianized, so, if you are driving, you will need to leave your car at one of the two official car parks and get a shuttle bus to the centre.
❷ **Bus station** Via Luigi Pirandello. Local bus services are run by **Interbus** (T0942-625301, interbus.it).
❸ **Train station** Stazione FS Taormina-Giardini (piazza dell Stazione, on the SS114, T0942-52189, trenitalia.it) is on the coast below Taormina, but is linked by a bus service (usually every 30 mins, fewer services on Sun) to the main town's bus terminal.
❹ **ATM** Most are clustered along corso Umberto I.
⊕ **Hospital** Ospedale San Vincenzo Taormina, via Crocefisso, T0942-579322.
✚ **Pharmacy** The British Pharmacy (with a full range of Italian pharmacy services as well), piazza IX Aprile 1, T0942-625866, Mon-Fri 0900-1300, 1700-1930, Sat 0900-1300.
➚ **Post office** Main post office, piazza Bucini' Medaglia d'Oro 1, T0942-213011, poste.it, Mon-Fri 0800-1830, Sat 0800-1230. In Giardini-Naxos, via Francavilla 42, T0942-58164, Mon-Fri 0800-1830, Sat 0800-1230.
❶ **Tourist information** Main tourist office in Palazzo Corvaja, piazza Santa Caterina, T0942-23243. There is also a tourist office at the train station, T0942-52189.

Along corso Umberto I

The spine of Taormina is bustling corso Umberto I, which stretches for 800 m from porta Messina in the north to porta Catania in the south. This is where the smartest boutiques and souvenir shops are concentrated, and where an endless stream of visitors ebbs and flows. Heading south from porta Messina (where shuttle buses disgorge visitors from the town's main car park), the street soon opens into the piazza Vittorio Emanuele, with a scattering of terrace cafés. Nearby, the Palazzo Corvaja, dating back to the 11th century, now houses the tourist office. Piazza IX Aprile, a vast sweep of chequered tiles, has plenty of enticing cafés and magnificent views across the bay. The handsome 17th-century Torre dell'Orologio rises above the terrace of the historic celeb-haunt Caffè Wunderbar, near the little porta di Mezzo ('halfway gate'). Beyond it is a clutch of fine monuments,

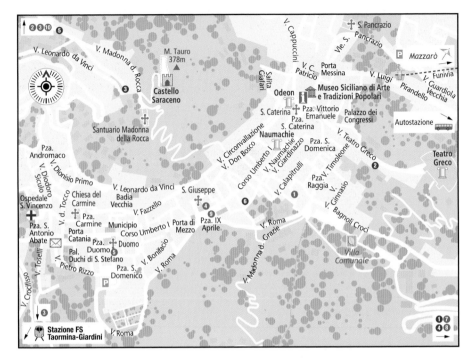

Taormina listings

❶ Sleeping

1 Casa Famiani B&B *via Millo 4, Letojanni*
2 Grand Hotel Timeo *via Teatro Greco 59*
3 Villa Angela *via Leonardo da Vinci*
4 Villa Carlotta *via Pirandello 81*
5 Villa Ducale *via Leonardo Da Vinci 60*
6 Villa Schuler *piazzeta Bastione*

❶ Eating & drinking

1 A'Zammàra *via Fratelli Bandiera 15*
2 Antico San Giorgio *piazza S Antonino, Castelmola*
3 Bar Turrisi *piazza Duomo, Castelmola*
4 Caffè Wunderbar *piazza IX Aprile 7*
5 Casa Grugno *via Santa Maria dei Greci*
6 Da Antonio *via Crocefisso 4*
7 Da Nino *via L. Rizzo 29, Letojanni*
8 La Capinera *via Nazionale*
9 Mocambo *piazza IX Aprile*
10 Pizzeria Ciccino *piazza Duomo, Castelmola*

Villa Comunale.

Mt Etna from Castelmola.

including the Norman Duomo, which is not really a cathedral despite the name, and bristles, slightly comically, with battlements. Down a stone staircase, the sublime, restrained 13th-century Palazzo dei Duchi de Santa Stefano is now used as a temporary exhibition space.

Villa Comunale

The via Roma, which makes two gentle swoops from piazza IX Aprile, offers heavenly views out across the coastline. It also leads to the Villa Comunale, Taormina's idyllic public gardens, which are filled with gorgeous blooms and shady trees. There's no better place to picnic, so find a spot beneath a magnolia tree and drink up the views.

Castelmola

From the streets of Taormina, you can just make out the ruins of a Saracen castle high above the town. The castle dominates Castelmola, a tiny knot of narrow streets with a smattering of cafés and restaurants, from where there are some of the best views in Sicily. The stunning but stiff 3-km hike up to Castelmola from Taormina takes about 45 minutes, or you could take the bus (roughly every hour) or grab a taxi.

The town, not large, is contained between two gates. Near the first of these, the Porto Messina, there is a small, tree-shaded square with a fountain and a stone wall along which village idlers are arranged like birds on a telephone wire.

Truman Capote, *A Capote Reader*, 1987

Fontana Vecchia

The Fontana Vecchia, a 17th-century villa of pinkish stone set amid rambling gardens, has sheltered some extraordinary literary talents over the years. DH Lawrence and his wife Frieda lived here from 1920 to 1922. During this time, Lawrence managed to complete a play and had three novels published, including *Women in Love* (1920). Almost 30 years later, in 1950, Truman Capote moved in to Fontana Vecchia with his lover Jack Dunphy. "It was like living in a ship trembling on the peak of a tidal wave," he would write of this clifftop eyrie. He too found it easy to write here, completing the *The Glass Harp* (1951), the novella that would cement his reputation (*In Cold Blood*, more than a decade later, would turn him into a household name). To peek at the villa from the outside, follow the winding via Cappuccini, which becomes the via Fontana Vecchia (also known as the via David Herbert Lawrence).

Isola Bella & the beaches

Taormina is linked to the beaches by a cable car (summer Mon-Sat 0800-0100, Sun 0900-0100, winter till 2015, €1.80 single, €3 return) which swings down to the Lido Mazzaró and a popular (pebbly) beach in just a few minutes. If you stroll a few hundred metres south you'll find a gorgeous little bay and the Isola Bella, a small island which is now a wildlife reserve.

Giardini-Naxos

Just below Taormina, Giardini-Naxos has a splendid beach, a pretty fishing harbour, and a swathe of modern villa developments. In July and August it gets crowded and hectic, but it is tranquil for the rest of the year. The resort is the modern heir to ancient Naxos, the oldest Greek colony on Sicily, which was established in 735 BC on the headland of Capo Schisò behind the harbour.

Isola Bella.

Around Taormina

Gole dell'Alcantara

Main entrance (with car park, bar and restaurant) signposted off the SS185, about 18 km from Taormina, 2 km before arriving at Francavilla di Sicilia. Interbus run 4 services daily (excluding Sun) from Taormina. Several tour operators, including the SAT travel group (see page 182), offer day trips from Taormina.

The Alcantara, the largest river in eastern Sicily, descends from its source near Floresta in the Nebrodi mountains to flow into the sea near Giardino-Naxos. Over millennia, the river has eroded a passage through an ancient lava flow from Etna, creating a series of gorges through silvery basalt cliffs. These gorges, the Gole d'Alcantara (part of the Parco Fluviale dell'Alcantara, parcoalcantara.it), are a popular attraction in summer, when you can hire waders to walk through part of the gorge (the water is icy even in summer) or join a guided tour to the heart of the canyon (strictly for those who are fit and in good health as it can involve negotiating rapids, scrambling over rocks and climbing slippery walls). Or, you can just admire from afar! You can reach the river by lift (€4.50) from the main entrance or take the free option and make your way down steep steps some 200 m from the car park.

For information on trails and other activities (such as birdwatching and horse riding) along this fertile river valley, visit the park information office in the pretty medieval village of Francavilla di Sicilia (in a converted church on the via dei Mulini, T0942-989911). There's another park information office at Randazzo, see page 171.

Sávoca

20 km northeast of Taormina.

Sávoca is one of several idyllic hilltop villages in the foothills of the Peloritani mountains, between Taormina and Messina. It was once one of the most important settlements on Sicily's eastern coast but has been crumbling picturesquely for centuries, which made it perfect as a substitute for the less photogenic Corleone in *The Godfather*. Michael Corleone was married to Apollonia in the church of Santa Lucia; the wedding party then celebrated at the Bar Vittelli, which is still dominated by a *granita* machine dating back to the 1930s, and remains a place of pilgrimage for movie buffs. Nearby, in the catacombs beneath the Convent of the Frati Cappuccini, you can ponder Sicily's strange custom of arranging its dead like waxworks.

Catania & around

Catania, Sicily's second city, is a bold, grubby, flamboyant and UNESCO-protected Baroque ensemble of black-and-white lava stone curved around a sea port. Its eternal rival is Palermo – dark and introverted where Catania is sunny and forward-looking. Its heady nightlife, fuelled by students from the 15th-century university and personnel from the nearby NATO military base, is legendary, particularly in summer. Known as the 'daughter of Etna', Catania's fortunes have often been determined by the great volcano, which looms over the city.

Piazza del Duomo, Catania.

Unsurprisingly, perhaps, Catania has been flattened and rebuilt countless times in its 3000-year history. First a Sikel trading post, then a Greek colony from 729 BC, it blossomed under the Romans to whom it fell in the second century BC. In 1669, the year of Etna's most terrible eruption, the lava flows reached Catania, which was then completely destroyed by a devastating earthquake in 1693. A new, gorgeously ornate, Baroque city was raised from the ashes in the early 18th century, but Catania's fortunes never really revived. The city was heavily bombed during the Second World War, and, despite bursts of economic optimism in the 1960s and early 1990s, it remains one of the poorest cities in Italy. In 2008, the local council was awarded an emergency aid package after the street lights went out because it was unable to pay the electricity bill.

Piazza del Duomo & around

The showcase square of Catania, the piazza del Duomo, is lined with Baroque buildings and home to the city's two best-loved monuments: the Duomo (see page 163) dedicated to Sant'Agata, Catania's adored patron saint, and the lavish **Fontana dell'Elefante**, which sits in the centre of the square. Designed by Sicilian Baroque architect Giovanni Battista Vaccarini (1702-1768) and erected in the 1730s, the fountain incorporates an ancient elephant made of lava stone and an Egyptian obelisk. The smiling elephant takes pride of place on Catania's coat of arms and, like the bones of St Agatha, is considered a talisman against the unpredictable fury of Etna. Several palazzi flank the square, including the handsome Palazzo Senatorio, better known as the Palazzo degli Elefanti, which is the city hall. Set back slightly is the graceful Badia di Sant'Agata, also the work of Vaccarini, which now contains the **Museo Diocesano** (via Etnea 8, T095-281635, museodiocesicatania.it, Tue-Sun 0900-1230, 1600-1930, €4.20), with a mildly

Essentials

❶ **Getting around** Most of Catania's main sights are clustered around the piazza del Duomo in the heart of the city and are easy to get around on foot. To visit the beaches, you'll need to take one of the local **AMT** city buses (T800-018696, amt.ct.it) from in front of the train station. The airport is located 5 km from the centre: the AMT 'Alibus' runs a service every 20 minutes to the city centre (€1). Catania also has a single-line metro system, which runs from Borgo in the north (where it connects with the Circumetnea railway), via the train station, to the port. It is not particularly useful to visitors, but the network is currently being expanded and should eventually link the airport with the city centre.

❷ **Bus station** Piazza Papa Giovanni XXIII, T095-7230511. Regional and local buses stop in the square opposite the train station.

❸ **Train station** Stazione Centrale, piazza Giovanni XXIII (Trenitalia T848-888088, trenitalia.it) is about a 15-minute walk from the centre. The private, narrow-gauge train around Mount Etna (the Ferrovia Circumetnea) departs from the **Stazione Catania Borgo**, via Caronda, T095-541250, circumetnea.it.

❹ **ATM** You're never far from an ATM in central Catania. There are several along via Etnea, particularly around piazza Stesicoro.

❺ **Hospital** Ospedale San Vincenzo Taormina, via Crocefisso, T0942-579322.

❻ **Pharmacy** Farmacia Consoli, via Etnea 400, T095-448317, Mon-Fri 0900-1300, 1700-1930, Sat 0900-1300.

❼ **Post office** Main post office occupies a grand palazzo at via Etnea 215, T095-715 5071, Mon-Fri 0800-1830, Sat 0800-1230.

❽ **Tourist information** There are information booths at the airport (T095-730 6266) and at the train station (T095-730 6255), but the main office is in the city centre at via Domenico Cimarosa 10, T095-730 6211, turismo.catania.it, Mon-Sat 0800-2000. The most useful local website is cataniacittametropolitana.it

interesting collection of religious art and liturgical objects. The flamboyant fountain of Amenano, named after the underground river that feeds it, guards the porta Uzeda, a gateway that leads into the peaceful **Villa Pacini** public gardens, where old men gather on tree-shaded benches.

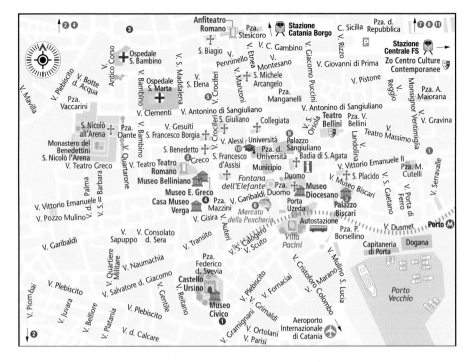

Catania listings

❶ Sleeping

1 5 Balconi *via Plebiscito 133*
2 Castello d'Urso Somma *via S.Giuseppe La Rena 15*
3 Liberty Hotel *via San Vito 40*
4 Rapa Nui Rooms *via Gagliani 13*

❶ Eating & drinking

1 Cordai Casa delle Crispelle *via Vittorio Emanuele 35-37*
2 Don Turiddu *via Musumeci 50*
3 I Crociferi *piazza S Francesco 14*
4 Il Sale Art Café *via S. Filomena 10-12*
5 Metrò *via Crociferi 76*
6 Osteria Antica Marina *via Pardo 29*
7 Savia *via Etnea 302*
8 St Moritz *viale Sanzio Raffaele 8-12*
9 The Other Place *via E Reina 18-20*
10 Tre Bicchieri *via San Giuseppe al Duomo 31*
11 Viscuso *via Re Martino 101*

Mercato della Pescheria.

The feast of Sant'Agata

Every year, between 3 and 5 February, hundreds of thousands of Catanesi flock to venerate a statue of their beloved patron saint, St Agatha. Bedecked in jewels, and surrounded by white-robed devotees, the statue is set atop a chariot and processed through the city. Agatha (AD 231-251) was a beautiful young woman who caught the eye of a Roman senator. She refused his advances, and was viciously punished. Among the horrible tortures the senator inflicted were slicing off her breasts and rolling her in hot coals. Sentenced to be burned at the stake for being a Christian, she was in prison awaiting death when Etna rumbled and the earth shook so terrifyingly that the senator was frightened into commuting her sentence. She has been the patron saint of fire and lightning ever since, and her relics are said to have stopped lava flow from Etna many times.

Duomo

Piazza del Duomo, T095-320044.
Daily 0800-1200, 1600-1900, free.

According to legend, St Agatha, Catania's revered patron saint, was martyred on this very spot in AD 251. The first cathedral dedicated to the saint was constructed in the 11th century under Norman Count Roger but subsequently flattened by the terrible earthquake of 1693. The replacement, a vast and elegantly proportioned Baroque edifice largely designed by Vaccarini, incorporates columns from the Roman amphitheatre in the handsome façade. The splendid interior contains the tombs of several Aragonese kings and that of composer Vincenzo Bellini, but the real draw is the **Cappella di Sant'Agata** which contains the martyr's relics and some of the church's treasures relating to her cult.

Mercato della Pescheria

Via Zappalà Gemelli and around.
Mon-Sat dawn till 1300.

Catania's fabulous fish market, the raucous, pungent and absolutely unmissable Pescheria, takes place every morning just off the piazza del Duomo around via Zappalà Gemelli. The sight of exuberant, chopper-wielding stallholders bellowing out the specials over the gaping heads of giant swordfish is one of Catania's most intense pleasures – and one that can have changed little since Catania was Katane, and the stallholders hawked their wares in Greek. Stalls selling

everything from hand-made cheeses to local herbs can be found along the side streets.

Museo Belliniano

Piazza San Francisco 3, T095-715 0535.
Mon-Sat 0900-1300, free.

Opposite the Chiesa di San Francisco (a short walk from piazza del Duomo along via Vittorio Emanuele), the handsome Palazzo Biscari contains the Museo Belliniano, dedicated to Vincenzo Bellini (1801-1835), the celebrated operatic composer. Bellini was born in Catania to a musical family, and could apparently sing operatic arias at the age of just 18 months. His most famous operas include *La Sonnambula*, *I Puritani*, and *Norma* – which was such a hit it even inspired a pasta dish, the famous Sicilian *pasta alla Norma*. Another section of the palazzo houses the **Museo Emilio Greco** (T095-317654, Mon, Wed, Fri, Sat 0900-1300, Tue and Thu 0900-1300, 1500-1800, free). It features paintings and graphic works by another local boy, Emilio Greco (1913-1995), whose sculpture can be found in many of the world's greatest museums.

Teatro Romano & Odeon

Via Vittorio Emanuele 260, T095-715 0508.
Mon-Sat 0900-1330, 1500-1700, €3/1.50 concession.

Behind the Bellini museum, around the corner on via Vittorio Emanuele, you'll find the humble entrance to Catania's best preserved ancient site, the Roman theatre. Built in the second century AD over an earlier Greek version, the theatre occupies a deep hollow in the middle of the city, now encircled by the Baroque buildings of central Catania. The adjoining Odeon (same ticket), a smaller theatre, was mainly used for rehearsals.

Via Crociferi

For a glimpse of how Catania might have looked in the heady, affluent years of the early 18th century, take a stroll down via Crociferi which preserves a splendid ensemble of Baroque churches and palazzi. Most are in dire need of restoration, but, even mouldering and splattered with graffiti, they are gorgeously theatrical. There are four churches in close succession: the Chiesa di San Benedetto, linked by a bridge to the Benedictine monastery opposite; the Chiesa di San Francesco Borgia; the Collegio dei Gesuiti (now an art institute); and the Chiesa di San Giuliano, considered the finest Baroque church in the city. Beyond is the Villa Cerami, once one of the city's most opulent residences, and now part of the university.

Tip...

If the Teatro Romano is closed, or you don't fancy the steep steps, you can peer down on it from via Teatro Greco.

Teatro Romano.

Via Etnea

This is the city's showcase avenue, a long, broad sweep from the foot of Mount Etna all the way down to the piazza Duomo. It's where you'll find most of the city's shops and cafés, overlooked by proud Baroque palazzi in genteel decline. Just a short walk from the Duomo, the avenue opens out into the elegant piazza Università, named after Catania's university, which was founded in the 15th century but now occupies the sumptuous Baroque palace constructed after the 1693 earthquake. Heading north, piazza Stesicoro is the heart of the modern city, although a great swathe of it is taken up with the scant remnants of the **Anfiteatro Romano** (Roman amphitheatre). Overgrown and uninspiring now, once it was one of the largest in the Empire, second only to Rome's Colosseum. A short stroll east will bring you to the **Palazzo Manganelli** with opulent salons that appeared in Visconti's film adaptation of *The Leopard*.

Castello Ursino

Piazza Federico II di Svevia, T095-345830. Mon-Sat 0900-1300. Free.

This castle looks like it might be home to a knight in armour and perhaps a dragon or two. Now it's marooned in a run-down neighbourhood (which also has a fantastic street market), a five-minute walk from the piazza del Duomo (take via Garibaldi, and turn left down via Castello Ursino). It was considered impregnable when it was built for Frederick II in the early 13th century, and is one of few buildings in Catania to have survived the earthquakes and volcanic eruptions that plague this coast. A royal residence and seat of the Sicilian parliament, it also played a crucial role in the Sicilian Vespers (see page 33). The castle's fortunes declined once the Sicilian capital was transferred to Palermo, and it was converted into a prison. Now restored, it houses Catania's Museo Civico, with a magpie collection that includes everything from Greek statuary to Baroque shoes, taking in armour, coins, paintings and Nativity scenes on the way.

Along the coast

Catania's main beach is at La Pláia, on the southern outskirts of the city, but you'll find nicer ones to the north along the **Riviera dei Ciclopi**, which gets its name from the jagged volcanic islets – the **Faraglioni del Ciclope** – which dot this coast. A Norman keep built entirely of black lava dominates **Aci Castello**, a fishing village 11 km from Catania overlooking a rocky bay and surrounded by lemon trees. **Aci Trezza**, 2 km up the coast, is a pretty fishing village with a boat-filled bay. It overlooks the most dramatic of the Faraglioni del Ciclope, which are protected as a natural reserve.

Acireale

17 km north of Catania.

Serene Acireale is beautifully strung out along a lava cliff overlooking the sea. The city has existed since Phoenician times, but, like Catania, has been flattened and rebuilt throughout its history. It owes its splendid Baroque core to the terrible earthquake of 1693, and is now a relaxing spot for a gentle amble and perhaps a dip in the thermal waters, which have been famous for millennia.

Acireale.

What the locals say

When I'm in Catania, I always pop in for *arancine* at one of the bars on the via Etnea: **Savia** at No 302 and **Spinella** at No 300 are the best. Both offer a fantastic range of fillings, from classic *ragù* (a tomato sauce with meat and vegetables), to swordfish, salmon or even pistachio.

Alessio Creta, from Taormina, co-founder of fuori-fase music label (see fuori-fase.com).

Acireale cathedral fresco.

It's a myth...

According to legend, Ulysses blinded the Cyclops Polyphemus at Aci Castello before escaping by ship. The Faraglioni del Ciclope are the very rocks thrown after the departing hero by the enraged Cyclops.

Mount Etna & around

Europe's highest and most active volcano, Mount Etna (around 3329 m) dominates the whole of eastern Sicily: its iconic silhouette ever present, the snow-clad slopes dazzling against a cobalt-blue sky. Despite the terrible destruction wreaked by Etna over the centuries (most recently in 2002, while eruptions in 2008 led to Catania's airport being closed in a flurry of dark ash), locals regard the volcano with a fierce mixture of love and awe. Unfazed by the danger that literally bubbles beneath them, numerous communities are gathered around Etna's base, drawn by the rich, fertile volcanic soil that continues to provide these towns with their livelihoods.

Mount Etna.

Etna essentials

Before you go You might want to check out the latest volcanic activity (ingv.it) and weather conditions at the summit (T095-9141) before setting off. Come prepared for freezing temperatures and heavy winds when visiting the summit, even in the height of summer. You'll also need suitable footwear to negotiate the slippery ground. Coats and boots can usually (but not always) be rented at the guide huts, but it's best to come prepared. You will also need sun hats and sun block.

Getting to Rifugio Sapienza A once-daily AST bus (T840-000323, aziendasicilianatrasporti.it) for Rifugio Sapienza from Catania via Nicolosi (departs 0815, returns 1630, journey time 2 hrs).

Cable car to upper station Cable cars run roughly every 20 minutes (summer 0900-1715, winter 0900-1530, T095-9141, funiviaetna.com, €30 return fare) to the upper station (2500 m). If it is windy or foggy, 4x4 minibuses make the journey to the upper station. In bad weather, all services are suspended. It's worth ringing in advance to check – weather conditions on Etna can vary dramatically from those on the coast.

Upper station to viewing area Take the 4x4 minibuses (with guide) which wait at the upper station. All-inclusive tickets, including the return journey by cable car plus the minibus journey to the viewing area, cost around €45, and the journey takes about 2½ hours. Note that it is, strictly speaking, forbidden for visitors to climb beyond the upper station, although many people do. Follow the jeep track (roughly 1 km) to reach the viewing area close to the summit.

Walks on the crater The standard 4x4 minibus tours from the upper station include the services of a driver-guide, who will give a brief description of the main features of the summit and stop briefly at the Valle del Bove, a huge depression in Etna's flank. A popular, signposted walking path descends from the Valle del Bove to emerge on the road about 3½ km south of Rifugio Sapienza. A number of tour companies (see below), including those found on site at the Rifugio Sapienza station, offer a range of guided tours of the summit area. Don't be tempted to walk alone.

Local guides and tour operators Numerous local tour operators (including Etna Trekking and Etna Guide, see page 183) offer well-priced one-day tours or hiking excursions to points of interest including the main craters and some of the fascinating caves that pock the volcano.

Information Parco dell'Etnea, Monastero di San Nicolò, via del Convent 45, Nicolosi, T095-821111; piazza Annunziata 5, Linguaglossa, T0956-43094; via Umberto 193, Randazzo, T0957-991611; via A Manzoni 21, Farnazzo-Milo, T095-955159. Information in Italian only at parcoetna.ct.it, but there is some info in English at parks. it (follow the links to Etna).

Winter hiking across Etna.

Silvestre craters of Etna.

Etna's summit

The upper reaches of Etna are thrillingly unlike anywhere else on earth. All greenery is banished, and the slopes unfold in an eerie sea of lava and volcanic ash in hues of grey, black and the occasional streak of fiery red, covered in patchy snow and ice for most of the year. The summit can be reached from the Rifugio Sapienza (where the cable car begins) to the south or from quieter Piano Provenzana to the north.

Rifugio Sapienza & South Etna

The main access towns for the southern approach to Etna's summit are **Nicolosi** (700 m) where there's an interesting little volcano museum (via C Battisti 28, T095-791 4589, Tue and Thu 0900-1230, 1530-1730, Wed, Fri-Sun 0900-1230), and **Zafferana Etnea** (574 m), which was almost wiped out by the lava flow from the 2002 eruption (a statue of the Virgin marks the point at which the lava stopped – or, as locals tell it, was turned back when confronted with a statue of the Madonna). Both make good bases for visiting Etna.

Access roads (well signposted but unnumbered) from Nicolosi and Zafferana Etnea wriggle up the southeastern and eastern flanks of the huge mountain respectively. Both twist and turn through an increasingly bare and otherworldly landscape as orchards give way to bare black rock before arriving at **Rifugio Sapienza** (1910 m). Here, emerging surreally from the empty wilderness, you'll find a huge car park (this is as far as cars are allowed), with huts selling souvenirs and offering guide services, and a couple of hotels (including the Rifugio Sapienza itself). It is often shrouded in mist or cloud, and the sudden wind and cold can be shocking, even if you left heat and sunshine on the coast. The menacing dunes of lava lapping at the fringes of the station are a vestige of the terrible eruption that destroyed the cable car and skiing facilities in 2002. Newly rebuilt, the cable car once again makes its ascent, catering to walkers for much of the year and to skiers from December to March.

The most common way to get from Rifugio Sapienza to the top of Etna is to choose a popular combined ticket, which includes a return fare on the cable car and a 4x4 minibus excursion with guide to the top of Etna from the upper cable car station. The minibuses climb to a viewing area at around 2900 m, from where the views stretch endlessly in all directions – at least when the clouds lift! On the clearest days, the Aeolian Islands are visible beyond the forested peaks of the Madonie mountains.

The most active and dangerous craters lie beyond this point, and you may see belching smoke, or perhaps, if you're lucky, a hissing jet of lava or a shower of molten rock. Several companies offer guided hikes beyond this point, with thrilling glimpses into the shifting, molten lava at the Bocca Nuova and southeast craters.

If you prefer to hike, it's possible to make the climb to the summit from Rifugio Sapienza (a stiff 3½ to 4 hour climb but a considerably faster descent), or to trek from the upper cable car station (follow the dirt road taken by the minibuses). There are several signposted trails, including a few which pass the Philosopher's Tower. According to legend, this was built by the philosopher Empedocles (c490-430 BC), who died by throwing himself into the seething crater in the mistaken belief that he was immortal.

Piano Provenzano & North Etna

Piano Provenzano was once Etna's main ski centre, but the resort was entirely wiped out during the 2002 eruption. Now, a new centre is slowly being rebuilt directly over the lava field, but it remains considerably quieter than Rifugio Sapienza. It's reached from Linguaglossa (see page 171), which sweeps up through the Ragubo pine forest, with walking trails and picnic tables. Although the lava laid waste to the green fields and forest that once made Piano Provenzano so attractive, the station is still the starting point of several excellent hikes. Kiosks sell souvenirs, snacks and drinks, and official guides with the ubiquitous 4x4 minibuses offer escorted trips to the summit (as on the southern side, an official guide is required to visit the summit area over 2900 m). Most people just

Tip...

Probably the easiest and most popular way to visit Etna is via Rifugio Sapienza, not least because it is accessible by public transport (unlike Piano Provenzano). Visibility is usually best in the mornings.

join the excursion when they arrive at Piano Provenzano, but you can book trips in advance with Guide Etna Nord (guidetnanord.com, see also page 183). There is no public bus to Piano Provenzano, but the tourist office in Linguaglossa (15 km away) can organize a taxi.

Etna from afar.

Around Etna

A ring of small towns circles the base of Mount Etna, linked by the delightful, narrow-gauge Ferrovia Circumetnea railway and a small provincial road (the SS284), which winds through citrus orchards and olive groves. Misterbianco has been swallowed up by Catania's grimy suburbs, but Paternò preserves a magisterial Norman castle and some elegant Baroque churches in its historic centre and, rather bizarrely, Italy's largest shopping mall on its outskirts. Kids might enjoy Etnaland (see page 181), a water park and adventure playground. Biancavilla concentrates on agriculture rather than tourism, and is set in a sea of orange and lemon trees, but neighbouring Adrano contains an 11th-century castle built of black lava and a delightful art nouveau theatre.

Bronte & around

The stretch of railway line and road between Adrano and Bronte offers some of the best glimpses of Etna along this route, as the terrain

Simply red

It used to be that pop stars partied hard and died young. Now, it seems, they make wine. Mick Hucknall of Simply Red has followed in the footsteps of Bob Dylan, Madonna and Sting and acquired a vineyard. His 18th-century estate sits on the northern slopes of Etna and produces a critically acclaimed red, Il Cantante ('the singer'). Etna's potent reds and whites were the first in Sicily to be awarded DOC (denomination of origin) status. Recent interest in indigenous grape varieties (plus the allure of celebrities like Hucknall) has revitalized Etna's historically humble wines. Award-winning wines include Cottanera (T0942-963601, cottanera. it), Tenuta delle Terre Nere (T095-924002) and Passopisciaro (T0578-267110, passopisciaro.it).

becomes increasingly rugged. **Bronte** is famous throughout Sicily – and in kitchens throughout the world – for the exquisite, intense green pistachios

It's a fact...

The Reverend Patrick Prunty was such a fervent admirer of Lord Nelson that he changed his surname to Brontë, although it was his literary daughters – Charlotte, Emily and Anne – who would make the name famous.

Castello Maniace.

cultivated here. They are harvested every second year but celebrated annually in the exuberant Sagra del Pistacchio (Pistachio Festival). **Maletto** is the highest village on this route, and emerges from a sea of vines and strawberry fields (there's an annual strawberry festival in June).

Castello Maniace

Castello di Nelson, T095-690018.
Daily 0900-1300, 1430-1900, €3 (park only €1.50).
8 km north of Maletto, signposted off the SS120.

Locally known and signposted as the Castello di Nelson, this venerable 18th-century mansion belonged to the Nelson family for two centuries. The estate was part of the specially created Duchy of Bronte, awarded to Admiral Horatio Nelson by Bourbon king Ferdinand IV in gratitude for his suppression of the bloody Naples rebellion of 1799. It now belongs to the town of Bronte, which has opened it to the public. The elegant salons ooze Englishness, with pretty wallpaper, portraits and nautical prints. The house dominates a hilltop first occupied by an Arabic fortress and then by a 12th-century Benedictine abbey whose original 13th-century chapel has been handsomely restored. Best of all are the lovely gardens, an fusion of English landscaping and Mediterranean abundance, and an idyllic spot for a picnic.

Randazzo

Loveliest of all the towns at Etna's feet, Randazzo was historically home to three communities, each with a different origin (Greek, Latin and Lombard), and each, until comparatively recently, with its own dialect. The town's finest monuments are a trio of medieval churches, which were the focus of these communities and took turns to act as Randazzo's cathedral. The most imposing is **Santa Maria**, which retains a 15th-century Catalan-Gothic portal and striking columns of black lava. The 13th-century apse is all that survives of the original church of **San Nicoló**, almost entirely rebuilt in the 16th and 17th centuries, while little **San Martino**

retains a charming campanile with stripes of black and white stone. Randazzo is an excellent base for walkers and those wanting a relaxed rural holiday as it is perfectly positioned for access to three wonderful natural parks: the Nebrodi mountains (see page 126), Etna, and the Alcantara river valley (see page 159). The town's helpful visitor centre provides information on all three parks.

Linguaglossa

Continuing east from Randazzo, the railway line and road both descend to Linguaglossa, the main access town for north Etna and a good base for hiking in summer and skiing in winter. It's a tidy, peaceful little town, with handsome houses trimmed with lava stone decoration.

San Martino church, Randazzo.

Circling Etna by train

Etna's famous narrow-gauge railway was built in 1895 in order to link the agricultural towns circling the mountain with the seaport at Catania. This 'great day out' takes in the whole circuit, with suggested stops at two of the prettiest towns, Bronte and Randazzo. Bring a sense of adventure, some reading material, plus plenty of snacks and water.

Catania to Bronte

Journey time 1 hr 40 mins, €4.20 adult single.

The first part of the train journey is uninspiring, but beyond Misterbianco the graffiti-smeared buildings give way to orchards and fields. The stretch between Adrano and Bronte is one of the most panoramic; with luck, and some sunshine, you'll see some striking views of Etna, glowering massively above the orchards. Lumpish grey rocks, from ancient lava flows, are scattered amid the trees. Bronte famously produces exquisite pistachios, and the final approach is characterized by grove upon grove of silvery nut orchards.

Bronte

Sitting in the shadow of Etna at 760 m and often dusted with snow in winter, Bronte is a busy country town. Time your arrival here for a spot of lunch. It has several simple restaurants to choose from, the best being the Albergo Parco dell'Etna (see page 179), but don't bother ordering dessert. Instead, head for one of the famous pasticceries selling delectable pistachio pastries and pick up some treats, including a big bag of pistachio biscuits to munch on the train. Conti Gallenti (see page 180) is a favourite pasticceria; it's also a good place for a snack from the tavola calda, if you'd prefer a lighter lunch.

Bronte to Randazzo

Journey time 25 mins, €2 adult single.

Hop back on the train and continue your journey to Randazzo. The train passes first through the empty plain of Contrada Difesa, scattered with pretty wild flowers in spring, before beginning a slow ascent through increasingly wild and rocky terrain. It reaches its highest point by the Rocca Calanna, which sits at almost 1000 m. Maletta, the highest village on the route, sits in a green plateau, and beyond it you can see the distant peaks of the Madonie and Nebrodi mountains. The train then descends towards Randazzo.

Randazzo

Graceful Randazzo (see page 171) is easily the most beautiful town in the Etna region. Try to allow at least two hours to soak up its atmosphere before embarking on your return to Catania.

Randazzo to Giarre

Journey time 65 mins, €3.10 adult single.

Be careful with train times from Randazzo: there are limited services from here to Giarre (for connections to mainline train services back to Catania). From Randazzo, the train heads east, and you can take in the last few glimpses of Etna through the orchards.

Giarre-Riposto to Catania

Journey time 30 mins, €2.55 adult single.

At Giarre, cross over from the Circumetnea to the adjacent mainline station, Giarre-Riposto. From here, the mainline train makes its way through Catania's suburbs, arriving in the city centre.

Ferrovia Circumetnea essentials

Options The train begins in Catania Borgo, circles the volcano for 114 km, and culminates at Giarre (which is linked to the mainline Giarre-Riposto train station), 30 km north of Catania. The Bronte–Randazzo leg is the most attractive, and takes about 2 hours (€4 single, €6.90 return). Catania to Giarre takes 3½ hours, plus another half-hour for the regional train to return you to Catania.

Depart Stazione Borgo, via Etnea, Catania, T095-534323; take the metro to Borgo.

Frequency There are 11 services Monday-Saturday (0550-1915) running clockwise from Catania to Randazzo; two of these make the full loop and continue to Riposto. There are seven services Monday-Saturday (0653-1805) running anti-clockwise from Riposto to Catania.

Selected stops Catania to Bronte (1 hr 40 mins), Randazzo (2 hrs 5 mins), Lingualossa (2 hrs 45 mins), Giarre (3 hrs 10 mins). Giarre to Randazzo (1½ hrs), Bronte (2 hrs), Catania (3 hrs 20 mins).

Special tours Circumetnea offers special tours, including day trips to the Castello di Nelson, winery visits, and vintage train tours.

Information and timetable From stations, tourist offices, or circumetnea.it, T095-541250.

Tip...

This journey circles Etna in a clockwise direction: for the best views, try to get a seat on the right-hand side of the train.

Sleeping

Hotel Sant'Elia €
Via 1 Settembre 67, T090-601 0082, hotelsantelia.com.
A functional but reliable three-star option, this is convenient for Messina's city centre and port, being just a five-minute walk from the port in one direction and the Duomo in the other. The rooms have air conditioning and satellite TV.

Grand Hotel Timeo €€€€
Via Teatro Greco 59, T0942-23801, grandhoteltimeo.com.
The sumptuous salons at Taormina's oldest and grandest hotel have played host to royalty and celebrities since the mid-19th century, and the hotel's luxurious amenities include extensive gardens and an excellent restaurant.

Villa Angela €€€
Via Leonardo da Vinci s/n, T0942-28138, hotelvillaangela.com.
Jim Kerr of Simple Minds is behind this modern stylish hotel, which occupies a stunning position high above Taormina. There's a pool in the gardens, an excellent restaurant, and a terrace-bar for views. You can take the free hotel shuttle bus down into town (about a 15-min stroll), or to the beaches.

Villa Carlotta €€€
Via Pirandello 81, T0942-626058, hotelvillacarlottataormina.com.
Surrounded by luxuriant tropical gardens, this appealing boutique hotel is set in a turn-of-the-century villa close to the heart of Taormina. Rooms and suites are elegantly furnished in pale tones, and there's a small pool in the gardens. Best of all is the stunning rooftop bar, where you can linger over a cocktail and gaze at Mount Etna.

Villa Ducale €€€
Via Leonardo da Vinci 60, T0942-28153, villaducale.com.
This former coaching inn, on the winding road uphill from central Taormina, is an absolute charmer. The rooms all have balconies. A buffet breakfast is served on a terrace with stunning views. A free shuttle bus takes guests to the beaches, 4 km away, and it's a 15-minute stroll into the centre of Taormina.

Villa Schuler €€
Via Roma, piazzetta Bastione, T0942-23481, villaschuler.com. Closed mid-Nov to early Mar, no credit cards.
Occupying a handsome, early 20th-century villa with palm-shaded gardens, this family-run hotel is well located in the centre of town. The 21 rooms are comfortably furnished, or you could splash out on the top-floor suites, which have private terraces with magnificent views over the bay or across to Etna. There is no restaurant, but you'll find plenty within a short stroll.

Casa Famiani B&B €
Via Millo 4, Letojanni, T347-753 1113, casafamiani.it.
This simple and friendly B&B in the seaside resort of Letojanni, 6 km north of Taormina, is run by the congenial Ignazio. It's an excellent budget option just five minutes' walk from the beach, and a shuttle bus for Taormina leaves from nearby. Rooms are very basic but spotlessly clean, and a plentiful breakfast is served family-style in the kitchen. They also have holiday apartments for rent (sleeping two €60-100 per night, four €120-180).

Le Case del Principe
Via Fondaco d'Accorso, T349-788 0906 (mobile), lecasedelprincipe.it.
The *principe* in question, Prince Gabriele Alliata of Villafranca, has renovated outbuildings on the family's Pietraperciata estate to create six elegant and well-equipped holiday villas. They sleep between 6 and 20 and are available to rent by the week (€350-5000 depending on season and house). Sleep amid olive groves and citrus orchards, with the sea (1 km) and Taormina (7 km) both within a short drive. Pool, bike rental and gardens.

Liberty Hotel €€
Via San Vito 40, T095-311651, libertyhotel.it.
A reliable option in central Catania, within five minutes' walk of via Etnea, the Liberty Hotel is set in a fine 19th-century villa on an otherwise unprepossessing street, and offers traditional rooms furnished with antiques. Staff can arrange excursions to Etna and transfers to and from the airport.

Castello d'Urso Somma €€-€
Via S Giuseppe La Rena 15, T095-713 9145, castellodursosomma.com.
A fabulous folly set in luxuriant gardens is the focus of this welcoming, family-run B&B in Catania's southern suburbs. While the family occupy the castle, guests stay in charmingly furnished rooms in the garden annexes. There's a huge pool, it's a short walk to the beaches, and it's just 5 km from the airport and the city centre.

5 Balconi €
Via Plebiscito 133, T095-723 4534, 5balconi.com.
This charming B&B has just four pretty rooms with two shared bathrooms in an old palazzo in the heart of Catania, just above Ursino castle. It's run by a delightful Anglo-Sicilian couple, who are happy to provide local

information and help with tours, trip ideas and more. The delicious breakfasts include home-made jams and pastries.

Rapa Nui Rooms €
Via Gagliani 13, T095-286 1243, rapanuirooms.com.
Close to piazza Duomo and Catania's wonderful fish market, this friendly budget-option B&B occupies a carefully restored 19th-century building. Rooms accommodating one to four people are bright and modern, if functionally furnished, and boast air conditioning and Wi-Fi. You can choose to have private bathrooms or share for a bit less. A voucher for coffee and *cornetti* at a nearby bar is included.

Hotel Airone €€
Via Cassone 67, località Airone, Zafferana Etnea, T095-709 1919, hotel-airone.it.
This big, modern, resort-style hotel looks a little out of place in the countryside (it would be more at home by a beach), but it is a good base for visiting Mount Etna, particularly if you are travelling with kids, thanks to the on-site restaurant, extensive grounds and swimming pool. Ask for a room with a sea view.

Hotel Corsaro €€
Piazza Cantoniera, Etna Sud, T095-914122, hotelcorsaro.it.
Enthusiastically run by the Corsaro family, the 'highest hotel on Etna' is located at the Rifugio Sapienza station, near the cable car. It offers double and family rooms with wonderful Etna

views and a good restaurant serving traditional fare at modest prices. It's the best bet on Etna, thanks to the friendly service, and is a tad more comfortable than the neighbouring Rifugio Sapienza.

Hotel Federico II €€
Via Maggiore Baracca 2, Castiglione di Sicilia, T0942-980368, hotelfedericosecondo.com.
This relatively new hotel occupies a restored 14th-century palazzo tucked away in the beguiling centre of medieval Castiglione di Sicilia. There are just nine modern rooms, which include family rooms for up to four, and two rooms equipped for disabled travellers. Staff are extremely welcoming, and it makes a comfortable and quiet base for visiting the Alcantara valley and its gorges, as well as Mount Etna and Taormina.

Il Nido dell'Etna €€
Via G Matteotti, Lingualossa, T095-643404, ilnidodelletna.it.
This recently built hotel in the centre of the village combines modern amenities with old-fashioned charm, offering crisp, contemporary rooms (some with fabulous views of Etna from their balconies), a good restaurant and copious buffet breakfasts. Lingualossa is the main base for access to north Etna, but it remains a quiet, enjoyably relaxed little town.

Tenuta San Michele €€
Via Zafferano 13, Santa Venerina, T095-950520, murgo.it.
Surrounded by snaking vines on the southeastern slopes of Mount Etna, with phenomenal views of both the volcano and the coast, this *agriturismo* offers comfortable B&B and self-catering accommodation (apartments from €80-160 per night). Enjoy a tour of the vineyard, then explore the full range of their Murgo wines in the excellent restaurant.

L'Aquila dell'Etna €€-€
Via Stabilimenti 107, Santa Venerina, T095-954364, laquiladelletnabandb.it.
This charming B&B is located in a pink-painted villa, in a small village halfway between the coast and Mount Etna (there are astounding views of the volcano from the panoramic terrace). Rooms are prettily furnished and the friendly owners (for whom nothing is too much trouble) can organize hiking, mountain-bike and horse-riding excursions.

Case Perrotta €
Via Andronico 2, Puntalazzo (near Sant'Alfio), T095-968928, caseperrotta.com.
An old stone convent is at the heart of this *agriturismo* complex, beautifully located in the hills between Taormina and Mount Etna. Now it offers simple rooms, excellent local cuisine and

beautiful views. You can pick up some of their award-winning olive oil too.

Hotel Rifugio Sapienza €
Piazzale Rifugio Sapienza, Etna Sud, T095-915321, rifugiosapienza.com.
The main lodge at the southern approach to Etna's summit, a few metres from the start of the cable car. The big Alpine-style chalet has functional but comfortable rooms, all with en suite facilities, and there's a café and restaurant downstairs.

La Giara B&B €
Viale della Regione 12a, Nicolosi, T095-791 9022, giara.it.
Friendly, cosy and perfectly located for exploring the Etna region, this pretty B&B is set in the centre of Nicolosi. There are four rooms, and the villa is shaded with palm trees. A sumptuous breakfast can be enjoyed out in the garden.

L'Antica Vigna €
Monte La Guardia, Randazzo, T095-924003, anticavigna.it.
Well placed for exploring both Etna and the Nebrodi, this olive oil *agriturismo* 4 km outside Randazzo offers simple but charming B&B accommodation. The farmhouse is surrounded by vines and olive trees, facilities include a tennis court, and the restaurant serves specialities and home-made bread and pastries.

Eating & drinking

Due Sorelle €€€
Piazza Municipio 4, T090-44720.
Mon-Fri 1300-1500, 2000-2400,
Sat 2000-2400, closed Aug.
This popular local eaterie is on
the city's main square, and is a
great place to try Sicilian classics
such as *cuscus dì pesce* (fish
couscous), or swordfish from the
Strait, all prepared with
spectacularly fresh seasonal
produce, with a creative twist.
The desserts are deliciously
inventive too – don't miss the
dark chocolate and hazelnut tart.

Cafés & bars
Bar Progresso
*Viale San Martino 33, T090-
673734.*
Sun-Fri 0800-2000.
This has been going strong since
1910, and is still the place to
come for a refreshing *granita*,
accompanied by *spongata*, a
delicious pastry prepared to an
old family recipe. It's handily
located for the port, the train
station and the Duomo.

Pasticceria Irrera
*Piazza Cairoli 12, T090-673823,
irrera.it.*
Tue-Sat 0800-1330, 1600-2000,
Sun 1600-2000.
The most famous pasticceria in
Messina, with a huge and well
deserved reputation for its
sumptuous cakes and ice creams.
The shelves are lined with

elegantly packaged treats,
including delicious *torrone*
(unctuous almond nougat) and
frutta martorana (astonishingly
realistic marzipan fruits), which
make great gifts.

Casa Grugno €€€€
*Via Santa Maria dei Greci,
T0942-21208, casagrugno.it.*
Mon-Sat 1300-1500, 2000-2300,
open Sun in Aug.
One of the best addresses in
Taormina, this restaurant is
housed in a 15th-century Gothic
palazzo with a summer terrace.
Chef Andreas Zangerl prepares
outstanding Michelin-starred
contemporary cuisine, including
seafood, *tagliolini* with rabbit
ragout and Salina capers, or
saddle of lamb in a *caponata*
crust with Modican chocolate.

Da Nino €€€€
*Via L Rizzo 29, Letojanni,
T0942-36147, danino.it.*
Daily 1230-1500, 1930-2400.
The modest appearance of this
restaurant on the seafront at
Letojanni, 6 km from Taormina,
belies the excellence of its
cuisine, which features the
freshest produce, including
swordfish and sea bass plucked
from the Ionian Sea, platters of
shellfish, or more exotic offerings
such as pasta with sea urchins.
Book in advance, particularly for
a coveted table on the terrace.

La Capinera €€€
*Via Nazionale 177, Spisone,
T0942-626247,
ristorantelacapinera.com.*
Tue-Sun 1300-1500, 1930-2300,
daily in Aug, closed Feb.
Halfway down the hill from
Taormina, in this restaurant with
a terrace overlooking the sea, the
chef prepares dishes based on
traditional recipes. Choose six,
seven or eight dishes from the
tasting menu, but save room for
dessert. Booking advised.

A'Zammàra €€
*Via Fratelli Bandiera 15,
T0942-24408, zammara.it.*
Daily 1300-1500, 1930-2400.
This restaurant offers reliable
local cuisine served inside or in a
charming courtyard with tables
set out under the orange trees.
Try the classic *pasta alla Norma*
and finish up with rich *cassata
siciliana*. Ancient Roman ruins are
visible through a glass floor.

Da Antonio €
Via Crocefisso 4, T0942-24570.
Daily 1200-1500, 1900-2400.
This relaxed pizzeria and trattoria
is one of few modestly priced
options in Taormina. The only
drawback is its location – at the
bottom of town, almost near the
junction with the main SS114
road. There is an enormous
range of pizzas (evenings only),
or you could try the fish of the
day. A great option for families.

What the locals say

Bar Mocambo was a fashionable haunt in the 1950s and 60s, which became *the* place to be seen in the 1970s when the new manager, my uncle Robertino Fichera, took over. Robertino knew everyone, including Truman Capote and Tennessee Williams. In the bar, you can see a huge mural on one wall. Robertino wanted to capture Taormina society at that moment forever, and asked Christian Bernard to paint the mural in 1978. Robertino is in the centre, surrounded by a crowd of famous Taormina characters. I'm in it too – the little girl standing just behind him on the left.

Giovanna Fichera, Taormina resident.

Pizzeria Ciccino €
Piazza Duomo, Castelmola,
T0942-28081.
Daily 1930-2400.
A classic in lofty Castelmola, this pizzeria is a local favourite. A good option for families.

Cafés & bars
Antico San Giorgio
Piazza S Antonino, Castelmola,
T0942-28228.
Daily 0900-2400 in summer, weekends only in winter.
This old-fashioned bar prides itself on its home-made almond wine. It overlooks the church on the main square. Castelmola is a stiff stroll up to the village from Taormina, but the views are truly breathtaking, particularly at dusk.

Bar Turrisi
Piazza Duomo, Castelmola,
T0942-281181, turrisibar.it.
Daily 1000-2400.
This is the second of the two immensely popular bars in

Castelmola. Watch the lights sparkle in the bay below from one of the balcony tables.

Caffè Wunderbar
Piazza IX Aprile 7, T0942-625302.
Daily 0830-0230, Nov-Feb closed Tue.
Once the haunt of intellectuals and film stars, this is now living on past glories and you might not think the high prices for its ice creams and *granite* justify the superb views.

Mocambo
Piazza IX Aprile, T0942-23350.
Daily 0900-2400.
Another historic bar, with a lovely terrace on Taormina's most panoramic square and red velvet armchairs inside, this is good for afternoon coffee or evening drinks, accompanied by picture-postcard views of the coast and Etna.

Catania & around

Tre Bicchieri €€€€
Via San Giuseppe al Duomo 31,
T095-715 3540,
osteriaitrebicchieri.it.
Mon-Sat 1300-1530, 2000-2300.
Catania's most elegant restaurant. Dine on sumptuous dishes such as lobster with artichokes in the salons upstairs or tuck into simpler fare downstairs in the wine bar. The restaurant is owned by the wine-producing Benanti family – try their acclaimed reds, Rovittello and Lamoremio.

Metrò €€€
Via Crociferi 76, T095-322098.
Mon-Sat 1300-1530, 2000-2300.
A sleek bistro on one of Catania's most important thoroughfares, this serves traditional fare with a modern twist. It's part of the Slow Food movement, and the menu changes with what's in season. Try the *timballetto di sarde e patate* if it's on the menu.

Osteria Antica Marina €€€
Via Pardo 29, T095-348197,
anticamarina.it.
Thu-Tue 1230-1530, closed Aug.
Overlooking Pescheria market and specializing in fish, this is one of the best restaurants in Catania. Don't miss the sea urchins, if they are available, and don't expect to see a menu. The chef prepares whatever is freshest at market. Book in advance.

Ristorante I Crociferi €€€

Piazza S Francesco 14, T095-715 2480, ristoranteicrociferi.com.
Mon-Sat 1300-1530, 2000-2200.
Overlooking one of the loveliest squares in the *centro storico*, this restaurant serves Sicilian cuisine with an emphasis on fish. Start with *risotto gamberetti e fiori di zucca*, with tiny prawns and courgette flowers, and follow with oven-baked sea bass. The wine list includes a good selection of regional wines.

Don Turiddu €€

Via Musumeci 50, T095-537844.
Mon-Sat 1300-1500, 1930-2300.
This pretty, traditional tavern can be found on the edge of the old centre, between piazza Repubblica and via Umberto I (about a 10-min walk from the Duomo). The smell of *pesce alla griglia* will draw you to its door: doused with a mixture of olive oil and lemon juice, the barbecued fish comes off the grill tender and succulent.

Il Sale Art Café €€

Via Santa Filomena 10-12, T095-316888.
Daily 2000-2400, closed Tue in winter.
Part bar, part restaurant and part art gallery, this is one of Catania's most fashionable and laid-back places to eat. The menu features pizzas, plus a few typical local dishes including fresh fish and *caponata*. Book early.

Cordai Casa delle Crispelle €

Via Vittorio Emanuele 35-37, Acireale, T095-763 1791.
Tue-Sun 1900-2400.
A classic stop for the Catanian speciality *crispelle* – deliciously light (and shockingly moreish) fritters, available here with savoury ricotta or sweet honey fillings. The shop occupies a Baroque palazzo in the old town.

Cafés & bars

Savia

Via Etnea 302, T095-31691, savia.it.
Daily 0900-2300.
Many believe that the *arancine* at Savia are the best in Catania. It's located opposite the Giardino Bellini botanic gardens, and there's a café upstairs, where you can try cakes and pastries.

St Moritz

Viale Sanzio Raffaello 8-12, T095-320936.
Daily 0900-2300.
Fans of the typical Sicilian dessert *cannoli* should make a pilgrimage to the St Moritz to stock up on their ricotta-stuffed pastry treats. There's a handy *tavola calda*, too. It's just a couple of blocks from the Catania-Borgo station (the start of the Circumetnea line), and easily found by metro (Borgo station).

Tip...

It's hard to find fresh *cannoli* in July and August, because the ricotta cheese sours quickly in the heat. But *cannoli*-flavoured ice cream is a great substitute!

The Other Place

Via E Reina 18-20.
Daily 2100-0200.
Long-standing and popular Brit-style pub with a friendly studenty crowd of locals, this is slap bang in the middle of Catania (about a block from the Duomo). Pizzas are served too.

Viscuso

Via Re Martino 101, Aci Castello, T095-271244.
Daily 0900-2000.
Known by the locals as Il Cavaliere, this bar-cum-pasticceria opposite Aci Costello's main church has been serving scrumptious cakes and pastries along with outstanding ice creams since the 1930s.

Entertainment

Mount Etna & around

Albergo Parco dell'Etna €€
Via Carlo Alberto dalla Chiesa 1,
T095-691907, parcodelletna.com.
Tue-Sat 1300-1500, 1930-2200,
Sun 1300-1500.
A 10-minute walk east of the
station, this friendly hotel-
restaurant serves traditional and
well-priced local cuisine.
Pistachios feature prominently
on the menu. You'll also find wild
mushrooms on the menu in
season (late autumn). Pizzas are
served in the evenings.

Ristorante Hosteria della
Stazione €€
Contrada Difesa, Bronte,
T329-023 6244.
Wed-Mon 1200-1500, 1930-
2300.
This restaurant overlooking a
plain occupies an old waiting
room in a disused Circumetnea
train station on the outskirts of
Bronte. The cuisine is superb: try
the tagliatelle with asparagus, or
the pork with polenta.

San Giorgio e Il Drago €€
Piazza San Giorgio 28, Randazzo,
T095-923972.
Tue-Sun 1230-1500, 1930-2200.
In the heart of Randazzo's
historic centre, this trattoria has
wooden tables and chairs,
brick-lined arches, and a menu of
delicious local recipes. Try roast
lamb cutlets and pistachio tart.

Trattoria Veneziano €€
Via Romano 8, Randazzo,
T095-799 1353,
ristoranteveneziano.it.
Tue-Sat 1200-1500, 1930-2300,
Sun 1200-1500.
This smart country restaurant on
the edge of Randazzo (about 1½
km from the town centre, just off
the SS120) specializes in wild
mushrooms, served simply
sauteed or with delicious
home-made pasta. Follow them
with some local meat grilled over
hot coals, washed down with
local Etna wine.

Cafés & bars
Conti Gallenti
Via Umberto 247, Bronte,
T095-691165.
Daily 0700-2100.
You'll be spoilt for choice in
Bronte, where there are countless
pasticceries selling sumptuous
pistachio-flavoured treats, but
the Conti Gallenti, on central
Bronte's main street, is perhaps
the best.

Vitale
Piazza A Longo 7, Nicolosi,
T095-914499.
Tue-Sat 0900-2000.
Vitale's famous ice cream is
available year-round, although
you'll find the best flavours are
seasonal – lots of fruit flavours
during the summer, with
chocolate and nuts
predominating in winter.

Children
Etnaland
Località Valcorrente, Belpasso
(near Paternò), T095-791 3333,
etnaland.eu.
Late Jun to early Sep 0900-
1800, €22 adults/teenagers, €13
children up to 140 cm, free for
children under 140 cm.
Sicily's only theme park, with
waterslides, laser show and an
adventure park. You'll need a car
as there is no public transport to
Etnaland (and no taxis from the
nearest train station).

Cinema
Cinema King
Via Antonio De Curtis 14,
Catania, T095-530218.
This centrally located cinema is
just a couple of blocks from the
train station. Showings are
dubbed into Italian.

Clubs
I Quattro Venti
Via Cardinale Dusmet 53-55,
Catania, T095-327477.
Wine bar open daily 1900-2400.
This sleek and fashionable wine
bar offers a huge range of wines,
with more than 200 labels from
Sicily and around the world.
There's an adjoining restaurant,
and a lounge bar, where
international DJs perform at
weekends. They also run a
summer-only outdoor restaurant
and disco at the Lido Bellatrix, via
Acireale, T393-925 7727.

Shopping

La Capannine
Viale Kennedy (SP53), Catania, T095-735235, lacapannine.it.
Thu-Sat 2100-0300, daily in Aug, closed mid-Sep to mid-Jun, €10 (includes a drink).
This popular *discoteca* is located on the beach stretching south of Catania's harbour.

La Chiave
Via Landolina 64, Catania, T347-948 0910, myspace.com/lachiavecatania.
Daily 1600-0200, free for gigs.
This atmospheric disco-bar (near the Teatro Massimo Bellini in the centre of Catania) has a wide-ranging programme of live gigs, plus DJ sessions. Jazz sessions on Sunday evenings. There's also an internet café.

Ma (Music Action)
Via Vela 6, Catania, T095-341153.
Thu-Sun 2300-0300, €10.
This is a very glamorous club near the Castello Ursino, where you'll have to dress to impress or you won't get in. Expect the best local and international DJs.

Mercati Generali
SS417 Km 69, T095-571458, Catania, mercatigenerali.org.
Nightly parties in summer, DJ sessions Fri and Sat in winter, 2200-0300.
You'll need a car (or a taxi) to get out to this gorgeous venue, which is set in a converted *baglio* a 15-minute drive from the city centre, and combines art gallery, exhibition space, disco and bar.

Gay & lesbian

Pegaso's Circus
Lungomare Presidente Kennedy 80, Catania, T095-735 7268, pegasos.it.
Fri-Sun 2300-0500, daily in summer.
This beachside gay disco takes place in a tent complex in winter, but the roof comes off in summer. With drag shows, live music, go-gos and more. Catania's biggest gay venue.

Music

Teatro Massimo Bellini
Via Perrotta 12, Catania, T095-730 6111, teatromassimobellini.it.
Catania's opera house was inaugurated in 1890 with a performance of *Norma*, by Catanian-born composer Bellini. The programme includes year-round opera (including 'Piccola Opera' which is geared towards children), plus classical music concerts.

Ferragosto
Messina and around.
15 Aug.
Messina's *Ferragosto* festival is huge, but all the surrounding villages also celebrate the Feast of the Assumption with parades and pilgrimages.

Beachwear & clothing

Marella Ferrera
Viale XX Settembre 25-27, Catania, T095-446751, marellaferrera.com.
Mon-Sat 1000-1230, 1700-2000.
Marella Ferrera is Sicily's doyenne of style, the most successful fashion designer to emerge from the island. Her creations range from Cinderella-style wedding dresses to sexy evening wear.

Books

Libreria Cavallotto,
Corso Sicilia 91, Catania, T095-310414, cavallotto.it.
Mon-Sat 0900-2000.
This bookshop stocks a good range of books with a Sicilian theme, including a small selection in English. It's a large store, and often organizes readings, shows for children, and other events.

Food & drink

Bottega della Carne di Francesco Cannavò
Via Roma 232, Linguaglossa, T095-643748.
Mon-Fri 0900-1230, 1700-1930, Sat 0900-1230.
Linguaglossa is famous for *zuzzu*, a kind of gelatinous, rustic sausage usually served in cubes and which is perhaps best suited to those with adventurous palates. This local butcher has won awards for his *zuzzu*.

Activities & tours

Dagnino Carlo
Via Etnea 179, Catania,
T095-312169.
Mon-Fri 0900-1300, 1630-1900,
Sat 0900-1300.
Everything you want for a picnic,
including cheeses, hams and
salame, as well as olives, some
gourmet pates made with olives
or capers, oil, wine and more. It's
a couple of blocks beyond the
piazza Stesicoro.

I Dolci di Nonna Vincenza
Piazza San Placido 7, Catania,
T095-715 1844,
dolcinonnavincenza.it.
Mon-Sat 0900-1300, 1700-1900,
Sun 0900-1300.
A Mecca for Sicilian desserts,
including *cassate* and *cannoli*,
this is handily located near the
cathedral. Nonna Vincenza has
been making these pastries for
more than 70 years!

Outdoor equipment
Zacca Sport
Via de Felice 30, Catania,
T095-327985.
Mon-Sat 0900-1300, 1700-2000.

If you haven't brought suitable
footwear or a coat, this sports'
goods shop just off via Etnea is a
good place to pick up the basics
for climbing Etna.

Souvenirs
Antica Bottega del Puparo
Fratelli Napoli, via Reitano 55,
Catania, T095-751 3076.
The Napoli family have been
making the famous Sicilian
puppets since the 19th century,
and are celebrated throughout
the island. The magnificent
puppets are almost life size, and
can weigh up to 30 kg. You may
be lucky and find the shop open,
but usually prior notice is
required.

Gran Bazar Artigianato Siciliano
Via Etnea 2, Catania,
T095-345360.
Mon-Sat 0900-1300, 1700-2000.
All kinds of Sicilian crafts are on
display here, including ceramics,
puppets and musical
instruments.

Cultural
SAT Group
Corso Umberto 73, Taormina,
T0942-24653, satgroup.it.
Well-priced coach tours
throughout the year to Etna, the
Alcantara gorges, Syracuse,
Agrigento, Palermo, Cefalù,
piazza Armerina as well as
additional tours in summer to
the Aeolian Islands and a wider
range of excursions to Etna.
Multilingual guides.

Cycling
Blue Stone
Via Felice Paradiso 62, Acireale,
T095-765 8945,
bluestonesicily.com.
This reliable tour operator offers
three- to seven-day self-guided
bike tours on and around Etna.
Prices for the week-long tour
(from €560 per person) includes
seven nights' B&B
accommodation, road map,
baggage transportation and a
24-hour helpline; bike hire can be
added for another €55. They can
also organize bike rental.

Food & wine
Blue Stone
(see above)
Acireale-based Blue Stone offers
a range of food and wine tours,
including visits to wineries,
participation in the grape
harvest etc.

Transport

Trekking

Etna Trekking

*Piazza Santo Calì 4,
Linguaglossa, T095-647877,
etnatrekking.com.*

Family company offering various
Etna excursions and treks
including a full day, moderate to
strenuous trek (seven hours)
across the top craters, ascending
from the south side (Nicolosi)
and descending on the north
side (Rifugio Citelli). Guided
groups of 10 to 15 people, €70
per person including cable car
and transfers to and from
Nicolosi.

Etna Guide

*Rifugio Sapienza, T095-791 4755,
etnaguide.com.*

These guides are based at
Rifugio Sapienza, and have a
wooden booth near the cable
car station. They offer a range of
guided tours, from easy
two-hour nature walks (around
€30 per person) to moderately
strenuous four-hour hikes to the
Valle del Bove (around €60) or
tough eight-hour day hikes to
the ice caves (around €100).

Messina & around

Messina is the main port for
ferries to mainland Italy. It's also
on the main northern train line
from Palermo (several services
daily, 3½ hrs). **SAIS** (T090-661754,
saisautolinee.it) bus services link
Messina to Catania (via Taormina,
Giardino-Naxos and Acireale) and
Palermo (2 hrs 40 mins, some
services stop at Castel di Tusa).
Giuntabus (T090-673782,
giuntabus.com) run a regular
service to Milazzo (1 hr). See also
Essentials, page 151.

Taormina & around

Taormina's train station
(Taormina-Giardini) is on the
coast near Giardino-Naxos on
the main Messina–Catania line
(Messina 70 mins, Catania 50
mins). Bus services from Messina
(1 hr 40 mins) and Catania (1 hr
10 mins) with **Interbus**
(T095-532716, interbus.it) drop
passengers at the main bus
terminal on via Luigi Pirandello.
See also Essentials, page 155.

Catania & around

Catania can be reached by direct
train from Messina (70 mins) and
Syracuse (75 mins), but you'll
need to change at Messina if
coming from Palermo. Bus
services are usually faster and
more convenient: **SAIS**
(T090-661754, saisautolinee.it)
runs services from Palermo (2 hrs
40 mins), while **AST** (T840-
000323, aziendasicilianatrasporti.
it) run regional services along the
coast to Acireale (50 mins) via Aci
Castello and Aci Trezza. See also
Essentials, page 161.

Mount Etna & around

A once-daily AST bus for Rifugio
Sapienza from Catania via
Nicolosi (departs 0815, returns
1630, journey time 2 hrs), but
you'll need your own car to reach
Piano Provenzano. See also
Essentials, page 167, and
Circumetnea, page 173.

Contents

Piazza Archimedes, Syracuse.

Southeastern Sicily

Introduction

The southeastern corner of Sicily is packed with outstanding attractions, from superb Graeco-Roman ruins to lavish Baroque cities. Syracuse and Noto are the biggest honeypots, attracting constant streams of visitors, but escape – in the form of the gentle Iblei mountains or the glorious beaches of the Vendicari nature reserve – is always close at hand.

Some of the largest and most resplendent ancient ruins in Europe can be found in Syracuse, once the most powerful city state in Magna Graecia. The highlight is a vast theatre carved into the rock two and a half thousand years ago, which still hosts a superb annual festival of classical drama. More dramatic ruins can be found on the enchanting little island of Ortigia, where the columns of an ancient temple form the skeleton of the beautiful cathedral.

A massive earthquake shook the entire southeastern corner of Sicily in 1693. Tragically, many thousands died and entire towns were reduced to rubble, but out of the ashes rose a string of beautiful new cities, built in an extravagant style that would become known as Sicilian Baroque. Now protected by UNESCO, these splendid cities, led by the golden triumverate of Noto, Ragusa and Modica, are among the loveliest in Sicily.

What to see in...

...one day
Arrive early (0900) to see ancient Syracuse's incredible **Teatro Greco** and the rest of the **Parco Archaeologico** before it gets too hot, then bone up on what you've seen at the archaeological museum. Have lunch by the water's edge in **Ortigia**, and spend the afternoon getting lost in the narrow streets and exploring the **cathedral**. Finish up with a cocktail on piazza del Duomo.

...a weekend or more
In a weekend, you could also explore the beautiful Baroque trio of **Noto**, **Ragusa** and **Modica** and take a dip in the sea at the stunning **Riserva Naturale di Vendicari**. With a bit more time, head to the **Vall d'Anapo** to see the Bronze Age necroplis of **Pantalica** and hike in the valley.

Left: Ortigia peninsula, Syracuse.

Syracuse & around

The Roman philosopher Cicero described Syracuse as "the greatest Greek city and the most beautiful of them all". Two natural harbours and a freshwater spring drew the first Greek settlers in the eighth century BC, and Syracuse grew to become the most important city-state in Magna Graecia: rich, powerful and replete with magnificent monuments. The remnants of the spectacular theatre survive today, a gigantic arc of stone that once accommodated up to 15,000 spectators. Modern Syracuse (Siracusa) is rather tired and dusty, dominated by an enormous sanctuary resembling a gigantic mound of piped concrete, built to house a much-venerated statue of the Madonna.

Piazza Archimedes, Syracuse.

Much prettier is the little island of Ortigia with its sinuous network of convoluted streets overlooked by the splendid Baroque Duomo, which incorporates the 2500-year-old columns of the Temple of Athena. Further afield, there are more ancient ruins, including Megara Hyblaea out on a quiet, green cape, and the extraordinary necropolis at Pantalica, where thousands of graves are hollowed out of the gorge.

Ortigia

A diminutive, drop-shaped island at the very tip of Syracuse, Ortigia (Ortygia) is the ancient heart of the city. Only a few metres separate it from the dusty modern city on the mainland, to which it is now permanently linked by bridge, but it has a completely different atmosphere.

Ortigia is dreamy and gentle, its battered yet enchanting little streets still scattered with ghostly reminders of its ancient history. Until surprisingly recently, Ortigia's stone palazzi and tidy town houses with their wrought-iron balconies were grimy and neglected, but the island's recent (and ongoing) rise in the fashion stakes has brought a sprinkling of boutique accommodation, chic stores and wine bars in its wake. Vestiges of its grittier past survive, particularly in the wonderful morning produce **market** that takes place by the port on and around via Trento. Come early to hear the traders in full voice, and to be dazzled by an extraordinary variety of goods. At the southernmost tip of the island, the hulking **Castello Maniace** (closed indefinitely for restoration) is named after the Byzantine general Georgios Maniakes who captured Syracuse from the Arabs in 1038; this version was built by Federico II between 1232 and 1240. Behind the defensive walls, little of this former royal residence has survived, although ongoing restoration has revealed some reminders of its glorious past, including the magnificent vaulted main hall.

Essentials

❶ **Getting around** The island of Ortigia is closed to tourist traffic, and visitors must park their cars at the car park near the Ponte Umberto. Free, electric shuttle buses (*navette*) make the circuit of the island from the *fermata* (bus stop) by the car park. The island of Ortigia is small and easy to get around on foot. The archaeological area is at the other end of the city, a dusty 2-km walk through central Syracuse (not particularly attractive), or you could take AST buses 1, 7, 8, 9 or 12 from the **Riva Nazario Sauro** in Ortigia (near the bridge). Useful AST bus timetables (for urban and regional services) can be found at comune.siracusa.it/TasportiAst/Trasporti.htm.

❷ **Bus station** Inter-urban bus services stop at the terminal on corso Umberto I, near the train station. The hub for urban bus services is the Riva Nazario Sauro, near the Umberto bridge, in Ortigia. Buy bus tickets at kiosks by the bus station, or at any *tabacchi*.

❸ **Train station** Stazione Centrale FS, piazzale Stazione, T0931-464467, trenitalia.it.

❹ **ATM** Many ATMs including at the train station; on corso Umberto; and several on Ortigia, including two on piazza Archimede: **Banco di Sicilia** at No 1, T0931-725111, and **Banca d'Italia** at No 7, T0931-46199.

❺ **Hospital** Ospedale Umberto I, Contrada Sirina, T0931-724033, ospedateumbertoprimo.

❻ **Pharmacy** Farmacia Centrale, via Maestranza 42, Ortigia, T0931-65320, is just one of numerous pharmacies.

❼ **Post office** Riva della Posta 1, T0931-79611, Mon-Fri 0800-1830, Sat 0800-1230.

❽ **Tourist information** The main city office is at via Maestranza 33, Ortigia, T0942-23243. There is also a provincial tourist office in mainland Syracuse at via San Sebastiano 43, apt-siracusa.it.

Tip…

When choosing accommodation in Syracuse, opt to stay in Ortigia. The nicest hotels and B&Bs are here, and it has considerably more atmosphere (as well as restaurants and bars) than the rest of town.

Syracuse listings

ⓞ Sleeping

1 Agriturismo La Frescura
  via Per Floridia 50
2 Algilà *via Vittorio Veneto 93*
3 Caol Ishka Hotel
  via Elorina, Contrada Pantanelli
4 Casa dello Scirocco
  contrada Piscitello, Carlentini
5 L'Approdo delle Sirene
  riva Garibaldi 15
6 Royal Maniace *lungomare di Ortigia 13*

ⓞ Eating & drinking

1 Al Mazzarì *via G Torres 7*
2 Bar Tabacchi Maestranza
  via Maestranza 15
3 Gran Caffè del Duomo
  piazza Duomo 18-19
4 Jonico 'a Rutta 'e Ciauli
  Riviera Dionisio Il Grande 194
5 Le Antiche Siracuse
  via delle Maestranza 2
6 Trattoria La Foglia
  via Giuseppe Maria Capodieci 21
7 Osteria da Mariano *vicolo Zuccalà 9*

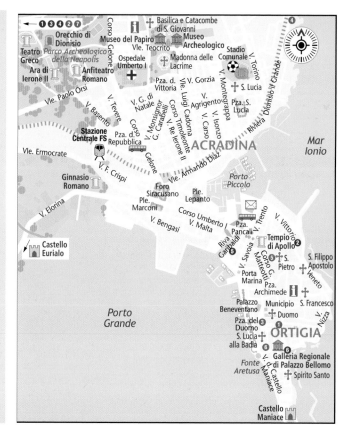

Piazza del Duomo, Ortigia.

Duomo

Piazza del Duomo, T0931-465179.
Daily 0800-1200, 1600-1900, free.

The piazza del Duomo is the showiest square in Ortigia, flanked on every side by the swooping lines of the city's finest Baroque monuments. First among them is the Duomo (Santa Maria delle Colonne), which, according to an inscription in the nave, is the oldest Christian church in Europe, though it still clearly preserves the skeleton of an ancient pagan temple (seen to most dramatic effect from via Minerva). The site was once occupied by the magnificent Temple of Athena, erected in the fifth century BC to celebrate the tyrant Gelon's victory over the Carthaginians. Vast, lavishly decorated with gold and marble, and presided over by an enormous statue of the goddess Athena, it was famous throughout Magna Graecia. The temple was converted into a Christian church under Byzantine rule in the seventh century AD, and the Duomo still preserves several superb columns, which have stood here for some 2500 years. The interior was stripped of its Baroque fittings in the first decades of the 20th century, and

the ancient columns stand out beautifully in the soft light of the modern stained-glass windows. One of the side chapels contains the silver statue of Santa Lucia, the city's much-venerated patron saint. She has two feast days, in May and December, when everyone turns out to watch the statue being paraded through the crowded streets to the Chiesa di Santa Lucia al Sepolcro (piazza Santa Lucia), which was erected over the spot on which Lucia was martyred.

Fonte Aretusa

The Fountain of Arethusa sits on the prettiest – western – stretch of seafront on Ortigia, and is the most popular destination for the evening *passeggiata*. This freshwater spring was legendary in antiquity, celebrated by Pindar and Virgil, and later described by the poets Milton and Pope. It was named after the nymph Arethusa, who fled the attentions of the river god Alpheus and was transformed into a spring by her mistress, the goddess Artemis. Now the spring flows into a small pool, little more than a murky duckpond. It's planted thickly with papyrus, which locals say was brought here by the Egyptians in the first century BC, and is still used by craftspeople to make souvenirs. Next to the spring, a tiny **aquarium** (daily 1000-2200, €3/2, accessed from the marina below) is a pleasant spot to spend an hour or two watching small tanks full of colourful fish from the Ionian Sea and farther afield.

Fonte Aretusa.

Walking tour of Ortigia

Begin at the piazza Archimede, with its lavish 19th-century fountain depicting the myth of Artemis, and head east along via Maestranza. Continue to the end, before turning right on via Alagona, once one of the main arteries of the former Jewish quarter, Giudecca.

An ancient mikvah (ritual bathhouse) survives in the basement of the Alla Giudecca hotel (via Alagona 52, T0931-22255, tours on the hour Mon-Sat 1100-1900, Sun 1100-1200, €5). At its height, in the mid-15th century, more than a quarter of the population of Ortigia was Jewish, but the entire community was exiled by Spanish decree in 1492. Turn right down via M Minniti, and right again onto via della Giudecca. On the right, the Baroque church of San Filippo Apostolo (closed for decades and badly neglected) was built over the former synagogue, and contains another ritual bath as well as a crypt with frescoes. Just beyond it, the Teatro dei Pupi, a traditional Sicilian puppet theatre, has regular summer performances. In front of the church, the narrow via del Crocifisso culminates in the via Roma, Ortigia's main shopping street, lined with chain stores from Benetton to Versace. Turn left and walk to the end of via Roma, and you'll see the Palazzo Bellomo (13th to 18th century) at the corner with via Capodeici; now seat of the regional art museum, it's currently being restored. Turn back down via Roma and turn left onto via Minerva, the Roman name for the goddess Athena, to whom a great temple was dedicated in the fourth century BC. Its fluted columns are visible on the left, incorporated into the wall of the Duomo (see page 190). Via Minerva emerges onto the piazza del Duomo, the grandest square in the city, which is overlooked by the superb main façade of the cathedral as well as several Baroque palazzi, including the Palazzo Benevantano del Bosco. Cafés spread a sea of tables across the square from where you can enjoy the views.

A small street at the southern end of the square, via P Picherali, leads to Ortigia's most famous and possibly least impressive monument, the **Fonte Aretusa** (see page 190). This freshwater spring brought the first settlers to the region and inspired one of the best-known classical myths, the flight of the nymph Arethusa, but it is decidedly dull in the flesh. Loop around the pond and follow the passeggio Adorno until you see the **porta Marina**, a 15th-century Gothic gateway built under the Spanish. From here, via Savoia leads to largo XXV Luglio, little more than a widening in the road rather than a fully fledged square. On the right, you'll see the remains of the **Tempio di Apollo** (Temple of Apollo), buried for centuries under later buildings until uncovered in the 19th century to reveal the oldest Doric temple in Sicily, dating back to the sixth century BC. Fragments of several columns survive. Across the piazza Pancali, a **market** takes place along the parallel streets of via Trieste and via Trento. Return to piazza Archimede via corso G Matteoti and reward yourself with an ice cream at the **Antiche Siracuse**, on the corner with via Maestranza.

Around the island

Galleria Regionale di Palazzo Bellomo

Via Capodieci 16, T0931-69511, regione.sicilia.it/beniculturali/palazzobellomo.
Closed for major restoration at time of going to press but due to reopen in late 2009 – check dates and times with tourist office. While restoration is in progress, a selection of works, including Antonello da Messina's *The Annunciation* (1474), is on display at the museum's temporary headquarters in the former Convento del Ritiro (via Mirabella 31, Ortigia, daily 0900-1900, €4).

The imposing Palazzo Bellomo, which dates back to the 13th century, once belonged to one of Ortigia's wealthiest and most powerful families. In 1725 it was sold to the Monastery of St Benedict, joined to the neighbouring Palazzo Parisi, and given a Baroque facelift. Fortunately its elegant Gothic courtyards, with their sweeping staircases and delicate archways, were left intact. Since the 1940s, the palace has been home to the city's art collection, which spans several centuries from the Middle Ages to the 19th century and was largely gleaned from the region's churches and monasteries. As well as sculpture and painting, the museum also has a fascinating collection of historic artefacts, including an array of beautifully painted traditional carriages. One of the museum's most famous paintings is Caravaggio's superb *Burial of St Lucy* (1608), in which two thuggish grave-diggers are about to bury the beautiful young martyr, Lucia, who was born and died in Syracuse in the fourth century AD and is the city's patron saint. The painting was commissioned for the altarpiece of the Basilica Santa Lucia al Sepolcro, where it can be seen while the museum is being restored.

The museum's greatest masterpiece, Antonello da Messina's *The Annunciation* (1474), has recently undergone major restoration. The painting, which was commissioned for a church in Palazzolo Acreide was very badly damaged even a century ago, when it was bought by the state for the Bellomo museum. The latest restoration has made an extraordinary difference, bringing to life the upper part of the canvas which was previously dim and patchy (the lower third, unfortunately, remains considerably degraded).

Mainland Syracuse

Parco Archeologico della Neapolis

Via del Teatro, T0931-66206.
Tue-Sun 0900 till 2 hrs before dusk, €6/3 concession, €10 combined ticket with Museo Archeologico.

Many of the most important ruins of ancient Syracuse – once rivalled only by Athens itself – are contained within the confines of the archaeological park on the northern fringes of town. This area was called Neapolis, meaning 'New Town', once a wealthy suburb of Syracuse.

The superb **Teatro Greco** (Greek Theatre), a sweeping arc of pale, sun-bleached rock, was one of the largest in antiquity. Of the original 52 rows of seating, only 11 are missing, and the great auditorium, gouged into the hillside, had a capacity for as many as 15,000 spectators. The theatre has a special place in the history of modern drama. The comedies of Greek dramatist Epicharmus (c540-450 BC) were enacted at the original wooden theatre that stood here from the sixth century BC, and the early stone theatre that replaced it was inaugurated with a drama by Aeschylus (c525-456 BC), considered the founder of tragedy. Hieron II (270-215 BC), who was responsible for most of Syracuse's grandest monuments, had the theatre expanded into one of the largest ever built under the Greeks, and it was remodelled further by the Romans. Although little survives of the main stage (the stone was plundered by Spanish troops in the 16th century in order to shore up the city's defences), you can still make out the little niches in the rock wall where votive offerings were presented to the gods.

The archaeological zone also includes the **Latomia del Paradiso** (Paradise Quarry), a rambling

Parco Archeologico della Neapolis essentials

It's a long, dusty walk from Ortigia to the **Parco Archeologico**, but there are regular buses (numbers 1, 7, 8, 9 or 12) from the Riva Nazario Sauro in Ortigia (near the bridge). The ticket office is down a small, well-signposted track, viale Augusto, off via Teracati. The little road is densely lined with souvenir stalls and snack kiosks; about halfway along is the Norman church of San Nicolò dei Cordari. The three main areas of interest (the Greek theatre, the Roman amphitheatre and the Latomie quarries) each have separate entrances off this main artery, although all are accessed with a single ticket. The ticket and information office is by the entrance to the Greek theatre at the end of the road. Another gate, almost adjacent, leads to the Latomie. The entrance to the Roman amphitheatre is further back, opposite the church.

The **Museo Archeologico** is located a 5-10 minute walk (about 500 m) east of the Parco Archeologico; walk down the viale Augusto, which becomes the viale Teocrito once it crosses the viale Teracati. The museum is on the left.

network of ancient quarries which over the centuries has been transformed into an extensive garden dotted with caves. Visit the **Orecchio de Dionisio** (Ear of Dionysios), a gloomy cavern where (if you can dodge the bat droppings) it's worth trying out the curious acoustics: even whispered words uttered in the depths of the cave are clearly audible at the entrance. Unfortunately, all of the other caves and most of the pathways have been closed to visitors because of safety concerns.

Access to the **Anfiteatro Romano** (Roman amphitheatre) is through a pretty, tree-shaded garden opposite the little Norman church of San Nicolò dei Cordari ('of the rope-makers'). Ancient sarcophagi stud the path leading to the arena, which was built in the first century BC and was the largest Roman amphitheatre on Sicily. Overgrown and tumbling into ruins, just enough has been preserved to offer an intriguing glimpse into the past – the faded names of former seat-holders etched into the marble balustrade are particularly evocative.

Tip...

Every year from early May to late June a **Festival of Classical Theatre** is held in Syracuse's Teatro Greco. The performances take place at sunset, just as they did in Greek times, so that the fiery sky becomes an element in the drama. Programme and information (currently in Italian only) at indafondazione.org.

Teatro Greco.

Around the island

Museo Archeologico Regionale Paolo Orsi

Viale Teocrito 66, T0931-464022,
regione.sicilia.it/beniculturali.
Tue-Sat 0900-1900 (Thu and Sat till 2200), Sun
0900-1900, €6/3 concession, €10 combined
ticket with Parco Archeologico.

Syracuse's archaeological museum gathers
together the most important treasures from
the city's glittering past. It is the best
archaeological museum in Sicily and one of the
largest in Europe. The collections are currently
divided into four sections.

    Section A This covers the most important
prehistoric finds, with stone, bone and pottery
fragments dating back to the fifth millennium BC.
Look for the astonishingly accomplished, finely
ribbed vase discovered in the 'royal' tomb in the
Pantalica necropolis (see page 198).

    Section B The story picks up around the
seventh and sixth centuries BC, with artefacts
collected from the earliest Greek colonies
including Megara Hyblaea (see page 199) and
Syracuse. Some of the museum's most famous
exhibits are in this section, including a captivating
gorgon that once leered from Syracuse's Temple of
Athena (now the cathedral); a strangely
contemporary stylized terracotta horseman, which
served as an elaborate roof tile in Kamarina; and a
serene statue of a plump, mysterious fertility
goddess suckling twins, from the necropolis at
Megara Hyblaea.

    Section C This covers the classical Greek
period, the fifth and fourth centuries BC, with
artefacts from Gela and Agrigento, as well as
Syracuse's sub-colonies, such as Akrai.

    Section D The final section contains finds
from Syracuse under Roman rule, with early
Christian sarcophagi, including the superb
Adelphia Sarcophagus (AD c.340), and some fine
statuary, including the celebrated and voluptuous
Venus Anadyomene (also called the *Landolina
Venus*, after the archaeologist who discovered it), a
first or second century AD copy of the Greek

original. This is the most famous of the museum's
treasures, and depicts the moment when the
goddess of love emerges from the sea, modestly
clasping her robe around her.

Catacombe di San Giovanni

Piazza San Giovanni, T0931-67955.
Daily 0930-1230, 1430-1800, all day in summer,
€5 by guided tour only.

Just around the corner from the archaeological
museum, the church of San Giovanni stands in
ghostly ruins, a delicate rose window gazing out
from its roofless walls. The first bishop of Syracuse,
St Marcian, was martyred here and his tomb is kept
in an underground crypt, still decorated with worn
Byzantine mosaics. St Paul is said to have preached
on this very spot, and it remains a redolent Catholic
pilgrimage site. An extensive network of
labyrinthine tombs spreads out from the chapel,
where thousands were buried during the fourth to
fifth centuries BC. The graves have been plundered
over the centuries, but one great treasure
miraculously survived: the elaborately carved
Adelphia Sarcophagus, which is now held in the
archaeological museum.

Basilica Santuario Madonna delle Lacrime di Siracusa

Via Santuario 3, T0931-21446,
madonnadellelacrime.it.
Mon-Fri 0700-1300, 1500-2000, Sat-Sun
0700-1300, 1500-2100, free.

You can't miss the enormous, concrete Dalek of a
structure that dominates the skyline of modern
Syracuse. This church, completed in 1994 and built,
supposedly, to resemble a teardrop, is dedicated to
the Madonna of the Tears, a small, factory-made
statue that shed tears of blood for four days in 1953
and is said to have been responsible for more than
200 miracles. Tour buses clog the city streets daily,
delivering surges of pilgrims intent on laying eyes
on the miraculous statue.

Archimedes (c287-c212 BC)

Archimedes of Syracuse is considered one of the greatest mathematicians of all time. The Archimedes' principle (which apparently came to him in the bath, and elicited the famous cry "Eureka!") explains why some large, heavy objects float and others don't: A body immersed in fluid is subject to an upward force equal in magnitude to the weight of fluid it displaces. He was also a skilled engineer, who designed sophisticated weaponry that may have included a giant claw for hooking enemy ships right out of the sea and a mirror device that could set distant sails aflame. Archimedes died during the Roman siege of Syracuse: he was so busy working out equations in the dust that he ignored a Roman soldier's commands, and was killed. His last words were "Don't touch the circles!"

Archimedes' claw.

Around Syracuse

Castello Euriàlo

Belvedere, 7 km northwest of Syracuse, T0931-711773.
Daily 0900 till 1 hr before dusk, €3. Buses 9 and 11, corso Gelone, outside Archaeological Park.

Above Syracuse, a winding road edged with prickly pear leads up to the Castello Euriàlo which dominates a lofty plateau, scattered with pale, limestone boulders. The views in every direction are staggering. The castle was built in the fourth century BC under Dionysos I (432-367 BC) in order to strengthen the city's defences. Dionysos was 'tyrant' of Syracuse when 'tyrant' meant simply 'absolute ruler'. Although the word wouldn't acquire its negative connotations for a few centuries, Dionysos was already trying them out for size. His cruelty and ruthlessness were legendary, but so too was his military genius. More than 60,000 slaves laboured to build the huge wall, which was said to have been completed in just 20 days. The walls extended for 27 km and were considered one of the great wonders of the ancient world. The fortress was further strengthed

in the third century BC, and it was from here, according to legend, that the great mathematician Archimedes angled his giant mirror and set fire to the sails of the Roman fleet that was massing against Syracuse. Now the castle is largely in ruins, overgrown and scattered with wild flowers, but scrambling over the old stones, with the city splayed out on the plain below and the vivid blue sea beyond, is a delight.

The ruins of Castello Euriàlo.

Palazzolo Acreide

42 km west of Syracuse.

Heading inland from Syracuse, the SS124 meanders through the Iblei foothills, a gentle and surprisingly empty landscape, with endless olive groves tucked behind low walls of pale stone. Eventually, it emerges at Palazzolo Acreide, an enchanting if rather dilapidated little town in shades of ochre, pink and cream. It was rebuilt in the 18th century after a devastating earthquake, and bristles with flouncy spires and Baroque swoops and flourishes.

Despite figuring on UNESCO's World Heritage list, the palaces are visibly crumbling, but Palazzolo Acreide still puts on a brave show, particularly along the main street, corso Vittorio Emanuele, and via Garibaldi, where the **Palazzo Iudica** boasts a long, sinuous Baroque balcony supported by hordes of *putti* and leering creatures. Come during Carnival if you can, when the town explodes into life. The **Museo di Antonino Uccello** (via Machiavelli 19, T0931-881499, daily 0900-1300, 1430-1900, free) is a gem of a museum dedicated to the life and work of peasant farmers.

The original settlement, ancient and still-impressive **Akrai** (daily 0900 till 1 hr before sunset, €3), dominates the hilltop above the town. The first sub-colony of Syracuse, it was founded in 664 BC and quickly rose to prominence thanks to its strategic location at the hub of trade and communication routes from the south of the island. It continued to flourish after the Roman conquest (when it was known as Acrae) and into the early Christian era, but was flattened by the Arabs in the early ninth century. Some poignant

Buscemi's living museum

Just to the north of Palazzolo Acreide, further into the Iblei monti along the SS124, the attractive little town of Buscemi has preserved many of its historic buildings as a fascinating folk museum (museobuscemi.org): among them, you can visit the shoemaker's, the blacksmith's and the wine press. Perhaps the most eye-opening house, highlighting the blistering rural poverty that continues to blight the island, is a *casa ro iurnataru* (day-labourer's house). Just 12 m square, six people shared this tiny space right up until the 1960s.

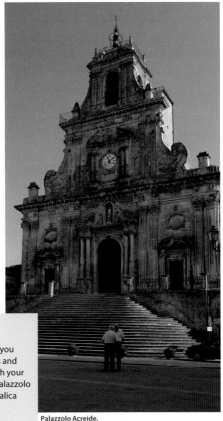

Palazzolo Acreide.

Tip...

Your own transport is advisable if you want to explore the smaller towns and villages of southeastern Sicily. With your own car, a circular tour taking in Palazzolo Acreide and the Necropoli di Pantalica makes for an enjoyable day out.

ruins survive, including a fine 800-seat theatre, built in the third century BC, which is still used for youth drama performances every May (see indafondazione.org for details); the *bouleterion*, a small council chamber; and two *latomie* (originally quarries, later used for cult worship and as necropoli), which still bear the remnants of a Greek bas-relief, with a banquet scene, and a Roman relief of a warrior.

On the road towards Ragusa, a turning will bring you to the famous **Santoni**, a series of 12 life-size statues of the goddess Cybele – beautiful in conception, but weathered almost beyond recognition over the centuries. Unfortunately, repeated acts of vandalism mean that they can only be visited by prior appointment: call the tourist office in Syracuse in advance to arrange a visit.

Necropoli di Pantalica

No visitor centre; administration office T0931-954805.
Permanently open, free. From Sortino (32 km northwest of Syracuse), follow signs for 'Pantalica' and 'Necropolis' to a car park about 5 km from the village at the eastern end of the valley. There is no public transport to Pantalica; the nearest buses go to Sortino.

A panoramic back road wriggles east of the pretty village of **Ferla** towards **Sortino** offering intriguing glimpses of the enclosed and secret gorges of the beautiful **Vall dell' Anapo**. This is a quiet and wonderfully little-visited natural park, where the steep, limestone cliffs are honeycombed with around 5000 niches. These ancient burial sites, some of which date back to the 13th century BC, comprise the Necropoli di Pantalica, a UNESCO World Heritage Site and the largest necropolis in Sicily. An easy footpath meanders through pine forest, taking in the most dramatic of the gorges, as well as the remnants of a Byzantine oratory, San Micidarios, set into the cliff and still adorned with faded frescoes.

The main hiking path in the Vall dell'Anapo is a converted train track, making it easily negotiable for wheelchairs and prams. There are smaller side paths for a more adventurous hike. Note that, strictly speaking (although rarely enforced), mountain bikes are only allowed on certain days or with special permission (by calling the head office on T0931-954805).

Megara Hyblaea

18 km north of Syracuse.

North of Syracuse, a string of huge and spectacularly ugly chemical plants clog the once-lovely bay, the Golfo di Augusta, which is now the most polluted stretch of coast anywhere in the Mediterranean. If you can block out the dismal backdrop by ensuring you face out to sea (and not back towards the smoke-belching refineries), the ruins of Megara Hyblaea are attractively set on a headland. These are the most complete surviving remains of any pre-Classical Greek colony, dating back to the mid-eighth century BC. Megara Hyblaea grew to become a major power, but it was crushed in 483 BC by the tyrant Gelon, who saw the city as a dangerous rival to Syracuse. There's a museum, but the best finds, including the sixth-century BC fertility goddess, are in the archaeological museum in Syracuse.

Lentini

46 km northwest of Syracuse.

Northwest of Augusta, Lentini, founded in 729 BC, may be one of the oldest Greek colonies on Sicily, but it's now a scruffy and cheerfully undistinguished agricultural town. Beyond it, the **Biviere di Lentini**, a marshy lake, is a haven for waterbirds, with more than 200 species resident year-round. Overlooking the lake, you'll find an unexpected oasis in a mellow aristocratic mansion, where the Princess Borghese has created a sumptuous Mediterranean garden, **Il Giardino del Biviere** (Contrada Il Biviere, Lentini, T095-783 1449, ilgiardinodelbiviere.it, autumn/winter 1000-1700, spring/summer 1000-1200, 1700-1900, €10).

Noto & around

Glorious, golden Noto is the queen of southern Sicily's dazzling Baroque cities. After the original settlement was razed by the terrible earthquake of 1693, the town was rebuilt in the valley below and Noto Antica was abandoned to its lonely hilltop. Thanks to the shared vision of the main architects – Vincenzo Sinatra, Paolo Labisi and Rosario Gagliardi – and their use of the local, honey-coloured tufa stone, Noto was endowed with a singular beauty, and locals still describe Noto as *un giardino di pietra* (a garden of stone). A short drive from the city, you'll find some delightful little resorts and fishing villages, as well as some of the most beautiful and deserted beaches on Sicily at the isolated reserve of Vendicari. There is some fine walking to be had in the silent hills near Noto Antica, and superb hiking in the dramatic gorge of Cavagrande.

Duomo, Noto.

Noto boasts the loveliest ensemble of Baroque palaces and churches in Sicily, all created from the same golden stone. The huge Duomo is the centrepiece of the historic town, built on an enlightened grid plan, with generous boulevards and and expansive squares. After a severe earthquake in 1990, Noto's churches and palazzi were dangerously shaken, requiring massive restoration that closed many of the city's finest buildings for years. The scaffolding finally came down in 2007, when Noto emerged as pristine and lovely as when it was first built 300 years ago.

Corso Vittorio Emanuele

The **porta Reale** offers a suitably regal introduction to Noto's main street, corso Vittorio Emanuele, where Noto's finest monuments are clustered, from the grandest palaces to the most splendid churches. Built in the style of a triumphal archway, the porta Reale was erected to honour the Bourbon king Ferdinand II who visited the city in 1838. (The three statues that top the gate – the dog, the swan and the tower – symbolize strength and loyalty, so it's rather ironic that just three decades later Noto would rebel against the Bourbons and open her gates to Garibaldi and his army.) Just beyond the gateway, an imposing flight of steps leads to the **Chiesa di San Francesco all Immacolata**, which has a frothy, wedding-cake façade. Beyond it, the **Museo Civico** (closed indefinitely for refurbishment, check with tourist office) contains some earthquake-battered remains from Noto Antica. The nearby **Monastero di Santa Chiara** contains the only part of the Museo Civico currently open to visitors, with a collection of works by Giuseppe Pirrone, who designed the bronze doors of the cathedral. Continue along corso Vittorio Emanuele until reaching the **Piazza del Municipio**, the monumental heart of the town, where the **Palazzo Ducezio** (1746) on one side and the lofty Duomo on the other take pride of place.

Essentials

❶ Getting around Noto is very small, and you won't need public transport to get around. Most of the main sights are concentrated along the central corso Vittorio Emanuele, although it's worth getting off the main drag to appreciate the quieter side streets.

❷ Bus station Buses (from Syracuse and the coast) stop at largo Pantheon, on via Ducezio, by the Giardino Pubblico.

❷ Train station Piazza Stazione Centrale, T0931-66640 (Trenitalia T848-888088), a 15-minute walk, 1 km from the centre.

❸ ATM There are several ATMs along corso Vittorio Emanuele, including **Banca Populare Italiana** at No 182, T0931-835001, and **Banco di Sicilia** at via Vittorio Emanuele 102-104, T0931-839786.

⊕ Hospital Ospedale Unico, Contrada San Giovanni, T0931-890111.

✛ Pharmacy Farmacia Pace, corso Vittorio Emanuele 161, T0931-835475, is one of numerous pharmacies.

❼ Post office Via Zanardelli 2, T0931-824411, Mon-Fri 0800-1830, Sat 0800-1230.

❶ Tourist information Piazza XVI Maggio, T0931-836744, comune.noto.sr.it.

The **Bishop's Palace** and the sumptuous **Palazzo Landolina** complete the ensemble. Inside the Palazzo Ducezio, now the seat of the town council, you can visit the **Sala degli Specchi** (Hall of Mirrors), a frankly dull, late-19th-century salon.

Duomo

Dominating Noto's skyline, the immense Duomo sits atop an immense flight of stairs. Completed in 1776, the magnificent cathedral is flanked by two restrained bell towers and topped with a huge dome. The 1990 earthquake left a network of cracks, which were ignored until the cathedral's iconic dome collapsed in 1996. By sheer luck, no one was hurt. The cathedral was painstakingly – and expensively – restored over the following decade and reopened in 2007. A small museum (access from via Cavour) shows how the restoration was carried out. Inside, a 16th-century urn contains the ashes of Noto's beloved patron saint, San

Around the island

Corrado Confalonieri, a 14th-century hermit, whose feast day (19 February) is celebrated with a moving procession attended by all the townspeople.

Around piazza XVI Maggio

Continuing along corso Vittorio Emanuele one passes the steep via Corrado Nicolaci on the right, framing fine views of the **Chiesa di Montevergine**. Duck up here to admire the **Palazzo Nicolaci Villadorata** (1733) with its intricate wrought-iron balconies supported by ranks of plump cherubs and leering monsters. Unfortunately, the lavish, if dilapidated, interior is closed indefinitely. The last of the grand squares on the corso Vittorio Emanuele is the **piazza XVI Maggio**, where a pretty 17th-century fountain, brought from Noto Antica, burbles in front of the exquisite little **Teatro Comunale**. Also here is the church of San Domenico, with a frothy, convex façade and five dainty cupolas, and the tourist information office.

Noto Alto

Noto Alto, reached by partly-stepped streets, was conceived as the new town's residential district. It is far less ornate than the monumental lower town. Nonetheless, its honey-coloured streets with their modest homes and churches, and wonderful views over the hills, make for an enchanting stroll.

Noto Alto.

Noto Antica

16 km north of Noto.

Drive out to the poignant remains of Noto Antica (follow signs for SS Maria della Scale, then continue for another 5 km beyond the convent). Behind a stretch of surprisingly grand, fortified walls lie the toppled stones of the ancient town, now overgrown and brambly. Quiet and dreamy, this contemplative spot affords some wonderful views.

Avola & the Riserva Naturale Cavagrande del Cassibile

Near the coast, **Avola** (9 km east of Noto) is a little town with fine Baroque monuments and a seaside satellite, **Avola Marina**, which is always lively during the summer. A short drive north, the most dramatic limestone gorge in Sicily is protected in the **Riserva Naturale Cavagrande del Cassibile** (follow signs for Convento di Avola Vechio, about 4 km from Avola, then continue until you reach the car park at the top of the gorge). A stiff, hour-long hike makes the steep descent to the bottom of the canyon, where a dip in the icy natural pools is an invigorating reward. There's a footpath along the base of the canyon if you want to hike further.

Lido di Noto

7 km southeast of Noto.

Lido di Noto is the town's modern beach resort, a long stretch of golden sand backed by concrete apartment blocks and a smattering of restaurants. The beaches stretch to the patchy remnants of ancient **Eloro**, a sub-colony of Syracuse founded in the seventh century BC.

Tip...

Visitors to Cavagrande del Cassibile are required to register at the hut in the car park in case of accidents.

Tip…

There are three entrances to the Vendicari reserve, all accessible from the main Noto–Pachino road (SP19), but the most convenient is the middle one of the three. Follow signs for the Torre di Vendicari and leave your car in the car park and then take the wooden boardwalk towards the beach. There is no entrance fee to enter the reserve.

Riserva Naturale Oasi Faunistica di Vendicari

12 km south of Noto.

The coastline south of Eloro is dominated by the magnificent Vendicari reserve, a marshy wetland spread around a pair of lakes and one of the wildest and most beautiful regions anywhere on the island. The reserve is a refuge for thousands of migratory and resident birds, including herons, swans, flamingos, spoonbills, and cormorants. A network of paths links hides, where birders can check off a few species on their lists. For a few weeks in the high season, the perfect Mediterranean beaches of golden sand might be occupied, but for the rest of the year you may have them entirely to yourself. The graceful silhouette of a ruined *tonnara* (tuna fishery) dominates Tonnara Beach, one of several that dot this stretch of coastline, ghostly reminders of a once-thriving industry. Tiny **Cala Mosche**, better known locally as Funni Musca, is a perfect arc of intense blue fringed with rocks. On the edge of the reserve, the **Villa Romana del Tellaro** (Contrada Caddeddi, T0931-836744, daily 0900-2000, €6/3 concession) was once a palatial residence belonging to a rich landowner and boasts some vibrant Roman mosaic decoration – less sophisticated than those at piazza Armerina (see page 224), but still remarkably fine.

Portopalo & around

Continuing south along the coast, tourism, albeit low-key, has joined fishing as a source of income in pretty **Marzamemi**, where colourful boats dot the curving bay and boho-chic bars and restaurants

Infiorata di Noto – Noto's flower festival

Every year, on the third weekend of May, the steep via Corrado Nicolaci is carpeted with flowers, laid out to form elaborate pictures. On the Monday, the children are allowed to stampede through the street, kicking the petals into the air.

cater to a stylish crowd in summer. **Pachino** is a little market town famous for its wines and tomatoes. The flat terrain of the surrounding cape is etched with vines, and huge, low greenhouses where the celebrated Pachino tomatoes are grown. At **Portopalo**, there's yet another ruined *tonnara*, and a sprinkling of hotels and restaurants, with views out to the Isola di Capo Passero, still topped by a 17th-century castle. The very tip of Sicily – and, indeed, of Europe – is the **Isola delle Correnti**, connected by an artificial wharf to the mainland. Low, scrubby and beautifully isolated, its empty beaches are the perfect spot to recharge. In winter, the wind-whipped waves attract surfers and windsurfers, but the waters are generally calmer in summer. There are more wetlands further along the coast in the **Oasi di Pantani Longarini**; although nominally 'protected', swathes are sadly polluted and rubbish-strewn.

Ragusa & around

Ragusa is another of the splendid Baroque cities erected after the terrible earthquake of 1693. The heart of the modern city is Ragusa Superiore (Upper Ragusa), but dreamy little Ibla, with its tangle of cobbled streets, is infinitely more appealing. There are more Baroque delights in Modica, which has a superb reputation for its gourmet restaurants and local produce (particularly the scrumptious chocolate). In Ispica, the Baroque is offset with a touch of *stile Liberty*, and in sleepy Scicli, you'll almost have the Baroque churches and palaces to yourself. Along the southern coast are small resorts with a couple of fine beaches for a spot of lazing, or you could head inland to explore gentle agricultural towns like Comiso and Vittoria, or even play the aristocrat for the day at the Castello di Donnafugata.

Ragusa.

A deep, narrow gorge is all that divides Ragusa Superiore (Upper Ragusa) from its ancient precursor, Ragusa Ibla (Lower Ragusa, or simply Ibla). Ragusa Ibla is an enchanting jumble of narrow streets winding up a small hill. Ragusa Superiore, the grand new city built across the ravine, has a swathe of Baroque monuments behind a ring of modern developments.

Ragusa Superiore

Corso Italia is the tree-lined main street of upper Ragusa, with a smattering of Baroque mansions amid the shops. Just off the Corso Italia, overlooking piazza San Giovanni, is the imposing, golden façade of the **Cattedrale di San Giovanni Battista** (daily 1000-1300, 1500-1800, free). Built between 1706 and 1778, this is Ragusa's most splendid monument, with a light-filled interior topped by a graceful cupola. Near the cathedral, the Baroque **Palazzo Zacco** (corner of via S Vito and corso Vittorio Venero) is famous for its wrought-iron balconies supported by curious characters from a mermaid to a monster sticking out its tongue.

The city's main museum is the **Museo Archeologico Ibleo** (via Natalelli, T0932-622963, 0930-1330, 1600-1900, €2), in need of modernization. The tired displays include ceramics and statuary, the best of which come from Kamarina, a Syracusan colony founded in 599 BC.

Corso Italia continues eastward, and begins to wriggle downwards towards the ravine, becoming via XXIV Maggio and then corso Mazzini. On the right stands the **Chiesa di Santa Maria delle Scale** (open for mass only), rebuilt after the 1693 earthquake but incorporating vestiges of the 14th-century original. There are magnificent views across to Ragusa Ibla from here. Continue to the old town by taking the wonderful sweep of steps, Le Scale, that descends past more battered palazzi to the piazza di Repubblica and the entrance to Ragusa Ibla.

Essentials

❶ Getting around It's a beautiful walk from Ragusa Superiore to Ragusa Ibla (better done that way around, as it's a really stiff climb in the opposite direction) but you can also take the shuttle bus (run by AST, Nos 1 and 3): pick it up on the corso Italia in Ragusa Superiore.

Ragusa and Módica are linked by bus and train. The train station is inconveniently located 1 km from the city centre, but regular (at least eight daily) AST buses (T840-000323, aziendasicilianatrasporti.it) deposit visitors on the central Corso Umberto I. You'll need to be in good shape to get up and down the steps between Modica Alta and Modica Bassa.

❷ Bus station AST and SAIS buses arrive at piazza Gramsci, by the train station, in Ragusa Superiore. Local buses, including the *navette* for Ragusa Ibla, depart from the piazza del Popolo.

❸ Train station Stazione Centrale FS, piazza Gramsci Antonio, T0932-682158.

⊕ Hospital Ospedale Civile, piazza Ospedale Civile, T0932-600111.

✚ Pharmacy Vitale Dr Carmelo Farmacia, corso Italia 228, T0932-621605, is one of several pharmacies, Mon-Fri 0900-1300, 1600-1900, Sat 0900-1300.

❓ Post office Main post office is on piazza S.N. Matteotti, T0932-232287, Mon-Fri 0800-1830, Sat 0800-1230.

❶ Tourist information Via Capitano Bocchieri 33, Ragusa Ibla, T0932-221529, ragusaturismo.it, Tue-Sun 0900-1400, 1600-1800.

Typical architecture of Ragusa.

Around the island

Ragusa Ibla

Ragusa Ibla is replete with graceful, Baroque churches and romantically crumbling palazzi. Explore the labyrinth of narrow streets and steps that link delightful squares and throw up a host of Baroque treasures. The jewel of Ragusa Ibla, the **Duomo di San Giorgio** (piazza del Duomo, Wed-Mon 1000-1330, 1600-1830, free) sits at the very top of the little town, and was designed by Rosario Gagliardi. The cathedral is topped with a huge neoclassical dome (completed in 1820), and overlooks a pretty square with some fine palaces including the Palazzo Arezzi and Palazzo Donnafugata. Ragusa Ibla is becoming increasingly fashionable, and contains some chic boutique-style accommodation and restaurants.

Around Ragusa

Modica & around

15 km south of Ragusa.

Captivating Modica sits astride a gorge in the Ibli mountains. At the top, Modica Alta clings precipitously to the lip of the gorge, with ranks of houses spilling down to Modica Bassa, strung out along the valley below. Prepare to huff and puff your way between the two, negotiating steep stairways. The original settlement was another victim of the devastating 1693 earthquake, but was rebuilt in the early 18th century in the late Baroque style that characterizes the Val di Noto.

First among the city's monuments is the magnificent **Chiesa di San Giorgio** (via San Michele, Modica Alta, T0932-941279, daily 0900-1200, 1600-1900, free), which sits atop a steep flight of some 250 steps, and is dedicated to the patron saint of Modica Alta. Considered the finest work of the celebrated architect Rosario Gagliardi (1698-1762), who was also responsible for many of Noto's best monuments, its lavish façade culminates in a single tower, emphasizing the impression of height. Before the earthquake, its rival claimant to the title of Modica's Chiesa Madre

---

Il Cioccolato Modicano

Modica's celebrated chocolate is curiously granular in texture. The secret lies in the process, which dates back centuries and is said to have been taught to the Conquistadors by the Aztecs. The ingredients are cooked over a very low heat, which means that the sugar never completely dissolves, thereby giving the chocolate its grainy texture. This also ensures that the spices and flavours – vanilla, cinnamon, orange or ginger are common – are not destroyed by the heat. Countless shops advertise *vero cioccolato Modicano* but, to really taste the best, head for **Antica Dolceria Bonajuto**, see page 213.

---

was the **Chiesa di San Pietro** (corso Umberto I, T0932-941074, daily 0900-1200, 1600-1900, free) in the lower town, which was also lavishly rebuilt and is dedicated to the patron saint of Modica Bassa. The longstanding rivalry between the two churches has never really been quashed, and each congregation vies to outdo the other on their respective feast days. But much of Modica's appeal lies in simply wandering through its streets.

Chiesa di San Giorgio.

Scicli, 10 km south of Modica, is an elegantly down-at-heel Baroque gem, rebuilt, like the other UNESCO towns of the Val di Noto, after the destruction caused by the 1693 earthquake.

Nearby Ispica, between Modica (17 km) and Noto (23 km), is another restored Baroque city, with a handsome historic heart hidden behind sprawling, modern development. Vincenzo Sinatra's majestic Basilica di Santa Maria Maggiore, near the piazza Regina Margherita, is a gorgeous whirl of gilt and marble, but the locals come to venerate the late-medieval statue of Cristo alla Colonna, with its frighteningly realistic wounds. Take a peek at the Palazzo Bruno di Belmonte (now the town hall, on the corso Umberto), the work of Sicily's most important exponent of *stile Liberty*, Ernesto Basile.

The Cave d'Ispica is a verdant 13-km-long gorge, where you can still make out the remains of Christian chapels cut into the rock, as well as cave dwellings that were used up until the earthquake struck in 1693. The gorge stretches almost to Modica and has some excellent walking trails.

West of Ragusa

West of Ragusa, Comiso (22 km) is scattered with florid Baroque churches and topped by a 15th-century Aragonese castle that only partly withstood the earthquake of 1693. More Baroque monuments cluster in the old centre, where a fountain of the goddess Diana tinkles on the main square. Further west, the town of Vittoria (22 km), famous for its wines and olive oil, has a fine theatre and a Baroque church in the piazza del Popolo.

Castello di Donnafugata

Donnafugata, 20 km southwest of Ragusa, T0932-619333.

Tue-Sat 0900-1400, Sun 0900-1330, 1430-1730, last entry 1 hr before closing. €5/2.50 concession; €3.50/2.50 *piano nobile* (first floor) and park; €2/1 *piano nobile*.

The splendid 19th-century country house surrounded by gardens was built over the remnants of a 13th-century tower and a 17th-century mansion. Some of its sumptuous salons can be visited (the rest are still being restored), including the rooms where Bianca di Navarra is said to have been imprisoned by the wicked count of Modica. Banish the ghost stories in the romantic gardens, with their dainty follies, pools and maze.

Coastal resorts

Along the coast, backed by a sea of plastic greenhouses in which the famous *pomodori di Pachino* are grown, there are several resorts and attractions within easy reach of Ragusa. Pozzallo (40 km) is a busy little port (there is a regular ferry service from here to Valletta in Malta) with some fine, sandy beaches, including the Spiaggia di Maganuco. West of Pozzallo, Donnalucata, a small resort with an attractive *lungomare*, is a much nicer option than grotty, concrete Marina di Ragusa (24 km). The scant remains of the Syracusan colony of Kamarina (T0932-826004, 0900 till dusk, €3), founded in 599 BC and destroyed by the Romans two and a half centuries later, are signposted just outside Scoglitti.

Sleeping

Algilà €€€€
Via Vittorio Veneto 93, T0931-465148, algila.it.
This luxury boutique hotel in Ortigia opened in 2008. Aristocratic Florentines purchased the historic palazzo and have refurbished it in style. Some rooms have four-poster beds, others have colourful local tiles in the bathrooms, while the rooftop executive suite boasts an outdoor jacuzzi with sea views. Off-season deals can make this a fantastic winter bargain.

Caol Ishka Hotel €€€
Via Elorina, Contrada Pantanelli, T0931-69057, caolishka.com.
Ultra-modern furnishings and gorgeous interiors have transformed the old *masseria* (farmhouse) into a super-stylish retreat, with amenities that include an excellent though expensive restaurant (Zafferano Bistrot) and a huge outdoor pool. The hotel is set in verdant countryside on the banks of the Anapo river, about 1½ km south of Syracuse.

Hotel Royal Maniace €€€
Lungomare di Ortigia 13, T0931-463815, maniacehotel.com.
With a perfect location overlooking the sea, this exquisitely renovated hotel is housed in an 18th-century townhouse on the quieter side of the small island. Some original details have been retained, including the exposed stone walls and brick arches, but they are brought up-to-date with contemporary furnishings and amenities. It's worth paying the small supplement for sea views. It's a tad overpriced in summer, but winter deals bring prices down considerably.

L'Approdo delle Sirene €€
Riva Garibaldi 15, T0931-24857, apprododellesirene.com.
A beautiful, light-filled B&B in a converted palazzo in Ortigia, with smart rooms. The best rooms have balconies with sublime views over the port. Breakfast is served on the panoramic roof terrace in summer. Book early.

Casa dello Scirocco €€
Contrada Piscitello, Carlentini, T339-490 7743, casadelloscirocco.it.
In the hills just outside Lentini, this 18th-century farmhouse is surrounded by orange orchards. It's an excellent accommodation choice if you are travelling with children. Facilities include a beautiful garden pool, a football pitch and a playground, while a host of activities, from helping out on the farm to horse riding, are also available. Choose from rooms furnished with antiques, or self-catering accommodation in a cottage. There's also a restaurant. Half or full board (required in high season, August to first week of September) €65-80 per person; B&B (rest of the year) €40 per person. Group bookings only from November to March.

Agriturismo La Frescura €
Via Per Floridia 50, T338-940 1937, lafrescura.com.
On the outskirts of Syracuse, this farmhouse consists of two buildings dating back to the 17th century. Choose from a suite with a kitchenette or simply a bedroom for B&B accommodation. All retain original details. There is no restaurant, but the owners prepare local food with their own organic vegetables. B&B accommodation from €60-100 per night, and apartments/suites from €80-300 per night, depending on the size and number of guests (between two and six).

Accommodation Syracuse
T339-298 3507, accommodation-syracuse.com.
A renovated 18th-century house in Ortigia has been divided into modern, well-equipped flats that can accommodate up to five people. The nicest has a private roof terrace, but others have balconies. There is a lift, a laundry room, and the owners are happy to provide tips on where to eat

and what to do. Prices are good value, particularly in the low season, with deals on their website. There is a minimum three-night stay, with a one-week minimum in August. €85-100 per night for a two-room apartment based on two adults and two children.

Terre di Vendicari €€€
Contrada Vaddeddi s/n Noto, T346-359 3845, terredivendicari.it.
A stylish retreat by the beaches of the Vendicari nature reserve. Built in 1848, the house has been exquisitely restored to provide five guest rooms. Best of all is the outdoor pool and the sun terrace. There's a restaurant, bar, and a shop selling local produce.

Avola Antica €
Contrada Avola Antica, Avola, T095-990362, avolaantica.it.
High on a hilltop, just inland from the resort of Avola, this *agriturismo* is surrounded by countryside. It's close to the Cavagrande del Cassibile reserve, with rock pools and gullies, and makes a good base for touring the Baroque cities and the beaches at Vendicari. A car is essential. B&B €38-55 per person.

San Pietro B&B €
Via Cosenza 9, T0931-836395, bbsanpietro.it.
Spacious, clean rooms and copious breakfasts make this a firm favourite in Noto. It's just a five-minute walk to all the main sights, yet the B&B is quiet and tranquil. The friendly owners are welcoming and always happy to give advice on what to see and do in their beautiful city. Parking is available.

Locanda don Serafino €€€
Via XI Febbraio 15, Ragusa, T093-222 0065, locandadonserafino.it.
This luxury designer hotel is hidden away in the heart of old Ragusa (Ragusa Ibla) in a 19th-century *palazzetto*. Don't bother with a poky smaller room: go for one of the suites. At the hotel's acclaimed restaurant (a short walk up the street in a former stables), award-winning chef Vincenzo Candiano prepares exquisite cuisine.

Casa Talía €€
Via Exaudinos 1/9, Modica, T0932-752075, casatalia.it.
Tucked away in one of the steep, labyrinthine streets of Modica, this chic and ultra-stylish little B&B offers sublime views across the Baroque city. It was created by a pair of Milanese architects, who converted a sprawl of abandoned ruins into an oasis of

peace (they live here with their little son). Rooms vary in size, but it's worth splashing out on one of the larger ones. Fabulous breakfasts are served on the tree-shaded terrace.

Hotel Novecento €€
Via Duprè 11, Scicli, T0932-843817, hotel900.it.
There are just seven rooms at this gorgeous little boutique hotel, which is tucked away in the Baroque town of Scicli in Monti Iblei. It's off the beaten track, but makes an excellent base for visiting the great Baroque jewels of southeastern Sicily, including Noto and Ragusa, as well as the superb beaches at Vindicari. The hotel prepares delicious traditional breakfasts, and there's an excellent restaurant for elegant dining. Staff are utterly delightful, and the hotel fills quickly in high season with repeat guests.

Villa Aurea €
Contrada Senna, Ispica, T0932-956575, villasara.it.
This immaculate B&B is located midway between Ispica and the beaches of Pozzallo. It offers pristine rooms, a fabulous pool set amid Mediterranean fruit trees, and glorious, sandy beaches are a five-minute drive away. They also offer bright, simple B&B accommodation in the heart of Pozzallo.

Eating & drinking

Jonico 'a Rutta 'e Ciauli €€€-€
Riviera Dionisio il Grande 194, T0931-65540.
Daily 1230-1500, 2000-2300.
A celebrated seafood restaurant, still more popular with locals than tourists, this is magnificently located in a lavish *stile-Liberty* villa on a clifftop overlooking a beautiful cove. It's some distance from Ortigia, so you'll need to get a taxi. Try typical dishes like *pasta con le sarde e finocchio selvatico* (pasta with sardines and wild fennel) or fresh swordfish. Pizza is also served in the evenings on a less formal, but still panoramic, terrace.

Al Mazarì €€
Via G Torres 7, T0931-483690, almazari.com.
Daily 1300-1500, 1930-2300.
An intimate and welcoming restaurant tucked down a tiny side street near the Duomo on Ortigia, this is run by the delightful Roccafiorita family. The Sicilian specialities are prepared with market-fresh seasonal ingredients and include *sàiddi a beccaficu* (boned sardines prepared with grapes, pine nuts and sweet tomatoes) and superb home-made desserts. Highly recommended.

Ristorante Andrea €€
Via Maddalena 24, Palazzolo Acreide, T0931-881488, ristoranteandrea.it.
Wed-Mon 1230-1500, 1930-2200.
Behind the peeling exterior of a tumbling palazzo is this bright, modern restaurant, which promises *sapore montani* (flavours from the mountains) and specializes in recipes from the Iblei Monti. Try ravioli stuffed with ricotta and Bronte pistachios or tender local lamb.

Trattoria La Foglia €€
Via Giuseppe Maria Capodieci 21, T0931-66233, lafoglia.it.
Daily 1230-1500, 2000-2300.
Sculptures by owner Beppe, black and white prints, bunches of dried flowers and a rustic beamed ceiling are all part of the charm of this quirky, family-run restaurant in the heart of Ortigia. Mediterrranean dishes on offer are based on old family recipes, including delicious soups.

Osteria da Mariano €€
Vicolo Zuccalà 9, T0931-67444, osteriadamariano.it.
Wed-Sun 1300-1500, 2000-2300.
This rustic trattoria, prettily set in a series of small rooms with wooden furnishings and checked tablecloths, is hidden down a side street on Ortigia. It specializes in dishes from the Iblei Monti, including platters of

chargrilled meats (lamb, local sausages, chops) or roast rabbit. The antipasti is excellent, and there's a good range of fish dishes as well.

Cafés & bars

Bar Tabacchi Maestranza
Via Maestranza 15, T0931-463740.
Mon-Fri 0600-2100, Sat-Sun 0600-2400.
A friendly Ortigia *tabacchi* at the front, but behind the shop area is a simple, untouristy café where locals come for breakfast, a lunch from the *tavola calda*, or a beer or two in the evenings.

Le Antiche Siracuse
Via Maestranza 2, T0931-483003.
Daily 0700-2100.
There's nothing 'antiche' about this modern café just off Ortigia's piazza Archimede, but it's the best place to come for breakfast because the pastries and *cornetti* are made by Corsino, a *pasticcerie* in Piazzolo Acreide.

Gran Caffè del Duomo
Piazzo Duomo 18-19, T0931-21544, grancaffedelduomo.com.
Daily 0700-2400.
This plush café has a superb location on Ortigia's main square, with a shaded terrace overlooking the Duomo. There's a restaurant, bar and a wide selection of ice creams to choose from, although prices reflect the sublime location.

Duomo €€€€
Via Capitano Boccheri 31,
T093-265 1265,
ristoranteduomo.it.
Oct-Apr Sun 1300-1500, Tue-Sat
1300-1500, 2000-2300; May-Sep
Mon 2000-2300, Tue-Sat
2000-2300 (in Aug, also open
Wed and Fri lunchtimes).
Closed 10 days in Jan, 10 days in
Jul, 10 days in Nov.
The restaurant everyone is
talking about: chef Ciccio
Sultano has won every major
European culinary award,
including Michelin stars. The
menu is a balanced fusion of
tradition and innovation, with
dishes such as octopus and
squid prepared with Burrata di
Andria (a mozzarella-like cheese),
or the classic dish of fettuccine
with lamb ragout. Finish up with
the *cannolo* with ricotta.

Fattoria delle Torri €€€€
Vico Napolitano 14, Modica,
T0932-751286.
Tue-Sun 1300-1500, 2000-2300.
An early 19th-century mansion
houses this smart restaurant,
with an elegant, light-filled
dining room and a terrace out in
a courtyard perfumed with
lemon trees. Sublime local dishes
include the Sicilian staple
caponata, prepared here with
roasted vegetables, and the
outstanding house speciality *u*
lebbru 'nciucculattatu, rabbit
cooked in chocolate.

Taverna La Cialoma €€
Piazza Regina Margherita 23,
Marzamemi, T093-184 1772.
Daily 1200-1500, 1900-2200.
This restaurant sits on the main
square of Marzamemi, a fishing
village 23 km south of Noto. Fish
features prominently on the
menu, which offers simple
Sicilian fare. Prices are reasonable,
and service is friendly. Book in
advance in summer.

Trattoria del Carmine €€
Via Ducezio 9, T0931-838705,
trattoriadelcarmine.it.
Mon-Sat 1200-1530, 1930-2400.
A simple trattoria serving classic
Sicilian cuisine. Start with their
antipasti, then follow up with
pasta *alla Norma* (pasta with an
aubergine and ricotta sauce) and
the fresh fish of the day. Booking
is recommended in summer.

**Trattoria Crocifisso Da
Baglieri €€**
Via Principe Umberto 48,
T0931-571151.
Thu-Tue 1230-1500, 1900-2400.
For excellent traditional Sicilian
cuisine, few places can beat this
old-fashioned trattoria, which is
run by the welcoming Baglieri
family. Delicious hand-made
pasta dishes include *ravioli di
ricotta* with a pork ragout, or you
could try the *insalata tiepida di
polpo, patate e olive* (octopus
salad, with potatoes and olives).

Cafés & bars
Alla Vecchia Fontana
Corso Vittorio Emanuele III 150,
T0931-839412.
Elegant café for coffee, cakes and
ice cream, handily located on
Noto's main drag and perfect for
a break from sightseeing.

Entertainment

La Gazza Ladra €€€€
*Via Blandini 5, Modica,
T0932-755655,
ristorantelagazzaladra.it.*
Sun 1300-1500, Tue-Sat
1300-1500, 2000-2300.
Part of the sumptuous Palazzo
Failla hotel in Modica Alta, this
award-winning restaurant ('the
thieving magpie') is one of the
best in Sicily. Assured, creative
cuisine based on the freshest
seasonal produce includes such
dishes as couscous with squid ink
and shellfish. Excellent
fixed-price menus showcase the
highlights: *La Tradizione* (€60, six
courses) or *La Gazza Ladra* (€75,
nine courses), excluding wines.

Monna Lisa €
*Via Ettore Fieramosca 1,
T0932-642250.*
Tue-Sun 1300-1500, 2000-2300.
A friendly, rustic restaurant
serving delicious pizzas, this has
a pretty internal courtyard for

outdoor dining. If you're on a
budget, this is the place to go.
The only drawback is that it's on
the very edge of Ragusa.

Cafés & bars
Bar Sicilia
*Corso Umberto I 6, Modica,
T0932-943651, barsicilia.it.*
Daily 0500-2000.
A local favourite for coffee, cakes
and ice cream – don't miss the
hot chocolate made with the
famous Modica chocolate.

Gelateria DiVini
*Piazza del Duomo, T0932-
228989, gelatidivini.it.*
Daily 0930-2200.
Every imaginable flavour and
then some: try saffron, liquorice
or honey from the Monti Iblei if
plain old chocolate and vanilla
doesn't do it for you. They also
have a little shop next door with
a good range of local wines.

Children
Piccolo Teatro dei Pupi
*Via della Giudecca 17, T0931-
465550, pupari.com.*
Museum Mar-Sep 1030-1300,
1600-1900, Oct-Dec 1100-1300,
1600-1800. Performances at
1830 and 2130 daily in Aug.
Check schedules for the rest of
the year.
This little theatre is a great place
to see popular Sicilian puppet
theatre (see box, page 85). Even if
there are no performances, you
can visit the museum which
contains historic puppets and
scenery, or check out puppets
being made at the adjoining
workshop.

Clubs
Le Piscine/Discoteca Caligola
*Viale dei Lidi, Fontane Bianche,
Syracuse, T0931-753633.*
Fri-Sat 2200-0330.
South of the city in Fontane
Bianche, a big outdoor disco
with three dance floors, a pool,
which is popular in summer. In
winter, it becomes Caligola.

La Nottola
*Via Gargallo 61, Syracuse,
T0931-60009.*
Mon-Thu 2000-0100, Fri-Sat
2000-0300.
Pizza restaurant, bar and disco
which this is very popular with a
young, studenty crowd.

Shopping

Cavalcata di San Giuseppe
Scicli.
19 Mar.
Horses parade in elaborate costumes made with flower petals.

Easter week
Lavish processions across the region, particularly in Ispica, Modica, Ragusa and Scicli.

Infiorata
Noto
Third Sun in May.
Enormous pictures made from flower petals carpet the streets in Noto's lavish spring festival.

Ciclo di Rappresentazioni Classiche
Syracuse
May-Jun.
Classical theatre festival held at the Teatro Greco.

Books

Biblios Café
Via del Consiglio Reginale 11, Syracuse, T0931-21491, biblios-cafe.it.
More of a café than a bookshop, but this does have a small selection of books on Sicily in English. Italian conversation classes are offered.

Food & drink

Antica Dolceria Bonajuto
Corso Umberto I 159, Modica, T0932-941225, bonajuto.it.
Tue-Sun 0900-1330, 1600-2030.
The oldest chocolate-maker in town and still the best, with a range of local specialities.

Antica Drogheria
Via XXV Aprile 57, Ragusa, T0932-652090.
Mon-Sat 1000-2030, daily in summer.
Sells all kinds of gourmet goodies from charcuterie, cheeses and olive oil to honey, jams and Modica chocolate.

Casa del Formaggio Sant'Anna
Corso Italia 387, Ragusa, T0932-227485, dipasqualeformaggi.it.
Daily 0730-1330, 1630-20, closed Wed afternoon.
Ragusano cheese, made from the milk of rare Razza Modicana cows, is hard to find, but this shop sells the best on the island. It also has a wide selection of other Sicilian cheeses.

Top picnic spots

Greek theatre, Syracuse There are few good picnic spots in central Syracuse, but the Greek theatre is outstanding by any standards, see page 194.

Passeggio Adorno, Syracuse This shaded walk, also known as the Foro Italico, near the Fonte Aretusa is great for a picnic, see page 191.

Castello Eurialo, Syracuse Tuck into your *panini* amid the old stones and wild flowers at this lofty castle, with views across the whole coast, see page 197.

Riserva Naturale Oasi Faunistica di Vendicari You'll have your pick of picnic spots in this magnificent coastal nature reserve, see page 203.

Riserva Naturale Cavagrande del Cassibile, Avola Sit on the river's edge and watch for kingfishers, see page 202.

Vall dell'Anapo, Sortino Famous for the Pantalica necropolis, this protected valley is full of excellent hiking trails and picnic spots, see page 198.

Greek theatre, Syracuse.

Activities & tours

What the locals say

My favourite place for a romantic meal in Ortigia is Oinos (via della Giudecca 69, T0931-464900, ristoranteoinos.com, closed Sun), which is really beautiful. The interior is all pale colours with white tablecloths, and you can eat outside in the garden in summer. The food is amazing, the wines are really good, and I love their home-made ice cream in summer. It's a little expensive, but worth it.

Alessandro Zito, Syracuse resident.

Gifts

Le Antiche Siracuse
Via Maestranza 2, T0931-483003.
Mon-Sat 0900-2000.
The celebrated *café-pasticceria* also has an adjoining gift shop, with a range of local ceramics, plus wines, oils and more.

Ortigia
Via Maestranza 12, Ortigia, Syracuse, T0931-461365.
Mon-Sat 0900-1300, 1600-2000.
Upmarket Ortigia toiletries, candles and more, with colourful and distinctive packaging (inspired by the Roman mosaics in Piazza Armerina).

Hypermarket

Carrefour Siracusa
Via Necropoli del Fusco, Syracuse, T800-650650.
Mon-Sat 0900-2100.
This huge hypermarket is handy for supplies if you are self-catering. It's also good for other basics – beach towels, flip-flops, plug adaptors, toys, etc.

Outdoor equipment

Hang Loose Surf Shop
Via E di Giovanni 66/68, Syracuse, T0931-441486.
Boards, clothing and everything you need if the waves at the Isola delle Correnti are calling.

Cultural

Hermes Sicily
T334-769 9195 (mobile), hermes-sicily.com.
Hermes offer a range of guided tours in Syracuse and southeastern Sicily. These include tours to Noto and Ragusa, as well as the Vendicari reserve and the Roman villa at Tellaro. Tours and prices vary.

Cycling

Hybla Biking
Via del Bagolaro 9, Contrada Fortugnello, Ragusa, T0932-667419, hyblabike.com.
This company offers mountain-bike rental, and also runs guided bike tours. These accommodate bikers of all levels, with simple rides for beginners to more demanding routes for experienced cyclists.

Food & wine

Love Sicily
Via Sicilia 72, Ispica, T0932-950222 (UK T+44 (0)208-133 6251).
This cookery school in Modica offers week-long group classes, including accommodation, as well as tailor-made cookery classes which can be as short as half a day.

Transport

Syracuse

Syracuse is on the main train line from Messina via Catania, with several departures daily (Messina 3 hrs, Catania 1 hr 45 mins). There are direct trains to Noto (30 mins) and, less frequently, to Modica (1 hr 40 mins) and Ragusa (2 hrs 20 mins). There are no direct trains between Palermo and Syracuse: you will need to change at Catania.

It is usually easier to get around the region by bus. **AST** (T840-323 0000) runs local bus services from Syracuse to Noto (1 hr), Ragusa (via Palazzolo Acreide, 2 hrs), Modica (1 hr 30 mins), Catania (including the airport, 2 hrs) as well as services to the smaller towns and villages, including Avola, Palazzolo Acreide and Lentini. AST bus services also link Pozzalo, Pachino, Scicli with Ragusa. **Interbus** (T091-342525, interbus. it) run bus services between Syracuse and Catania (including the airport, 2 hrs) and Messina.

Noto

Regional trains depart regularly from Noto to Syracuse (at least 6 daily, 30 mins). There are three direct trains a day to Ragusa (1 hr 40 mins) plus a couple of slow services with a change (usually at Modica). There are at least five services daily to Modica (1 hr 10 mins).

AST (T840-000323, aziendasicilianatrasporti.it) is the main bus company in the area. It operates services from Noto to Syracuse (roughly every hour, about 10 daily, 55 mins), with stops at Avola (15 mins) and Cassibile (25 mins); Ispica (about 6 daily, 1 hr 25 mins); Ragusa (about 6 daily, 2 hrs); Comiso (2 hrs 25 mins); and Vittorio (2 hrs 45 mins). It also runs direct buses to Catania (1 hr 40 mins) and Catania airport (1 hr 25 mins).

Ragusa

Trains link Ragusa with Syracuse (3 services a day, 2 hrs). There are three trains a day to Noto (1 hr 40 mins); five a day to Gela (1 hr 15 mins); three a day to Avola (1 hr 30 mins); and three a day to Syracuse (2 hrs).

AST buses (see details above) offer services from Ragusa to Syracuse (at least 4 daily, 2 hrs 20 mins); Pachino (at least 2 daily, 1 hr 30 mins), for connections to Marzamemi and Portopalo; Modica (9 daily, 30-45 mins); Scicli (8 daily, 1 hr 15 mins) and Ispica (3 daily, 1 hr 15 mins). All bus services are considerably reduced on Sundays. There are at least two buses a day to Palermo (5 hrs 15 mins). There are summer-only buses between Modica and Modica Marina and the other beach resorts along the Ragusan coast.

Contents

Central & Southern Sicily

Palace of Filipo Bentivegna.

Introduction

What to see in...

...one day
Spend the morning at the **Villa Romana** in **Piazza Armerina**, then return to **Enna** after lunch for an afternoon stroll around its old quarter, and sunset views from the castle. Alternatively, consider spending the morning exploring the **Valley of the Temples**, perhaps with a picnic lunch in the **Kolymbreta Garden**, and then a lazy afternoon swimming by the **Scala dei Turchi**.

N owhere is the divide between Sicily's ancient glories and modern privations more obviously pronounced than in its heartland. This region contains two of the island's top attractions in the magnificent Valley of the Temples in Agrigento and the Villa Romana in Piazza Armerina – as well as some of its poorest communities (where the Mafia, unfortunately, still holds sway).

Central Sicily, with its gentle peaks and endless fields of wheat, is the region which has changed least since Giuseppe di Lampedusa so lyrically described its pastoral beauty in *The Leopard*. Its capital is lofty Enna, the 'belvedere of Sicily', and a string of time-worn villages are scattered amid the hills. There are more serene and solitary ancient ruins at Morgantina, and some less poetic reminders of recent Sicilian history in the defunct sulphur mines that scar the hillsides. The southern coast boomed thanks to sulphur, and Porto Empedocle and Gela remain busy (if decidedly unattractive) port towns.

Fortunately, swathes of this coastline have been left undeveloped, and it has some heavenly, empty beaches, particularly those around the colourful little resort of Sciacca. The prize for most beautiful beaches in Sicily may well go to the sun-bleached trio of Pelagie Islands, where giant loggerhead turtles come to nest.

...a weekend or more
With more time you could combine the above itineraries, and add a day or so exploring the hill towns north of Enna, or the beaches and resorts of Agrigento. With at least a long weekend to spare, consider a trip to the Pelagie Islands for some diving and sunbathing.

Agrigento Bay.

Enna & around

Perched high on a cloud-shrouded mountain top at the very centre of Sicily, Enna is the highest provincial capital in Europe and one of the oldest continually inhabited cities on the island. It is often called the belvedere of Sicily for the tremendous views over rippling, wheat-covered hills, a landscape that has changed little since the days when much of the grain for the Roman Empire came from around Enna. This quiet, agricultural region makes an excellent base for a relaxed holiday and a taste of genuine Sicilian rural life. For those passing through, the must-see sight is the Villa Romana del Casale at Piazza Armerina, with its wonderful mosaic decoration.

Enna.

In Enna Alta – a straggle of little squares, churches and worn palazzi strung out along a lofty ridge – the narrow streets still retain their medieval feel. Almost all of the important sights are clustered around the via Roma, Enna's main artery, which sweeps up to the city's grandest monument, the 13th-century Castello di Lombardia, from where there are glorious views across to the Madonie mountains.

Castello di Lombardia & Rocca di Cerere

Daily 0900-1300, 1500-1800, free.

The huge, stark ruins of Sicily's largest castle remain a stirring sight. An ancient Arab fortress, it was substantially enlarged under the Normans and the Aragonese. Just six of the original 20 towers have survived, and only one, the Torre Pisana, can be climbed. The views are extraordinary, encompassing a great swathe of central Sicily and even – on cloudless days – stretching all the way to Etna. There are a couple of stone benches, good for picnic lunches, and the main courtyard is used as an open-air theatre in summer. Just outside is a statue of Eunus, leader of the first Slave Revolt against the Romans (see History, page 31).

Below the castle, a path leads to the **Rocca di Cerere** (Rock of Ceres, perhaps better known by her Greek name Demeter), where a famous shrine to the great earth mother goddess once stood. Its size and beauty were legendary in ancient times: it was said to contain a statue of such beauty that many believed it to be Demeter herself.

Duomo

Via Roma/piazza Mazzini, T0935-500940.
Daily 0900-1200, 1600-1900, free.

Enna's handsome cathedral, the most elaborate of the city's many churches, is a Baroque restoration of a 14th-century original, constructed over the remnants of an ancient temple to Persephone. The main façade rises grandly over the piazza Mazzini,

Essentials

❶ Getting around The tiny centre of Enna Alta is easy to get around on foot; visitors won't need (or want) to spend time in Enna Bassa, the modern sprawl which spreads beneath the old town.

❷ Bus station Most local and inter-urban bus services (SAIS, T800-211020, saisautolinee.it) stop at the piazza Vittorio Emanuele, on the edge of Enna Alta.

❸ Train station The train station is located 5 km from the city centre, at the base of the steep hill. There are taxis outside the station, or you can catch the infrequent (hourly) local shuttle bus up the hill to the town centre.

❹ ATM Banco di Sicilia, piazza Umberto I 1, T0935-48111.

❺ Hospital Azienda Ospedaliera Umberto I, Contrada Ferrante, T0935-516111, (emergencies T0935-516152), ospedaleenna.it.

❻ Pharmacy Farmacia del Centro, 315 via Roma, T0935-500650, Mon-Sat 0900-1300, 1630-1900.

❼ Post office Via Agira 2, T0935-519501, Mon-Fri 0800-1330, Sat 0800-1230.

❽ Tourist information Via Roma 413, T0935-528288, ennaturismo.info.

and is topped with an elegant bell tower. Inside, an elaborate carved and gilded ceiling in the nave is supported by black basalt columns with fantastical creatures writhing around the bases and capitals. One chapel contains the Nave d'Oro – the 'golden boat' in which the statue of the Madonna della Visitazione, Enna's beloved patron saint, is paraded around the city every year on 2 July.

Just behind the Duomo, the **Museo Alessi** (via Roma 465, T0935-501365, closed indefinitely) contains the cathedral treasury, including the magnificent 17th-century Crown of the Madonna, created for the city's patron saint (held in the Duomo), and studded with gems. The nearby **Museo Archeologico** (piazza Mazzini, T0935-528127, closed at the time of writing) is notable more for its splendid setting, the sumptuous Palazzo Varisano, than for its rather thin collection.

Easter in Enna

There's a distinctly Spanish flavour in Enna during Holy Week (*Settimana Santa*). The Aragonese, who ruled Sicily from the 15th to 17th centuries, organized the city's existing local guilds into confraternities, and the traditions established all those centuries ago have survived intact to this day. Enna now has 15 confraternities (originally there were 34), each attached to a different church, which together boast more than 2000 members. Solemn processions take place throughout the week, but the main event begins on the evening of Good Friday. Dressed in their traditional garb of cloaks and hoods, the men (no women are admitted) carry two spectacularly heavy floats bearing images of the Dead Christ and Our Lady of Sorrows through the crowded yet eerily silent streets. Easter Sunday is all about celebration, and the church bells begin to peal joyously at the meeting of the statues of the Resurrected Christ and Mary. On Albis Sunday, a week later, in a tradition that pre-dates the Aragonese occupation, or even the guilds, the confraternity of the Holy Saviour blesses Enna's abundant and fertile fields from the Castello di Lombardia.

Torre di Federico II

Via Torre di Federico.
Daily 0800-1800, free.

At the western extreme of the via Roma, the sturdy octagonal tower named after Federico II sits in public gardens above the ugly jumble of modern Enna Bassa. It's the only survivor of the ancient city walls, which once bristled with fortifications and ensured Enna's legendary impregnability.

Around Enna

Around Enna are a clutch of sleepy medieval villages, set amid the lonely peaks of the Monti Erei. Also here is Sicily's only natural lake, and some of the most beautiful and isolated ancient ruins on the island at Morgantina. The biggest draw by far, however, is the Villa Romana di Casale at Piazza Armerina, a luxurious Imperial retreat, with the finest late Roman mosaic decoration to be found anywhere.

North & east of Enna

From Enna, you will have spotted the picturesque outline of medieval **Calascibetta**, on a hilltop overlooking a sea of olive groves and cornfields, 6 km from the provincial capital. From here the scrubby, empty peaks of the Monti Erei unfold. Beyond vertical **Leonforte**, with a creamy Baroque church and a 17th-century fountain with 24 spouts, are quiet villages like medieval **Assoro**, lofty **Agira**, and lovely, remote **Centuripe**. Further north, **Nicosia**, a shabby but appealing ancient town huddled beneath a jutting crag, sits on the southernmost reaches of the Madonie natural park (see page 118). To the east of Nicosia, **Troina**, with a tiny crooked heart, is, at 1121 m, one of the highest villages in Sicily. From here, the vast silhouette of Mount Etna seems to fill the entire sky.

South of Enna

Sicily's only natural lake, the **Lago di Pergusa** (5 km south of Enna, bus No 5 from the city centre) is where Demeter's daughter Persephone is said to have descended into the underworld in the ancient legend. In the 1960s, insanely, this idyllic spot was chosen as the location for a motor-racing track, the Autodromo di Pergusa, which still hugs the lake shores – even though the area is now a nature reserve and a protected bird sanctuary.

Continuing south along the S117b, the sun-bleached fields give way gradually to luxuriant forest and orchards. In this green corner, 35 km southeast of Enna, the tranquil country town of **Piazza Armerina** is splayed over three gentle hills and topped with a medieval castle and a huge Baroque cathedral. The old town is sprinkled with Baroque churches and faded palazzi of golden stone, which make a theatrical setting for the annual Palio dei Normanni (14-15 August), a medieval festival which recreates the entrance of the first Norman ruler, Roger I (1031-1101) with costumed jousting and parades.

Caltagirone

30 km south of Piazza Armerina.

Spread over three hills, this large town is famous throughout Italy for the colourful, hand-painted ceramics produced here since Arabic times. The celebrated **La Scala,** a grand staircase of 142 ceramic-encrusted steps, links the upper and lower parts of town, and is flanked on either side by shops selling local crafts. Come in May to see the steps carpeted with flower petals, or on 24-25 July, when they are beautifully lit with glowing lanterns in honour of San Giacomo, the city's patron saint. The **Museo Regionale della Ceramica** (via Giardino Pubblico, T0933-58418, 0900-1830, €3/2 concession) contains ceramics from across Sicily, with examples dating back to the Middle Ages. The **Duomo** sports a *stile-Liberty* façade.

Morgantina

Contrada Morgantina, Aidone, T0935-87955.
Daily 0800 till 1 hr before dusk, free.
20 km northeast of Piazza Armerina.

The ruins of ancient Morgantina are dreamily set in green hills 2 km east of the pretty town of Aidone. This beautiful spot enticed settlers as early as 1300 BC, and later became a wealthy and influential Syracusan colony. It was razed during the Punic wars, subsequently rebuilt by the Romans, but, by the first century BC, it had lost its importance and was gradually abandoned. Enough survives to give visitors a sense of the grandeur of the ancient city, particularly the theatre which is built into the hillside and is still occasionally used for concerts (the acoustics are said to be perfect). Behind it are the remnants of the Sanctuary of Demeter, and beyond, on the hilltop, the House of Ganymede, which contains some early mosaics. Some of the finds from the site are displayed in the **Museo Archeologico di Aidone** (Largo Torres Trupia, T0935-587307, Tue-Sun 0800-1830, €3/2 concession), a small archaeology museum housed in a restored convent in nearby Aidone.

Mosaic at Piazza Armerina.

Caltanissetta

36 km southwest of Enna.

This raffish provincial capital, with its serpentine streets, petite Baroque cathedral and raucous street market (via Benitendi), maintains a cheerful air despite the odds, for this is one of the most poverty-stricken regions in Sicily. It was the centre of the dangerous and exploitative sulphur industry for many years, but when production collapsed in the 1950s the jobs disappeared. Caltanissetta was heavily bombed during the Second World War, and a grim belt of concrete towers surrounds it, but the old town, with its sprinkling of battered churches, and old-fashioned shops, cafés and bars (where you can try the local Amaro Averna liqueur, a bitter-sweet *digestivo*) is an authentic delight. There are a couple of museums: the interesting **Museo Archeologico di Caltanissetta** (via S Spirito, T0934-25936, 0900-1300, 1530-1900, €2.50), with ceramics, jewellery and votive offerings dating back to the third millennium BC, and the **Museo Mineralogico** (viale della Regione 71, T0934-591280, Mon-Fri 0900-1300, €1.50) which describes the local mining industry. Impossibly perched on a sheer jagged rock on the outskirts of town are the sparse remnants of the **Castello di Pietrarossa,** an Arabic fortress expanded by the Normans.

Mosaics at Villa Romana del Casale

❶ **Corridoio della Grande Caccia** The Corridor of the Great Hunt is the largest and most impressive of the villa's mosaic scenes.

❷ **Sala Ragazze in Bikini** The Room with the Bikini-clad Girls depicts 10 athletic young women in suprisingly modern-looking outfits.

❸ **Diaeta di Orfeo** In the Hall of Orpheus, all kinds of animals fall under the spell of the god's lyre.

❹ **Vestibolo di Polifemo** The Vestibule of Polyphemus contains a superb depiction of the famous scene from the *Odyssey* when Ulysses offers drugged wine to the Cyclops Polyphemus.

❺ **Triclinio** The entire floor of this Banquet Hall, more than 250 sq m, is covered with mosaic scenes.

Detail from the Corridor of the Great Hunt.

Mosaic restoration at Villa Romana del Casale.

Villa Romana del Casale

Piazza Armerina, T339-265 7640, villaromanadelcasale.it.
Daily, €3, free for EU citizens under 18 and over 65. About 5 km from the centre of Piazza Armerina, linked by local bus Apr-Sep.

Listed as a UNESCO World Heritage Site, the Villa Romana del Casale is one of the most important surviving Roman monuments. The palatial residence is crammed with dazzling and extensive mosaics – room after room of exquisitely rendered scenes of extraordinary naturalism and vivacity. The extent and quality of the decoration has led some scholars to believe that it belonged to Maximian (Maximianus Herculeus) (AD 286-305), Diocletian's co-emperor and ruler of the Western Empire; others contend that it belonged to an important landowner. The villa was built during the first decades of the fourth century AD, when Sicily, after two centuries of decline, was once again a power to be reckoned with, thanks to its strategic location on new trans-Mediterranean trade routes. Rich landowners built huge country villas at the centre of their vast estates, and embellished them extravagantly. None was more lavish than the villa at Casale: more than 3500 sq m of mosaics survive, the most extensive group to survive in situ anywhere. The villa was gradually abandoned, and finally, in the 12th century, it was buried by a mud slide, and forgotten for hundreds of years. The earliest excavations in the early 1800s gave little indication of the riches buried under the earth, and it wasn't until the early 20th century that the full extent of the find became apparent. The most extensive excavations took place in the 1950s, but work is ongoing. Until recently, the villa was covered with a clear roof, but this caused a greenhouse effect which damaged the mosaics. A new, more controversial, shelter was unveiled in early 2009, made of contemporary materials, but suggests the form of the original roof in its form.

Visitors entered the villa through the atrium, a forecourt overlooked by the remains of a triumphal arch. Beyond the atrium, the main reception hall leads to the peristyle at the heart of the complex, an elegantly proportioned courtyard which would once have been filled with sweet-smelling herbs and flowers. The Salone del Circo, a small gym for use before entering the baths, is vividly decorated with a circus scene from the Circus Maximus in Rome. Another vestibule contains a fascinating portrait mosaic of the mistress of the house on the way to the baths (possibly Eutropia, wife of Maximianus, flanked by her children, Maxentius on the right and Fausta to the left). The guest rooms, linked to the peristyle, are profusely decorated with dozens of lively scenes, including a small but action-packed hunting scene.

This is merely a taster for the villa's most spectacular mosaic series, which spans the length of an entire hall: the **Corridoio della Grande Caccia** (Corridor of the Great Hunt), which depicts the capture of wild beasts from across the Roman empire for the *venationes* (bloody spectacles held in honour of Diana, the goddess of hunting, at the Colosseum in Rome). The corridor itself represents the entire Roman Empire, with female allegories at either end symbolizing Mauritania and India (the boundaries of the known world), and Rome itself at the centre. Even after all these centuries, the mosaic pulses with life, and the stories it depicts are as enthralling (and gory) as ever. At the furthest extremes of the hall, the hunt begins in the most remote corners of the empire, with hunters baiting a leopard, or being attacked by a wounded lion, and moves gradually through increasingly civilized regions (note the houses in the background)

before reaching the port. Here, slaves drag the animals on to a boat, which is seen docking at Rome in the central scene. Each scene is depicted with extraordinary energy and naturalism, from the coiled spring of the leopard leaping on to the antelope's back to the gush of scarlet blood.

Beyond a small anteroom is the famous **Sala Ragazze in Bikini** (Room of the Bikini-clad Girls) with 10 bikini-clad women lifting weights, throwing the discus, and accepting prizes. In the **Diaeta di Orfeo** (Room of Orpheus), a music room, Orpheus holds the animals spellbound with his lyre. The grandest room of all is the **Triclinio** (Banquet Hall), with a superb mosaic floor measuring over 250 sq m vigorously describing the 12 labours of Hercules. Other legendary scenes occupy the apses. The private apartments contain more rich decoration, notably the bed chambers. Look for Ulysses offering the cyclops Polyphemus a glass of wine in the **Vestibolo di Polifemo** (Vestibule of Polyphemus), and beyond it, in another bedroom, a steamy mosaic of a semi-naked couple embracing.

Agrigento & around

Wrapped in the dirt-grey tentacles of a highway on stilts, Agrigento, at first glimpse, is a miserable sight. But hidden behind these concrete horrors is a rambling old town of cobbled streets and pretty squares high on a hilltop, and, strung out along a ridge dominating the valley below, the magnificent Valley of the Temples, a UNESCO World Heritage Site and the most impressive surviving temple complex outside mainland Greece. More superb archaeological sites dot this coast, including Eraclea Minoa, which boasts a panoramic theatre overlooking the sea. Further west, Sciacca is tucked behind medieval walls and overlooks a busy fishing port. Its long beaches of golden sand are a big favourite with Sicilian families.

Agrigento bay.

Ancient Akragas, which would become known as Agrigentum under the Romans, was one of the most powerful colonies of Magna Graecia. Brace yourself for the shocking intrusion of illegal construction, with shoddy concrete apartment buildings and hotels encroaching on the protected heritage site. This grim sight is relieved only by the orchards of almond trees, which burst into clouds of palest pink in February and March.

Valle dei Templi

Piazzale dei Templi, off the passeggiata Archeologica, T0922-497226, parcovalledeitempli.it.
Collina dei Templi daily 0830-1900, Nov-Apr 1000-1730, Area di Zeus May-Oct 0830-1700, Nov-Apr 1000-1700, €8/4 concession, €10/5 combined ticket for temples and archaeological museum. Kolymbetra Garden 1000 till dusk, €2. Illuminated hill Jul-Aug Mon-Fri 2000-2200, Sat-Sun 2000-2130, €8, no concessions.

In the entire Mediterranean world, few sights evoke the splendour of ancient Greece like the great temple complex of Agrigento. Despite the name, the temples are actually set above the valley, where they loom imposingly from a high ridge and once beckoned to sailors. Sadly, creeping illegal development has substantially blighted their beauty, which once induced Goethe to sigh: "We shall never in our lives be able to rejoice again, after seeing such a stupendous view in this splendid valley." Akragas was founded in the sixth century

Essentials

❶ Getting around While the historic centre of Agrigento is small and easy to get around on foot (if rather steep in places), the Valley of the Temples is 2 km from the centre – it's served by city buses 1, 2 or 3, which leave regularly from outside the train station.
❷ Bus station The main inter-urban bus station is on piazza Rosselli. Local buses depart from the piazza Marconi, outside the train station.
❸ Train station Agrigento Central, piazza Guglielmo Marconi.
❹ ATM Banco di Sicilia, via Atenea 119, T0922-402748; Banco d'Italia, via Crispi Francesco 6, T0922-20589.
❺ Hospital Ospedale S Giovanni di Dio, Contrada Consolida, T0922-441846, agrigento-hospital.it.
❻ Pharmacy Farmacia Averna Dottor Antonio, via Atenea 325, T0922-26093, Mon-Sat 0900-1300, 1700-1930.
❼ Post office Via Antonino Pancamo 10, T0922-604546, Mon-Fri 0800-1330, Sat 0800-1230.
❽ Tourist information AAPIT, viale della Vittoria 225, T0922-401352; AAST, via Cesare Battisti 15, T0922-20454.

Tip...

The best time to visit Agrigento is in spring, when the almond blossom is in bloom. The main temple site (Collina dei Templi) is very exposed and extremely hot in summer. Late autumn is also a good time to come, when the weather is mild and there are no crowds.

Concordia temple, Agrigento.

Doric temple, Agrigento.

> ❝
> The most beautiful of mortal cities.
> *Pindar, Ancient Greek poet, speaking of Akragas.* ❞

Valle dei Templi essentials

The main area of the archaeological park is divided into three sections: the Collina dei Templi, the Area di Zeus and the Giardino dell Kolymbetra. The first two are accessed with the same ticket, while the Kolymbetra Garden has separate admission. The main entrance gates to all three sections are on the piazzale dei Templi, passeggiata Archeologica, 2 km from the centre: take city buses 1, 2 or 3 from outside the train station. There is also a small ticket office at the eastern end of the via Sacra, near the Temple of Hera, on the via Panoramica dei Templi. There is a small café at the main entrance, and another on the via Sacra by the Temple of Hera. More ruins, including the Hellenistic-Roman district, are located near the archaeological museum. This is not open to the public but can be viewed from the road.

BC, as a subcolony of Gela, but became one of the richest and most powerful colonies in Magna Graecia. After it was destroyed by the Carthaginians in 406 BC, it didn't regain its former influence until the Romans captured it in 210 BC and renamed it Agrigentum. At its height, Agrigento boasted a population of 200,000: four times the current number of inhabitants.

The finest surviving monuments of ancient Akragas are found along the via Sacra, where several temples in the Doric style were erected during the sixth and fifth centuries BC. Closest to the entrance gate by the piazzale dei Templi is the **Tempio di Ercole** (Temple of Heracles), whose eight intact columns were re-erected in the 1920s, while fragments of the rest are scattered nearby. Beyond it is the supremely graceful, golden **Tempio della Concordia** (Temple of Concord), which is the best preserved of the group, probably because it was converted into a Christian church in the sixth century AD. At the end of this section of the via Sacra is the **Tempio di Giunone** (Temple of Hera/Juno), smaller than the Temple of Concord but remarkably intact and exquisitely located. This trio is spectacular in the evening, burnished gold by the setting sun and beautifully illuminated after nightfall. There are two more temples at the other end of the via Sacra, accessed via a gate on the piazzale dei Templi. The massive stones on the right are all that remain of the **Tempio di Giove Olimpico** (Temple of Olympian Zeus/Jupiter), which archaeologists believe was once the largest Doric temple ever built (although it was never completed). Beyond it are the remnants of the **Tempio di Castore e Polluce** (Temple of Castor and Pollux), with a group of columns re-erected in the early 19th century.

An entrance near the Temple of Olympian Zeus/Jupiter leads to the **Giardino della Kolymbetra** (Kolymbetra Garden), the most recent archaeological area to be opened to visitors, and perhaps the most poetic. It was once a beautiful lake, dug out by slaves for the tyrant Theron, and surrounded by gardens, but it was later filled in and then used as an orchard by the Arabs. Now, huge stones are half-hidden by luxuriant greenery, and trees frame beautiful views of the distant temples.

Museo Regionale Archeologico

Contrada San Nicola, via dei Templi, T0922-497111, parcovalledeitempli.it.
Tue-Sat 0900-1900, Sun-Mon 0900-1300, €6/3 concession, €10/5 combined ticket with archaeological zone, €5 audio guide.

Agrigento's excellent archaeological museum is bright, modern and – almost uniquely in Sicily – provides visitor information in several languages. The museum is organized chronologically and contains finds dating back to the earliest Neolithic settlements, as well as those from ancient Akragas and other important Greek colonies in the region, such as Gela and Eraclea Minoa. In **Room III**, there is an outstanding collection of red-figure and black-figure Attic vases from the sixth to fifth centuries BC, including the famous *Crater of*

Luigi Pirandello (1867-1936)

Luigi Pirandello was born in Agrigento in 1867, although he moved to Palermo with his family in 1880. He was a prolific writer, producing novels, plays and short stories, but he shot to fame with *Sei personaggi in cerca d'autore (Six Characters in Search of an Author)*, which appeared in 1921. This split the critics on its first appearance, but would become profoundly influential in the development of contemporary drama. In 1934, Pirandello was awarded the Nobel prize for literature. His birthplace in the suburb of Caos, south of Agrigento, is now a small museum (T0922-511826, daily 0900-1200, 1500-1900, €2).

Dionysios. **Room VI** contains the huge *telamones* (colossal human figures) which once decorated the massive temple of Olympian Zeus. One, which is more than 7 m high, has been reconstructed from the remnants found at the site, while three massive heads sit by the wall. **Room X** contains the famous marble statue of *Ephebus of Agrigento*, a young athlete who lived in the fifth century BC. There are Roman sarcophagi in **Room XI**, including a tiny one which belonged to a child, and a red-figured crater from Gela in **Room XV**.

The museum sits in a garden next to the graceful 13th-century **church of San Nicola**. This was built with volcanic rock taken from the great Temple of Olympian Zeus, and contains a beautiful Roman sarcophagus of white marble, depicting the tragic story of Phaedra and Hippolytus. Excavations next to the museum have revealed the remnants of the **Bouleuterion**, which housed the *boule*, or council of citizens. Across the main road, the fenced-off remains of the Hellenistic-Roman quarter can be viewed from a distance. This residential area was probably developed from the second century BC (first by the Greeks and then by the Romans) and it's possible to make out the remnants of houses with mosaic decoration and even heating arrangements.

Around the island

Agrigento town

The Greek acropolis once occupied the hilltop where Agrigento's old town is now clustered. Barbarian invasions and pirate raids sent the local inhabitants scuttling up from the valley below, and a walled city developed first under the Saracens and then the Normans. Although Agrigento's old town now draws visitors on their way to the temples, rather than for any intrinsic attractions, it is still an enjoyable spot for an amble. From the central piazza Vittorio Emanuele, the via Atenea begins its sinuous ascent. This is the heart of local life, a (usually) pedestrianized street lined with shops, cafés and *pasticcerie*. Off the via Atenea is the **Monastero di Santo Spirito** (Salida Santo Spirito, T0922-590371), a medieval complex containing a florid Baroque church (usually closed) and a folk museum (Mon-Fri 0900-1300, 1500-1800, €2.50); just off the cloister, you can order delicious almond and pistachio *dolci* baked by the nuns. The grand 19th-century **Teatro Pirandello** is named after Agrigento's most famous son, Luigi Pirandello, and there's a small **Museo Civico** (Mon-Fri 0900-1300, 1500-1800, €2.50) in a restored convent on the nearby piazza Pirandello. The 13th-century **Chiesa di Santa Maria dei Greci** was built over the ruins of an ancient Greek temple; the recycled columns are visible in the nave. At the very top of town, up an impressive flight of steps, the severe

Inspector Montalbano

Andrea Camilleri's hugely enjoyable novels featuring the detective Inspector Montalbano are set in the fictional towns of Vigàta (based on Porto Empedocle) and Montelusa (Agrigento). In 2003, the harbour town changed its name officially to Porto Empedocle Vigàta – although you'll only find the name in tourist brochures. Camilleri, who was born in Porto Empedocle in 1925 but lives in Rome, published his first Montalbano novel *La forma dell'Acqua (The Shape of Water)* in 1994. The series has been a huge success, and the fantastic television show, starring Luca Zingaretti, has brought the books to an even wider audience.

lines of Agrigento's **Cattedrale di San Gerlando** (via Duomo, T0922-490011, usually open for mass only) betray its 12th-century Norman origins, although it was significantly remodelled in the 16th and 17th centuries.

Around Agrigento

East to Gela

Ferries for the Pelagie Islands (see page 234) depart from busy **Porto Empedocle**, which was named after the Greek philosopher Empedocles but has recently become famous for its association with another writer, Andrea Camilleri. Just west of Porto

Greek temple at Agrigento.

Empedocle, there is a popular beach by the stunning **Scala dei Turchi**, a huge 'staircase' of the palest stone which has been eroded by the wind and time. Heading east towards Gela, there are more wild and beautiful coves to be found at the base of the Punta Bianca, and near the little resort of **Marina di Palma**. The coastal SS115 continues to **Licata**, a large seaport, with a sprinkling of archaeological remains from ancient **Phintias**, and a likeable, if unremarkable, old centre. Gourmets take note: this humble town is home to what many consider to be the best restaurant on Sicily (see Eating & drinking, page 239). There are some attractive dune-backed beaches on the quiet coastline between Licata and Gela, including one overlooked by a castle at **Falconara** and another, with a couple of beach bars, at **Manfria**.

Gela

72 km east of Agrigento.

Poor Gela may win the prize for ugliest city in Sicily, owing to the presence of a gargantuan oil refinery and unchecked concrete post-war development. It wasn't always thus: Gela was once one of the most powerful city states in Magna Graecia, which conquered a huge swathe of eastern Sicily during the fifth century BC. Only Syracuse withstood its mighty armies, by brokering a truce that offered the Gelans the colony of Kamarina (see page 207). Finds discovered during excavations are displayed in the excellent **Museo Archeologico** (corso Vittorio Emanuele 2, T0933-912626, 0900-1300, 1400 till 1 hr before sunset, €3), which has a superb collection of ceramics and coins, as well as a masterfully carved horse's head that once adorned a fifth-century BC temple, and three exquisite terracotta altars. There are also items salvaged from a Greek trading ship, which sank around 500 BC and was discovered in 1988. It is believed to be the largest of its kind and was finally raised from the sea, to great excitement, in 2008. It was taken to the UK for restoration, and there is a talk of a new museum in Agrigento to house it. Just outside the museum are the remnants of the acropolis.

Gela was badly damaged by bombs during the Second World War but a remarkably intact stretch of third-century BC fortifications, the **Mura Timoleontee di Capo Soprano** (0900 till 1 hr before sunset, €3, includes admission to Gela's Museo Archeologico, see left) have survived on a beautifully unspoilt headland at Capo Soprano.

The concrete eyesores that blight the city are a painful reminder of the stranglehold which the Mafia has long had over the city. This, however, is becoming a thing of the past, thanks in no small part to the determined efforts of Gela's charismatic (and openly gay) mayor, Rosario Crocetta. After a Mafia plot was revealed in 2008, Crocetta was forced to double his bodyguard escort, and now travels with six guards at all times.

On the eastern fringe of the city is a small nature reserve, the **Biviere di Gela**, a marshy wetland with two small lakes which is a haven for birds. There are some beautiful hill towns near Gela, particularly **Butera**, a medieval stronghold up a squiggly mountain road, and **Mazzarino**, with the crumbling remains of a huge 17th-century mansion and a clutch of fine churches.

North of Agrigento

Fourteen km northeast of Agrigento, **Favara** is a handsome little town, with a clutch of Baroque monuments overlooking the central piazza Cavour. Nearby, lost in the hills, **Naro** dominates the

Castle of Chiariamonte, Naro.

Five of the best

Beaches

❶ **Marina di Palma** The stretch of coast near Marina di Palma is characterized by cliffs pierced with a series of delightful, pebbly coves overlooking transparent waters.

❷ **Oasi WWF di Torre Salsa** Wild, sandy beaches backed by dunes, part of a nature reserve.

❸ **Eraclea Minoa** Quite possibly the most photographed beach in southern Sicily, this is backed by pine forest and tall, white cliffs.

❹ **Sciacca** Sciacca's town beach has great facilities, shallow waters, and swathes of pale sand, making it perfect for families.

❺ **Spiaggia dei Conigli, Lampedusa** The most famous beach on the island, where the loggerhead turtles come to breed, and where tourists roast on the whitest, finest sand in Sicily.

Eraclea Minoa.

surrounding countryside from its lofty hilltop. Now a quiet agricultural town overlooking a huge reservoir, it was once a medieval citadel prized for its strategic location. A sturdy 14th-century castle and a handful of faded palazzi and churches are poignant reminders of its glorious past. Perhaps the strangest sight around Agrigento is the black, bubbling landscape of the **Vulcanelli di Maccalube** (15 km north of Agrigento, 3 km outside Aragona). These strange craters belch black clay every few seconds, creating mini-volcanoes up to a metre high and intricate patterns in the sun-baked soil.

West to Sciacca

Back along the coast, **Siculiana** (18 km west of Agrigento) sits on a gentle hill overlooking the sea, surrounded by lush fields of grapes, olives and wheat. The town is topped by the huge Baroque Chiesa Madre. The sandy beaches between Siculiana Marina and Realmonte are beautiful, and a section, the **Oasi WWF di Torre Salsa** (T0922-818220, wwftorresalsa.it) is protected as a nature reserve by the WWF. Seven loggerhead turtles were born here in 2008.

Eraclea Minoa

Contrada Minoa, Eraclea Minoa, T0922-846005. Daily 0900-1900 in summer, otherwise until 1 hr before dusk, €3.
Signposted off the SS115/E931, 6 km west of Siculiana Marina.

The isolated ruins of ancient Eraclea Minoa are magnificently set on a lonely clifftop overlooking the brilliant blue sea. According to legend, King Minos of Crete landed here in pursuit of Daedalus, who had helped Theseus and Ariadne find their way out of the labyrinth. The local king refused to hand over Daedalus, and murdered Minos instead. This panoramic spot was inhabited in Neolithic times, and it was a Phoenician settlement before Greeks from Selinunute (see page 30) arrived in the sixth century BC. It was conquered by the Romans

during the third century BC, but gradually declined over the following centuries. The theatre, built in the third century BC, is the best surviving monument, poised on the cliff edge, and still occasionally used for performances. A museum on site contains finds from the excavations. Below the ruins, there is a stunning, long sandy beach backed by pines, and more secluded coves around the headland of Capo Bianco.

Sciacca

61 km northwest of Agrigento.

Sciacca was founded by the Greeks in the fifth century BC as a spa town for nearby Selinunte (see page 258); its pungent, sulphurous waters are still held to have curative properties. The lovely old town, a tumble of narrow streets overlooking a colourful fishing port, is tucked behind the remnants of 15th-century walls. At the centre of town, the expansive piazza Scandaliato – dotted with palm trees and with pretty views of the higgledy-piggledy harbour and out to sea – is the focal point of the evening *passeggiata*. On the outskirts of town, Sciaccamare is a popular holiday resort, with ranks of concrete hotels overlooking sandy beaches.

Just east of town, signposted off the SS15, the **Castello Incantato** ('Enchanted Castle', Tue-Sat 0900-1300, 1500-1700, free) is actually an old *baglio* (country house), once inhabited by Filippo Bentivegna, who went to America to seek his fortune, and fell in love but was badly beaten by a rival. He returned to Sciacca *"non proprio sano di mente"* (not quite right in the head), as the tourist office frankly puts it, and began to create a fantastical and alluring sculpture garden, chiselling strange stone busts of everyone from his former love to Mussolini and Garibaldi.

The Pelagie Islands

The Pelagie archipelago, a tiny trio of islands comprising Lampedusa, Linosa and Lampione, lies about 210 km south of Agrigento between Tunisia and Malta. In 2002, the three islands were grouped together under the Area Marina Protetta Isole Pelagie nature reserve, which protects the flora, fauna and wildlife with special consideration for the endangered loggerhead turtles which nest here. Lampione, little more than a scrubby rock, is uninhabited, but its rugged coastline is a paradise for snorkellers and divers. Quieter Linosa is the only volcanic island of the three, with black-sand beaches and swirling lava rock formations. Lampedusa, the largest and most developed of the islands, attracts most visitors for its magnificent, Caribbean-style beaches of pristine white sand and spectacularly clean and clear waters. But it isn't just affluent tourists from the north who are drawn to these isolated islands: as the gateway to Europe, Lampedusa also attracts huge numbers of desperate immigrants, who cross from Africa in flimsy boats.

Lampedusa.

Lampedusa

From a distance, Lampedusa is a pale, scrubby rock, tilted sharply, which emerges from a turquoise sea. The northeast has high cliffs and dramatic coves, while the flatter, southwestern coast boasts some of the most beautiful beaches in Sicily. The stunning stretches of white sand lapped by calm, clear waters attract enormous crowds of tourists (mainly from northern Italy), which can triple or even quadruple the island's permanent population. During the peak season of late July and August the tiny island (just 21 sq km) is frankly overwhelmed.

Lampedusa town is a scruffy, low-rise jumble of hotels, restaurants, bike and scooter rental outlets, shops and other services gathered around the busy harbour and adjoining bays. From the port, stretching west along the southern coast, is a succession of breathtaking coves, including Cala Croce, Cala Galera and Cala Greca. Beyond them is the Baia dei Coniglia, a dazzling azure bay fringed with white sand, which gazes across to the **Isola dei Conigli**, named after long-vanished rabbits but now a nature reserve dedicated to the protection of the endangered loggerhead turtle (*caretta caretta*). The island is one of very few places left in the Mediterranean where the sea turtles still regularly lay their eggs, which usually takes place between July and August. Dolphins are a common sight, and fin whales (also endangered in the Mediterranean) can be spotted in spring, when they migrate along Lampedusa's southern coast.

Linosa

Linosa is prettier and greener than big sister Lampedusa, but its volcanic beaches of black sand don't draw the same crowds. A cluster of pastel-coloured cubes are huddled around the port, and the miniature coves are a paradise for scuba-divers. Linosa also boasts a nesting beach for the Mediterranean loggerhead turtle at Cala Pozzolana di Ponente.

Lampione

The smallest of the Pelagie islands is little more than bare rock topped by an unused lighthouse. It's home to a large colony of Cory's shearwater, and the submarine coves and caves are popular with divers (trips depart from Lampedusa).

Linosa.

Sleeping

Villa Gussio-Nicoletti €€€
Contrada Rossi, SS121 Km 94.75 (Stazione Pirato), Leonforte, T0935-903268, villagussio.it.
This pink, listed villa set in extensive grounds 12 km southwest of Leonforte is now a gracious spa hotel, with elegant rooms and a wide range of sports facilities, including archery, canoeing, pool, tennis and a nine-hole golf course. There is also a choice of restaurants and a beauty centre.

Hotel Sicilia €€
Piazza Napoleone Colajanni 7, Enna, T0935-500850, hotelsiciliaenna.it.
Enna has few hotels, and none of them stand out, but the modern Grande Albergo Sicilia is very central (100 m from the Duomo), the staff are friendly and the rooms are pristine – and offered at bargain prices on the website. Family rooms are good value.

Masseria Mandrascate €€
SP4 Km 9.80, Valguarnera, T0935-958502, masseriamandrascate.it.
This magnificent 17th-century fortified farm of cool grey stone is beautifully set midway between Piazza Armerina and Caltagirone amid olive groves and green hills. The bedrooms here have stone walls, wooden beams, and plush modern furnishings in shades of cream and beige. The gardens contain a large pool, and you can taste the farm's own fabulous olive oil and wines. There's no restaurant, but charming Rosita will prepare dinner on request (once tasted, you may never want to eat anywhere else).

Suite d'Autore €€
Via Monte 1, Piazza Armerina, T0935-688553, suitedautore.it.
A designer art hotel is probably the last thing you'd expect to find in Piazza Armerina, but Ettore Massina has developed exactly that. The hotel has been decorated and furnished by up-and-coming artists from around the world, and if you see a painting, a lamp, or a table that you fancy, they're all available for sale. There are seven spacious rooms, the best with stunning views over the Duomo.

La Casa sulla Collina d'Oro €€-€
Via P Mattarella, Piazza Armerina, T0935-89680, lacasasullacollinadoro.it.
Guests find it hard to leave this wonderful, welcoming B&B, run by a charismatic and expansive couple. It sits on the hill above Piazza Armerina (a 10-minute walk from the centre), and offers five stylish rooms, some with magnificent views. Breakfast, which includes home-made jams, cheeses, and fabulous pastries, is served in the kitchen.

Azienda Agrituristica Savoca €
Contrada Polleri 13, Piazza Armerina, T348-842 0337, agrisavoca.com.
This large, comfortable farmhouse 3 km east of Piazza Armerina offers B&B accommodation in traditional, antique-furnished rooms. Peacocks roam the well-kept gardens, which also contain a pool. There's a range of organic products to sample, including wine, oil and their delicious home-made *limoncello*, and horse-riding and cookery lessons can be arranged. There is also a camping area and a reasonably priced restaurant serving home-cooked food. Buses stop outside the farm.

Le Querce di Cota €
Bivio Ciappulla (off the SS575, SP55), Troina, T0935-356266, lequercedicota.it.
A remote, peaceful farmhouse 6 km southeast of the lofty village of Troina. The rooms all boast stunning views over the hills or across to Etna, and it's an excellent base for walkers with numerous trails in the vicinity.

Falconara Charming Resort €€€-€€
Località Falconara, Butera, T0934-349012, designhotels.com.
Open May-Sep.

On the seafront, about 8 km east of Licata, this 'chic' hotel incorporates an outbuilding from the adjacent (private) Norman castle which guards the headland. It's a small resort, offering tennis, a pool, small spa and a private beach, but your own transport is recommended if you want to explore the area.

Farm Ospitalità de Campagna €€
Contrada Strada, Butera, T0934-346600, farm-ospitalitadicampagna.it.
A gorgeous rural retreat in the hills above Gela, with quirky, art-filled rooms, a small outdoor pool, and a host of pampering treatments and courses, including massages and yoga classes. There's also a restaurant.

Hotel Amici €
Acrone 5, Agrigento, T0922-402831.
Simple rooms with air conditioning plus a convenient location near the train station make this budget hotel a good bet. The buses for the Valley of the Temples depart from close by, and it's great value. Triple and quadruple rooms also available.

Camere a Sud B&B €
Via Ficani 6, off via Alenea, Agrigento, T349-638 4424, camereasud.it.
Tucked away in the heart of Agrigento's old quarter, this arty little B&B has just three pretty rooms (two doubles and a triple), all with air conditioning and en suite bathrooms. Breakfast is served on a tiny terrace overlooking the rooftops.

Camera con Vista €
Via Porta Aurea 4, Agrigento, T0922-554605, cameraconvista.it.
Many hotels promise views of Agrigento's famous temples, but few actually deliver: this inn has views over the valley to the temples high on their imposing ridge. The eight rooms are simply furnished but all have fridges and air conditioning, and most boast balconies or terraces on which you can soak up the views.

Terrazze di Montelusa B&B €
Piazza Lena 6, Agrigento, T0922-28556, terrazzedimontelusa.it.
This elegant B&B in a 19th-century town house in Agrigento's old quarter contains three bedrooms, two suites (for only €10 extra) and welcoming owners. A delicious breakfast is served on a panoramic terrace, with views stretching down to the temples and out to sea.

Self-catering
Mandranova €€
Palma di Montechiaro, SS115 Km 217, T393-986 2169, mandranova.it.
This *agriturismo* with restaurant is located amid olive groves, a 20-minute drive from Agrigento

(the main coast road is by the gate – a blessing and a curse). Choose from a traditionally furnished room in the main house or the converted former railway station, or self-catering accommodation in a separate villa (sleeps up to six, weekly rates €1200-2700). There are gardens, a pool, a restaurant, and cookery lessons are offered.

Fattoria Mose
Via M Pascal 4, Agrigento, T0922-606115, fattoriamose.com.
Peacefully located about 4 km from the Valley of the Temples and 3 km from the sea, this *agriturismo* offers B&B (€) accommodation in the owners' 19th-century manor house or self-catering in simple apartments (sleeping two to six people, €450-1100 per week, one week minimum in high season) converted from old estate buildings. The farm produces citrus fruits and olive oil, a home-cooked dinner can be prepared, and breakfast includes home-made bread and jams.

Hotel i Dammusi di Borgo Cala Creta €€€
Lungomare Luigi Rizzo, Cala Creta, Lampedusa, T0922-970883, calacreta.com.
Closed mid-Nov to mid-Apr.
This small hotel complex overlooks a beautiful rocky cove, Cala Creta (there's no beach, but

Eating & drinking

you can swim from the rocks). Accommodation is in 23 *dammusi* – traditional, domed 'bungalows' built of creamy stone. The complex also contains a diving centre and restaurant. Prices drop dramatically outside the peak season. One week stay minimum in high season.

Hotel La Perla €€
1-5 Lungomare Rizzo, Lampedusa, T0922-971932, laperlahotel.net.
A simple, whitewashed hotel overlooking the harbour, this has attractive rooms decorated in nautical shades of blue and white. The best boast private balconies or terraces (worth the extra), and the hotel has a good, reasonably priced restaurant with a terrace offering sea views. In high season, half-board is obligatory. Open year round.

Linoikos €€-€
Via Alfieri, Linosa, T0922-972212, linoikos.it.
Closed Oct-May.
Run by a co-operative that restores abandoned churches, this small, modern hotel has 14 simple rooms (doubles and triples) painted in bright, local colours. All have en suite bathrooms, but no TVs or radios. Prices include breakfast, which is served on the roof terrace.

Enna & around

Al Fogher €€€€
Contrada Bellia, SS117 bis, Piazza Armerina, T0935-684123, alfogher.net.
Tue-Sat 1230-1500, 1930-2230, Sun 1230-1500.
Settle down to some gourmet cuisine at this beautiful country restaurant on the outskirts of Piazza Armerina, this serves delicious gourmet cuisine. Part of the Slow Food movement, you can rely on the freshest seasonal produce. Try dishes such as red mullet with a pistachio crust, or suckling pig with asparagus.

Antica Hostaria €€€
Via Castagna 7, Enna, T0935-22521.
Wed-Sun 1300-1500, 1930-2200, Mon 1300-1500.
An 18th-century palazzo houses the finest restaurant in Enna, which serves rich country dishes such as *orecchiette alla carbonara con asparagi* ('little ear' pasta with carbonara sauce and asparagus tips) or the house speciality, *pasta con ragù di maiale all'ennese* (pasta served with a rich pork ragout).

La Littorina €€
Tren Museo Villarosa, Stazione Ferroviaria, Villarosa, T0935-32002.
Tue-Sun 1230-1500, 1930-2200.
This unconventional restaurant on the platform at Villarosa's quirky train station-cum museum, 10 km west of Enna, offers delicious traditional Sicilian home cooking, all served with home-made bread, local olives, cheeses and cured meats..

Cafés & bars
Caffè Marro
Piazza Vittorio Emanuele 22, Enna, T0935-591184.
Daily 0800-2200.
This historic café (although you wouldn't guess it from the modern fittings) serves superb hazelnut pastries, ice creams and other treats. In summer there's a terrace on the square.

Pasticceria Gelateria di Catalano
Piazza Garibaldi 16, Piazza Armerina, T0935-680167.
Tue-Sun 0900-2000.
A range of *dolci*, including traditional cakes and biscuits and ice creams and more, are the staple fare at this *pasticceria*.

Pick of the picnic spots

Castello di Lombardia.

Castello di Lombardia, Enna Pick up some choice cheeses from Formaggi Di Dio and make for this lofty vantage point, see page 221.

Morgantina These lonely ruins are perfect for picnics and philosophical ruminations, see page 223.

Giardino della Kolymbetra, Agrigento Take lunch to this shady corner and ponder on the past, see page 229.

Scala dei Turchi A gorgeous swoop of pale stone steps overlooking an azure sea, page 230.

Eraclea Minoa Clumps of wild grass make lovely cushions at these panoramic ruins. Bring provisions, see page 232.

Agrigento & around

Hosteria del Vicolo €€€€
Vicolo Sammaritano 10, Sciacca, T0925-23071.
Tue-Sun 1230-1530, 1930-2200.
A local classic in the historic heart of Sciacca. Its refined cuisine takes traditional Sicilian recipes and reinvents them with contemporary flair.

La Madia €€€€
22 Corso Filippo di Re Capriata, Licata, T0922-771443, ristorantelamadia.it
Mon, Wed-Sun 1300-1530, 1930-2200; also closed Sun lunch in Aug.
This restaurant has won countless awards, including a Michelin star for chef Pino Cuttaia, and the Best Restaurant in Sicily award in 2008. Go for the smoked cod with pine nuts, or the couscous with plump Sicilian prawns. Around €70 per head, booking recommended.

Spizzulio €€
Via Panoramica dei Templi 23, Agrigento, T0922-20712, spizzulio.it.
Mon-Sat 1900-2300.
An intimate *enoteca*, serving Sicilian wines, platters of charcuterie, cheeses and olives, as well as a selection of more substantial dishes.

Cafés & bars
Infurna Pasticceria
Via Atenea 96, Agrigento, T0922-595959.
Mon-Sat 0900-2100, Sun 1230-1900.
A good place for cappuccino and some pistachio cream-filled *cornetti* before hitting the sights.

Pelagie Islands

Trattoria La Risacca €€€-€€
Via Roma, Lampedusa, T0922-975798, trattorielampedusa.it
Daily 1300-1500, 1900-2300.
Closed winter.

A central trattoria with fresh tuna and calamari among the seafood specialities on the menu.

Terra del Sole €€
Via Vittorio Emanuele 28, Lampedusa, T0922-970072, terradelsolelampedusa.com.
Daily 1300-1500, 1900-2300.
Weekends only in winter.
Fun and informal, with a wide interior patio. Fresh fish is prepared on the barbecue.

Cafés & bars
Bar 13.5
Via Roma 45-47, Lampedusa, T0922-971798.
Daily 1000 till late. Closed winter.
One of the best cafés in town with pastries and ice creams. In the evenings, it turns into a bar and is lively until very late.

Entertainment

Festivals & events

Easter week
Enna, Agrigento and Caltanisetta are all famous for their solemn Easter celebrations.

Kubbaita
Troina.
Jun.
A medieval-style horse race in honour of Count Roger's capture of Troina's castle, followed by the distribution of *torrone* (nougat sweets).

Rappresentazioni Pirandelliane
Agrigento.
Jun-Aug.
Agrigento's summer-long drama festival dedicated to the works of Luigi Pirandello.

Festa di San Giacomo
Caltagirone
24-25 Jul.
Caltagirone's famous ceramic staircase is beautifully lit with lanterns.

Palio dei Normanni
Piazza Armerina.
13-14 Aug.
Medieval festival re-enacting the arrival of Count Roger in the city.

Shopping

Ceramics

Ceramiche Cascio
Corso V Emanuele 115, Sciacca,
T0925-82829.
Mon-Sat 0900-1300, 1700-1900.
Sciacca is famous for its ceramics, and this is just one of many craft shops to be found in the town.

Food & drink

Caffè Italia
Piazza Garibaldi, Enna,
T0935-501111.
Daily 0900-2200.
This popular café has an eye-popping range of outstanding pastries, biscuits and cakes. Fabulous gifts – if you can bear to give them away.

Salumeria Enoteca Delizie di Diliberto Bruno
Via Madonna di Fatima 4,
Caltanissetta, T0934-951621.
Mon-Fri 0900-1300, 1630-1900,
Sat 0900-1300.
Salami and other *charcuterie*, Sicilian wines and a range of local delicacies make this a great stop for picnic supplies.

Salumeria del Buon Sapore
Via Cappuccini 20, Agrigento,
T0925-26562.
Mon-Sat 0900-1300, 1630-1900.
Cured hams and sausages, cheeses, oils, wines and much more.

Five of the best
Food festivals (*sagre*)

❶ Sagra Arancia Rossa di Sicilia, Centuripe (late March) A celebration of Sicily's delicious blood oranges.

❷ Sagra del Maccherone, Nicosia (third Sunday in May) Macaroni dishes celebrate the feast of Nicosia's patron saint.

❸ Sagra della Vastedda cu Sammuccu, Troina (June) Troina is famous for its focaccia-style bread stuffed with local cheese and ham and flavoured with elderflowers.

❹ Sagra della Salsiccia, Aragona (second Sunday in September) Aragona links its Saint's day festival (San Vincenzo) with a celebration of its flavoursome sausages.

❺ Sagra del Buccellato, Enna (19-21 December) Enna's sweet biscuits, *buccellato*, are filled with dried figs and served at Christmas.

Formaggi di Dio
Via Mercato Sant'Antonio 34,
Enna, T0935-25758.
Mon-Sat 0900-1300, 1700-1900.
A must for cheese addicts, this sells all kinds of unusual local specialities such as Piacentinu (flavoured with black peppercorns and saffron), as well as hams, oils, wine and other necessary picnic items.

Activities & tours

Diving

The Pelagie Islands are a popular diving destination. Among the subaquatic wonders are corals, sponges and myriad colourful fish. There are many diving agencies on the islands, offering trips to suit everyone from beginners to experienced divers. Prices are fairly standard: a single dive costs around €50 including equipment hire, and a ten-dive pass is around €370. Recommended companies include:

Tortuga Diving
Contrada Cala Creta (c/o Villaggio Albergo 'Borgo Cala Creta'), T0922-970394, tortugadiving.com.

Pelagos Diving Center
Vicolo Linosa 3, Contrada Guitgia, T335-660 9443, pelagoslampedusa.it

Lo Verde Diving Center
Via Sbarcatoio, T0922-971986, loverdelampedusa.it.

Blue Dolphins
Via Madonna 1, T339-740 3490, bluedolphins.it.

Sailing
L'Altro Mare
Via G Morone 6, Milan, T338-868 5279, altromare.com. Week-long sailing trips around the Pelagie Islands. Accommodation and food provided on board.

Transport

Enna & around

Enna is on the main train line from Palermo to Catania, but trains stop 5 km from the old town at the bottom of the steep hill. There's an infrequent (hourly) local bus up the hill, or take a taxi. There are several trains daily to **Caltanissetta** (45 mins). Regular bus services (considerably fewer on Sunday) run by **SAIS** (T0935-524111) link Enna with Palermo (1 hr 45 mins), Catania (1 hr 45 mins) and Piazza Armerina (45 mins).

Agrigento & around

There are daily train services between Agrigento and Palermo (2 hrs 10 mins), and Caltanissetta (1 hr 30 mins). The main train station (Agrigento Centrale) is conveniently central, as is the bus station. Different companies run services to most Sicilian cities, including Palermo (**Cuffaro**, T0922-418231, 2 hrs) and Catania

(**SAIS**, T0922-595260, 3 hrs), and to Palermo airport (**Sal**, T0922-401360). Sal also run services between Agrigento, Porto Empedocle, Licata and Gela.

Pelagie Islands

There are flights to Lampedusa from most major mainland Italian airports in summer, including Palermo (about 1 hr), with **Meridiana/Eurofly** (meridiana.it), **Air Italia** (alitalia.com), **Club Air** (clubair.it), and **Air One** (flyairone.it). Lampedusa airport (T0922-970006) is a short walk (5 mins) from the town centre. Daily overnight ferries (**Siremar**, T892 123, call centre from within Italy or T091-7493111, siremar.it, Linosa 5 hrs 45 mins, Lampedusa 8 hrs) and seasonal hydrofoils (**Ustica Lines**, T0922-970003, usticalines. it, Linosa 3 hrs, Lampedusa 4 hrs 15 mins) depart from Porto Empedocle, near Agrigento. Note that visitors cannot take cars to Linosa from June to September.

Contents

Arco dell'Elefante, Pantelleria.

Western Sicily

Introduction

What to see in...

...one day
Take the cable car up to hilltop **Erice** (the earlier the better to enjoy cloudless skies), and stroll around the little town. After a lazy lunch, return to **Trapani** to take in the sights, and perhaps a romantic evening drive along the salt flats to see the sunset.

Western Sicily feels distinctly different from the rest of the island. It's not just the landscape – wider, flatter and emptier than anything in the east – but in the almost intangible legacy of the Arabs who ruled for 200 years. You'll feel it in the languid rhythm of life, in the delicately spiced cuisine, and in the generous hospitality of the people. For a little *dolce far niente* (carefree idleness), there's nowhere better.

Sicilians like to remind visitors that the eastern part of the island looks to Europe and the west to north Africa, but the cliché rings truest in Trapani and Mazara del Vallo, both of which recall the port towns of the Maghreb with their low, cube-shaped dwellings. These, along with the wine-producing town of Marsala, are the only sizeable communities in the laid-back west.

...a weekend or more
With more time, you shouldn't miss the **Zingaro Reserve**, with its gorgeous hikes and coves. Or perhaps a spot of wine-tasting around **Marsala, Erice or Alcamo**. To kick back, take a ferry to the **Egadi Islands**, and to relax in style, head for **Pantelleria**.

Sleepy and slow-paced it may be, but Western Sicily is packed with some outstanding sights. Just for starters, there's the magnificent Zingaro nature reserve, with its unspoilt coastline; the sublime temple at Segesta, poetically set amid pristine hills; and the perfect medieval time-capsule of Erice, lost in clouds on its lofty pinnacle. And to drop the pace yet another notch or two, there are the unspoilt Egadi islands, or the chic little celebrity retreat of Pantelleria.

Left: Windmill near Trapani.

Trapani & around

Trapani is an inviting harbour town spread along a slender headland. It was founded by the Elymians as a port for Eryx, modern Erice, a magical hill town just inland. To the south stretches a delicate network of salt pans, overlooked by the tiny island of Mozia, once a powerful Carthaginian city. A dramatic cape juts north, dividing Trapani from the fishing villages cum seaside resorts of Castellammare del Golfo and San Vito Lo Capo; between them stretches the Zingaro Reserve, perhaps the most beautiful stretch of coast in Sicily. Inland, the temple of Segesta is sublimely set in a pristine valley.

At Trapani's saltworks.

Ignore the scruffy sprawl on Trapani's outskirts: the city's historic heart is a charmer. Compact and surprisingly elegant, it boasts a minuscule core of winding medieval streets, and a couple of Baroque avenues with splendid palazzi. Trapani's main monuments were thoroughly scrubbed up in 2005, when it hosted the trials for the prestigious America's Cup sailing competition, although the port is still gritty.

Old Town (Cenni Storici)

Corso Vittorio Emanuele is old Trapani's main street, a handsome, pedestrianized boulevard. Its eastern end is dominated by the enormous **Cattedrale di San Lorenzo** (daily 0800-1600), built in 1421 but entirely remodelled in the 18th century; it contains an *Annunciation* attributed to Anton van Dyck (1599-1641). At the tip of the headland, by the squat Torre di Ligny, there are fabulous views out to the Egadi Islands. The finest Baroque church in Trapani is the **Chiesa di Maria SS del Soccorso**, better known as Badia Nuova, on via Torrearsa. Some resplendent Baroque palazzi and churches line via Garibaldi. The 16th-century **Palazzo Ciambra** (also known as the Torre Giudecca) is an exquisite example of the Spanish Plateresque style – it overlooks the main street of the former Jewish quarter (Giudecca). At the corner of via Garibaldi and via Torrearsa, the 19th-century **Mercato del Pesce** (Mon-Sat 0800-1500) is a splendid setting for Trapani's famous fish market. The sweeping via XXX Gennaio marks the eastern boundary of the old town. Just beyond it are Trapani's leafy public gardens, the 19th-century **Villa Margherita**, with an outdoor theatre and a pond.

Santuario dell'Annunziata

Via Conte Agostino Pepoli 178, T0923-539184. Daily 0800-1200, 1600-1900.

Modern Trapani, otherwise bland and uninteresting, is redeemed by two monuments

Essentials

❶ Getting around The centre of Trapani is tiny and easy to get around on foot; a free shuttle bus runs from the train station to the sanctuary and adjoining art museum. Bus No 23 takes you to the start of the cable car for Erice.

❷ Bus station Near the train station at piazza Ciaccio Montalto. AST information on T0923-23222.

❸ Train station In the centre of town at piazza Umberto I, T0923-540416.

❹ ATM There are several banks along corso Italia and via Garibaldi, including **Banco di Sicilia**, via Garibaldi Giuseppe 9, T0923-821111.

⊕ Hospital Azienda Unità Sanitaria, via Staiti, T0923-543011.

✚ Pharmacy Farmacia Marini Sofia Maria, corso Vittorio Emanuele 117, T0923-21204, Mon-Sat 0900-1300, 1630-1930.

❓ Post office Piazza Vittorio Veneto 11, T0923-872016, Mon-Sat 0800-1830.

❶ Tourist information Casina delle Palme, via Regina Elena 1, T0923-29000, apt.trapani.it, trapaniwelcome.it.

Santuario dell'Annunziata.

I Misteri di Trapani

Trapani's Easter processions are among the most famous in Sicily. A series of floats topped with scenes from the Passion of Christ (the events leading up to the Crucifixion) are processed through crowd-lined streets on Good Friday and Holy Saturday. Even if you're not here at Easter you can see the figures in the little Chiesa del Purgatorio (via San Francesco d'Assisi, daily 1600-1830), murky with incense.

that stand side by side on a square 2 km east of the old centre. The Santuario dell'Annunziata contains the venerated *Madonna di Trapani*, a 14th-century statue by Nino Pisano or his school. At the Madonna's feet are a poignant heap of ex-votos from miracle-seeking parishioners.

Museo Regionale Pepoli

Via Conte Agostino Pepoli 200, T0923-553269. Tue-Sat 0900-1330, Sun and holidays 0900-1230, €4, free for EU citizens, under 18 and over 65.

Next door to the Sanctuary, a former convent is a beautiful setting for an enjoyably eclectic collection of painting, sculpture and decorative arts, including curiosities made from coral.

East of Trapani

Some of Sicily's most beautiful sights are easily accessible from Trapani, including the dreamy hill town of Erice (see Great days out, page 252), the temple at Segesta, and the magnificent coastal nature reserve at Zingaro. There are also great beaches at San Vito Lo Capo and Castellammare del Golfo.

Castellammare del Golfo

53 km east of Trapani.

Castellammare del Golfo, a pretty tumble of ochre and yellow houses clustered around a bay, forms the nucleus of a popular summer resort with long sandy beaches. The town was founded by the Elymians as a port for Segesta (see page 250), and its heart is still the harbour. The *tonnara* (tuna fishery), long closed, is now a smart hotel, but fishermen from the dwindling fleet still sit on the quay to mend their nets. The harbour is guarded by the squat **Castello Arabo-Normanno** (Mon-Sat 0900-1300, 1500-1900, daily in Aug, T0924-30217) which houses the local museum, as well as a tourist information office (open same hours as museum).

Castellammare del Golfo.

Scopello

8 km northwest of Castellammare del Golfo.

Scopello is a picture-postcard village of rosy stone clustered around an 18th-century *baglio* (country house). It overlooks a bewitching stretch of coastline, with tiny coves dotted with rocks and islets. Its permanent population numbers only 80: in August, that can swell tenfold, and it's standing room only in the pretty *baglio* courtyard, with its popular restaurants and bars. The village is the main access point for the magnificent Riserva Naturale dello Zingaro.

Riserva Naturale dello Zingaro

Southern entrance at Scopello, northern entrance at San Vito Lo Capo, T0924-35108, riservazingaro.it. Apr-Sep 0700-2100, Oct-Mar 0800-1600, €3, free under 10.

The Zingaro nature reserve occupies the eastern part of the spectacular headland that culminates in San Vito Lo Capo, and includes 7 km of breathtakingly beautiful coastline. Inland, the scrub-covered slopes are home to a wealth of flora and fauna, including one of the last pairs of Bonelli's Eagle on Sicily. There are several wonderful hiking paths, marked on the plan obtainable at the park entrances, but the most popular is the coastal path.

Scopello.

San Vito Lo Capo

Tourist information at via Savoia 57, T0923-974300, comune.sanvitolocapo.tp.it.

The long rocky finger that juts north beyond Trapani culminates dramatically in Monte Cofano. Beyond this crag is San Vito Lo Capo (38 km north of Trapani), a former fishing village surrounded by a modern sprawl of apartment buildings. Every summer, visitors descend in droves to colonize the fabulous white beaches – formed from tiny shells. San Vito Lo Capo is famous for its *couscous di pesce*, a celebrated North African dish given a Sicilian twist with the addition of fresh fish, which gets its own festival in September (couscousfest.it).

Alcamo

55 km east of Trapani.

Alcamo, a trim little agricultural town surrounded by snaking vines, is the capital of one of Sicily's best known winemaking regions. Some of the local vineyards accept visitors; check with the tourist office. The seaside satellite, Alcamo Marina, has more fine sandy beaches.

San Vito Lo Capo.

Around the island

Segesta

Signposted off the A29 Palermo–Trapani autostrada, 36 km east of Trapani, 7 km west of Calatafimi, T0924-952356.
Entrance tickets (€6/3 concession) and bus tickets (€1.20) for the shuttle to the top of the hill are available from the café-bar and shop by the car park.

Nothing quite prepares you for the first glimpse of Segesta. There's a crook in the country road, and suddenly the vast temple appears from the folds of the green hills like a mirage.

Little is known about the Elymians, one of the earliest peoples on Sicily, nor about the founding of Segesta, their most important city. It enters recorded history only around 500 BC, but had been founded centuries earlier. The city was destroyed by its rival Selinunte (see page 258) in 409 BC and never recovered its former power and influence. Segesta was one of the first cities to ally with the Romans, who invaded Sicily in the third century BC, and was later destroyed by Vandals. What little remained was shattered by an earthquake.

The highlight is the temple, built around 430 BC, one of the best-preserved Doric temples in the world. Curiously, there is no roof, which has given rise to a number of different theories. The most captivating of these is that the temple was only built to dazzle the Athenians, whom the Segestans wanted as allies in their war with arch-rival Selinunte. Once the Athenians left, having satisfied themselves of the wealth and taste of the Segestans, the locals didn't bother to finish it.

A steep path winds up through scrub and wild herbs to the top of the hill in 20-30 minutes, or you can take the shuttle bus from just outside the bar. Crowning the hill is a superb Greek theatre, carved into the pale stone in the third century BC, and looking out over undulating hills all the way to the coast. A festival of Greek theatre is held here every summer (end July to end August, festivalsegesta. com). The Arabs and then the Normans occupied the site briefly, and remnants of a mosque and a church are visible just beyond the theatre.

The roofless but well-preserved Doric temple at Segesta.

South of Trapani

Via del Sale (the Salt Route)

The silvery outline of Trapani's famous salt lagoons stretch south to Marsala, dotted with the silhouettes of wooden-sailed windmills. The SP21 – the 'Via del Sale' – is a panoramic back road that skirts the coast. Trapani salt is highly regarded as a gourmet item thanks to its rich mineral content and the traditional, chemical-free process by which it is made. There are two main areas of production: the **Saline di Trapani**, around the hamlet of Nubia about 6 km south of Trapani, and the hauntingly beautiful **Stagnone di Marsala**, 20 km south of Trapani, a vast lagoon dotted with islands, which is a protected nature reserve.

In the coastal hamlet of **Nubia**, a picturesque windmill contains the **Museo del Sale** (via delle Saline, T0923-867442), where you can learn about the history of salt-making. It sits on the edge of the **Riserva Saline di Trapani e Paceco** (visitor centre, Mulino Maria Stella, via Garibaldi 138, Contrada Nubia, T0923-867700, riservewwfsicilia.it), a WWF-run Mecca for birdwatchers.

The southern salt pans fringe the edge of the **Stagnone di Marsala**, the largest lagoon in Sicily, which averages just 1 m in depth, now a nature reserve. By the water's edge (follow signs for the Saline Ettore e Infersa) there's another restored (and functioning) windmill (Contrada Ettore Infersa, T0923-733003, 0900-1300, 1500 till dusk, €3). It overlooks the slip for boats to the Isola di San Pantoleo, which is more commonly known as Mozia for the important Phoencian settlement of Motya (see below) which once occupied the island.

Mozia (Isola di San Pantoleo)

Follow signs for Imbarcadero Saline Infersa off the SP21 to reach the jetty.
Boats €5 return, summer 0900-1930, winter 0900-1830.

It's hard to believe that great swathes of the Mediterranean were controlled from this little island, but ancient Motya was once a powerful city state. It was founded during the eighth century BC by the Phoenicians, but reached the peak of its power under the Carthaginians during the fifth and fourth centuries BC. In 397 BC it was razed after a siege by Dionysos I, tyrant of Syracuse, who slaughtered every inhabitant. It was recaptured a year later, but never regained its former influence. For the last 2000 years or more, it has been home only to a handful of fishermen, apart from a brief period during the 11th century when Basilian monks established a small community and dedicated the island to San Pantoleo.

The island has been owned by the Whitakers (the British family who made a fortune through Marsala wine) since Joseph 'Pip' Whitaker, an enthusiastic amateur archaeologist, heard that

The ruins at Mozia.

some unusual finds had been discovered by locals. He uncovered one of the best preserved Phoenician sites anywhere in the Mediterranean. Some remarkable finds are on display in the small **Museo Whitaker** (summer 0900-1245, 1400-1900, winter 0900-1245, 1500-1800, T0923-712598, €7) which now occupies the lovely, tree-shaded villa. Pride of place goes to the celebrated fifth-century BC statue, *Il Giovane di Motia*, of a young man with confident pose and beautifully rendered garments, one of the finest pieces of Greek sculpture in Sicily. There are lots of finds from the Tophet burial ground, including urns which contained the ashes of sacrificed animals or cremated children (opinion is divided on whether the Phoenicians sacrificed children to their gods, or whether these are the remains of children who died naturally), and grinning masks placed in burial sites to ward off evil spirits.

Outside the villa, look for the **Casa dei Mosaici**, with faded designs picked out in black and white stones. A pathway makes a loop around the island, passing the ancient **Kothon** (port) and dry dock, and the underwater vestiges of the Roman-built causeway that once linked the city to the mainland (and was in use right up until 1971).

Tip...

It takes about an hour to stroll around the entire island, but it's well worth bringing a picnic, along with a sunhat (there's little shade) and plenty of water (limited supplies on the island), and spending the day there.

Erice: a walk in the clouds

Erice is a perfectly preserved medieval town, literally lost in the clouds atop Monte San Guliano (750 m). It was founded by the Elymians in the seventh century BC, and has been associated with the goddess of love since the Elymians erected a temple to Venus. The huge Noman Castello di Venere, which still dominates the southeastern flank of the mountain, was built from the ruins of the once-celebrated temple. Although the tight maze of narrow alleys recalls an Arabic casbah, most of what survives today was built under the Normans and the Spanish. It's easy to get lost – but getting lost is the best way to discover Erice's secret courtyards (*cortiles*) with their flowers and fountains.

Enter the pedestrianized old quarter through the imposing **porta Trapani**. Just beyond it, overlooking a little cobbled square to the left, is the restrained Gothic **Real Duomo** (1000-1230, 1500-1800, mornings only in winter, €2 admission to treasury) with a graceful portal. The unusual detached bell tower, the **Torre Campanario** (1000-1230, 1500-1800, mornings only in winter, €1) is also known as the Torre di Re Federico II, and can be climbed for outstanding views.

Continue up the steep, cobbled **corso Vittorio Emanuele**, the little town's main drag, lined on every side with cafés, souvenir shops and restaurants (don't miss Maria's famous pastry shop and café, on the left at No 14). Many of the shops display the colourful local carpets, *frazzate*, which are typical of Erice and are made of tightly woven coloured rags in geometric designs. The street opens out onto the **piazza Umberto I**, the main square with a handful of terrace cafés and the town hall, which contains the **Museo Cordici** (Mon, Thu 0800-1400, 1430-1700, Tue-Wed, Fri 0800-1400, free). This enjoyably old-fashioned museum has a collection of archaeological finds and a few paintings, notably Antonello Gagini's *Annunciation*.

From piazza Umberto I, turn right down **via Cordici** to reach the pretty **piazza San Domenico**, overlooked on one side by the church of the same name and on the other by a line of handsome palazzi. Take via Filippo Guarnotti, opposite the church, and stroll down until you come to the **Chiesa di San Pietro** and its adjoining monastery: the latter contains the **Ettore Majorana Foundation and Centre of Scientific Culture** (EMFCSC) run by the physicist Antonino Zichichi. He is a well-known, if controversial, Italian media personality, famous for making science accessible to millions and for his strong Catholic faith.

Via Filippo Guarnotti curves around to meet **piazza San Giuliano**, named after another fine Baroque church. From here, the via Roma sweeps down to Erice's beautiful public gardens, the **Giardino del Balio**, which offer breathtaking views. From the gardens, a series of steep steps lead up to the **Castello di Venere** (0900-1700, donations requested), the most spectacular of Erice's surviving fortifications, with more heart-stopping views from its walkways and battlements.

Left: Vintage cars line the town walls.
Right: Look out for the small details as you walk around the town; an impressive Baroque facade.

Tip...

Erice has been pedestrianized and visitors must leave their cars at the main car park by the porta Trapani, for which there is a charge during August and early September. There's a free car park 400 m away, with a free shuttle bus to the porta Trapani.

Erice cable car

Erice is most easily reached via a cable car (Funivia), which swings up from Trapani below in about 15 hair-raising minutes (bus 23 from the bus station on piazza Vittorio Emanuele to terminal on via Caserta, departures daily Tue-Fri 0740-2030, Sat-Sun 0940-2400, usually closed for a period between mid-Jan to mid-Mar for maintenance, €2.70 single, €5 return, funiviaerice.it). If you are taking the cable car up to Erice, start early to enjoy the best views. The cloud tends to gather later in the day.

Marsala & around

Sicily's southwestern corner gazes out across the Strait of Sicily to Africa, and is still deeply imbued with a North African influence. Marsala owes its modern name to ninth-century Arabic rulers, and its recent prosperity to the eponymous dessert wine, popularized during the 19th century. The Arabic influence is strongest in Mazaro del Vallo, a vibrant harbour town that shelters one of Italy's largest fishing fleets. East of Mazaro del Vallo is Selinunte, another of Sicily's sublimely beautiful ancient sites. Inland, a string of interesting country towns are scattered across the Val de Belice.

Piazza della Repubblica, Marsala.

Marsala is an appealing port town, slightly frayed at the edges, but still lively and even occasionally elegant. During the 19th century Marsala was famous around the globe for its amber dessert wine popularized by enterprising British businesses, the profits of which paid for the construction of lavish *stile-Liberty* villas which still dot the area.

Centro storico

Marsala's grandest square in the old centre is the **piazza Repubblica**, overlooked by the 18th-century **Palazzo Comunale** (city hall) and the lavish **Duomo** (daily 1000-1200, 1500-1800), which is dedicated to San Tommaso di Canterbury (Thomas à Becket). The frilly façade was only completed in 1956, thanks to a donation from a returning emigrant; inside there are several fine artworks including a *Madonna del Popolo* (1490) by Domenico Gagini. A lively fish market takes place behind the city hall every morning except Sunday.

Museo con gli Arazzi Fiamminghi

Via G Garaffa 57, T0923-711327.
Tue-Sat 0900-1300, 1600-1800, Sun 0900-1300, €2.50.

Behind the cathedral, this small museum contains eight exceptional 16th-century Flemish tapestries depicting scenes from the Jewish revolt against the Roman Empire (AD 66-70). They were presented to Antonio Lombardo (1523-1595), Archbishop of Messina, who is buried in the cathedral. Lombardo, who was born in Marsala, was an ambassador to Spain, where he was given the tapestries by King Felipe II.

Essentials

❶ **Getting around** The centre of Marsala is small and compact. Regular bus and train services link it with Trapani and Mazara del Vallo. Mazara, also easily negotiable on foot, is the starting point for buses to Selinunte, Ghibellina and Salemi.
❷ **Bus station** Piazza del Popolo, in the centre.
❸ **Train station** Viale Amerigo Fazio, about a 10-minute walk to the town centre.
❾ **ATM** Banco di Sicilia, via XI Maggio 91, T0923-766111.
⊕ **Hospital** Ospedale San Biagio, piazza San Francesco 1, T0923-782111.
✛ **Pharmacy** Farmacia Calcagno, via XI Maggio 126, T0923-953254.
❷ **Post office** Via G Garibaldi 9, T0923-763014.
❶ **Tourist information** Via XI Maggio 100, T0923-714097, comune.marsala.it.

Holy week, Marsala.

Around the island

Complesso San Pietro – Museo Garibaldino

Via XI Maggio, T0923-718741.
Tue-Sun 0900-1300, 1600-2000, €2.

Marsala entered the history books in 1860 when Garibaldi landed here with his famous *Spedizione dei Mille* (Expedition of a Thousand) in one of the culminating episodes of the Risorgimento. Marsala's municipal museum is dedicated to the event.

Museo Archeologico Baglio Anselmi

Lungomare Boeo, T0923-952535.
Tue-Sat 0900-1900 last entry 1800, Sun 0900-1300, €3.

Marsala was founded by the Phoenicians after the destruction of Motya with the sonorous name of Lilybeo. It became the most important Carthaginian stronghold on Sicily, before falling to the Romans during the First Punic War. The museum, located in a wine warehouse on the seafront contains finds from ancient Lilybeo, but the highlight is the Punic warship discovered in the Stagnone lagoon. It went down around the time of the Battle of the Egadi Islands, which concluded the First Punic War in 241 BC, and was recovered in 1971. Other highlights include a pair of Roman mosaics, some gold jewellery, and the *Venus of Marsala*, a battered statue of the goddess of love (a Roman copy of a Greek original) which was mutilated by Christians.

Chiesa di San Giovanni & the Grotto of the Sibyl

Usually closed – ask at the tourist office.

This 16th-century church was built over the remnants of a cave with a natural spring where the famed Sibyl of Lilybeo dwelt in ancient times. Her accuracy as a seer was renowned, but the practice of consulting oracles dwindled after the arrival of the Romans. However, the faithful still visit the church on 24 June, feast day of San Giovanni, to ask the Sibyl to grant them luck and good fortune.

Five of the best

Ancient treasures in western Sicily

❶ *Il Giovane di Motia*, **Museo Whitaker, Mozia** Sicily's most beautiful Greek statue depicts a confident youth in a tunic, page 251.

❷ **Punic ship, Museo Archeologico, Marsala** This third-century BC ship was sunk during the First Punic Wars, see page 256.

❸ *La Venere di Marsala (Venus of Marsala)*, **Museo Archeologico, Marsala** A graceful, if battered, statue of Venus emerging from the waves, see page 256.

❹ **Gold bracelet, Museo Archeologico, Marsala** This exquisite golden bracelet dates from the third century BC, see page 256.

❺ *Il Satiro Danzante (Dancing Satyr)*, **Museo del Satiro, Mazara del Vallo** An ecstatic, writhing satyr discovered in fishing nets in 1998, see page 257.

Around Marsala

Mazara del Vallo, a busy harbour town with a huge fishing fleet, has a pretty if battered core, and a reminder of its ancient importance under the Arabs in the redolent Casbah. East of Mazaro del Vallo is ancient Selinunte, where the bones of temples are submerged in scrub. Inland, the beautiful Val di Belice, although devastated by an earthquake in 1968, is still dotted with sleepy country towns like Salemi and Santa Margherita.

Mazara del Vallo

23 km southeast of Marsala.

One of the oldest settlements in Sicily, Mazara del Vallo is a cheerful town with a busy port, a palm-lined *lungomare*, and a small historic kernel. Just an archway survives of the Norman castle where the Sicilian parliament was called for the first time in 1097, but the 11th-century cathedral, rebuilt in the 17th century, still dominates the old town.

Mazara del Vallo.

Marsala wines & the Cantine Florio

The Marsala region has always been famous for its grapes but it was the Englishman John Woodhouse who saw the possibilities for a fortified-wine business and set up shop in 1773. By the end of the 18th century Marsala wine was being drunk on all of the British navy's ships. More British businesses, including Ingham, Good and Whitaker, joined the industry, which peaked in the second half of the 19th century. The Florio family set up a firm in 1831, which was bought by Cinzano in 1924, along with the Woodhouse and Ingham-Whitaker wineries. The Cantine Florio, built of tufa stone in the 1830s, is now Marsala's biggest tourist attraction, with more than 30,000 visitors annually. **Cantine Florio**, via Vincenzo Florio 1, T0923-781306. Visits Monday-Friday 1000, 1100, 1530, 1630, Sat 0930, 1030, 1100, €5-10 depending on whether you choose the guided tour or not (tours must be booked in advance).

Mazara was founded as a trading post by the Phoenicians in the ninth century BC, but it reached the peak of its influence under the Arabs, who landed here in AD 827. Mazara quickly became one of the wealthiest cities on the island, but lost its status after the arrival of the Normans in the 11th century. Now, the Arabs are back. In the northern section of the old centre, Arabic and French are more likely to be heard than Italian, and Halal butchers and tea shops line the streets.

Most of the North African community work on the trawlers: Mazara shelters one of Italy's largest fishing fleets (although business is down as it gets harder to recruit fishermen). It was a local fisherman who landed Mazara's greatest claim to fame: the *Satiro Danzante (Dancing Satyr)*, a bronze statue found tangled in nets in 1998. The figure, probably dates from the third or second century BC, and is exhibited at the excellent **Museo del Satiro** (piazza Plebiscito, T0923-933917, Tue-Sun 0900-1800, €6.50), where a visit includes an entertaining short film with footage of the exultant fisherman who found the statue.

Greek ruins at Selinunte.

Selinunte essentials

Getting there Signposted off the SP56, 2 km east of Marinella di Selinunte, 22 km south of Mazara del Vallo. Local AST and Marinella buses link Mazara del Vallo with Marinella di Selinunte, and stop at the site entrance.

Orientation The excavations are laid out in three main areas: the temples on the **Collina Orientale** (East Hill), closest to the visitor centre; the **Acropoli** (Acropolis), across the bay; and the **Santuario di Demetra Malophoros** (Sanctuary of Demeter Malophorus), beyond the acropolis, across the dry bed of the Modione River. The unofficial website selinunte. net has a great interactive map.

Getting around The site is very pleasant to explore on foot. It's about 1½ km from the visitor entrance to the furthest ruins. A shuttle service in electric carts is available between the three main areas of the site (€5 per person): arrange pick-up times with the driver.

Selinunte

Via Selinunte, Marinella di Selinunte, T0924-46251, selinunte.net
Daily 0900-1700 (last entry 1600), €6/3 concession.

Wild, beautiful Selinunte is curved around a quiet bay, once the colony's port. The vast ruins of a large temple dominate one hillside, while the remnants of the acropolis are strewn across another. The name comes from *selinon*, the Greek word for wild celery, which is still abundant.

Selinunte was founded in the seventh century BC by settlers from Megara Hyblaea (see page 199) and reached the height of its influence in the fifth century BC. Selinunte wanted to expand north and access the gulf of Castellammare but the Elymian city of Segesta stood in its path. This rivalry would lead to the destruction of Selinunte by the Carthaginians, allies of Segesta, in 409 BC. Selinunte would never fully recover. It supported Syracuse against the Carthaginians at the end of the fourth century BC, but finally submitted to Carthage in 276 BC. Only 25 years later, the city was

evacuated and its people sent to Lilybeo (see Marsala, above). Selinunte was abandoned, although there were small settlements during the Arab and Norman occupations.

East Hill The most immediately impressive ruins are those of the East Hill temples, which are usually referred to by letters as their dedication is still uncertain. There are three temples in the group, of which the most complete is **Temple E** (closest to the visitor centre). Some of its exquisitely carved *metopes* can be seen in Palermo's archaeological museum (see page 88). Beyond it are the sparse remnants of **Temple F**, which was the oldest of the trio, reduced now to little more than a tumble of overgrown stones. A splendid line of huge columns are all that remains of **Temple G**, which would once have been one of the largest and most imposing temples of antiquity.

Acropolis A path winds down the valley from the temples, skipping over brooks, to emerge at the road which leads to the second area of excavations, the acropolis. This is the real heart of the city, where the people of Selinunte lived, worked and prayed. It is thought a population of around 20,000 lived within the ancient walls. The ruins are beautifully set overlooking the sea, but are very sparse: it is possible to make out the two main thoroughfares, one running north-south, the other east-west, but of the five temples that once stood within the city walls, only **Temple C** can be discerned.

Sanctuary   West of the acropolis, the third set of excavations occupy a gentle hill above a second bay which would also have served as a port. Very little survives of the **Sanctuary of Demeter Malophoros** (Malophoros means 'the pomegranate-bearer', and refers to a fertility goddess), which was built on the route to the necropolis, so that the bereaved could pray to the earth mother goddess, deity of life and death.

Santa Margherita di Belice

68 km east of Marsala.

Fans of Giuseppe di Lampedusa's extraordinary novel *Il Gattopardo* (The Leopard) should make the pilgrimage to the quiet country town of Santa Margherita di Belice. The author spent idyllic childhood summers at his grandmother's palace, the Palazzo Filangeri-Cutò, which was the inspiration for Donnafugata in the novel. Sadly, the palace was destroyed by the 1968 earthquake, although remnants have been incorporated into the town hall, where a small museum contains the original manuscript, plus photographs and costumes. The ruins of the Baroque church of Santa Margherita, also described by Lampedusa, long left poignantly unroofed, are being converted into a **Museo della Memoria** (Mon 0930-1400, 1530-1830, Tue, Wed and Fri 0900-1400, Sat-Sun 0930-1300, 1530-1830, free) to those who lost their lives in the earthquake that shattered the valley on 15 January 1968.

Il Gattopardo (The Leopard)

Giuseppe di Lampedusa (1896-1957), the 11th and last Prince of Lampedusa, set his tale during the 1860s, the tumultuous years of the Risorgimento. The novel describes the decline of an aristocratic Sicilian family, as seen through the unflinching eyes of Fabrizio, Prince of Salina, who was based on Lampedusa's great-grandfather, Prince Giulio. The manuscript was rejected by several leading publishers and was finally published posthumously to become the best-selling Italian novel of the 20th century.

Salemi & Gibellina

Sleepy little hilltop **Salemi** (45 km north of Mazara del Vallo) found itself briefly at the centre of the world's attention in 1860, when Garibaldi declared it the capital of newly unified Italy. Its moment of glory lasted just three days, but the event is commemorated in the Museo del Risorgimento, one of three small museums gathered together in the much-restored 13th-century **Castello di Salemi** (T0924-982248, Tue-Sun 0900-1400, 1600-1900, free). Salemi hit the news recently, when enterprising mayor Vittorio Sgarbi offered a thousand crumbling but historic houses for sale at just €1. **Gibellina Nuovo**, 6 km east of Salemi, was supposed to be an ideal modern town, built by artists and architects after the terrible earthquake of 1968 devastated the original city. Unfortunately, the site is exposed and unshaded, and the construction proved to be so shoddy that the town, and all its famous public art, is literally falling apart. The ruins of old Gibellina, **Ruderi di Gibellina**, can be found 20 km east along the SS119 in the beautiful Val di Belice. The greeness is suddenly shattered by a sea of white cement smothering the hillside: this is Alberto Burri's controversial sculpture, *Cretto (Crevice)*, which covers the entire remains of the village.

The Egadi Islands & Pantelleria

The unspoilt Egadi Islands of Favignana, Levanza and Marettimo sit just off the western coast of Sicily. Favignana, the largest and closest (just 17 km from Trapani), is the busiest, but little Levanzo and Marettimo remain refreshingly unhurried. All offer the essentials for an idyllic holiday – endless sunshine, crystal-clear waters, and a relaxed pace of life. There are no beaches, but the rocky coves are perfect for swimming and diving. Fishing is still an important industry, and ancient methods have been preserved, including the annual *Mattanza* (tuna slaughter).

Pantelleria, a volcanic island 100 km from the Sicilian mainland, is sometimes called the 'black pearl of the Mediterranean', and is famous for its celebrity visitors (Madonna, Sting and Giorgio Armani among them) and its exquisite dessert wines.

Favignana Island.

Egadi Islands.

The Egadi Islands

Favignana

The most accessible of the Egadi Islands, Favignana is just 17 km from the coast of mainland Sicily. Commonly described as shaped like a butterfly, one 'wing' is largely flat, the other forested, while the centre is dominated by the great hump of the Montagna Grossa (315 m). On weekends, the ferries do brisk business, depositing an endless stream of Sicilian families who come for long lunches at the island's restaurants or elaborate picnics in the beautiful rocky coves.

The main town, **Favignana Città**, is a sea of white and ochre buildings spread around the port at the centre of the 'butterfly'. The vast Florio

tonnara, once the largest tuna-processing factory in Sicily, sits on the water's edge, and is currently being elegantly (and expensively) restored into a cultural centre. The rosy Palazzo Florio (1874), built for the scions of the dynasty that once owned the Egadis, is now part of the town hall. Piazza Matrice is the heart of the *città*, and the focus of the evening *passeggiata*. Café terraces spill their tables out onto the square, which is overlooked by the simple façade of the Chiesa Madre. The shabby fortress that stands on the hill above the town was built by the Arabs, and later expanded by the Bourbons to contain a prison – a function it fulfilled until 1860. Until recently it was used by the Italian military, but is now abandoned. The rest of the island is pocked with the scars of tufa quarries, which etch the cliff with geometrical patterns around the stunning **Cala Rossa** (in the north of the island). This is now Favignana's most beautiful bay, but got its name, according to legend, after the seas turned red with blood during the final naval battle of the First Punic War in 241 BC. There is some excellent diving around this cape. The best swimming cove is the breathtaking **Cala Azzurra** at the southeastern tip.

La Mattanza

Every year, from late April to early June, the waters turn red once again around the island of Favignana during the annual *Mattanza* (tuna slaughter). Using an ancient method, introduced by the Arabs and largely unchanged, the bluefin tuna are guided into a series of netted chambers, culminating in the *camera della morte*. Once the tuna are trapped in this final chamber, they are stabbed by the waiting fishermen (the *tonnaroti*) and hauled on to the boats. The sight has become a tourist attraction in recent years, and boat tours and underwater diving excursions are organized (ask at the tourist office for details).

Levanzo.

Levanzo

Levanzo, the smallest of the Egadi islands, lying 15 km from Trapani, is an empty, arid outcrop with a rocky coastline overlooking a cobalt sea. The only village, which overlooks the tiny port at Cala Dogana, is a simple straggle of white houses at the foot of a tall crag. There is just one road, but a series of wonderful footpaths criss-cross the island. One of the best of these leads to the celebrated **Grotto del Genovese** (locked after vandal attacks: organize tours at least a day in advance through the custodian, T0923-924032/T339-741 8800, grottadelgenovese.it; from €15 per person, including return journey by boat or jeep), which contains some extraordinary prehistoric paintings, discovered only by accident in 1949. Some date back to the Upper Palaeolithic era (around 10,000 BC), while the incised drawings were probably executed around 8000 BC during the Neolithic era. The paintings, among the earliest cave paintings in Italy, depict fishermen (chasing tuna, even then), farmers, and wonderful dancing figures. This is just one of numerous caves that riddle the island, many of which are only accessible by boat. It's a paradise

Tip...

There's a wonderful coastal path leading to Cova del Genovese, by the Grotto of the same name, which is a good place for a picnic.

for divers, and there have been several important submarine finds dating back to the time of the Punic wars between the Romans and the Carthaginians. Fishing remains an important industry, and the fishermen of Levanzo also participate in the annual *Mattanza*.

Marettimo

The greenest and most remote of the Egadis (24 km from Trapani), Marettimo is a rugged island paradise. Accommodation is limited, and should be booked well in advance during the peak summer season, but even then this deliciously uncommercialized spot is rarely overwhelmed. The island is a protected nature reserve, and there are some superb hikes. One of the best leads to the remnants of a fortress (which served as a prison until the mid-19th century) right at the top of Punta Troia, with wonderful views. Fishermen offer boat trips to some of the loveliest coves, many of which are only accessible by boat; ask around at the harbour, or at your accommodation.

Marettimo harbour.

The chic little celeb haunt of Pantelleria is a small volcanic island closer to Africa than to Sicily (the Tunisian coast is just 70 km away, while Marsala is 100 km in the opposite direction). It's the largest of Sicily's offshore islands (83 sq km), and preserves a strong Arabic influence, not just in the place names – Khamma, Gadir, and Bukkuram – but also in the low, domed buildings of stone called dammusi which dot the countryside. Vineyards planted largely with the Zibibbo grape (the Sicilian name for the Muscat of Alexandria) produce the lusciously sweet moscato and passito dessert wines (see page 270 for details of wineries offering tours), and the tangy Pantelleria capers are a delicacy beloved by gourmets.

The island was heavily bombed during the Second World War, and the main town, **Pantelleria**, is modern and scruffy. Piled up higgledy-piggledy around the harbour, it's not particularly pretty, but the narrow streets are appealingly lively, especially in summer. There are more picturesque hamlets at **Scauri**, **Nikà** and **Gadir**, which all boast harbours with volcanic springs (the latter is home to Giorgio Armani's lavish summer home). Out at the tip of the panoramic headland (the **Punto dell'Arco**) is a spectacular natural arch of putty-coloured lava that resembles the head of an elephant (the **Arco dell'Elefante**). Inland, the **Montagna Grande**, the island's highest peak at 836 m, is part of a protected nature reserve, and a beautiful region to hike. During the migrating seasons, the island attracts numerous bird species including flamingos, herons and avocets. On its northeastern flank is a volcanic lake known as *Lo Specchio di Venere* (Venus's Looking Glass) where the goddess of love apparently once admired herself and which is fed by thermal springs. The stunning coastline, with its glittering black rocks and secret coves, is perfect for submarine exploration and there are several diving companies on the island.

Sleeping

Torri Pepoli €€€
Giardini del Ballo, viale Conte Pepoli, Erice, T0923-860117, torripepoli.it.
For sheer romance, few places can beat this beautifully restored medieval castle which dominates the magical hilltop town of Erice. Go for the Tower Room with spectacular 360-degree views which reach as far as the Egadi Islands (be sure you're in shape – it's at the top of a long, steep staircase).

NH Tonnara di Bonagia Resort €€
Piazza Tonnara, Bonagia, Valderice, T0923-431111, nh-hotels.com.
Closed mid-Oct to mid-Apr.
A 17th-century tuna fishery in a tiny seaside village has been magnificently restored to house this comfortable hotel, which offers rooms, suites and small self-catering apartments which are a good deal for families. Active kids will enjoy a football pitch, tennis, pool and children's entertainment, and there's a restaurant and a small spa with beauty treatments.

Hotel Cetarium €€-€
Via Don Leonardo Zangara 45, Castellammare del Golfo, T0924-533401, hotelcetarium.it.
Sitting right on the piquant little port, with views over the working fishing boats and yachts, this former *tonnara* has been converted into a stylish hotel. Rooms are small but comfortable, with contemporary furnishings, and there's a restaurant and fashionable bar.

Ai Lumi €
Corso Vittorio Emanuele 71, T0923-872418, ailumi.it.
A lovely palazzo on Trapani's elegant (pedestrianized) main street houses this appealing B&B, with rooms distributed around a patio. There's a restaurant downstairs (see page 266), where guests are given a 15% discount. Simple self-catering apartments are also available.

Almaran B&B €
Via S Cristoforo 8, T0923-549847, almaran.it.
A very friendly little B&B in the old quarter of Trapani, this offers a handful of simple rooms at a bargain price. Rooms are bright and spotless, all boasting private bathrooms and air conditioning, and the owner is full of great tips.

Baglio la Luna €
Riserva dello Zingaro, San Vito Lo Capo, T335-836 2856, bagliolaluna.com.
Open Apr-Nov.
On the edge of the Zingaro Reserve, this B&B enjoys a breathtaking location high above the sea. There are three pretty rooms, a fabulous garden with a play area, and a magnificent terrace. Home-cooked dinners can be served on request, and the friendly owners can arrange cookery classes, guided walks and diving excursions.

Self-catering
Le Chiavi di San Francesco Hotel
Via Tartaglia 18-20, T0923-438013, lechiavidisanfrancesco.com.
This smart apart-hotel is tucked away in a converted palazzo in the heart of Trapani's old centre (although the original interior has been replaced with modern furnishings). It offers attractively, if simply, furnished apartments for two to four people with basic kitchenettes (€80-150/€90-180 per night respectively). Breakfast is served on a panoramic roof terrace, with wonderful views over the old town with its spires and domes.

Tarantola
Contrada Tarantola, Alcamo, T329-271 3073, gorgodeldrago.it.
Set amid a sea of vines, this tranquil *agriturismo* and working wine estate offers accommodation in attractively refurbished outbuildings. Choose from B&B (€€-€) or one of the self-catering apartments (€120-200, sleeps 4). Their own produce is used in the restaurant.

Kempinski Hotel Giardino di Costanza €€€€

Via Salemi Km 7.1, Mazara del Vallo, T0923-675000, kempinski-sicily.com.

This was the fanciest resort on the island until the arrival of Rocco Forte's Verdara Resort, but it's still gloriously relaxing and luxurious. There's a spa, a pool in tropical gardens, a children's programme, plus a choice of restaurants for fine dining, and even a private beach (a minibus makes the 15-minute drive).

Carmine Hotel €€

Piazza Carmine 16, T0923-711907, hotelcarmine.it.

A beautifully restored former convent, complete with original tiles and wooden beams, now houses this boutique hotel in Marsala. The nicest rooms have balconies overlooking the courtyard garden. Breakfast is served on a terrace gazing out over the gardens.

Gadir B&B €

Corso Umberto 1, Mazara del Vallo, T334-837 1408, bbgadir.it.

Well located on the edge of town, this little B&B makes a good base to explore the southwestern corner of the island. Rooms are crisply decorated and air conditioned, and breakfast includes local pastries.

Hotel Centrale €

Via Salinisti 19, T0923-951777, hotelcentralemarsala.it.

A simple little two-star hotel in the heart of Marsala, this offers impeccably clean if functionally furnished rooms set around a plant-filled courtyard. It's a great deal with free bike hire and free parking.

La Finestra sul Sale €

Contrada Ettore Infersa 158, 5 km north of Marsala, near Isola San Pantaleo, T0923-966936.

This little B&B, just a handful of rooms over a gloriously isolated café, is located by the pier where the boats leave for Mozia – there are spellbinding views over the lagoon. Midweek is best for quiet, but come at weekends (Thu-Sun) to enjoy live music at the bar (see Caffè Mamma Caura, page 268) downstairs.

Self-catering

Baglio Calia €

Contrada Serroni, Mazara del Vallo, T0923-909390, bagliocalia.it.

A big, rambling country farm, this has been converted into a friendly *agriturismo*, with a range of apartments and bedrooms set in the converted outbuildings. It's 2 km from the centre of town, and from the beaches. The estate produces its own wines, which you can try in the excellent restaurant.

Monastero €€€€

Contrada Kassa, Scauri Alta, Pantelleria, T0923-916304, monasteropantelleria.com.

This exclusive and ultra-luxurious hotel is a bolt hole for the rich and famous (Sting and Madonna are among its past guests) but, if you've got a few thousand euro to spare, one of their artily furnished *kassas* can be yours. There's no restaurant, but a private cook can rustle up anything your heart desires.

Casa di Gloria B&B €€

Contrada Penna, T328-277 0934, Pantelleria, dammusidigloria.it.

This relaxed and stylish B&B on chic Pantelleria is run by a wonderful couple, Gloria and Saura, who want every guest to feel at home. Rooms are located in a collection of beautiful *dammusi* set around an enormous pool.

Santa Teresa €€

Contrada Monastero Alto, Scauri Siculo, Pantelleria, T0923-916389, santateresa.it.

This is a stunningly stylish *agriturismo* in the Monastero valley in the centre of Pantelleria. The elegantly restored *dammusi* of traditional stone are set within vineyards, olive groves and orchards.

Eating & drinking

Albergo Egadi €€-€
*Via Cristoforo Colombo 17,
Favigana, T0923-921232,
albergoegadi.it.*
Just 50 m from the sea, this little
inn has oodles of style. Bed and
breakfast starts at €50 per person
in the low season, but prices
double in August. The rooms are
set above a restaurant serving
excellent Mediterranean cuisine.

Villaggio Albergo l'Oasi €€-€
*Contrado Camaro, Favignana,
T0923-921635, loasifavignana.it.*
A quiet complex of buildings set
in a tropical garden, this
hotel-village offers a selection of
rooms and mini-apartments
sleeping four to six people
(€70-130 per night) by the sea.
The staff can arrange excursions,
diving trips and more.

Self-catering
Marettimo Residence
*Via Telegrafo, Marettimo,
T0923-923202,
marettimoresidence.com.*
The island's only hotel, this offers
pristine, well-equipped
apartments decorated in
Mediterranean blue and white
(sleeping two to six people,
€50-100 in low season, €100-225
in July and August). The
apartments are distributed in
low, whitewashed bungalows
overlooking the sea, each with
an olive-shaded terrace.

Trapani & around

Dal Cozzaro €€€
*Via Savoia 15, San Vito Lo Capo,
T0923-972777, dalcozzaro.it.*
Daily 1230-1530, 1900-2330.
A long-established classic, this
buzzy restaurant serves a wide
range of couscous dishes (served
with vegetables, meat or fish),
plus wonderfully fresh fish of the
day, and excellent salads. Prices
are moderate, and good value
for the quality on offer.

Ristorante del Golfo €€€
*Via Segesta 153, Castellamare del
Golfo, T0924-30257.*
**Wed-Mon 1230-1500, 1930-
2200. Closed 2 weeks in Oct.**
Book early for a table at this
minuscule but well regarded
restaurant, where you will be
served whatever came in on the
fishing boats that morning. Fresh
seafood is prepared to traditional
recipes.

Taverna Paradiso €€€
*Lungomare Dante Alighieri 22,
Trapani, T0923-22303,
tavvernaparadiso.com.*
**Mon-Sat 1300-1500, 1930-2230.
Closed 3 weeks in Nov.**
An elegant seafood restaurant in
a series of antique-furnished
dining rooms, this Trapani
favourite offers local specialities
including *cuscus di pesce* and
fresh tuna in season (end April to
early June). They make their own
creamy *cassata* for dessert.

Ai Lumi €€
*Corso Vittorio Emanuele 71,
Trapani. T0923 872418, ailumi.it.*
**Mon-Sat 1900-2300, Aug daily.
Closed Nov.**
Rustic wooden tables and
checked tablecloths belie the
sophistication of this Trapani
tavernetta, which serves some of
the best food in town. Start with
antipasti and home-made bread,
and follow up with grilled fish.
They also run a charming B&B.

Cantina Siciliana €€
*Via Giudecca 32, Trapani,
T0923-28673, cantinasiciliana.it.*
Daily 1230-1500, 1930-2200.
A long-established and
atmospheric *trattoria* in Trapani's
old Jewish quarter, this serves
market-fresh cuisine like *rotolini
gamberetti e uovo di tonno* – a
pasta pocket stuffed with tiny
shrimp, hazelnuts and tuna roe.
Order *cassatelle* (fried pastry
parcels with ricotta and
cinnamon) for dessert.

Monte San Giuliano €€
*Vicolo San Rocco 7, Erice,
T0923-869595.*
**Mon-Sat 1300-1500, 1900-2200.
Closed 3 weeks in Jan and 3
weeks in Nov.**
Tucked away in Erice's beautiful
stone heart, this pretty restaurant
is a great place to try *cuscus di
pesce* (fish couscous) or a wide
range of flavoursome, home-
made pasta dishes. Book a table
on the plant-shaded terrace.

Five of the best

Places for *granite*

❶ Minaudo, San Vito Lo Capo The *granita di arance rosse*, made with blood oranges, is deservedly famous here.
❷ Enzo e Nino, Marsala This old-fashioned bar is the best place to join the locals for a granita.
❸ Gelateria Coppetta, Mazara del Vallo Try the unusual, fruity *granita di gelsi* (mulberry).
❹ Due Colonne, Favignana Order a *granita di caffè* (like a frozen espresso) to go with the view of Favignana's square.
❺ Scaletta, Marettimo Take the edge off the island heat with a refreshing, fruity *granita*.

Trattoria del Porto da Felice
€€
Via Ammiraglio Staiti 45, Trapani, T0923-547822.
Mon-Sat 1300-1500, 1930-2200.
Tuck into large portions of tasty home cooking at this deightful family-run restaurant that overlooks Trapani's port. Fresh fish is the highlight, including fish couscous, but their *spaghetti al pesto Trapanese* – with tomato and almond pesto – is also very good. Finish up with *cassatelle con ricotta*.

Cafés & bars
Bar Pasticceria Scopello
Via A Diaz 13, Scopello, T0924-541149.
Mon-Sat 0800-2000, daily in summer.
A classic for breakfast cappuccino and *cornetti* in this charming seaside village.

Il Gelato di Michele
Viale Regina Margherita 25, Trapani, T0923-873942.
Daily 0900-1900, weekends only in winter.
If you can't make up your mind which flavour to choose, go for the intense dark chocolate.

Minaudo
Via Gioacchino Amico 12, San Vito Lo Capo, T349-463 8074.
Daily 1100-2100. Closed in winter.
Widely considered the best gelateria in town, with a huge range of flavours to choose from. Try the fantastic *granita di arance rosse*, made with blood oranges.

Marsala & around

Il Pescatore €€€€
Via Castelvetrano 191, Mazara del Vallo, T0923-947580, ristorantedelpescatore.com.
Tue-Sun 1230-1500, 2000-2200.
Book early on summer weekends if you want one of the sought-after terrace tables at this restaurant on the outskirts of town, in a modern residential neighbourhood. Beautifully fresh fish is the highlight of the menu, including swordfish prepared in several different ways.

Osteria Il Gallo e L'Innamorata €€€
Via S Bilardello 18, Marsala, T0923-195 4446, osteriailgalloelinnamorata.com.
Wed-Mon 2000-2200.
A highly recommended choice in central Marsala, serving fish so fresh it melts in the mouth. Go for the bruschetta topped with *bottarga* (dried tuna roe, a pungent local speciality), and follow with pasta with *ragù di tonno* (when in season).

Alla Kasbah €€
Via Itria 10, Mazara del Vallo,
T0923-906126.
Tue-Sun 1300-1500, 1930-2230.
This popular trattoria is another
excellent place to try western
Sicily's signature dish, *cuscus di
pesce*, prepared here with a
slightly more exotic array of
spices. Many of the recipes come
from the island of Pantelleria and
have a distinct North African
influence.

La Bettola €€
Via Francesco Maccagnone 32,
Mazara del Vallo, T0923-946422,
ristorantelabettola.it.
Thu-Tue 1300-1500, 1930-2200.
Closed 2 weeks in Jul.
In the historic centre, with a small
terrace behind wooden shades,
this is an elegant spot for local
cuisine. As you might expect in
one of Italy's busiest fishing
ports, the fish is superbly fresh;
have it simply grilled, or in
ghiotto, a sturdy fish stew.

La Pineta €€
Marinella di Selinunte,
T0924-46820.
Mid-Mar to end Sep 1000-2300
(hours erratic, advance booking
advised).
Dine with your toes in the sand
at Bar Ristorante La Pineta, which
is located east of Marinella di
Selinunte in the Belice River
nature reserve. Leave your car in
the car park and follow the sandy
path for the last 200 m. Despite
the plastic tables, La Pineta offers

serious cooking, particularly the
seafood. Try the spaghetti with
cozze (mussels) and follow up
with the fish of the day. May
close in bad weather.

Cafés & bars
Enzo & Nino
Via XI Maggio 130, Marsala,
T0923-951969.
Daily 0800-2000.
A long-established
neighbourhood favourite on
Marsala's main drag, this is an
essential stop for coffee, snacks,
or a refreshing ice cream.

Gelateria Coppetta
*Corso Umberto I 27, Mazara del
Vallo, T0923-90737.*
Daily 1000-2200.
Among the flavours at this
award-winning ice-cream
parlour is luscious peach.

Caffè Mamma Caura
*Contrada Ettore Infersa 158, 5 km
north of Marsala, near Isola San
Pantaleo, T0923-966936.*
Summer daily 1000-0100,
phone for winter opening
hours.
Near the embarkation point for
boats to Mozia, this charming,
and simple café-bar has
magnificent views over the salt
flats and is a romantic place to
soak up the sunsets. Live jazz and
pop at weekends. It also has B&B
accommodation (see La Finestra
sul Sale, page 265).

(see La Finestra sul Sale, page 265).

Egadi Islands & Pantelleria

La Nicchia €€€
Via Messina 22, Pantelleria town,
T0923-912968, lanicchia.it.
Daily 1900-2200 in summer.
Closed Oct to Easter.
One of the island's most
fashionable restaurants, set in a
beautifully restored *dammuso*
overlooking a delightful garden.
Nearby, the owners have opened
a simple *enoteca*, La Nicchia sul
Mare, serving a wonderful range
of wines accompanied by
tapas-style treats.

Paradiso €€€
Via Lungomare 8, Levanzo,
T0923-924080, isoladilevanzo.it.
Daily 1230-1500, 1900-2300.
Closed mid-Nov to mid-Mar.
This classic seaside restaurant
doesn't look up to much but has
long been considered the best
on the island. Unsurprisingly, fish
predominates on the menu, with
linguine con polpo (linguine with
octopus), and fresh tuna during
the *Mattanza* season.

Il Veliero €€
Via Umberto 22, Marettimo,
T0923-923142.
Daily 1200-1500, 1900-2200.
On the water's edge, this
traditional, family-run trattoria is
the best place to fill up on big
plates of home cooking. Try the
busiati (a plump, long pasta
typical of western Sicily) with a
tuna sauce if it's on the menu.

Entertainment

La Bettola €€
*Via Nicotera 47, Favignana,
T0923-921988, isoleegadi.it/
labettola.php.*
Fri-Wed 1230-1500, 1900-2300,
daily in Aug.
A good, old-fashioned trattoria
serving excellent fresh seafood
(try the lobster salad), excellent
couscous, and fabulous
home-made desserts.

Donne Fugate €€
*Corso Umberto 10, Pantelleria
town, T0923-912688.*
Daily 1200-1500, 1900-2200.
A charming little restaurant
serving excellent cuisine
prepared with superb local
ingredients. The antipasti is
especially recommended,
particularly the carpaccio of
aubergine with *bottarga* (dried
tuna roe), as well as the *cuscus di
pesce* (Thursdays only).

Scaletta €
*Via Telegrafo 3, Marettimo,
T0923-923233.*
Daily 0900-2200.
This manages to combine a little
of everything – *pasticceria*, bar,
café and an excellent, informal
restaurant. Come for breakfast, a
seafood lunch, or just ice cream.

Cafés & bars
Due Colonne
*Piazza Matrice 76, Favignana,
T0923-922291.*
Daily 0800-2200.
Grab a fruit *granita* or ice cream,
and watch the world go by.

Clubs
Muna Café
*Via Giuseppe Garibaldi, Trapani,
T329-166 8547.*
Tue-Thu 1900-2400, Fri-Sat
1900 till late.
This arty café-bar is a quiet place
for a coffee and a chance to
catch up on emails during the
evening, but becomes livelier at
night. It occasionally features live
acoustic acts.

Up & Down Pub
Via Marsala 305/307, Trapani.
Daily 2000-0200.
This newish venue has a little of
everything, from live gigs, to
theme parties, salsa nights and
even karaoke. It's a favourite with
the student crowd.

Oxidiana
*Contrada Kuddie Rosse,
Pantelleria, T0923-912319.*
A summer-only *discoteca* for
dancing under the stars.

Festivals & events
Estate a Marsala
Marsala.
Jul.
Outdoor concerts for the
'Summer in Marsala' festival
(comune.marsala.tp.it).

Luglio Musicale Trapanese
Trapani.
Jul.
Opera festival held at the Villa
Margherita public gardens.

Zampogna d'Oro
Erice
Early Dec.
Folklore music festival.

Music
Cine Impero
*Piazza della Vittoria, Marsala.
T0923-993393,
comune.marsala.tp.it.*
Cinema and theatre with all kinds
of performances including
regular concerts. Contact tourist
office for info.

Easter procession, Marsala.

Shopping

Activities & tours

Pick of the picnic spots

Torre Ligny, Trapani Perch on the rocks on the causeway leading to the Torre Ligny.

Villa Margherita, Trapani Trapani's shady public gardens are perfect for picnics, and the Renda deli is very handy for supplies.

Giardino del Balio, Erice Grab a bag of sublime pastries at Maria's and head to the castle gardens for panoramic views.

Scopello The little beach just beyond the *tonnara* in Scopello is a heavenly picnic spot, and great for a post-prandial swim.

Segesta There are picnic tables in the shade by the café-bar at Segesta, but a spot in the grass next to the beautiful temple is more atmospheric.

Capo Feto, Mazara del Vallo The protected Capo Feto headland, at the western edge of Mazara del Vallo, is only accessible on foot, but the long sands, backed by scrub, are really stunning.

Food & drink
E&N Pasticceria
Via XI Maggio 130, Marsala, T0923-951969, pasticceriaen.com.
Thu-Tue 0900-2000.
A selection of marzipan fruits, plus a mouthwatering range of traditional *dolci*. Try their *cassata*.

Gerardi Gastronomia
Piazza Mameli 14, Marsala, T0923-952240.
Mon-Tue, Thu-Sat 0800-1300, 1630-2000, Wed 0800-1300.
A gourmet deli, with Sicilian and international fresh produce, including cheeses and hams.

La Nicchia Bottega delle Specialità
Via Messina 24, Pantelleria, T0923-912968.
Mon-Sat 1000-2000, daily in Aug. Closed Nov to Easter.
The best restaurant in town prepares gourmet delicacies, including pâtés and pesto made with Pantelleria capers, jams, sauces, and of course the best Pantelleria wines.

Pasticceria Maria Grammatico
Corso Vittorio Emanuele 14, Erice, T0923-869390, mariagrammatico.it.
Daily 0800-2100.
A superb pastry shop (and café), which is famous throughout Sicily. Maria's story is told in *Bitter Almonds* by Mary Taylor Simeti.

Renda
Via Giovanbattista Fardella 82, Trapani, T0923-22270, renda.it.
Mon-Sat 0900-1300, 1630-2000.
This deli has all kinds of local specialities, including olive oils, wines, jars of Trapanese pesto, plus cheeses, hams, salami and everything you need for a picnic.

Diving
Cetaria Diving
Via Marco Polo 3, Scopello, T0924-541177/T368-386 4808, cetaria.com.
Diving and snorkelling in the protected Zingaro nature reserve. A half-day boat excursion with stops for snorkelling and swimming costs from around €50.

Diving Cava Levante
Pantelleria, T0923-915174, calalevante.it.
A reliable PADI dive centre, which offers a range of courses, including an underwater archaeology course (from €220). A single dive is €35.

Food & wine
Cantina Casano
Contrada Kamma, Pantelleria, T0923-912948, casanovini.it.
This wine producer, famous for its Marsala wines, also produces Zibibbo wines on Pantelleria.

Cantine Florio
Via Vincenzo Florio 1, T0923-781306, cantineflorio.it.
See box, page 257, for guided tours of Marsala's biggest tourist attraction.

Fazio
Via Capitano Rizzo 39, Fulgatore (near Erice), T0923-811700, faziowines.it.
Visits by prior appointment at this award-winning winery.

Transport

Feudo Bucari

Contrada Bucari, Mazara del Vallo, T339-8662060, feudobucari.it.

Tastings and tours at this small but interesting winery, which produces some excellent reds, whites and the local Marsala.

Salvatore Murana

Contrada Khamma 276, Pantelleria, T0923-969673, salvatoremurana.com.

Produces superb Pantelleria wines. Tours offered.

Trapani & around

Trapani is linked by train to Palermo (2½ hrs, 4 daily), Castellammare del Golfo (45 mins, 4 daily), Segesta-Tempio for Segesta (25 mins, 4 daily). There are at least 8 trains a day to Marsala (30 mins), and to Mazara del Vallo (50 mins). For Erice, take the cable car, or the regular AST or Lumia bus (45 mins). There are infrequent trains to Salemi-Gibellina station (1½ hrs). For Mozia (Motya), take the bus or train to Marsala, and then take a local bus from there. **AST buses** (aziendasicilianatrasporti. it) link Trapani with San Vito Lo Capo (1½ hrs, at least 8 daily except Sun), as well as Marsala (30 mins, regular weekday services, limited at weekends), Mazara del Vallo (2½ hrs, 3 services daily), Castellammare del Golfo (1 hr) and the airport at Trapani-Birgi (also known as Vincenzo Florio airport). AST, Tarantola and Segesta buses connect Trapani with Segesta (45 mins); Segesta buses continue to Palermo (2½ hrs). Russo buses link Castellammare del Golfo with Scopello and San Vito Lo Capo.

Marsala & around

There are no direct trains from Palermo to Marsala; you will need to change at Trapani or Alcamo (average journey time is 3½ hrs). There are direct trains to Trapani and Mazara del Vallo (see above). AST and Marinella buses link Mazara del Vallo with Marinella di Selinunte. There is only one bus a day from Marsala to Gibellina (1½ hrs) where there are connections for Salemi (20 mins from Gibellina). Gibellina is also served by buses from Alcamo (45 mins, 3 daily).

Egadi Islands & Pantelleria

Ferries and hydrofoils link the Egadi Islands with Trapani and Marsala. **Siremar** (siremar.it) runs daily car ferry services to Favignana (45 mins) all year round. **Ustica** (usticalines.com) runs a ferry service from Marsala to the Egadi Islands, and another from Mazara del Vallo to Pantelleria. Siremar and Ustica lines run faster hydrofoils to all three islands during the summer season (Favignana, 20 mins; Levanzo, 20 mins; Marettimo, 1 hr), and to Pantelleria (ferry 7 hrs, hydrofoil 2½ hrs). Pantelleria can also be reached by air: **Meridiana** (meridiana.it) fly daily from Trapani and Palermo during the summer, and **AirOne** (flyairone. com) operates flights from Palermo.

Contents

Practicalities

Signs in Stromboli.

Getting there

Air

From UK and Ireland

There are three international airports in Sicily: Palermo, Catania and Trapani. **British Airways** and **Air Malta** fly directly from London Gatwick to Catania; **easyJet** operates direct services from London Gatwick to Palermo; **Ryanair** flies directly from London Stansted, London Luton, Birmingham and Dublin to Trapani airport, and from London Stansted to Palermo. There are summer-only charter flights to Catania with **Avro**, **Monarch Charter**, and **Thomas Cook**. **Alitalia** offers services from London Heathrow to Palermo and Catania via Rome or Milan.

From North America

Eurofly operate direct flights from New York (JFK) to Palermo Airport. **Eurofly**, **Delta**, **United**, **Continental**, **US Airways**, **Alitalia** offer direct flights from the US to mainland Italian airports. Canadian travellers will have to change in the US, or fly to another European city for a connection. **Alitalia** fly directly from Toronto to Rome.

From rest of Europe and mainland Italy

Direct flights to Sicilian airports depart from most major European cities. These are operated by **Air Berlin**, **Brussels Airlines**, **ClickAir**, **easyJet**, **Ryanair**,

SkyEurope, ThomasCook, Transavia, TUI, and Vueling. Check the company websites and whichbudget.com for specific routes.

There are numerous flights from most mainland Italian airports (including Bologna, Florence, Milan, Palma, Pisa, Rome, Turin, Venice and Verona) with **Alitalia-Air One**, **Wind Jet**, **easyJet**, and **Ryanair**, and the joint company **Meridiana-Eurofly** (meridiana.it).

Airport information

Palermo Falcone Borsellino Airport (T800-541880, gesap.it) is at Punta Raisi, 35 km west of central Palermo. An airport bus departs every 30 minutes (0645-2400, €5, buy tickets onboard, journey time 55 mins) for piazza Politeama and the train station in central Palermo. There is also an hourly train service, **Trinacria Express** (0540-2340, €5.50, 55 mins). Taxis cost €30-40.

Catania Fontanarossa Airport (T095-723 9111, aeroporto.catania.it), 5 km southeast of the city, is connected to the central train station by AMT Alibus bus (0500-2400, every 20 mins, €1). A metro line is under construction. A taxi to the centre costs €15-20. There are also direct bus services to other towns on the east coast, including Syracuse and Taormina.

Trapani Birgi Airport (T0923-842502, airgest.it), 15 km southeast of Trapani and 15 km north of

Going green

Dutch **Motorail** (autoslaaptrein.nl in Dutch, or through Railsavers at railsavers.com) operate a daily service from s'Hertogenbosch in Holland to Bologna. This arrives at 1000, and another service, operated by **Trenitalia** (trenitalia.com), departs daily at 2148 for Catania (arrives the following day at 1216). There is also a motorail service from Rome to Catania (Sun, Wed and Fri, summer only). Prices vary widely, but start at around €500 one way for a car and two passengers from s'Hertogenbosch to Bologna, and around €400 from Bologna to Catania.

A section of the train continues to Palermo (11 hrs from Rome). Tickets at **raileurope.com** (T0870-584 8848), useful information at seat61.com. From destinations in the rest of Europe, there are also direct passenger trains to Milan and Rome where you can change for services to Sicily.

Road

Car
It's a 2450-km journey from London to Messina, or about 25 hours of driving time. You could halve the drive by taking the ferry from Genoa or Livorno to Palermo (see above). **Autostrade** (T055-420 3200, autostrade.it) provides information on Italian motorways while **Automobile Club Italiana** (T06-49981, aci.it) gives general driving information.

Bus/coach
Eurolines (T0870-580 8080, nationalexpress.co.uk) operate two services per week from London Victoria to Naples with a travel time of around 35 hours. There are bus connections from Naples to several points in Sicily with **SAIS** (T800-211020, saisautolinee.it).

Sea

The main Sicilian ports are Messina (northeast), Palermo (northwest) and Trapani (west). Travel by ferry is usually comfortable, but often considerably pricier than a budget flight.

Ferry from mainland Italy
Caronte (T0965-751413, carontetourist.it) and **FS ferries**, run by Italian State Railways (ferroviedellostato.it) operate ferry (25 mins) and hydrofoil (15 mins) services between Messina and Villa San Giovanni. **Ustica** (T0923-873813, usticalines.it) runs ferries and hydrofoils from

Marsala, is a hub for budget airlines and the main gateway to western Sicily. There are bus links to Trapani (every 30 mins, €3.50, journey time 25 mins), to Agrigento (1-2 services daily, €10.60) and to Marsala (2-4 services daily, €3.50)

The islands of **Lampedusa** and **Pantelleria** have small airports (both managed by Palermo's Falcone Borsellino airport, T091-702 0619, enac-italia.it), used for summer flights.

Rail

You can travel with **Eurostar** (eurostar.com) from London to Paris, before joining an overnight sleeper from Paris Bercy to Rome. This connects with a direct train to Sicily, which stops at Messina (8 hrs from Rome), Taormina, Catania and Syracuse.

Getting around

Getting around Sicily can be an adventure. Public transport is erratic, and you'll need patience and a whole sheaf of Plan Bs. Don't bother with a car if you are in Sicily on a city break (parking and driving are a nightmare in all Sicilian cities, particularly Palermo) but a car is essential to explore the hidden corners of this beautiful island. If you're spending time on Sicily's offshore islands, leave the car behind (there are strict restrictions on bringing vehicles to certain islands during the summer season). The best road maps for the island are published by Touring Club Italiano and Michelin.

Air

The islands of Lampedusa and Pantelleria have small airports, with regular flights from Palermo, Trapani and mainland Italian airports in summer. Panarea, in the Aeolian Islands, is linked by helicopter taxi service, see page 145 .

Rail

Reggio di Calabria to Messina. **Tirrenia** (T02-2630 2803, tirrenia.it) and **SNAV** (T081-428 5555, snav.it) operate daily Naples–Palermo crossings (9 hrs 45 mins – 10½ hrs). SNAV also runs crossings between Civitavecchia (Rome) and Palermo (11 hrs) and between Naples and the Aeolian Islands. **Grandi Navi Veloci** (T010-209 4591, gnv.it) run daily (excluding Sunday) services between Genoa and Palermo (20 hrs). Ustica operate summer-only hydrofoils from Naples to Trapani (6½ hrs) and Favignana (7 hrs). Tirrenia runs ferries between Cagliari (Sardinia) and Trapani (13 hrs). **Grimaldi** (T089-253202, grimaldi-lines.com) operate several routes: Genoa–Catania, Civitavecchia–Catania, Civitavecchia–Trapani, Livorno-Palermo, Salerno–Palermo, Tunis–Palermo, Tunis–Trapani, Malta–Catania.

Mainland Italy has an extensive and efficient rail network, but Sicily's is decidedly patchy. The train is worth taking between Palermo and Messina; between Trapani, Marsala and Mazara del Vallo; and from Messina to Syracuse via Catania. Services within other areas are slow or require a change (there is no direct train from Palermo to Catania, for example). Almost everywhere else is best reached by bus (see below). For this reason, none of the usual European rail passes represent good value in Sicily, unless the island is just one stage of a longer Italian or European trip.

There are several different train services, of which the most common are the plush InterCity (IC) services and the more common regional trains (REG). (Sicily has no Eurostar Italia trains.) All can be booked at **trenitalia.com**, where the type of train is indicated with the initials IC or REG. 'Amica' fares are cheaper advance tickets (if you can find one);

flexi-fare costs more but is flexible; and standard fare is just that. Booking and buying tickets at the counter or via machines in train stations is convenient if you can't access the internet. Tickets must be validated at the yellow stamping machines before boarding.

Sicily also has a private train line, the **Circumetnea**, which circles the base of Mount Etna (see page 173).

Road

Car

Driving in Sicily is not for the timid. Sicilians drive with reckless disregard for road markings, traffic lights, and pedestrians. Around Palermo, for example, the road markings dictate that there should be two lines of traffic in either direction. You will see three. Keep to your 'lane' (ie follow the car in front of you), and you will emerge unscathed. Don't hesitate (or you will be lost) and remember that the golden rule of Sicilian driving is to keep the traffic flowing.

Italy has strict laws on drink driving: the legal limit is 0.5 g of alcohol per litre of blood, so steer clear of alcohol to be safe. The use of mobile telephones while driving is illegal. Children under 1.5 m are required to sit in the back of the car, and a reflective jacket must be worn if your car breaks down on the carriageway in poor visibility. On-the-spot fines for minor traffic offences are now legal – typically €150-250. Always get a receipt if you incur one.

Speed limits are 130 kph (motorways), 110 kph (dual carriageways) and 50 kph (towns). Limits are 20 kph *lower* on motorways and dual carriageways when the road is wet. *Autostrade* (motorways) are toll roads, so keep cash in the car as a back-up even though you can use credit cards on the blue 'viacard' gates. **Autostrade** (T055-420 3200, autostrade.it) provides information on motorways in Italy while **Automobile Club d'Italia (ACI)** (T06-49981, aci.it) provides general driving information. ACI offers roadside assistance with English-speaking operators on T116. Unleaded petrol is *benzina*, diesel is *gasolio*.

Car hire

Car hire is available at all of Italy's international airports and many domestic airports. Book as early as possible for popular destinations and at busy times of year. Check in advance the opening times of the car hire office. Car hire comparison websites and agents are a good place to start a search for the best deals. Try **easycar.com**, **carrentals.co.uk**, **thinksicily.com** (which has a good price comparison engine).

Check what documents are required. Some companies will ask for an International Driving Licence, with your normal driving licence, if the language of your driving licence is different from the country you're renting the car in. Others are content with an EU licence. You'll need to produce a credit card for most companies. If you book ahead, make sure that the credit card holder is the same as the person renting and driving the car to avoid any problems. Most companies have a lower age limit of 21 years and require that you've held your licence for at least a year. Many have a young driver surcharge for those under 25. Confirm insurance and any damage waiver charges and keep all your documents with you when you drive. Always take a printed copy of the contract with you, regardless of whether you have a booking number and a 'confirmed' booking.

Bicycle

Cycling is madness in Sicilian cities and in general the island is poorly equipped for cyclists. Bike rental outlets are few and far between, even in the biggest resorts, and there are almost no cycling lanes anywhere. However, there are some superb cycling routes for experienced road cyclists, particularly in the Madonie mountains and around Mount Etna, and some flatter routes, more suitable for less experienced bikers, in the west. These are popular with foreign visitors, most of whom bring their own bikes or come on organized holidays.

Tip...

EU nationals driving their own car need an International Insurance Certificate (also known as a Green Card). Those holding a non-EU licence need an International Driving Permit.

Bus/coach

Buses are the most popular – and often the only – means of public transport in Sicily. There are four main bus companies which cover most of the island: **AST** (aziendasicilianatrasporti.it); **SAIS** (saisautolinee.it); **Interbus** (interbus.it); and **Giuntabus** (giuntabus.com). These are supplemented by numerous local bus services. Tickets can usually be bought on board, or at kiosks near bus stops or bus stations in larger towns. Tickets for city buses should be purchased before boarding and must be validated once you get on (or risk a fine). Tickets are generally purchased at ticket booths, tobacco shops (*tabacchi*), or newspaper kiosks.

Sea

Ferry and hydrofoil

Sicily's offshore islands are linked by ferry and hydrofoil. Milazzo (see page 123) is the main port for the Aeolians; Porto Empedocle (see page 230) for the Pelagie Islands; and Trapani (see page 247) for the Egadi Islands and Pantelleria. The Egadi Islands and Pantelleria can also be reached from Marsala (see page 255) and Mazara del Vallo (see page 256). The main ferry lines are operated by **SNAV** (snav.it), **Ustica** (usticalines.it) and **Siremar** (siremar.it).

Directory

Customs and immigration

UK and EU citizens do not need a visa, but will need a valid passport to enter Italy. A standard tourist visa for those from outside the EU is valid for up to 90 days.

Disabled travellers

Italy is rather behind when it comes to catering for disabled travellers, and Sicily, which is one of the poorest regions in Italy, is worse than almost anywhere else. There is an interesting and inspiring article describing a trip to Sicily by a pair of independent wheelchair-users at globalaccessnews.com/sicilyedwards08.htm. Before departure, contact a specialist association or agency for more details, such as **Accessible Italy** (accessibleitaly.com) or **Society for Accessible Travel and Hospitality** (sath.org).

Emergency numbers

Ambulance T118; Fire T115; Police T112 (with English-speaking operators), T113 (*carabinieri*); Roadside assistance T116.

Etiquette

Projecting a good image is important to Sicilians. Smart casual dress is expected, even in summer when other countries dress down. At clubs and fashionable restaurants in the cities and resorts, you'll need to dress up to get in. Take note of public notices about conduct: sitting on steps or eating and drinking in certain historic areas is not allowed. Covering arms and legs is necessary for admission into some churches. Punctuality is apparently not mandatory in Italy, so be prepared to wait – even at government-run sights where opening times are treated as a suggestion.

Families

Whether for a traditional beach break or an afternoon in a gelateria, families are well accommodated in Italy. The family is highly regarded in Italy and *bambini* are indulged and there's plenty to do for children besides endless museum visits. Do note that sometimes lone parents or adults accompanying children of a different surname may need evidence before taking children in and out of the country. Contact your Italian embassy for current details: in London T020-7312 2200, in Washington DC T202-612-4400, in Dublin T353-1-660-1744, in Ottawa T613-232-2401, in Canberra T612-6273-3333.

Health

Comprehensive travel and medical insurance is strongly recommended for all travel. EU citizens should apply for a free **European Health Insurance Card** (ehic.org) which replaced the E111 form and offers reduced-cost medical treatment.

Pharmacies are identified by a large green cross outside. The **Farmacie di Turno** (duty pharmacies, which take it in turn to open 24 hours) are listed on the front door. T1100 for addresses of the nearest open pharmacies. The accident and emergency department of a hospital is the *pronto soccorso*. Local hospital details are in the Essentials boxes for each destination.

Insurance

Comprehensive travel and medical insurance is strongly recommended for all travel – the EHIC is not a replacement for insurance. You should check any exclusions, and that your policy covers you for all the activities you want to undertake. Keep details of your insurance documents separately – emailing yourself with the details is a good way to keep the information safe and accessible. Ensure you have full insurance if hiring a car, and you might need an international insurance certificate if taking your own car (contact your current insurers).

Money

The Italian currency is the Euro (€). Throughout Sicily there are ATMs that accept major credit and debit cards. To change cash or travellers' cheques, look for a *cambio*. Most larger restaurants and shops take major credit cards, but smaller establishments, museums and art galleries rarely accept them. Sicily is still a cash-based society. Paying directly with debit cards such as Cirrus is almost impossible, so withdrawing from an ATM and paying cash is better. Keep plenty of cash for toll roads if you're driving. See Essentials boxes for each destination for advice on where to find ATMs.

Police

While it appears that there are several different types of police in Italy (and several uniforms for each), there are two you will see most often: the *polizia* (T113) and the *carabinieri* (T112). The *polizia* are the 'normal' police under the control of the Interior Ministry, while the *carabinieri* are a de facto military force. Both will respond if you need help.

Post

Italian post has a not entirely undeserved reputation for being unreliable, particularly for handling postcards. Overseas post will require *posta prioritaria* (priority mail) and a postcard stamp will cost from €0.60. You can buy *francobolli* (stamps) at post offices and *tabacchi* (look for T signs). Post office locations are listed in the Essentials boxes for each destination.

Telephone

The dialing codes for the main towns in the region are: Palermo 091; Messina 090; Catania 095; Syracuse 093; Agrigento 0922; Trapani 0923; Enna 0935. You need to use these local codes even when dialling from within the city or region. The prefix for Italy is +39. You no longer need to drop the initial '0' from area codes when calling from abroad. For directory enquiries call T12.

Time difference

Italy uses Central European Time, GMT+1.

Tipping

Most waiters in the region expect a tip from foreigners; 10-15% is the norm if you're really happy with the service. Leaving change from the bill is appropriate for cheaper *enotecas* and osterias. Taxis may add on extra costs for luggage etc but an additional tip is always appreciated. Rounding up prices always goes down well, especially if it means avoiding having to give change – not a favourite Italian habit.

Tourist information

See Essentials boxes for each destination.

Voltage

Italy functions on a 220V mains supply and the standard European two-pin plug.

Safety

The crime rate in Italy is generally low, but rates of petty crime higher. Take general care when travelling: don't flaunt your valuables, take only what money you need and split it, and don't take risks you wouldn't at home. Beware of scams and con artists, and don't expect things to go smoothly if you partake in fake goods. Car break-ins are common, so always remove valuables and open the glove compartment to show that there is nothing valuable inside the car. Take care on public transport where pickpockets or bag-cutters might operate. Do not make it clear which stop you're getting off at – it gives potential thieves a timeframe to work in (most work in groups). Female travellers will find Sicily quite safe, apart from some attention from local Lotharios, who are generally harmless.

Language

In the main tourist resorts, at least in the larger hotels and restaurants, you'll usually find that some English is spoken. The further you go from the tourist centres, however, the more trouble you will have, unless you have at least a smattering of Italian. Syracuse is probably the most English-friendly town; throughout much of the rest of the island's interior English is often hard to come by or non-existent.

You will also find that Sicily's first language, *Sicilianu*, is widely spoken in much of the island, although, with the exception of the very elderly, all Sicilians also speak Italian. We've included a few simple Sicilian phrases on page 284. If you are interested in learning more, visit the website **linguasiciliana.org**.

Stress in spoken Italian usually falls on the penultimate syllable. Italian has standard sounds: unlike English you can work out how it sounds from how it's written and vice versa.

Vowels

a like 'a' in cat
e like 'e' in vet, or slightly more open, like the 'ai' in air (except after c or g, see consonants below)
i like 'i' in sip (except after c or g, see below)
o like 'o' in fox
u like 'ou' in soup

Consonants

Generally consonants sound the same as in English, though 'e' and 'i' after 'c' or 'g' make them soft (a 'ch' or a 'j' sound) and are silent themselves, whereas 'h' makes them hard (a 'k' or 'g' sound), the opposite to English. So *ciao* is pronounced 'chaow', but *chiesa* (church) is pronounced 'kee-ay-sa'.

The combination 'gli' is pronounced like the 'lli' in million, and 'gn' like 'ny' in Tanya.

Basics

thank you   *grazie*
hi/goodbye   *ciao* (informal)
good day (until after lunch/ mid-afternoon)   *buongiorno*
good evening (after lunch)   *buonasera*
goodnight   *buonanotte*
goodbye   *arrivederci*
please   *per favore*
I'm sorry   *mi dispiace*
excuse me   *permesso*
yes   *sì*
no   *no*

Numbers

one	*uno*	17	*diciassette*
two	*due*	18	*diciotto*
three	*tre*	19	*diciannove*
four	*quattro*	20	*venti*
five	*cinque*	21	*ventuno*
six	*sei*	22	*ventidue*
seven	*sette*	30	*trenta*
eight	*otto*	40	*quaranta*
nine	*nove*	50	*cinquanta*
10	*dieci*	60	*sessanta*
11	*undici*	70	*settanta*
12	*dodici*	80	*ottanta*
13	*tredici*	90	*novanta*
14	*quattordici*	100	*cento*
15	*quindici*	200	*due cento*
16	*sedici*	1000	*mille*

Gestures

Italians are famously theatrical and animated in dialogue and use a variety of gestures.

Side of left palm on side of right wrist as right wrist is flicked up   Go away

Hunched shoulders and arms lifted with palms of hands outwards   What am I supposed to do?

Thumb, index and middle finger of hand together, wrist upturned and shaking
  What are you doing/what's going on?

Both palms together and moved up and down in front of stomach   Same as above

All fingers of hand squeezed together   To signify a place is packed full of people

Front of side of hand to chin   'Nothing', as in 'I don't understand' or 'I've had enough'

Flicking back of right ear   To signify someone is gay

Index finger in cheek   To signify good food

Questions

how?   *come?*
how much?   *quanto?*
when?   *quando?*
where?   *dove?*
why?   *perché?*
what?   *che cosa?*

Problems

don't understand   *non capisco*
don't know   *non lo so*
don't speak Italian   *non parlo italiano*
How do you say ... (in Italian)?
  come si dice ... (in italiano)?
Is there anyone who speaks English?
  c'è qualcuno che parla inglese?

Shopping

this one/that one   *questo/quello*
less   *meno*
more   *di più*
How much is it/are they?   *quanto costa/costano?*
Can I have ...?   *posso avere ...?*

Travelling

one ticket for...   *un biglietto per...*
single   *solo andate*
return   *andate ritorno*
does this go to Palermo?
  questo va per Palermo?
airport   *aeroporto*
bus stop   *fermata*
train   *treno*
car   *macchina*
taxi   *tassi*

Hotels

a double/single room
una camera doppia/singola
a double bed   *un letto matrimoniale*
bathroom   *bagno*
Is there a view?   *c'è una bella vista?*
Can I see the room?   *posso vedere la camera?*
When is breakfast?   *a che ora è la colazione?*
Can I have the key?   *posso avere la chiave?*

Time

morning   *mattina*
afternoon   *pomeriggio*
evening   *sera*
night   *notte*
soon   *presto/fra poco*
later   *più tardi*
What time is it?   *Che ore sono?*
today/tomorrow/yesterday   *oggi/domani/ieri*

Days

Monday   *lunedi*
Tuesday   *martedi*
Wednesday   *mercoledi*
Thursday   *giovedi*
Friday   *venerdi*
Saturday   *sabato*
Sunday   *domenica*

Conversation

alright   *va bene*
right then   *allora*
who knows!   *bo! / chi sa*
good luck!   *in bocca al lupo!* (literally, 'in the
   mouth of the wolf')
one moment   *un attimo*
hello (when answering a phone)
   pronto (literally, 'ready')
let's go!   *andiamo!*
enough/stop   *basta!*
give up!   *dai!*
I like ...   *mi piace ...*
how's it going?   (well, thanks) *come va?* (bene, grazie)
how are you?   *come sta/stai?* (polite/informal)

Some Sicilian phrases

Good morning   *Bon giornu*
Good afternoon/evening   *Bona sira*
Good-bye   *Addiu*
Pleased to meet you   *Piaciri di canuscirvi*
How do you say in Sicilian...?   *Comu si dici in
sicilianu...?*
It's a beautiful day   *È na bedda jurnata*
Let's go   *Ammunì*

Index

Index

Footprint credits

Text editor: Tim Jollands
Assistant editor: Alice Jell
Picture editors: Rob Lunn, Kevin Feeney, Kassia Gawronski
Layout & production: Davina Rungasamy
Maps: Compass Maps Ltd

Managing Director: Andy Riddle
Commercial Director: Patrick Dawson
Publisher: Alan Murphy
Editorial: Sara Chare, Ria Gane, Jenny Haddington, Felicity Laughton, Nicola Gibbs
Cartography: Sarah Sorensen, Kevin Feeney, Emma Bryers
Design: Mytton Williams
Sales & marketing: Liz Harper, Hannah Bonnell
Advertising: Renu Sibal
Business Development: Zoë Jackson
Finance & Administration: Elizabeth Taylor

Print

Manufactured in Italy by EuroGrafica
Pulp from sustainable forests

Footprint feedback

We try as hard as we can to make each Footprint guide as up to date as possible but, of course, things always change. If you want to let us know about your experiences – good, bad or ugly – then don't delay, go to footprintbooks.com and send in your comments.

Every effort has been made to ensure that the facts in this guidebook are accurate. However, travellers should still obtain advice from consulates, airlines etc about travel and visa requirements before travelling. The authors and publishers cannot accept responsibility for any loss, injury or inconvenience however caused.

Publishing information

FootprintItalia Sicily
1st edition
© Footprint Handbooks Ltd
June 2009

ISBN 978-1-906098-59-9

CIP DATA: A catalogue record for this book is available from the British Library

® Footprint Handbooks and the Footprint mark are a registered trademark of Footprint Handbooks Ltd

Published by Footprint
6 Riverside Court
Lower Bristol Road
Bath BA2 3DZ, UK
T +44 (0)1225 469141
F +44 (0)1225 469461
www.footprintbooks.com

Distributed in North America by
Globe Pequot Press